Towards Understanding the Qur'ān

Vol. III

SŪRAHS 7–9

English version of
Tafhīm al-Qur'ān

SAYYID ABUL A'LĀ MAWDŪDĪ

Translated and edited by
Zafar Ishaq Ansari
assisted by
A.R. Kidwai

MARKAZI MAKTABA ISLAMI PUBLISHERS, DELHI-6

Translated and edited by Zafar Ishaq Ansari

Cover illustration: Rashid Rahman

British Library Cataloguing in Publication Data

Maududi, Sayyid Abul A'la
Towards Understanding the Qur'an
Vol. 3, Surahs 7-9
Pages 344
1. Islam, Koran: Critical Studies
I. Title. II. Ansari, Zafar Ishaq
III. Islamic Foundation.
IV. Tafhim al-Qur'an. English 297' 1226

ISBN 0 -86037-206-5
ISBN 0-86037-205-7 Pbk

Human Welfare Trust Publication No. 146

First Edition Feb 1998 (2000)

Published by
Markazi Maktaba Islami Publishers
1353 Chitli Qabr, Delhi - 110 006
Ph. 3262862
[redacted]

Printed at Dawat Offset Printers, Delhi - 110 006

بسم الله الرحمن الرحيم

Contents

TRANSLITERATION TABLE

Consonants. Arabic

initial: unexpressed
medial and final:

ء	ʼ	د	d	ض	ḍ	ك	k
ب	b	ذ	dh	ط	ṭ	ل	l
ت	t	ر	r	ظ	ẓ	م	m
ث	th	ز	z	ع	ʻ	ن	n
ج	j	س	s	غ	gh	ه	h
ح	ḥ	ش	sh	ف	f	و	w
خ	kh	ص	ṣ	ق	q	ي	y

Urdu and Persian the same except the following:

پ	p	ڈ	d̲	ژ	z̲
ٹ	t̲				
چ	ch	ڑ	r̲	گ	g

Vowels, diphthongs, etc.

short: ـَ a; ـِ i; ـُ u.

long: ـَا ā ـُو ū ـِي ī ـِيّ īy

diphthongs: ـَوْ aw

ـَيْ ay

Introduction

Islam is unique as a religion based on a Book – the Qur'ān. So is the Islamic *Ummah*, whose identity and historical personality have been derived from and fashioned by the Qur'ān. No influence has been greater than the Qur'ān in shaping the spirit and ethos of Muslim culture and civilization. If we look at the long history of religions and civilizations, it may be said, without reservation, that if ever there was a book that produced a religion, a community, a culture and a civilization, it is the Qur'ān. For this reason, the origins and destiny of the Muslim *Ummah* rest with the Qur'ān.

It would be no exaggeration to suggest that *Tafsīr* literature mirrors Muslim religious and social thought at its best. The real genius of the Muslim mind has expressed itself in its unceasing efforts to understand and interpret the word of God as enshrined in the Qur'ān and as exemplified in the *Sunnah* of the Prophet (peace be on him). And just as the Qur'ān deals with all aspects of human life, thought and behaviour, so *Tafsīr* literature constitutes a spectrum reflecting Muslim ideas in all areas of human thought and behaviour. From eschatology and metaphysics to prayer and worship, from epistemology to individual conduct and social behaviour, from social philosophy to the problems of familial and societal organization, from theology to law and morality, from the most sensitive aspects of motivation to the explicit problems of war and peace, to justice and *Iḥsān*, to history and futurology. A meaningful history of Muslim thought cannot be written without delving deep into *Tafsīr* literature. This is the reason why most of the histories of Muslim thought, written either in the West or which have drawn primarily upon sources other than *Tafsīr* literature, have failed to capture the richness and originality of Muslim contributions to human thought and society.

The Prophet Muḥammad (peace be on him) was not only the recipient of the Divine Revelation contained in the Qur'ān; he was also its most authentic interpreter and expounder. The *Sunnah* represents the Qur'ān in practice. It embodies and radiates the model in both space and time.

The prophetic model is not only the realization of the ideal; it also inaugurates a process through which those who have followed in the footsteps of the Prophet throughout the ages have continued to strive to understand, interpret, explain and implement the Word of God. Succeeding generations strived to follow the model and learn from the efforts of their predecessors. The text of the Qur'ān was preserved and protected in its totality; it was spared human interpolation. The translation of the Qur'ān into other languages was accepted as an aid to the understanding of the Qur'ān, but it was never accepted as a substitute for that text. A translation is a ***human effort*** and constitutes a form of *tafsīr* (*bayān*). Efforts were made in every age to understand the meaning of the Qur'ān and to discover its teachings' relevance to the problems faced by the people in particular situations. The eternal has continued to provide guidance for the temporal in all times and climes. Similarly, efforts to implement the teachings were made at both individual and collective levels, which did not lose sight of the specific problems of the age. In facing these challenges, meticulous care was taken to see that the Word of God and the Word of man remained distinct. Every effort to understand the intent of the Master and its relevance to changing situations remained a human effort, despite the fact that, in the context of Islamic thought and literature, these represented the best of the Muslim genius. Over a thousand *tafsīrs* are available in the Arabic language and a similar number in other Muslim languages taken together. Fresh contributions have been made in every age and from all areas of the Muslim world.

The science of *Tafsīr* is a very specialized discipline. It is impossible to make even an elementary effort, in this brief introduction, to capture the most distinct aspects of its subject. Yet it would be worthwhile to highlight at least three areas of special concern.

First and foremost, I would like to make reference to the Muslim scholars and savants who have strived to find the meaning to verses of the Qur'ān by reference to other verses of the Qur'ān itself and to the *Sunnah* of the Prophet Muḥammad (peace be on him). These efforts have been supplemented by attempts to find out how the Companions of the Prophet understood different verses of the Qur'ān. While using the tools of lexicon – the Arab idiom and usage at the time of the Prophet and the literary tradition which constituted the intellectual universe in which the Qur'ān was revealed – their real effort was to understand the meaning of the Qur'ān in light of the interpretation given by the Prophet, his Companions and the early savants. In the typology of *Tafsīr*, this is known as the tradition of *Tafsīr al-Ma'thūr*.

The second area of concern I have chosen relates to the *fiqhī tafsīr*. The primary concern, in this context, was to find out the divine commandments (*Aḥkām*) in relation to the different aspects of individual and collective life and behaviour. This covered not only whatever was available in the form of direct and explicit injunctions but also what was derived by applying the principles of *tafsīr* and the inference of law (*Istinbāṭ al-Aḥkām*). Efforts were made to apply Qur'ānic injunctions to new problems with the aim of deriving the intent of law for situations not explicitly covered. As Qur'ānic guidance comprehends all aspects of life, this effort became all-embracing. *Fiqhī Tafāsīr* lay primary emphasis on spelling out Qur'ānic guidance on the multifarious aspects of human life, and apply, in particular, general principles to actual problems and infer the law for issues and areas not directly covered in the text.

The third major area of concern covers the wide spectrum of *tafāsīr* written to highlight the wisdom contained in the Qur'ān, the rationale behind its beliefs as well as its commands, the vision of the man and the society the Qur'ān builds and how it differs from the vision of man and society in other religions, ideologies and philosophies. These *tafāsīr* also deal with doubts and suspicions and objections and criticisms voiced in respect of some of the teachings of the Qur'ān. Efforts were also made to show the relevance of the Qur'ān to the problems of the age and how these problems could be solved by recourse to the Qur'ān. This category is known as *Kalāmī Tafsīr*.

Although these three perspectives are not exclusive, Qur'ānic studies have nevertheless progressed in every age as a result of them. Muslim scholars, in their attempts to search out Qur'ānic answers to the challenges of their times have always tried to fathom Qur'ānic depths. Every age has its own outstanding contributions which testify to the inner strength and vitality of the Islamic traditions. For example, the latter half of the twentieth century will be remembered for two seminal contributions to *tafsīr* literature; namely *Fī Ẓilāl al-Qur'ān* by Shahīd Sayyid Quṭb and *Tafhīm al-Qur'ān* by Sayyid Abul A'lā Mawdūdī.

The Qur'ān held a unique fascination for Sayyid Mawdūdī. To him it was not simply a sacred book which had to be believed in as an article of faith. It was something more, something vitally different and something very special. Let me spell out his relationship with the Book in his own words.

It was in 1946 that an interesting book appeared under the title *Mashāhīr Ahl-e-'Ilm kī Muḥsin Kitāben* (Books that Moved the

Intellectual Luminaries, literally 'their Benefactor Books'). It was an anthology of essays and memoirs written by over two dozen top-ranking scholars and statesmen of the Indo-Pakistan subcontinent. Each one recapitulated and reflected upon the books that had influenced him most. In this myriad galaxy, which highlighted outstanding books from Rūmī's *Mathnawī* to the *Ṭilism-e-Hushrubā* (A Book of Magic and Fairy Tales), the shortest yet the most moving contribution was from Sayyid Mawdūdī. He was alone in identifying only one book, strangely enough the one not mentioned by any of the other distinguished scholars; it was the Qur'ān: 'I have studied a large number of books, particularly in the days of my early gropings in the dark (*Jāhilīyah*). It would not be an exaggeration to submit that I have tried to imbibe quite a library – books dealing with philosophy, old and new, science (natural and social), economics, politics and what not. But when I studied the Qur'ān with the eyes of my soul it opened up a new world before me. The spell of all that I had read in my age of gropings was cast asunder. Then only, I realized that now I have had access to the roots of knowledge, and the world of reality; Kant, Nietzsche, Hegel, Marx and other secular thinkers began to look like pygmies. In fact, I began to pity them, for they could not resolve issues, despite grappling with them throughout their life and producing thereon huge volumes. This Book has resolved these in a few words. This Book alone is my true benefactor. It has changed me altogether. It has transformed the animal in me into a human. It has conducted me from darkness into light. It has endowed me with a beacon which illumines every dismal corner of life into which I now venture to move. Now reality glows before my eyes without any mask. The key that can open every locked door is called a "master-key". So to me, the Qur'ān constitutes the master-key which resolves every problem of human life. It has opened up for me glorious avenues of life and progress. Words fail me to thank the Lord, Allah, *subḥānahū wata'ālā*, Who bestowed upon us this Blessed Book.'

The Qur'ān is the key to Sayyid Mawdūdī's life and mission. In his view, where the Muslims have failed is in the weakening or pollution of their relationship with the Qur'ān. It was the Qur'ān that made them masters of the world. It is the Qur'ān which can once again set their house in order and enable them to win back their rightful place in the world.

It is significant that the journal through which Sayyid Mawdūdī launched his intellectual crusade was called *Tarjumān al-Qur'ān* (Spokesman of the Qur'ān). And when the Islamic Movement of the *Jamā'at-i-Islāmī* was formally launched, in August 1941, he devoted most of his energies to writing the *Tafhīm al-Qur'ān* so that this movement would imbibe the message of the Qur'ān and engage in the struggle to establish the world order that the Qur'ān wants to be established. That is why *Tafhīm al-Qur'ān* occupies a very central position in Sayyid Mawdūdī's strategy for Islamic revolution.

Sayyid Mawdūdī is one of the chief architects of contemporary Islamic resurgence. He was a prolific writer. He authored more than 150 books and treatises on different aspects of Islam, ranging from *al-Jihād fī al-Islām* to the Manifesto of the *Jamā'at-i-Islāmi*. His *magnum opus*, however, remains the *Tafhīm al-Qur'ān*, his translation and *tafsīr* (exegesis) of the Qur'ān. This alone epitomizes his elegant literary style, his vast erudition, the clarity and brilliance of his thought and the candour of his commitment to change the world in the image of the Qur'ān. It was in the maturity of his youth, in February 1942, at the age of thirty-nine, that he began the writing of this *tafsīr*; it was not until May 1973, when his hair had run white and he had sought retirement from the active leadership of the *Jamā'at*, that he completed the work. *Tafhīm al-Qur'ān* is the choicest product of a lifetime – a life dedicated to the glory of the Lord, a life engaged in honest intellectual inquiry, in robust scholarship, in all round *Jihād* to establish the supremacy of the truth as revealed by Allah and as practised by His prophet. *Tafhīm al-Qur'ān* has been published in six volumes. The first volume appeared in 1950, when Sayyid Mawdūdī was in prison, and the last one appeared in 1973, six years before he breathed his last. The *Tafhīm al-Qur'ān* is the most widely read *tafsīr* in our times.

Tafhīm is a unique contribution to contemporary *tafsīr* literature. For this reason, some of its distinct aspects deserve to be highlighted.

The uniqueness of *Tafhīm* lies in the fact that it looks upon the Qur'ān as a book of guidance (*hidāyah*). There is no denying that the Qur'ān does deal with aspects of history, geography, socio-economic relations, natural phenomena, etc., but it is not primarily concerned with any of these subject areas. It is a masterpiece of higher literature, but it is not meant to be used as a mere piece of literature. As such, the Qur'ān has been approached as the main-spring for guidance, destined to play a decisive role in the reconstruction of thought and action, of institutions and society; as was the case when it was revealed to the Prophet Muḥammad (peace be on him). The function of *Tafhīm* is not to dwell primarily or mainly on literary beauties and legalistic niceties – which have not been ignored – but to develop an understanding of the Qur'ān as the source of guidance.

Sayyid Mawdūdī also emphasizes that the Qur'ān is a book of a movement. It presents a message, invites the whole human race to a view of reality and society, organizes those who respond to this call into an ideological community and enjoins upon this community the necessity to strive for the socio-moral reconstruction of humanity, both individually and collectively. The Qur'ān wants to produce a universal ideological movement and constitutes a guide-book for this movement. Much of the Qur'ān cannot be properly understood unless it is studied in the context of this framework. The Prophet was assigned to play a historical role as the leader of this Islamic movement. The Qur'ān was revealed to him piecemeal during the twenty-three years of his prophetic career, guiding his steps throughout his struggle. This guaranteed guidance has a particular, as well as a general and universal, aspect. In its particular aspect, this entire milieu provides an illustration of the movement and change which the Qur'ān wants to bring about. In its general and universal aspect, the Qur'ān abstracts from the specific time-space context and presents the model which can and should be applied in different time-space situations. Sayyid Mawdūdī approached the Qur'ān as the guide-book for this movement of Islamic reconstruction. As such, the internal evidence of the Qur'ān, revealing as it does different aspects and situations of this *Da'wah* and movement, the *Sunnah* of the Prophet and of his Companions and the evidence on *Asbāb al-Tanzīl*, assumes great significance in his understanding of the Qur'ān.

The Qur'ān presents a complete way of life – a code of conduct and a scheme for organizing the total gamut of human life – belief, action and society. It does not divide itself into water-tight material and spiritual, this-worldly and that-worldly, compartments. It creates only one supreme loyalty – to Allah and His prophet; and tries to organize the whole fabric of human life on this basis. Sayyid Mawdūdī suggests that the key concepts of the Qur'ān are *Ilāh, Rabb, 'Ibādah* and *al-Dīn*. The Qur'ān invites man to accept the Creator as *Rabb*, the Sustainer and Sovereign, to harmonize his will with the Will of Allah in all its aspects (*'ibādah*) and to establish the Will of Allah over the totality of life (*dīn*). This is the path through which man can seek the fulfilment of his real nature. This is the approach that the *Tafhīm* has expounded.

In his unique style, Sayyid Mawdūdī emphasizes that the key to the understanding of the Qur'ān lies in its style and methodology. These are distinct and unique – suited to its purpose and mission – and consequently do not fit any framework developed by human scholarship. Its purpose is *Hidāyah* (guidance). It addresses itself to man. Its target is to develop a new consciousness of reality to mould the character and personality of the individual on the prime value of *taqwā* (God-consciousness) and to generate a new social movement to establish a new culture and civilization. To achieve this objective, it has adopted a direct and straightforward method of heart-to-heart conversation between God and man. Its style is that of brief and precise *Khuṭubāt* addressed by God to man but containing all the elements of a meaningful dialogue between the two. Individually, every *āyah* of the Qur'ān serves this purpose, and in the context in which it occurs. Sayyid Mawdūdī develops a new concept of the (*Naẓm*) system and sequence within the Qur'ān. Earlier *Mufassirūn* have tried to elaborate on the relationship between the different *sūrahs* of the Qur'ān. Some have studied *Naẓm* within every *sūrah*. Sayyid Mawdūdī attempted to study the *Naẓm* of the whole of the Qur'ān and of each *sūrah*, and the relationship between different *sūrahs* and between verses within the *sūrah* in light of the overall objectives of the Qur'ān, and has shown how they are woven together into one glorious pattern. The apparent diversity is permeated with a purposive unity. To Mawdūdī, the style and methodology of the Qur'ān are not secondary to its purpose, rather they are its essential instruments. Instead of presenting an apology for the methodology of the Qur'ān or trying to justify it logically or rhetorically, he has presented this methodology of the Qur'ān as a unique and essential key to the understanding of the message and mission of the Qur'ān.

These propositions form the framework in which Sayyid Mawdūdī has endeavoured to study the Qur'ān. He has written a *Muqaddimah*, prolegomena, to the *Tafhīm al-Qur'ān*, wherein he has discussed his approach to the study of the Qur'ān and the principles of interpretation he has followed, and a treatise on the key concepts of the Qur'ān: *Ilāh, Rabb, 'Ibādah* and *al-Dīn*. Every *sūrah* has been prefaced by an introduction giving the subject matter of the *sūrah*, its relevance to the overall scheme of the Qur'ān, its historical setting and a summary of the questions and issues discussed in it.

The *Tafhīm* offers a new translation of the Qur'ān which is neither literal nor liberal. It is an interpretative translation in direct, forceful and modern Urdu. In the first place, this translation conveys the meaning of the Qur'ān in a forceful style nearest to the spirit of the original. Secondly, it renders the spoken word of the Arabic into the written word of Urdu. With this translation, Sayyid Mawdūdī has tried to provide for the ordinary Urdu reader an almost direct access to the Qur'ān.

Another distinctive aspect of this translation is the use of paragraphs. In the text of the Qur'ān, there are no paragraphs. The division of the Qur'ān into *Manzil, Juz'* and *Rukū'* is only for the convenience of recitation. They are not meaningful divisions. The introduction of paragraphing in translation is a major innovation and to the best of my knowledge, Sayyid Mawdūdī has been the first scholar to do so in Urdu, and perhaps in any language of the world.

The translation is followed by explanatory notes elaborating the meaning of the Qur'ān, giving historical and other information wherever necessary, pin-pointing the relevance of a verse to the message and spirit of the Qur'ān and the needs of the Islamic movement, explaining the *ḥikmah* (rationale) behind different injunctions and their import for our own times. Through these notes, Sayyid Mawdūdī has tried to develop a new *'ilm al-Kalām* based upon the Qur'ān and utilizing the developments of modern knowledge, the principles of historical criticism, comparative religion and ideologies. In using the methodology of the Qur'ān to develop a new *'ilm al-Kalām* Mawdūdī has added grist to his mill. His effort is to use these notes as an aid to the understanding of the Qur'ān and to dispel doubts and difficulties which a modern-educated Muslim may face in his efforts to study the Qur'ān. He has been only too eager to avoid any issues which may distract the reader's attention from the word of the Qur'ān. The notes are functional and not just ornamental.

He has also used these notes to delineate and elaborate the broad outlines of the total scheme of life adumbrated in the Qur'ān and to suggest how this can be translated into the reality of the present time.

While dealing with the *Aḥkām*, he has avoided sectarian controversies. Although he generally follows the Ḥanafī school, he has usually in his explanatory notes stated the viewpoint of all major schools of Islamic thought, including that of the *Shī'ah*. This helps the reader appreciate how a certain verse has been explained or approached by scholars belonging to different schools. It also identifies the flexibility of Islamic law, and paves the way for bridging the gap between the different schools of thought. In so doing, it lays the foundations for an ecumenical movement within Islam.

In his exegesis, Sayyid Mawdūdī tries not only to capture the original meaning and impact of the Qur'ān but also to throw light on the model that emerges from that, as a guide for the present and for the future.

Another distinct feature of the *Tafhīm al-Qur'ān* is its index. Running into some three hundred pages it is, perhaps, the most elaborate and exhaustive concordance of the Qur'ān. It deals with the concepts, themes, personalities and events in the Qur'ān and is an extremely useful aid to any researcher.

Tafhīm al-Qur'ān is a major contribution to *Tafsīr* literature. It is difficult to measure it with the yardsticks of modernism or traditionalism. It may, more correctly, be described as revivalist and revolutionary. Its emphasis is on movement, activism and dynamism, without taking liberties with the Word of God or equating the concepts of the Qur'ān with the thought-content of modern ideologies. It is permeated with respect for tradition in thought and practice without completely identifying the Qur'ān with the institutional structures produced by the Muslims during the course of history. It is a plea for purposive change and tries to develop the faculty to discriminate between the essential and the incidental, between the divine, and as such permanent, and the human, and as such changeable. The *Tafhīm al-Qur'ān* is, itself, a human effort and is subject to all the possibilities and limitations of a human effort to understand and explain the Divine Word. It has its own contemporary flavour and this constitutes its merit as well as its limitation.

The need to produce a complete translation of the *Tafhīm* in the English language has been felt ever since its publication in Urdu. To fulfil this need, Islamic Publications, Lahore has published an English translation of the *Tafhīm*. Although this rendered a useful service, it was commonly realized that the translation could not capture the real force and elegance of the *Tafhīm al-Qur'ān*, which is not only a masterpiece of scholarship, but also a rare piece of literary excellence. The text of the Qur'ān, as translated in Urdu by Sayyid Mawdūdī, could not be effectively reproduced in the English translation. Explanatory notes were abridged in a number of places. Editorial language standards and the physical production of the book left much to be desired. Sayyid Mawdūdī realized these limitations and wanted a new and more forceful translation of the *Tafhīm al-Qur'ān* in modern English and was eager that the same be printed to professional and international standards. It was with this ambition that the late Chaudhri Ghulam Muhammad and the present writer discussed with Sayyid Mawdūdī the plan for a new translation of the *Tafhīm*. We all agreed that Dr. Zafar Ishaq Ansari would be the most competent person to undertake this onerous task. His command of Arabic, Urdu and English and his deep understanding and insight into the thought and style of Sayyid Mawdūdī qualified him for the job. It was in deference to the wish of Sayyid Mawdūdī that Chaudhri Ghulam Muhammad and I persuaded Dr. Zafar Isháq Ansari to commit himself to this assignment, a responsibility that he shouldered with some reluctance. It is unfortunate that both Sayyid Mawdūdī and Chaudhri Ghulam Muhammad are no longer with us to see the fruit of Dr. Ansari's heroic effort to recreate the *Tafhīm* in English. Their souls would, however, be happy to see that their dream is now coming true.

The Islamic Foundation is publishing this new translation in fulfilment of the command of Sayyid Mawdūdī, with the co-operation of his family, and with the permission of the Idārah Tarjumānul Qur'ān which holds the copyright of the original. The Foundation has established a permanent cell to prepare and oversee the production of the *Tafhīm al-Qur'ān* in the English language. We have tried to achieve the highest standards of accuracy, literary elegance and aesthetic production. The translation of the entire Urdu *Tafhīm* is expected to be completed in twelve volumes of almost equal size. The thirteenth volume will contain an exhaustive index of the entire work. It is hoped that one volume will appear every year. May Allah enable us to achieve this target and may Allah make this translation as instrumental in spreading the message and mission of the Qur'ān all over the world as He has blessed the Urdu *Tafhīm* to rekindle the spark of faith in the lives of hundreds of thousands of people and committed them to the Islamic mission. And may Allah give the best rewards to all those who have been engaged or who have been helpful in producing this English version of the *Tafhīm al-Qur'ān*.

Leicester **Khurshid Ahmad**
22 Dhu al-Ḥijjah, 1410 A.H.
16 July, 1990

Editor's Preface

This is the third volume of *Towards Understanding the Qur'ān* and comprises *Sūrahs* 7–9 (*al-A'rāf, al-Anfāl* and *al-Tawbah*). It is unfortunate that the time lapse between the publication of the second and third volumes is perceptibly more than that between the publication of the first and second volumes. I fervently pray that the publication of the fourth volume may take less time. All that depends, however, on God's benign help.

As compared to the previous two volumes, which were entirely the work of this writer, the present volume represents a collaborative effort. The notes, which form the bulk of the work, were first translated into English by Dr. A.R. Kidwai of the Islamic Foundation. That draft served as the base out of which the present manuscript developed after a long process of editing and re-editing. While credit for painstaking assistance and constant counsel goes to Dr. Kidwai, it deserves to be noted that the responsibility for whatever inadequacies remain in the final version rests with the present writer alone. As for the English rendering of the meaning of the text of the *sūrahs* that have gone into this volume, the work is exclusively this writer's.

In this volume, as in the previous ones, we have attempted to provide adequate documentation. In documenting *Ḥadīth* we have followed the system of A.J. Wensinck in his *Concordance*. However, instead of referring to the number of the 'Bāb' of a tradition – a practice followed by Wensinck – we have preferred to mention the title of the 'Bāb'. It may also be noted that while referring to explanatory notes from different works of *Tafsīr,* we have referred to the verse and *sūrah* in connection with which the notes in question were written rather than to the volume and page numbers of the *Tafsīr* work cited. As for the Bible, all quotations have been taken from its *Revised Standard Edition*. In this volume too we have retained the features of the previous two volumes which were our additions to the original work *Tafhīm al-Qur'ān* viz. Glossary of Terms, Biographical Notes and Bibliography.

In finalizing the manuscript, I have benefited greatly from the editorial suggestions of Miss Susanne Thackray. Dr. Manazir Ahsan and Dr. A.R. Kidwai also kindly looked at the draft at the final stage and favoured me with several useful comments. In providing documentation to those parts of the work which needed documentation as well as in preparing the Biographical Notes and Glossary of Terms, I have received invaluable assistance from my colleague, Mr. A.R. Ashraf Baloch of the Islamic Research Institute. Mr. Amjad Mahmud of the Islamic Research Institute assiduously typed the manuscript many times before it could be sent to the press. Mr. E.R. Fox rendered valuable assistance in technical editing and proofreading and Mr. Naiem Qaddoura in setting the Arabic material. To these and many others who assisted and encouraged me, I record my profound sense of gratitude. May Allah bless them all.

Islamabad **Zafar Ishaq Ansari**
10 Dhu al-Ḥijjah, 1410 A.H.
2 July, 1990

N.B. ► *refers to the continuation of the paragraph adopted by Mawdūdī in the Urdu translation.*

Sūrah 7

al-A'rāf

(The Heights)

(Makkan Period)

Title

As verses 46–8 of this *sūrah* mention 'the Heights' and the 'People of the Heights' *(al-A'rāf)*, the *sūrah* is called *al-A'rāf*. Giving this title to the *sūrah* simply signifies that it is the *sūrah* in which the 'Heights' have been mentioned.

Period of Revelation

This *sūrah* was revealed, as is borne out by a close study of its contents, in the same period as *Sūrah al-An'ām*. It is not definitely known, however, which of the two *sūrahs* was revealed earlier. For a better appreciation of the historical context surrounding the revelation of this *sūrah* it is sufficient to take a look at the background information provided by us in the introductory statement about *al-An'ām*. (See *Towards Understanding the Qur'ān,* vol. II, pp. 209–13 – Ed.)

Main Themes

The central theme of the *sūrah* consists in urging people to follow the Prophets. The dominant tenor of this urging, however, is that of a warning. For the people of Makka to whom the Qur'ānic message was addressed had paid no heed to it even after a long period of time. The Makkans had rather shown such inveterate hostility that not long after the revelation of this *sūrah,* the Prophet (peace be on him) was directed to turn his attention to people other than the Makkans. Hence, this admonishment to the Makkans to accept the Guidance of the Prophet (peace be on him), was accompanied by a stern warning reminding them that other nations had earlier met their doom by following much the same attitude towards their Prophets.

As the Message had been repeatedly conveyed to the Makkans and that they would now have no excuse left before God for not embracing Islam, the last part of the *sūrah* would seem to be mainly addressed to the People of the Book, and on one occasion, to all mankind, rather than to the Makkans. This marks the proximity of the Migration *(Hijrah)*; of the fact that the phase in which a Prophet addresses only those close to him was about to finish.

In the course of delivering the basic Message, the Qur'ān also addresses the Jews. At the same time as they are invited to the basic Message of the Prophets, they are reminded of the dire consequences attendant upon their indulgence in hypocrisy, their frequent breach of the covenant, and their consciously clinging to falsehood in preference to the truth.

Towards the end of the *sūrah,* the Prophet (peace be on him) and his Companions are favoured with a few vital directives as to how they should disseminate their message with wisdom, and especially how they should bear the persecution and provocation of their opponents and so refrain from acting under emotional stress which could harm their cause.

In the name of Allah, the Merciful, the Compassionate.

بِسْمِ ٱللَّهِ ٱلرَّحْمَٰنِ ٱلرَّحِيمِ

(1) *Alif-Lām-Mīm-Ṣād.* (2) This is a Book revealed to you.[1] Let there be no impediment in your heart about it.[2] (It has been revealed to you) that you may thereby warn [the unbelievers], and that it may be a reminder to the believers.[3]

الٓمٓصٓ ﴿١﴾ كِتَٰبٌ أُنزِلَ إِلَيْكَ فَلَا يَكُن فِى صَدْرِكَ حَرَجٌ مِّنْهُ لِتُنذِرَ بِهِۦ وَذِكْرَىٰ لِلْمُؤْمِنِينَ ﴿٢﴾

---

1. The word 'Book', in this context, signifies this very *sūrah, al-A'rāf.*

2. The Prophet (peace be on him) is directed to preach his Message without fear and hesitation, and to disregard his opponents' response. Such opponents may well be offended by his preaching of the Message, or may hold it to ridicule, or go about maliciously twisting it, or acting with greater hostility. All this notwithstanding, the Message of Islam must be preached.

The Arabic word *haraj* (which we have translated as straitness), signifies an intractable bush. (See Ibn Manẓūr, *Lisān al-'Arab* and Fīrūzābādī, *al-Qāmūs,* q.v. 'Ḥarajah'.) 'Straitness or constriction in the breast' refers to the reluctance of a person to go ahead in the face of opposition. The following Qur'ānic verse would seem to allude to this mental state of the Prophet (peace be on him): 'We do indeed know how your heart feels distressed at what they say' (*al-Ḥijr* 15: 97). What painfully concerned the Prophet (peace be on him) was to find out how he could direct a people, whose adamance and opposition to truth had reached such high proportions, to the Right Way. The same state of mind is again reflected in the Qur'ānic verse: 'Perhaps you might feel inclined to part with a portion of what has been revealed to you, and your heart feels straitened lest they say: "Why is a treasure not sent down unto him; or why does an angel not come with him?"' (*Hūd* 11: 12).

3. The main purpose of this *sūrah* is to jolt the people out of their heedlessness and to warn them of the dire consequences that will follow if they reject the call of the Prophet (peace be on him). Additionally, this *sūrah* also seeks to serve as a reminder to the believers – a purpose which is achieved, incidentally, by the warning made to the unbelievers.

(3) [O men!] Follow what has been revealed to you from your Lord and follow no masters other than Him.[4] Little are you admonished.

(4) How many a township We have destroyed! Our scourge fell upon them at night, or when they were taking midday rest. (5) And when Our scourge fell upon them their only cry was: 'We are indeed transgressors.'[5]

اتَّبِعُوا مَا أُنزِلَ إِلَيْكُم مِّن رَّبِّكُمْ وَلَا تَتَّبِعُوا
مِن دُونِهِۦٓ أَوْلِيَآءَ قَلِيلًا مَّا تَذَكَّرُونَ ﴿٣﴾
وَكَم مِّن قَرْيَةٍ أَهْلَكْنَٰهَا فَجَآءَهَا بَأْسُنَا
بَيَٰتًا أَوْ هُمْ قَآئِلُونَ ﴿٤﴾ فَمَا كَانَ
دَعْوَىٰهُمْ إِذْ جَآءَهُم بَأْسُنَآ إِلَّآ أَن قَالُوٓا۟
إِنَّا كُنَّا ظَٰلِمِينَ ﴿٥﴾

4. The central theme of the whole *sūrah*, and of the present discourse, is the guidance which man needs in order to live a wholesome life, the knowledge which he requires in order to understand the reality of the universe and his own being and the purpose of his existence; the principles which he needs to serve as the basis for morality and social life as well as culture and civilization. In this regard man should look to God alone and follow exclusively the Guidance which He has communicated to mankind through His Messenger. To look to anyone other than God is dangerous for it has always spelled disaster in the past, and will always spell disaster in the future. In this verse the word *awliyā'* (masters) refers to those whom one follows, regardless of whether one idolizes or curses them, and whether one acknowledges their patronship or strongly denies it. For further explanation see *Tafhīm al-Qur'ān, al-Shūrá* 42, n. 6.

5. People can learn a lesson from the tragic fate of those nations that spurned God's Guidance, and instead followed the guidance of others; and they became so degenerate that their very existence became an intolerable burden on the earth. Eventually, God's scourge seized them, and the earth was cleansed of their filthy existence.

The words uttered by the evil-doers: 'We are indeed transgressors', emphasizes two points. First, that it is pointless for one to realize and repent of one's wrong-doing after the time for such repentance is past. Individuals and communities who allow the term granted to them to be wasted in heedlessness and frivolity, who turn a deaf ear to those who invite them to the truth, have so often been overtaken in the past by God's punishment. Second, there are numerous instances of individuals as well as communities which incontrovertibly prove that when the wrong-doings

(6) So We shall call to account those to whom Messengers were sent,[6] and We shall call to account the Messengers (to see how dutifully they conveyed the Message, and how people responded to it).[7] ►

فَلَنَسْـَٔلَنَّ ٱلَّذِينَ أُرْسِلَ إِلَيْهِمْ وَلَنَسْـَٔلَنَّ ٱلْمُرْسَلِينَ ﴿٦﴾

of a nation exceed a certain limit, the term granted to it expires and God's punishment suddenly overtakes it. And once a nation is subjected to God's punishment, there is no escape from it. Since human history abounds in such instances, there is no reason why people should persist in the same iniquity, and repent only when the time for repentance has passed.

6. The words 'call to account' refers to the questioning people will be subjected to on the Day of Judgement. For it is the reckoning on the Day of Judgement that really matters. Punishment dealt upon corrupt individuals and communities in this world does not constitute their true punishment. Punishment in this world is no more than what happens when a criminal, who has been strutting scot-free, is suddenly arrested. The arrest constitutes no more than depriving the criminal of the opportunity to perpetrate further crimes. The annals of history are filled with instances where corrupt nations have been punished, proving that man has not been granted absolute licence to go about doing whatever he pleases. Rather, there is a Power above all that allows man to act freely but only to a certain extent, no more. And when man exceeds those limits, that Power administers a series of warnings in order that he might heed the warnings and give up his wickedness. But when man fails totally to respond to such warnings, he is punished.

Anyone who considers the events of history will conclude that the Lord of the universe must have certainly appointed a Day of Judgement in order to hold the wrong-doers to account for their actions and to punish them. That the Qur'ān refers to the recurrent punishment of wicked nations as an argument in support of the establishment of the final judgement in the Hereafter is evidenced by the fact that the present verse – verse 6 – opens with the word 'so'.

7. This shows that on the Day of Judgement Prophethood will be the main basis of reckoning. On the one hand, the Prophets will be questioned about the efforts they made to convey God's Message to mankind. On the other hand, the people to whom the Prophets were sent will be questioned about their response to the message. The Qur'ān is not explicit about how

(7) Then We shall narrate to them with knowledge the whole account. For surely We were not away from them. (8) The weighing on that Day will be the true weighing:[8] those whose scales are heavy will prosper, (9) and those whose scales are light will be the losers,[9] for they are the ones who have been unjust to Our signs.

فَلَنَقُصَّنَّ عَلَيْهِم بِعِلْمٍ وَمَا كُنَّا غَآئِبِينَ
﴿٧﴾ وَٱلْوَزْنُ يَوْمَئِذٍ ٱلْحَقُّ فَمَن ثَقُلَتْ
مَوَٰزِينُهُۥ فَأُو۟لَٰٓئِكَ هُمُ ٱلْمُفْلِحُونَ
﴿٨﴾ وَمَنْ خَفَّتْ مَوَٰزِينُهُۥ فَأُو۟لَٰٓئِكَ ٱلَّذِينَ
خَسِرُوٓا۟ أَنفُسَهُم بِمَا كَانُوا۟ بِـَٔايَٰتِنَا
يَظْلِمُونَ ﴿٩﴾

judgements will be made with regard to individuals and communities who did not receive God's Message. It seems that God has left judgement – to borrow a contemporary judicial expression – reserved. However, with regard to individuals and communities who did receive God's Message through the Prophets, the Qur'ān states explicitly that they will have no justification whatsoever to put forward a defence of their disbelief and denial, of their transgression and disobedience. They are doomed to be cast into Hell in utter helplessness and dejection.

8. This means that when the Balance is fixed on the Day of Judgement, 'truth' and weight will be identical. The more truth one has to one's credit, the more the weight in one's scale; and vice versa. One will be judged solely on the basis of this weight. In other words, no consideration other than *truth* will enter into the calculation. A life of falsehood, however long it lasted, and however full of worldly achievements, will carry no weight at all. Weighed in the Balance, the devotees of falsehood will discover that their life-long deeds do not even weigh so much as a bird's feather. The same point has been expatiated upon in *al-Kahf* 18: 103–5: 'Shall We tell you of those who are greatest losers in respect of their deeds? It is those whose efforts have been wasted in this life, while they kept believing that they were acquiring good by their deeds. They are those who deny the Signs of their Lord and the fact of their having to meet Him (in the Hereafter). So their works are in vain and we shall attach no weight to them on the Day of Judgement.'

9. For a full appreciation of this point it is necessary to remember that man's deeds will be classified into positive and negative categories. The positive category will consist of knowing the truth, believing in it, acting

(10) We assuredly established you in the earth and arranged for your livelihood in it. Little do you give thanks.

(11) We initiated your creation, then We gave you each a shape, and then We said to the angels: 'Prostrate before Adam.'[10] They all prostrated except Iblis: he was not one of those who fell prostrate. ▶

وَلَقَدْ مَكَّنَّٰكُمْ فِى ٱلْأَرْضِ وَجَعَلْنَا
لَكُمْ فِيهَا مَعَٰيِشَ قَلِيلًا مَّا تَشْكُرُونَ ﴿١٠﴾
وَلَقَدْ خَلَقْنَٰكُمْ ثُمَّ صَوَّرْنَٰكُمْ ثُمَّ قُلْنَا
لِلْمَلَٰٓئِكَةِ ٱسْجُدُوا۟ لِءَادَمَ فَسَجَدُوٓا۟
إِلَّآ إِبْلِيسَ لَمْ يَكُن مِّنَ ٱلسَّٰجِدِينَ ﴿١١﴾

upon it, and striving to make it prevail. It is such acts alone which will have weight in the Hereafter. Conversely, whenever someone follows and goes afte lusts or blindly follows other humans or satans, his acts will be reckoned as 'negative'. Such acts will not only be of no value at all, but will also have the effect of reducing the total weight of one's positive acts.

Thus, a man's success in the Hereafter requires that his good acts outweigh his evil ones to such an extent that even if his evil acts cause the effacement of some of his good acts, he should still have enough left in his credit to ensure his scale is inclined towards the positive. As for the man whose evil acts outweigh his good acts, he will be like the bankrupt businessman who, even after spending all his assets, remains under the burden of debt.

10. These verses should be read in conjunction with *al-Baqarah* 2: 30–9. The words in which the command to prostrate before Adam is mentioned may give rise to the misapprehension that it was Adam as such who is the object of prostration. This misapprehension should be removed by what has been said here. The text makes it very clear that prostration before Adam was in his capacity as the representative of all mankind and not in his personal capacity.

The successive stages of man's creation mentioned in the present verse ('We initiated your creation, then We gave you each a shape'), means that God first planned the creation of man, made ready the necessary materials for it, and then gave those materials a human form. Then, when man had assumed the status of a living being, God asked the angels to prostrate before him. The Qur'ān says:

> And recall when your Lord said to the angels: 'I am about to create man from clay. When I have fashioned him (in due proportion) and breathed into him of My spirit then fall you down in prostration before him' (*Ṣād* 38: 71–2).

Mention has been made in these verses, though in a different way, of the same three stages of creation: man's creation from clay; giving him a proportionate human shape; and bringing Adam into existence by breathing into him God's spirit. The following verses also have the same import:

> And recall when your Lord said to the angels: 'I am about to create man, from sounding clay moulded into shape from black mud. When I have fashioned him (in due proportion) and breathed into him of My spirit, fall you all down in prostration before him' (*al-Ḥijr* 15: 28–9).

It is quite difficult for one to appreciate fully the details of the origin of man's creation. We cannot fully grasp how man was created out of the elements drawn from the earth; how he was given a form and a well-proportioned one at that and how God's Spirit was breathed into him. It is quite obvious, though, that the Qur'ānic version of man's creation is sharply at odds with the theory of creation propounded by Darwin and his followers in our time. Darwinism explains man's creation in terms of his evolution from a variety of non-human and sub-human stages culminating in *homo sapiens*. It draws no clear demarcation line that would mark the end of the non-human stage of evolution and the beginning of the species called 'man'. Opposed to this is the Qur'ānic version of man's creation where man starts his career from the very beginning as an independent species, having in his entire history no essential relationship at all with any non-human species. Also, man is conceived as having been invested by God with full consciousness and enlightenment from the very start of his life.

These are two different doctrines regarding the past of the human species. Both these doctrines give rise to two variant conceptions about man. If one were to adopt the Darwinian doctrine, man is conceived as essentially a species of the animal genre. Acceptance of this doctrine leads man to derive the guiding principles of his life, including moral principles, from the laws governing animal life. Given the basic premises of such a doctrine, animal-like behaviour is to be considered quite natural for man. The only difference between man and animal lies in the fact that animals act without the help of the tools and instruments used by humans, and their behaviour is devoid of culture.

Were one to accept the other doctrine, man would be conceived as a totally distinct category. Man is no longer viewed simply as a talking or gregarious animal. He is rather seen as God's vicegerent on earth. What distinguishes man from other animals, according to this doctrine, is not his capacity to speak or his gregariousness but the moral responsibility and trust with which he has been invested. Thus, one's whole perspective with regard to man and everything relating to him is changed. Rather than

(12) Allah said: 'What prevented you from prostrating, when I commanded you to do so?' He said: 'I am better than he. You created me from fire, and him You created from clay.' (13) Allah said: 'Then get you down from here. It does not behove you to be arrogant here. So be gone. You will be among the humiliated.'[11] (14) Satan replied: 'Give me respite till the Day they shall be raised.' (15) Allah said: 'You are granted respite.' (16) Satan said: 'Since You have led me astray, I shall surely sit in ambush for them on Your Straight Path. (17) Then I will come upon them from the front and from the rear, and from their right and from their left. And You will not find most of them thankful.'[12]

قَالَ مَا مَنَعَكَ أَلَّا تَسْجُدَ إِذْ أَمَرْتُكَ قَالَ أَنَا۠
خَيْرٌ مِّنْهُ خَلَقْتَنِي مِن نَّارٍ وَخَلَقْتَهُۥ مِن طِينٍ
﴿١٢﴾ قَالَ فَٱهْبِطْ مِنْهَا فَمَا يَكُونُ لَكَ أَن
تَتَكَبَّرَ فِيهَا فَٱخْرُجْ إِنَّكَ مِنَ ٱلصَّٰغِرِينَ
﴿١٣﴾ قَالَ أَنظِرْنِيٓ إِلَىٰ يَوْمِ يُبْعَثُونَ ﴿١٤﴾ قَالَ
إِنَّكَ مِنَ ٱلْمُنظَرِينَ ﴿١٥﴾ قَالَ فَبِمَآ أَغْوَيْتَنِي
لَأَقْعُدَنَّ لَهُمْ صِرَٰطَكَ ٱلْمُسْتَقِيمَ ﴿١٦﴾ ثُمَّ
لَءَاتِيَنَّهُم مِّنۢ بَيْنِ أَيْدِيهِمْ وَمِنْ خَلْفِهِمْ وَعَنْ
أَيْمَٰنِهِمْ وَعَن شَمَآئِلِهِمْ وَلَا تَجِدُ أَكْثَرَهُمْ
شَٰكِرِينَ ﴿١٧﴾

---

looking downwards to species of being lower than the human, man will turn his gaze upwards. It is claimed by some that however dignified the Qur'ānic doctrine might be from a moral and psychological point of view, Darwinism should still be preferred on the basis of its being scientifically established. However, the very claim that Darwinism has been scientifically established is itself questionable. Only those who have a very superficial acquaintance with modern science can entertain the misconception that the Darwinian theory of evolution has been scientifically established. Those who know better are fully aware that despite the vast paraphernalia of evidence in its support, it remains merely a hypothesis. The arguments marshalled in support of this theory at best succeed in establishing it as a possibility, but certainly not as an incontrovertible fact. Hence at the most

(18) Allah said: 'Go away from here – disgraced and expelled. I shall fill the Hell with all those that follow you. (19) O Adam! Live you and your spouse in the Garden and both of you eat from it wherever you will, but never approach the tree or you shall become wrong-doers.'

قَالَ اخْرُجْ مِنْهَا مَذْءُومًا مَّدْحُورًا لَّمَن تَبِعَكَ
مِنْهُمْ لَأَمْلَأَنَّ جَهَنَّمَ مِنكُمْ أَجْمَعِينَ ﴿١٨﴾
وَيَا آدَمُ اسْكُنْ أَنتَ وَزَوْجُكَ الْجَنَّةَ فَكُلَا
مِنْ حَيْثُ شِئْتُمَا وَلَا تَقْرَبَا هَٰذِهِ الشَّجَرَةَ
فَتَكُونَا مِنَ الظَّالِمِينَ ﴿١٩﴾

what can be said is that the evolution of the species is as much a possibility as its direct creation.

11. Implicit in the Qur'ānic expression *(ṣāghirīn)* is the idea of contentment with one's disgrace and indignity, for *ṣāghir* is he who invites disgrace and indignity upon himself. Now, Satan was a victim of vanity and pride, and for that very reason defied God's command to prostrate himself before Adam. Satan was, therefore, guilty of self-inflicted degradation. False pride, baseless notions of glory, ill-founded illusions of greatness failed to confer any greatness upon him. They could only bring upon him disgrace and indignity. Satan could blame none but himself for his sordid end.

12. This was the challenge thrown down by Satan to God. What it meant is that Satan would make use of the respite granted to him until the Last Day, and he would do so in order to prove that man did not deserve a position superior to his and this had after all been bestowed upon him by God. So doing he would expose how ungrateful, thankless and disloyal a creature man is.

The respite asked for by Satan and granted to him by God includes not only the time but also the opportunity to mislead man and to prove his point by appealing to man's weaknesses. The Qur'ān makes a pointed statement about this in *Banū Isrā'īl* 17: 61–5. These verses make it clear that God had granted Satan the opportunity to try to mislead Adam and his offspring. At the same time it has also been made quite clear that Satan was not granted the power to lead men into error against their will. 'As for my servants', says the Qur'ān, 'you shall have no power over them' (*Banū Isrā'īl* 17: 65). Thus all that Satan can do is to cause misunderstanding, to make people cherish false illusions, to make evil and error seem attractive, and to invite people to evil ways by holding out to them the promise of immense pleasure and material benefits. He would have no

(20) But Satan made an evil suggestion to both of them that he might reveal to them their shame that had remained hidden from them. He said: 'Your Lord has forbidden you to approach this tree only to prevent you from becoming angels or immortals.' (21) And he swore to them both: 'Surely I am your sincere adviser.'

(22) Thus Satan brought about their fall by deceit. And when they tasted of the tree, their shame became visible to them, and both began to cover themselves with leaves from the Garden. Then their Lord called out to them: 'Did I not forbid you from that tree, and did I not warn you that Satan is your declared enemy?'

فَوَسْوَسَ لَهُمَا ٱلشَّيْطَٰنُ لِيُبْدِيَ لَهُمَا
مَا وُۥرِيَ عَنْهُمَا مِن سَوْءَٰتِهِمَا وَقَالَ
مَا نَهَىٰكُمَا رَبُّكُمَا عَنْ هَٰذِهِ ٱلشَّجَرَةِ إِلَّآ
أَن تَكُونَا مَلَكَيْنِ أَوْ تَكُونَا مِنَ ٱلْخَٰلِدِينَ ﴿٢٠﴾
وَقَاسَمَهُمَآ إِنِّي لَكُمَا لَمِنَ ٱلنَّٰصِحِينَ
﴿٢١﴾ فَدَلَّىٰهُمَا بِغُرُورٍ فَلَمَّا ذَاقَا ٱلشَّجَرَةَ
بَدَتْ لَهُمَا سَوْءَٰتُهُمَا وَطَفِقَا يَخْصِفَانِ
عَلَيْهِمَا مِن وَرَقِ ٱلْجَنَّةِ وَنَادَىٰهُمَا رَبُّهُمَآ
أَلَمْ أَنْهَكُمَا عَن تِلْكُمَا ٱلشَّجَرَةِ وَأَقُل
لَّكُمَآ إِنَّ ٱلشَّيْطَٰنَ لَكُمَا عَدُوٌّ مُّبِينٌ ﴿٢٢﴾

---

power, however, to forcibly pull them to the Satanic way and to prevent them from following the Right Way. Accordingly, the Qur'ān makes it quite plain elsewhere that on the Day of Judgement, Satan would address the men who had followed him in the following words: 'I had no power over you except to call you; but you listened to me: then reproach me not, but reproach your own selves' (*Ibrāhīm* 14: 22).

As for Satan's allegation that God Himself caused him to fall into error (see verse 16) it is an attempt on the part of Satan to transfer the blame which falls squarely on him to God. Satan's grievance seems to be that God was responsible for his deviation insofar as He hurt Satan's pride by asking him to prostrate before Adam, and that it was this which led him to disobey God. It is thus clear that Satan wanted to continue enjoying his vain arrogance and that he was incensed that his weakness – arrogance – was seen through and brought to full light. The underlying stupidity of the statement is too patently obvious to call for any refutation, and hence God took no notice of it.

(23) Both cried out: 'Our Lord! We have wronged ourselves. If You do not forgive us and do not have mercy on us, we shall surely be among the losers.'[13]

قَالَا رَبَّنَا ظَلَمْنَآ أَنفُسَنَا وَإِن لَّمْ تَغْفِرْ لَنَا
وَتَرْحَمْنَا لَنَكُونَنَّ مِنَ ٱلْخَٰسِرِينَ ﴿٢٣﴾

13. The narrative sheds light on the following significant points:

(i) Modesty and bashfulness are inherent in human nature. The primary manifestation of this instinct is seen in the sense of shame that one feels when one is required to expose the private parts of one's body in the presence of others. According to the Qur'ān, this bashfulness is not artificial, nor an outcome of advancement in human culture and civilization. Nor is it something acquired as some misguided thinkers contend. On the contrary, modesty has been an integral part of human nature from the very beginning.

(ii) The very first stratagem adopted by Satan in his bid to lead man astray from the Right Path consisted of undermining man's sense of modesty, to direct him towards lewdness and make him sexually deviant. In other words, the sexual instincts of man were taken by Satan as the most vulnerable aspect of human nature. Accordingly, he sought to weaken man's natural instincts of modesty and bashfulness. This devilish stratagem is still followed by the disciples of Satan in our time. For them, progress is inconceivable without exposing woman to the gaze of all and making her strip before others in one form or another.

(iii) Such is human nature that man scarcely responds to an unambiguous invitation to evil. Those who seek to propagate evil are, therefore, forced to present themselves as sincere well-wishers of humanity.

(iv) Man is naturally drawn towards lofty ideals such as the attainment of superhuman positions and the securing of immortality. Satan achieved his first victory in his bid to mislead man by appealing to the latter's inherent desire to attain immortality. Satan's most effective weapon is to promise man a more elevated position than his present one, and then set him on a course that leads instead to his degradation.

(v) Here the Qur'ān refutes the fairly popular view that Satan first misled Eve and later used her as an instrument to mislead Adam. (See Ibn Kathīr's comments on verses 22–3 – Ed.) The Qur'ānic version of the story is that Satan attempted to mislead both Adam and Eve, and in fact both fell prey to his guile. At first sight, this might seem of trivial significance. However, all those who are acquainted with the impact of this version of Adam's fall on the moral, legal and social degradation of women will appreciate the significance of this Qur'ānic statement.

(vi) There is hardly any basis to assume that the forbidden tree had certain inherent qualities which could result in the exposure of Adam and Eve's private parts as soon as they had tasted its fruit. Instead of the forbidden tree possessing any extraordinary qualities, it was rather man's disobedience to God which led to his fall from his original state. Initially, Adam and Eve's private parts had remained hidden on account of special arrangements made by God. Once they disobeyed, they were deprived of that special Divine arrangement, and were left to themselves to cover their nakedness if they so wished.

This was a way of conveying to mankind for all time that whenever he disobeys God, he will sooner or later be exposed; that man will enjoy God's support and protection only so long as he remains obedient to Him. Once man transgresses the bounds of his obedience, he will be deprived of God's care and protection and left to his own self. This idea is also embodied in many traditions from the Prophet (peace be on him). According to a tradition, the Prophet (peace be on him) prayed:

اللّهمّ رحمتكَ أرجو، فلا تكِلْني إلى نفسي طَرفةَ عينٍ.

'O God! I seek Your Mercy. Do not leave me to my own care even for the wink of an eye!' (Aḥmad b. Ḥanbal, *Musnad,* vol. 5, p. 42 – Ed.)

(vii) Satan wanted to prove that man did not deserve, not even for a moment, the superior status which had been granted to him by God. However, Satan failed in the very first round of his efforts to discredit man. Granted, man did not fully succeed in obeying God's command; rather, he fell prey to the machinations of his arch-enemy, Satan, and deviated from the path of obedience. Nevertheless, it is evident even in the course of this first encounter that man is a morally superior being. This is clear from many a thing. First, whereas Satan laid claim to superiority, man made no such claim. Rather a superior status was bestowed upon him by God. Second, Satan disobeyed God out of sheer pride and arrogance. But far from openly revolting against God out of his own prompting, man was disobedient under Satan's evil influence. Third, when man disobeyed God, he did so unwittingly, not realizing that he was committing a sin. Man was beguiled into disobedience by Satan who appeared in the garb of man's well-wisher. It was Satan who persuaded him to believe that

(24) Allah said: 'Go down;[14] you are enemies one of the other. For you there is dwelling and provision on the earth for a while.' (25) He continued: 'You shall live there, and there shall you die, and from it you shall be raised to life.'

قَالَ ٱهْبِطُوا۟ بَعْضُكُمْ لِبَعْضٍ عَدُوٌّ وَلَكُمْ فِى
ٱلْأَرْضِ مُسْتَقَرٌّ وَمَتَٰعٌ إِلَىٰ حِينٍ ﴿٢٤﴾
قَالَ فِيهَا تَحْيَوْنَ وَفِيهَا تَمُوتُونَ وَمِنْهَا
تُخْرَجُونَ ﴿٢٥﴾

---

in the fruit of the forbidden tree lay his good, that his action would lead him to the heights of goodness, not to the depths of evil. Fourth, when Satan was warned, rather than confessing his mistake and repenting, he clung even more adamantly to disobedience. But when man was told that he had sinned, he did not resort to continued transgression as Satan did. As soon as man realized his mistake, he confessed his fault, returned to the course of obedience and sought refuge in God's mercy.

(viii) This story draws a clear line between the way of Satan and the way that befits man. Satan's way is characterized by rebellion against God, by arrogantly persisting in that rebellion even after having been warned, and by trying to mislead the righteously disposed towards sin and disobedience. As opposed to this, the way that befits man is to resist the evil promptings of Satan and to be constantly vigilant against Satanic machinations. But, if in spite of all these precautions, a man does swerve from the course of obedience, he should turn, as soon as he realizes his fault, to God in penitence and remorse and make amends.

This is the lesson that God conveys to man through this anecdote. The Qur'ān seeks to impress upon the opponents of the Prophet (peace be on him) that the way they are following is the way of Satan. To become indifferent to God's Guidance, to take satans among men and *jinn* as their protectors and to persist in disobedience despite repeated warnings, amounts to adopting a Satanic attitude. It demonstrates that they have fallen prey to the snares of the arch-enemy and have been totally overpowered by him. This attitude will lead to their total undoing just as it led to Satan's undoing. Anyone who has even an iota of understanding should heed and emulate the example of his foreparents – Adam and Eve – who repented and made amends after their disobedience.

(26) O Children of Adam![15] Indeed We have sent down to you a garment which covers your shame and provides protection and adornment. But the finest of all is the garment of piety. That is one of the signs of Allah so that they may take heed. (27) Children of Adam! Let not Satan deceive you in the manner he deceived your parents out of Paradise, pulling off from them their clothing to reveal to them their shame. He and his host surely see you from whence you do not see them. We have made satans the guardians of those who do not believe.[16]

يَٰبَنِيٓ ءَادَمَ قَدۡ أَنزَلۡنَا عَلَيۡكُمۡ لِبَاسٗا يُوَٰرِي
سَوۡءَٰتِكُمۡ وَرِيشٗاۖ وَلِبَاسُ ٱلتَّقۡوَىٰ ذَٰلِكَ
خَيۡرٞۚ ذَٰلِكَ مِنۡ ءَايَٰتِ ٱللَّهِ لَعَلَّهُمۡ
يَذَّكَّرُونَ ٢٦ يَٰبَنِيٓ ءَادَمَ لَا يَفۡتِنَنَّكُمُ
ٱلشَّيۡطَٰنُ كَمَآ أَخۡرَجَ أَبَوَيۡكُم مِّنَ ٱلۡجَنَّةِ
يَنزِعُ عَنۡهُمَا لِبَاسَهُمَا لِيُرِيَهُمَا سَوۡءَٰتِهِمَآۚ
إِنَّهُۥ يَرَىٰكُمۡ هُوَ وَقَبِيلُهُۥ مِنۡ حَيۡثُ لَا تَرَوۡنَهُمۡۗ
إِنَّا جَعَلۡنَا ٱلشَّيَٰطِينَ أَوۡلِيَآءَ لِلَّذِينَ
لَا يُؤۡمِنُونَ ٢٧

14. God's command that Adam and Eve 'go down' should not be misunderstood to mean that their departure from Paradise was by way of punishment. The Qur'ān has made it clear many a time that God accepted Adam and Eve's repentance and pardoned them. Thus the order does not imply punishment. It rather signifies the fulfilment of the purpose for which man was created. (For elaboration see *Towards Understanding the Qur'ān*, vol. I, *al-Baqarah* 2: nn. 48 and 53, pp. 63–4 and 66 – Ed.)

15. By referring to an important aspect of Adam and Eve's story, the attention of the people of Arabia of those days was drawn to the evil influence of Satan upon their lives. Under Satan's influence they had begun to see dress merely as a shield of protection against the inclemencies of the weather and as a means of adornment. The basic purpose of dress – to cover the private parts of the body – had receded into the background. People had no inhibition about the immodest exposure of the private parts of their body in public. To publicly take a bath absolutely naked, to attend to the call of nature on thoroughfares, were the order of the day. To crown it all, in the course of Pilgrimage they used to circumambulate around the

(28) And when such people commit an indecent act they say: 'We found our fathers doing that, and Allah has enjoined it on us.'[17] Say: 'Surely Allah never enjoins any indecency.[18] Do you say things regarding Allah that you do not know?' (29) Say to them (O Muḥammad): 'My Lord enjoins justice; and that you set your faces aright at the time of every Prayer; and that you call upon Him, exclusively dedicating your faith to Him. You shall return to Him as you were created.'[19] ▶

وَإِذَا فَعَلُوا۟ فَٰحِشَةً قَالُوا۟ وَجَدْنَا عَلَيْهَآ
ءَابَآءَنَا وَٱللَّهُ أَمَرَنَا بِهَا ۗ قُلْ إِنَّ ٱللَّهَ
لَا يَأْمُرُ بِٱلْفَحْشَآءِ ۖ أَتَقُولُونَ عَلَى ٱللَّهِ
مَا لَا تَعْلَمُونَ ﴿٢٨﴾ قُلْ أَمَرَ رَبِّى
بِٱلْقِسْطِ ۖ وَأَقِيمُوا۟ وُجُوهَكُمْ عِندَ
كُلِّ مَسْجِدٍ وَٱدْعُوهُ مُخْلِصِينَ
لَهُ ٱلدِّينَ ۚ كَمَا بَدَأَكُمْ تَعُودُونَ ﴿٢٩﴾

Ka'bah in stark nakedness. Women even surpassed men in immodesty. In their view, the performance of religious rites in complete nudity was an act of religious merit.

Immodesty, however, was not an exclusive characteristic of the people of Arabia. Many nations indulged in it in the past, and many nations continue to indulge in it even now. Hence the message embodied in these verses is not directed just to the people of Arabia. It is rather directed to all men. Mankind, which is the progeny of Adam, is warned against this particular aspect of Satanic influence on their lives. When men show indifference to God's Guidance and turn away from the Message of the Prophets, they virtually place themselves at the mercy of Satan. For it is Satan who makes them abandon ways that are consistent with true human nature and who leads them to immodesty in the same way he did with Adam and Eve. Were man to reflect on this, it would become quite evident that when he is deprived of the guidance of the Prophets, he cannot even appreciate, let alone fulfil, the primary requirements of his true nature.

16. These verses bring into focus several important points.

First, that the need to cover oneself is not an artificial urge in man; rather it is an important dictate of human nature. Unlike animals, God did not provide man with the protective covering that He provided to animals. God has rather endowed man with the natural instincts of modesty and bashfulness. Moreover, the private parts of the body are not only related to sex, but also constitute سوأة that is, something the exposure of which is felt to be shameful. Also, God did not provide man with a natural covering in response to man's modesty and bashfulness, but has inspired in him (see verse 26) the urge to cover himself. This is in order that man might use his reason to understand the requirements of his nature, use the resources made available by God, and provide himself a dress.

Second, man instinctively knows that the moral purpose behind the use of dress takes precedence over the physical purpose. Hence the idea that man should resort to dress in order to cover his private parts precedes the mention of dress as a means of providing protection and adornment to the human body. In this connection man is altogether different from animals. With regard to the latter, the natural covering that has been granted serves to protect them from the inclemencies of weather and also to beautify their bodies. However, that natural covering is altogether unrelated to the purpose of concealing their sexual organs. The exposure of those organs is not a matter of shame for them and hence their nature is altogether devoid of the urge to cover them. However, as men fell prey to Satanic influences, they developed a false and unhealthy notion about the function of dress. They were led to believe that the function of dress for human beings is no different from that for animals, viz., to protect them from the inclemencies of weather and to make them look attractive. As for concealing the private parts of the body, the importance of that function has been belittled. For men have been misled into believing that their private parts are, in fact, like other organs of their body. As in the case of animals, there is little need for human beings to conceal their sex organs.

Third, the Qur'ān emphasizes that it is not enough for the dress to cover the private parts and to provide protection and adornment to the human body. Man's dress ought to be the dress of piety. This means that a man's dress ought to conceal his private parts. It should also render a man reasonably presentable – the dress being neither too shabby and cheap nor overly expensive and extravagant relative to his financial standing. Nor should dress smack of pride or hauteur, or reflect that pathological mental state in which men prefer characteristically feminine dresses and vice versa; or that the people belonging to one nation mimic people of other nations so as to resemble them, thereby becoming a living emblem of collective humiliation and abasement. The Qur'ānic ideal can only be achieved by those who truly believe in the Prophets and sincerely try to follow God's Guidance. For as soon as man decides to reject God's Guidance, Satan assumes his patronage and by one means or another manages to lead him into error after error.

Fourth, the question of dress constitutes one of the numerous signs of God which is visible virtually throughout the world. When the facts mentioned above are carefully considered it will be quite clear as to why dress is an important sign of God.

17. This refers to the pre-Islamic Arabian practice of circumambulating around the Ka'bah in stark nakedness. The people of those days thought that nakedness during circumambulation had been enjoined by God.

18. The simple and succinct Qur'ānic statement that 'Allah never enjoins any indecency' (verse 29) stands as the overwhelming argument against many false beliefs that were entertained by the people of Arabia. For a fuller appreciation of this argument, the following points should be kept in mind:

First, that the people of Arabia totally stripped themselves while performing certain religious rites under the mistaken notion that it had been so enjoined. But on the other hand they were agreed that nudity was a shameful thing so that no Arab of any standing could ever approve of appearing naked in any respectable assembly or market-place.

Second, notwithstanding their reservation about nudity, they stripped themselves totally while performing certain religious rites on the ground that religion was from God. Hence there was nothing objectionable about performing a religious act in a state of nakedness for God had so enjoined them regarding the performance of that rite. Here the Qur'ān confronts them with a clear question: How can they believe that God could order them to do something which involves nakedness and which they know to be inherently shameful? What is implied is that God could not command them to commit indecency, and if their religion contained elements of indecency then this is positive proof of its not being from God.

19. The verse seeks to suggest that God has nothing to do with their foolish rituals. So far as the religion truly prescribed by Him is concerned, its fundamental principles are the following:

(1) That man should base his life on justice and righteousness.

(2) That man's worship should have the right orientation, i.e. that it should be directed to God alone and should be free of every trace of devotion to others than God, that man should reserve his absolute enthralment and bondage for the One True God alone. All these should have only one direction – the One that is truly worthy of worship.

(3) Man should invoke God alone to keep him rightly directed, to grant him help and succour, to favour him with protection and security. This should be done provided one's life is oriented to serving God. Invoking help from God would be ludicrous if man's life is based on unbelief, polytheism, disobedience to God, or serving a variety of gods other than the One True God. Such a prayer would amount to asking God's help in strengthening one in one's rebellion against Him.

(30) A party He has guided to the Right Way, and for another party straying is justly its due for they have taken satans, rather than Allah, as their guardians, even though they think that they are rightly-guided.

(31) Children of Adam! Take your adornment at every time of Prayer;[20] and eat and drink without going to excesses. For Allah does not like those who go to excess.[21]

فَرِيقًا هَدَىٰ وَفَرِيقًا حَقَّ عَلَيْهِمُ
الضَّلَٰلَةُ إِنَّهُمُ اتَّخَذُوا الشَّيَٰطِينَ
أَوْلِيَآءَ مِن دُونِ اللَّهِ وَيَحْسَبُونَ
أَنَّهُم مُّهْتَدُونَ ﴿٣٠﴾ يَٰبَنِيٓ ءَادَمَ
خُذُوا زِينَتَكُمْ عِندَ كُلِّ مَسْجِدٍ وَكُلُوا
وَاشْرَبُوا وَلَا تُسْرِفُوٓا إِنَّهُ لَا يُحِبُّ
الْمُسْرِفِينَ ﴿٣١﴾

(4) That man should have full conviction that in the same way as God caused him to be born in the world, He will also restore him to life after death and will make him stand before Himself so as to render an account of his life.

20. The word *zīnah* which occurs in this verse refers to full and proper dress. While performing Prayer people are required not only to cover the private parts of their body, but also to wear a dress that serves the two-fold purpose of covering and giving one a decent appearance.

The directive to pray in a proper and decent dress is aimed at refuting the misconception entertained by ignorant people down the ages that man should worship God either in a nude or semi-naked state, or at least have a shabby and unkempt appearance while worshipping. In this verse people are being told the opposite of this. At the time of worship they should not only be free from all kinds of nudity and indecency, but should also be in a decent dress.

21. God does not want to subject man to want and misery or starvation, or to deprive him as such of the good things of this worldly life. On the contrary, it pleases Him that man should appear in good, decent dress and enjoy the clean food provided for him by God. There is nothing sinful in that. As for sin, it consists in transgressing the bounds set by God. This

(32) Say (O Muḥammad): 'Who has forbidden the adornment which Allah has brought forth for His crcatures or the good things from among the means of sustenance?'[22] Say: 'These are for the enjoyment of the believers in this world, and shall be exclusively theirs on the Day of Resurrection.'[23] Thus do We clearly expound Our revelations for those who have knowledge.

قُلْ مَنْ حَرَّمَ زِينَةَ ٱللَّهِ ٱلَّتِىٓ أَخْرَجَ
لِعِبَادِهِۦ وَٱلطَّيِّبَٰتِ مِنَ ٱلرِّزْقِ ۚ قُلْ هِىَ
لِلَّذِينَ ءَامَنُوا۟ فِى ٱلْحَيَوٰةِ ٱلدُّنْيَا خَالِصَةً
يَوْمَ ٱلْقِيَٰمَةِ ۗ كَذَٰلِكَ نُفَصِّلُ ٱلْءَايَٰتِ
لِقَوْمٍ يَعْلَمُونَ ﴿٣٢﴾

---

transgression could be committed in both ways: by making the unlawful lawful, or by making the lawful unlawful.

22. Since it is God Himself Who has created all good and pure things for man, it obviously could not have been His intent to make them unlawful. Now, if there is any religion, or any ethical or social system which forbids those things, or considers them an insurmountable barrier to man's spiritual growth, it has an intellectual orientation which itself is evident proof of its not having been prescribed by God.

This is an important argument which the Qur'ān advances in refutation of false creeds. An appreciation of this argument would help one understand the Qur'ānic line of argumentation as such.

23. All the clean and beautiful things created by God are meant, in principle, for the believers even in this world, for they are God's faithful subjects, and it is fidelity to God that makes one deserve enjoyment of the things which are God's. However, all men are under a test in this world. Hence even those who are disloyal to God have been granted respite to mend their ways and are, therefore, not denied His worldly bounties. In fact with a view to testing those disloyal to God these bounties are at times lavished upon them even more abundantly than on God's faithful servants. But the character of the Next Life will be totally different. For one's station there will be determined entirely by one's righteousness and justice. God's bounties in the Next Life, therefore, will be for the faithful alone. As for the unfaithful, those who were disloyal to God even though every fibre of their being was nourished by the sustenance provided by Him, they will have no share whatsoever of those bounties in the Next Life.

(33) Tell them (O Muḥammad): 'My Lord has only forbidden indecent acts, whether overt or hidden;[24] all manner of sin;[25] wrongful transgression;[26] and [He has forbidden] that you associate with Allah in His divinity that for which He has sent down no sanction; and that you ascribe to Allah things of which you have no sure knowledge that they are from Him.'

(34) For every community there is an appointed term; and when its term arrives, they cannot tarry behind a moment, nor can they get ahead.[27] ►

قُلْ إِنَّمَا حَرَّمَ رَبِّيَ ٱلْفَوَٰحِشَ مَا ظَهَرَ مِنْهَا وَمَا
بَطَنَ وَٱلْإِثْمَ وَٱلْبَغْيَ بِغَيْرِ ٱلْحَقِّ وَأَن
تُشْرِكُوا۟ بِٱللَّهِ مَا لَمْ يُنَزِّلْ بِهِۦ سُلْطَٰنًا وَأَن
تَقُولُوا۟ عَلَى ٱللَّهِ مَا لَا تَعْلَمُونَ ﴿٣٣﴾ وَلِكُلِّ
أُمَّةٍ أَجَلٌ فَإِذَا جَآءَ أَجَلُهُمْ لَا يَسْتَأْخِرُونَ
سَاعَةً وَلَا يَسْتَقْدِمُونَ ﴿٣٤﴾

---

24. For an elaboration of hidden and overt indecencies see *Towards Understanding the Qur'ān*, vol. II, *al-An'ām*, 6: nn. 128 and 131, pp. 290–2.

25. The word *ithm* denotes negligence, dereliction of duty. *Āthimah* signifies the she-camel which, though capable of running at a fast pace, deliberately moves slowly. The meaning of the word, therefore, carries the idea of sin. Viewed in the context of man, the word conveys the sense of man's deliberate neglect of his duty to God, his failure to pursue God's good pleasure despite his having the capacity to obey and follow Him.

26. To exceed the limits set by God and to enter an area which has been declared out of bounds for man constitute rebellion and transgression. According to this definition of *baghy*, the charge of rebellion will apply to all those who act according to their whims rather than in accordance with the directives of God. It is applicable to those who behave as though they are the true masters of God's Kingdom, claiming for themselves the prerogatives of God. It also applies to all those who usurp the rights of others.

27. The expression 'fixed term' used in the verse should not give rise to the misconception that the term of a nation expires on a definite day,

(35) Children of Adam! If Messengers come to you from amongst yourselves who rehearse to you My signs, then those who shun disobedience and mend their ways shall have nothing to fear, nor shall they grieve. (36) And those who reject Our revelations as false and turn away from them in arrogance, they shall be the inmates of Hell; and there shall they abide.[28] (37) Who is more unjust then he who invents a falsehood, ascribing it to Allah, or who rejects His revelation as false? Their full portion of God's Decree shall reach them,[29] until Our deputed angels come to them to take charge of their souls, and say: 'Where are the deities now, those whom you invoked besides Allah?' They will say: 'They are all gone away from us.' And they shall bear witness against themselves that they were unbelievers. ▶

يَٰبَنِيٓ ءَادَمَ إِمَّا يَأۡتِيَنَّكُمۡ رُسُلٞ مِّنكُمۡ
يَقُصُّونَ عَلَيۡكُمۡ ءَايَٰتِي فَمَنِ ٱتَّقَىٰ وَأَصۡلَحَ
فَلَا خَوۡفٌ عَلَيۡهِمۡ وَلَا هُمۡ يَحۡزَنُونَ ٣٥
وَٱلَّذِينَ كَذَّبُواْ بِـَٔايَٰتِنَا وَٱسۡتَكۡبَرُواْ
عَنۡهَآ أُوْلَٰٓئِكَ أَصۡحَٰبُ ٱلنَّارِۖ هُمۡ فِيهَا
خَٰلِدُونَ ٣٦ فَمَنۡ أَظۡلَمُ مِمَّنِ ٱفۡتَرَىٰ
عَلَى ٱللَّهِ كَذِبًا أَوۡ كَذَّبَ بِـَٔايَٰتِهِۦٓۚ أُوْلَٰٓئِكَ
يَنَالُهُمۡ نَصِيبُهُم مِّنَ ٱلۡكِتَٰبِۖ حَتَّىٰٓ إِذَا
جَآءَتۡهُمۡ رُسُلُنَا يَتَوَفَّوۡنَهُمۡ قَالُوٓاْ أَيۡنَ
مَا كُنتُمۡ تَدۡعُونَ مِن دُونِ ٱللَّهِۖ قَالُواْ
ضَلُّواْ عَنَّا وَشَهِدُواْ عَلَىٰٓ أَنفُسِهِمۡ أَنَّهُمۡ
كَانُواْ كَٰفِرِينَ ٣٧

---

month or year. What the statement really means is that God has laid down a minimum proportion between the good and evil deeds of a nation. As long as that nation is able to maint... that minimum proportion, its existence is tolerated in order that it might be able to show its performance. Once a nation crosses that minimum limit, it is denied any further respite. (For further explication of this point see *Nūḥ* 71: 4–10 and 12.)

28. Reference to the continuous unremitting punishment of the unbelievers occurs invariably on occasions where the Qur'ān narrates the coming

(38) Allah will say: 'Enter the fire of Hell and join the nations of *jinn* and men that have gone before you.' As a nation enters Hell, it will curse the one that went before it, and when all are gathered there, the last of them shall say of the first: 'Our Lord! These are the ones who led us astray. Let their torment be doubled in Hell-Fire.' He will answer: 'Each will have a doubled torment; although you do not know.'[30] ▶

قَالَ ٱدۡخُلُواْ فِيٓ أُمَمٖ قَدۡ خَلَتۡ مِن قَبۡلِكُم
مِّنَ ٱلۡجِنِّ وَٱلۡإِنسِ فِي ٱلنَّارِۖ كُلَّمَا دَخَلَتۡ
أُمَّةٞ لَّعَنَتۡ أُخۡتَهَاۖ حَتَّىٰٓ إِذَا ٱدَّارَكُواْ فِيهَا
جَمِيعٗا قَالَتۡ أُخۡرَىٰهُمۡ لِأُولَىٰهُمۡ رَبَّنَا
هَٰٓؤُلَآءِ أَضَلُّونَا فَـَٔاتِهِمۡ عَذَابٗا ضِعۡفٗا
مِّنَ ٱلنَّارِۖ قَالَ لِكُلّٖ ضِعۡفٞ وَلَٰكِن
لَّا تَعۡلَمُونَ ٣٨

down of Adam and Eve from Paradise. (See *al-Baqarah* 2: 38–9; *Ṭā Hā* 20: 123–4.) What has been said here should be considered in relation to the fact that at the very start of man's earthly life he was informed of the evil results of unbelief. (See *Towards Understanding the Qur'ān*, vol. I, *Āl 'Imrān* 3: n. 69, pp. 268–9 – Ed.)

29. All men, whether good or bad, have been granted a definite term in this world which they will spend and obtain their share of worldly happiness and misery.

30. As it is, each group of people is followed, even as it is preceded, by others. A group which inherits an error of outlook and conduct from its predecessors passes on the same, in turn, to future generations. In addition, whereas a group owes its wrong-doing partly to the wrong-doing of its predecessors, it will also be held responsible for leaving behind an evil legacy for the future generations. The Qur'ān, therefore, pronounces a double punishment on such a group: it will incur punishment for its own misdeeds and also for leaving behind such a legacy for the coming generations. A number of traditions elucidate this point. According to one such tradition the Prophet (peace be on him) said: 'He who introduces a misleading innovation which does not please God and His Messenger shall be held guilty for the sins of all those who follow that innovation without lessening in the least the burden [of sins] of those who followed the innovation.' (Cf. Ibn Mājah, *Muqaddimat Bāb Man Aḥyā Sunnah qad*

umītat, where the words are slightly different – Ed.) According to another tradition, he said: 'The responsibility for all the murders committed in the world is shared by the first son of Adam [i.e. Cain] for he was the first to have innovated murder.' (See Bukhārī, *Kitāb al-Janā'iz, Bāb Qawlih 'alay al-Salām Yu'addhab al-Mayyit bi Ba'ḍ Bukā'i ahlih 'alayh* – Ed.)

We thus know that the individual or group responsible for introducing a wrong idea or practice is not only responsible to the extent of those sins, but shares the responsibility of the sins of all those who are influenced by him. As long as the evil effects of that influence continue, their sins will be continually added to his account. This also shows that a person is not only accountable for the good or bad deeds that he commits. In fact he is also accountable for the influence of those deeds on others.

This may be illustrated by considering the case of someone who indulges in unlawful sex. All those whose bad examples, evil company, and inducements to evil caused a man to indulge in such an act have a share in the sin that he committed. The persons who influenced him in turn had been influenced by others. Were this chain of influence traced back to its ultimate origin, the blame would be fixed on the first person who demonstrated this unlawful way for satiating the sexual urge.

This does not detract from the fact that anyone who indulged in fornication is also accountable for the sin he committed. This is so because when he committed a sin he did so because he failed to make proper use of his capacity to distinguish between good and evil with which he had been endowed. He also did not pay due heed to the voice of his conscience, and mobilize the power of self-control given him. Nor did he benefit from the knowledge of good and evil transmitted to him by pious men nor was he inspired by the noble examples of the God-fearing. Nor did he learn any lesson from the evil consequences of sexual misconduct. Instead, he totally succumbed to blind sexual lust which sought gratification at all cost. This much relates to the responsibility of the person who indulged in sexual misconduct.

But there is another dimension of that person's evil conduct – his propagation of that same evil among others which ruined the lives of countless people belonging to his own generation and to the generations that follow. It is also possible that he might have been afflicted by some general disease which he then communicated to his own generation and also to the generations that followed. His sexual misconduct might also have given birth to illegitimate children, unjustly passing on the burden of their upbringing to others, and making his offspring – without any justification – co-sharers in the fortunes and even the inheritance of others. The wrong that is thus perpetrated persists for many generations. Likewise, it is also possible that the said criminal might, by his cunning, have led an innocent girl to sexually corrupt behaviour. That in turn is likely to awaken evil propensities in her which wreck the lives and homes of countless families, even generations. Also, by setting an evil example for his children, relatives, friends and the society at large a fornicator is likely to cast a bad influence on people around him and infect others with moral corruption. The evil consequences of such an act thus linger on for a long time. The moral corruption that ultimately engulfs the society owes its origin to the person who initially introduced an evil. Justice, therefore, demands that such a culprit should also be held responsible for the subsequent evils which may be traced back to his initial act of corruption.

The same holds true for good deeds. The reward for the heritage of goodness left behind by our predecessors from the earliest times should inevitably go to the credit of those men of the past who have continually transmitted that heritage to posterity down to our own time. If our own generation takes good care of that heritage, enriches it and passes it on to the coming generation, it also deserves due reward for that. As long as our good acts leave a trace of good influence on history and continue to cast a good influence on people, mankind will reap the benefits of those acts.

This is the Qur'ānic view of retribution. Every sensible person will agree that such a dispensation alone can ensure perfect justice. Appreciation of this concept should dispel the idea of those who believe that men can be fully rewarded or punished for their deeds within the confines of this worldly life. Likewise, such an appreciation should also dispel the views of those who believe that the transmigration of souls alone can ensure full justice to all men. Such people have blundered because they have neither grasped fully the nature and consequences of human acts nor the nature and requirements of perfect justice. It is obvious that the consequences of individuals' acts are not visible during their life-span – say sixty or seventy years or so. Instead, human activities, both good and evil, influence the lives of countless people belonging to countless generations. One cannot, therefore, be brought to justice during one's own lifetime, since only a small part of the consequences of those acts have yet come to the surface. Moreover, the limited possibilities available in the present world are quite inadequate for bringing people to justice. Just consider the hideous crime of someone who pushes us to a world war. As things stand, the catastrophic consequences of such a crime would affect the lives of billions of men through the ages. Is there any punishment – physical, spiritual or material – which can be deemed even remotely proportionate to that crime? Likewise, no worldly reward, however valuable, can adequately recompense for the noble services rendered by a philanthropist which will benefit numerous people for thousands of years.

Having viewed the question from this angle, one readily concludes that there must necessarily be life in the Hereafter such that full justice can be meted out to everyone. Here all human beings are brought together, their full records are made available, and the reckoning is made by God Himself Whose knowledge embraces literally everything. Additionally, men should be granted unlimited spans of life, and infinite possibilities should be made available for receiving compensation.

A little reflection on this will help us see how false the doctrine of the transmigration of souls is. Those who subscribe to this doctrine fail to

(39) Then the preceding ones will say to the succeeding ones: 'You were in no way superior to us; taste, then, this torment for your deeds.'[31]

(40) Surely the gates of Heaven shall not be opened for those who reject Our signs as false and turn away from them in arrogance; nor shall they enter Paradise until a camel passes through the eye of a needle. Thus do We reward the guilty ones.

وَقَالَتْ أُولَىٰهُمْ لِأُخْرَىٰهُمْ فَمَا كَانَ
لَكُمْ عَلَيْنَا مِن فَضْلٍ فَذُوقُوا۟ ٱلْعَذَابَ
بِمَا كُنتُمْ تَكْسِبُونَ ﴿٣٩﴾ إِنَّ ٱلَّذِينَ
كَذَّبُوا۟ بِـَٔايَـٰتِنَا وَٱسْتَكْبَرُوا۟ عَنْهَا
لَا تُفَتَّحُ لَهُمْ أَبْوَٰبُ ٱلسَّمَآءِ وَلَا يَدْخُلُونَ
ٱلْجَنَّةَ حَتَّىٰ يَلِجَ ٱلْجَمَلُ فِى سَمِّ ٱلْخِيَاطِ
وَكَذَٰلِكَ نَجْزِى ٱلْمُجْرِمِينَ ﴿٤٠﴾

---

realize that eternal life is needed to mete out recompense to people for the deeds they commit during their relatively brief spans of life. If one were to believe in the unending cycle of life and death, it would become impossible to reward or punish anyone for his actions, for each span of life would go on accumulating endlessly. The arrears would never be cleared.

31. In addition to the above verse, the Qur'ān elsewhere recounts the mutual incriminations of the dwellers of Hell. For example, it occurs in *Sūrah al-Saba'* in the following words: 'Could you but see when the wrong-doers will be made to stand before their Lord, throwing back the word (of blame) on one another! Those who had been abased will say to the arrogant ones: "Had it not been for you, we should certainly have been believers!" The arrogant ones will say to those who had been abased: "Was it we who kept you back from Guidance after it reached you? Nay, rather it was you yourselves who transgressed" ' (*al-Saba'* 34: 31–2).

This means that since the misguided people themselves were not keen on receiving the right guidance, they fell victims even more to the forces of misguidance. Out of their own excessive worldliness they chose to follow their ungodly leaders. Granted that it was the forces of misguidance which had invented ideologies such as materialism, excessive worldliness, and nationalism. But when people were attracted to these false ideologies, they did so out of their own weaknesses. These forces of evil achieved success because what they offered was to the utmost liking of the people. Again, the people who were tempted to embrace counterfeit religious ideologies were themselves to blame for falling prey to them since there was an inner

(41) Hell shall be their bed, and also above them their covering. Thus do We reward the wrong-doers. (42) And those who believe and do good – We do not impose upon any of them a burden beyond his capacity. They are the people of Paradise. And there they shall abide. (43) We shall strip away all rancour from their hearts,[32] and rivers shall flow beneath them, and they shall say: 'All praise be to Allah Who has guided us on to this. Had it not been for Allah Who granted us guidance, we would not be on the Right Path. Surely the Messengers of our Lord did indeed come down with truth.' Then a voice will cry out to them: 'This is the Paradise which you are made to inherit as a reward for your deeds.'[33]

لَهُم مِّن جَهَنَّمَ مِهَادٌ وَمِن فَوْقِهِمْ
غَوَاشٍ ۚ وَكَذَٰلِكَ نَجْزِى ٱلظَّٰلِمِينَ
﴿٤١﴾ وَٱلَّذِينَ ءَامَنُوا۟ وَعَمِلُوا۟
ٱلصَّٰلِحَٰتِ لَا نُكَلِّفُ نَفْسًا إِلَّا وُسْعَهَآ
أُو۟لَٰٓئِكَ أَصْحَٰبُ ٱلْجَنَّةِ ۖ هُمْ فِيهَا
خَٰلِدُونَ ﴿٤٢﴾ وَنَزَعْنَا مَا فِى صُدُورِهِم
مِّنْ غِلٍّ تَجْرِى مِن تَحْتِهِمُ ٱلْأَنْهَٰرُ ۖ وَقَالُوا۟
ٱلْحَمْدُ لِلَّهِ ٱلَّذِى هَدَىٰنَا لِهَٰذَا وَمَا كُنَّا
لِنَهْتَدِىَ لَوْلَآ أَنْ هَدَىٰنَا ٱللَّهُ ۖ لَقَدْ جَآءَتْ
رُسُلُ رَبِّنَا بِٱلْحَقِّ ۖ وَنُودُوٓا۟ أَن تِلْكُمُ
ٱلْجَنَّةُ أُورِثْتُمُوهَا بِمَا كُنتُمْ
تَعْمَلُونَ ﴿٤٣﴾

urge in them to accept such ideologies. Rather than submitting to the One True God and to rigorous moral discipline, they looked for deities that would help them to achieve their worldly purposes. Naturally, they invented deities of their own liking. They also desired the intercession of those who would let them grow in worldliness and godlessness, and yet who would also ensure their redemption in the Next World. As they preferred a religion that would not make their life a bit dry, permissive religious cults which did not object to any kind of self-indulgence were developed. This establishes clearly that the external forces of evil alone are not to blame. The people who succumb to evil and error equally share the blame. This neither condones the role of those who seek to mislead others, nor detracts from the responsibility of those who choose to be misled.

(44) And the people of Paradise shall cry to the people of Hell: 'Surely we have found our Lord's promise to us to be true; have you also found true what your Lord has promised you?' 'Yes', they shall answer; and a herald shall cry out among them: 'Allah's curse be upon the wrong-doers'; (45) upon those who hinder men from the path of Allah and seek to make it crooked; and disbelieve in the Hereafter.'

وَنَادَىٰٓ أَصْحَـٰبُ ٱلْجَنَّةِ أَصْحَـٰبَ ٱلنَّارِ أَن قَدْ
وَجَدْنَا مَا وَعَدَنَا رَبُّنَا حَقًّا فَهَلْ وَجَدتُّم
مَّا وَعَدَ رَبُّكُمْ حَقًّا قَالُوا۟ نَعَمْ فَأَذَّنَ مُؤَذِّنٌۢ
بَيْنَهُمْ أَن لَّعْنَةُ ٱللَّهِ عَلَى ٱلظَّـٰلِمِينَ ﴿٤٤﴾
ٱلَّذِينَ يَصُدُّونَ عَن سَبِيلِ ٱللَّهِ وَيَبْغُونَهَا
عِوَجًا وَهُم بِٱلْـَٔاخِرَةِ كَـٰفِرُونَ ﴿٤٥﴾

---

32. If there develops any rancour or ill-will among good people during the course of their worldly lives, such rancour and ill-will will be removed in the Hereafter. Their hearts will be purged of all hostile feelings and they will enter Paradise as cordial friends. They will not feel envious towards those who had formerly been opposed or hostile to them that they share with them the bounties of Paradise. Significantly, 'Alī once recited this very verse and remarked: 'I wish that I and 'Uthmān and Ṭalḥah and al-Zubayr will be among those about whom God has said: "And We shall take away all rancour from their hearts" ' (verse 43). (See Qurṭubī's comments on verse 43 – Ed.)

Reflection on the verse leads one to conclude that out of His mercy God will first purge the righteous of their blemishes. This will be done before admitting them to Paradise. Thus they will enter Paradise in a state of untainted purity.

33. This refers to something of a fine and delicate character that will take place in Paradise. Instead of boasting about their virtuous deeds which led them to Paradise, the righteous will thank and praise God profusely and acknowledge His grace and mercy without which they could never have entered Paradise. On the other hand, God will not impress His bounty upon the righteous; He will rather emphasize that Paradise is granted to them by way of compensation for their righteous conduct, that it is the fruit of their hard labour; that it is not like the crumbs of charity but a fair recompense for their striving. The subtlety involved here is further brought into relief by the fact that the above response will not be made by God. It will rather be just announced to them.

(46) And between the two there will be a barrier, and on the Heights will be men who will recognize each person by his mark and will cry out to the people of Paradise: 'Peace be to you.' These will be the ones who had not yet joined them in Paradise, though they long to do so.[34] (47) And when the eyes of the people of the Heights will be turned towards the people of Hell they will say: 'Our Lord! Do not cast us among the wrong-doing people.' ►

وَبَيْنَهُمَا حِجَابٌ وَعَلَى ٱلْأَعْرَافِ رِجَالٌ
يَعْرِفُونَ كُلًّا بِسِيمَٰهُمْ وَنَادَوْا۟ أَصْحَٰبَ ٱلْجَنَّةِ أَن
سَلَٰمٌ عَلَيْكُمْ لَمْ يَدْخُلُوهَا وَهُمْ يَطْمَعُونَ ﴿٤٦﴾
۞ وَإِذَا صُرِفَتْ أَبْصَٰرُهُمْ تِلْقَآءَ أَصْحَٰبِ
ٱلنَّارِ قَالُوا۟ رَبَّنَا لَا تَجْعَلْنَا مَعَ ٱلْقَوْمِ ٱلظَّٰلِمِينَ ﴿٤٧﴾

What is said above about the Hereafter may be discerned in the attitude of the righteous in the world itself. The wicked and arrogant ones take great pride in their worldly attainments and ascribe them to their own efforts. They firmly believe that what they have achieved is the fruit of their labour. Swayed by such notions, they continue to act even more haughtily. Conversely the righteous look upon all the bounties which they receive as favours from God. Accordingly, they thank and praise Him out of gratitude. The more they are lavished with worldly favours, the more humble and generous they become. Moreover, they do not suffer from the illusion that their righteousness will certainly earn them their salvation. On the contrary, they consistently repent over their lapses and earnestly turn to God in the hope that He will pardon them out of His grace and mercy. They are always fearful of God's reckoning lest their evil deeds are found to outweigh their good deeds. According to a tradition, the Prophet (peace be on him) said: 'Know well that none will be able to enter Paradise by dint of his good deeds.' When asked if that would apply to him as well, the Prophet (peace be on him) replied: 'Yes, in my case as well; unless God covers me with His mercy and favour.' (Bukhārī, *Kitāb al-Riqāq*, *'Bāb al-Qaṣd wa al-Mudāwamah 'alá al-'Amal'* – Ed.)

(48) And the people of the Heights will cry out to the men whom they would recognize by their marks, saying: 'Neither your numbers nor the riches of which you were proud availed you. (49) Are these not the ones of whom you swore that Allah shall grant them nothing of His mercy?' To such it will be said: 'Enter Paradise. You have no cause to fear, nor shall you grieve.'

(50) And the people of the Fire will cry out to the people of Paradise: 'Pour out some water on us or throw at us something of what Allah has bestowed upon you.' They will reply: 'Allah has forbidden them to the deniers of the truth, (51) who have made their religion a sport and play, and whom the life of the world has beguiled. So on that Day We shall forget them in the manner they forget their meeting of this Day with Us and persist in denying Our revelations.'[35]

وَنَادَىٰٓ أَصْحَٰبُ ٱلْأَعْرَافِ رِجَالًا يَعْرِفُونَهُم
بِسِيمَٰهُمْ قَالُوا۟ مَآ أَغْنَىٰ عَنكُمْ جَمْعُكُمْ
وَمَا كُنتُمْ تَسْتَكْبِرُونَ ﴿٤٨﴾ أَهَٰٓؤُلَآءِ ٱلَّذِينَ
أَقْسَمْتُمْ لَا يَنَالُهُمُ ٱللَّهُ بِرَحْمَةٍ ۚ ٱدْخُلُوا۟
ٱلْجَنَّةَ لَا خَوْفٌ عَلَيْكُمْ وَلَآ أَنتُمْ تَحْزَنُونَ
﴿٤٩﴾ وَنَادَىٰٓ أَصْحَٰبُ ٱلنَّارِ أَصْحَٰبَ
ٱلْجَنَّةِ أَنْ أَفِيضُوا۟ عَلَيْنَا مِنَ ٱلْمَآءِ
أَوْ مِمَّا رَزَقَكُمُ ٱللَّهُ ۚ قَالُوٓا۟ إِنَّ ٱللَّهَ
حَرَّمَهُمَا عَلَى ٱلْكَٰفِرِينَ ﴿٥٠﴾
ٱلَّذِينَ ٱتَّخَذُوا۟ دِينَهُمْ لَهْوًا وَلَعِبًا
وَغَرَّتْهُمُ ٱلْحَيَوٰةُ ٱلدُّنْيَا ۚ فَٱلْيَوْمَ
نَنسَىٰهُمْ كَمَا نَسُوا۟ لِقَآءَ يَوْمِهِمْ
هَٰذَا وَمَا كَانُوا۟ بِـَٔايَٰتِنَا
يَجْحَدُونَ ﴿٥١﴾

---

34. The people of *A'rāf* (Heights) will be the people who are neither righteous enough to enter Paradise nor wicked enough to be cast into Hell. They will, therefore, dwell at a place situated between the two.

35. The trialogue between the People of Paradise, the People of the Fire, and the People of the Heights gives some indication of the tremendous

(52) Surely We have brought them a Book which We expounded with knowledge;[36] a guidance and a mercy to those who believe.[37] (53) Are they waiting for the fulfilment of its warning?[38] On the Day that warning is fulfilled, those that have neglected it before will say: 'The Messengers of Our Lord did indeed bring forth the truth. Are there any intercessors who will now plead on our behalf? Or, can we be restored to life that we might perform differently from that which we did?'[39] They surely ended in utter loss, and the lies they had fabricated failed them.

وَلَقَدْ جِئْنَٰهُم بِكِتَٰبٍ فَصَّلْنَٰهُ عَلَىٰ عِلْمٍ
هُدًى وَرَحْمَةً لِّقَوْمٍ يُؤْمِنُونَ ﴿٥٢﴾ هَلْ
يَنظُرُونَ إِلَّا تَأْوِيلَهُۥ يَوْمَ يَأْتِى تَأْوِيلُهُۥ يَقُولُ
ٱلَّذِينَ نَسُوهُ مِن قَبْلُ قَدْ جَآءَتْ رُسُلُ
رَبِّنَا بِٱلْحَقِّ فَهَل لَّنَا مِن شُفَعَآءَ
فَيَشْفَعُوا۟ لَنَآ أَوْ نُرَدُّ فَنَعْمَلَ غَيْرَ ٱلَّذِى كُنَّا
نَعْمَلُ ۚ قَدْ خَسِرُوٓا۟ أَنفُسَهُمْ وَضَلَّ عَنْهُم
مَّا كَانُوا۟ يَفْتَرُونَ ﴿٥٣﴾

---

range of human faculties in the Next World. These faculties would increase to such an extent that the People of Paradise, the People of the Fire and the People of the Heights will be able to see, hear and talk to one another. Other Qur'ānic statements about the Hereafter enable us to realize that the laws operating in the Next World will be altogether different from those in the present. Notwithstanding this, men's personalities will not undergo any such change.

Those who cannot perceive anything beyond the present limited world and who are incapable of imagining scales bigger than the ones relating to the present world, make fun of the statements in the Qur'ān and *Ḥadīth* about life in the Hereafter. This only betrays their poverty of understanding and imagination. The fact, however, is that the possibilities for life are not as narrow and limited as their minds.

36. The Qur'ān has spelled out in some detail what constitutes the fundamental reality, explained the attitude that man ought to adopt, and laid down the fundamentals of the way of life that he ought to follow. The details laid down in the Book in this regard are based on sound knowledge rather than on conjecture and fancy.

(54) Surely your Lord is none other than Allah, Who created the heavens and the earth in six days,[40] and then ascended His Throne;[41] Who causes the night to cover the day and then the day swiftly pursues the night; Who created the sun and the moon and the stars making them all subservient to His command. Lo! His is the creation and His is the command.[42] Blessed is Allah,[43] the Lord of the universe. ▶

إِنَّ رَبَّكُمُ ٱللَّهُ ٱلَّذِى خَلَقَ ٱلسَّمَٰوَٰتِ
وَٱلْأَرْضَ فِى سِتَّةِ أَيَّامٍ ثُمَّ ٱسْتَوَىٰ عَلَى
ٱلْعَرْشِ يُغْشِى ٱلَّيْلَ ٱلنَّهَارَ يَطْلُبُهُۥ حَثِيثًا
وَٱلشَّمْسَ وَٱلْقَمَرَ وَٱلنُّجُومَ مُسَخَّرَٰتٍۭ
بِأَمْرِهِۦٓ ۗ أَلَا لَهُ ٱلْخَلْقُ وَٱلْأَمْرُ ۗ تَبَارَكَ ٱللَّهُ
رَبُّ ٱلْعَٰلَمِينَ ﴿٥٤﴾

37. The contents and teachings of the Book are perspicuous enough to show one the right way. Moreover, the life-style of those who believe in this Book also bears out, by the beneficial effects it produces on human life, how well it guides man. The blessings of the Qur'ān become evident if man first notes the healthy changes that it brings about in his outlook, character and morals.

The above verse in fact alludes to the wonderful effect belief in the Qur'ān had on the lives of the Companions of the Prophet (peace be on him).

38. The position of the people in question is as follows. The difference between good and evil was first explained to them, and yet they turned a deaf ear to it. Then some people established a good example by following the right path notwithstanding the dominant trend towards error. The wholesome effect of righteous conduct became evident from the lives of such people, but it made no impression on the people concerned. Their persistence in error could only mean one thing: that they would only learn the lesson the hard way when they saw the painful effects of their error. Such people are like stupid patients who neither follow the directions of the physician, nor learn any lesson from their own observations of the many patients who have been cured of their diseases by following the directions of physicians. These people will realize – if they realize at all – on their death-bed that their ways were foolish and fatal.

39. Such people will long to return to the world, pleading that they will believe in the truth which they had rejected since they have now witnessed it. They will also ensure that their attitude will be different from that which had been before. For a fuller discussion of this plea and the rejoinder to it see *al-An'ām* 6: 27–8; *Ibrāhīm* 14: 44 and 45; *al-Sajdah* 32: 12–13; *al-Fāṭir* 35: 37; *al-Zumar* 39: 56–9; and *al-Mu'min* 40: 11–12.

40. The word 'day' in the above verse has been used either in the usual sense of the twenty-four hour unit of time, or in a more general sense of 'period' of time such as in the following verses of the Qur'ān:

> Verily a Day in the sight of your Lord is like a thousand years of your reckoning (*al-Ḥajj* 22: 47).
>
> The angels and the Spirit ascend unto Him on a Day the measure of which is fifty thousand years (*al-Ma'ārij* 70: 4. For further explanation see *Fuṣṣilat* 41, nn. 12–15.)

41. It is quite difficult to appreciate fully the exact nature of the Qur'ānic statement: '(Allah) ascended the Throne.' One possibility is that after the creation of the universe God focused His effulgence at a particular point in His Kingdom which is known as the Throne, from where He showers the blessings of life and power, and governs the whole universe.

It is possible that the word 'Throne' stands for dominion and authority and that God's ascending the Throne signifies His actual taking over the reins of the universe after having created it. Whatever the exact meaning of the expression '(Allah) ascended the Throne', the main thrust of the verse is that God is not just the creator of the universe, but is also its sovereign and ruler; that after creating the universe He did not detach Himself from, nor become indifferent to, His creation. On the contrary, He effectively rules over the universe as a whole as well as every part of it. All power and sovereignty rest with Him. Everything in the universe is fully in His grip and is subservient to His will. Every atom is bound in obedience to Him. The fate of everything existent is in His Hands. Thus the Qur'ān undermines the very basis of the misconception which leads man at times to polytheism, and at others to self-glorification and so to rebellion against God. This is the natural corollary of considering God divorced from the affairs of the universe. In such cases, there are two possibilities. One, that beings other than God are considered to have the power to make or mar man's destiny. Here, man is bound to turn to those beings in devotion and subservience. The second possibility is for man to consider himself as the master of his own destiny. Here, man considers himself independent of, and indifferent to, any higher being.

It is significant that the words and figures of speech employed by the Qur'ān to denote the relationship between God and man are closely related to kingship, dominion, and sovereignty. This is too conspicuous a fact to be missed by any careful student of the Qur'ān. It is strange, however, that it has led some superficial critics and persons of biased outlook to conclude that the Qur'ān reflects the milieu in which man's outlook was dominated by monarchical concepts, and that therefore its 'author', who in their view was the Prophet Muḥammad (peace be on him), presented God as a sovereign ruler, an absolute monarch.

Quite contrary to this is the fundamental truth which the Qur'ān emphatically affirms – God's sovereignty over the heavens and the earth. It negates, with equal emphasis, that sovereignty belongs to anyone else. Such a doctrine demolishes the very assumption on the basis of which the above erroneous conclusion was derived. The Qur'ānic concept of God's sovereignty is in sharp contrast to the idea that creatures of God may lay claim to sovereignty and kingship. In contrast to the weak, mortal kings of the world, God is eternal and all-powerful. This undermines the very basis of the misconceived criticism that Islam has a monarchical basis since no human being can conform to the Islamic description of the sovereign. All sovereignty vests in the One True God. Hence, all those who claim total or partial sovereignty either for any person or group of people are merely cherishing an illusion. It is evident, therefore, that it is totally inappropriate for man, who is a part of the universe created and governed by God, to adopt any other attitude than that of acknowledging God as the only object of worship and as the only sovereign in a societal and political sense.

42. This is an elaboration of the idea propounded in the note immediately above explaining the meaning of God's ascension to the Throne. To reiterate, God is not merely the sole creator but also the only One Who commands and governs. He has not detached Himself from His creation, leaving it to the care of others who might rule over it as they please. Nor has He granted independence to His creation or any part of it so that they might function as they wish. On the contrary, His grip over the entire universe is very firm. He rules over it according to His sovereign will. If we find alternation taking place between day and night, it is a result of God's command. God has full power both to hold that process in abeyance, or to alter the very system which causes the alternation. The heavenly bodies – the sun, the moon, and the stars – are all absolutely powerless. They are totally subservient to God's overpowering will, and have been yoked to function according to His command.

43. The word *barakah* signifies growth and increase. The notions of elevation and greatness as well as of permanence and stability are also an essential part of the word's meaning. Besides these the word inalienably carries nuances of goodness and beneficence. To say that God is full of *barakah* means that His goodness knows no bounds; that endless beneficence emanates from Him; that He is the Exalted One Whose loftiness knows no end; that His beneficence and loftiness are permanent, and thus

(55) Call upon your Lord with humility and in secret. Surely He does not love transgressors. (56) And do not make mischief in the earth after it has been set in order,[44] and call upon Him with fear and longing.[45] Surely Allah's mercy is close to those who do good.

ٱدْعُوا۟ رَبَّكُمْ تَضَرُّعًا وَخُفْيَةً إِنَّهُۥ
لَا يُحِبُّ ٱلْمُعْتَدِينَ ﴿٥٥﴾
وَلَا تُفْسِدُوا۟ فِى ٱلْأَرْضِ بَعْدَ
إِصْلَٰحِهَا وَٱدْعُوهُ خَوْفًا وَطَمَعًا إِنَّ
رَحْمَتَ ٱللَّهِ قَرِيبٌ مِّنَ
ٱلْمُحْسِنِينَ ﴿٥٦﴾

they will never vanish or suffer decline. (For further elaboration see *Tafhīm al-Qur'ān, al-Furqān* 25: nn. 1 and 19.)

44. The command not to make mischief in the earth means not to vitiate the right order of life. What basically constitutes 'mischief-making' is to surrender oneself to one's lusts, to commit acts in subservience to other human beings and to subscribe to base morals, social orders, civilizations, principles and laws derived from sources other than God's Guidance. This is the essential mischief from which innumerable evils issue and which the Qur'ān seeks to eradicate. The Qur'ān also emphasizes that sound order is the original condition, and disorder and mischief occurred later as accidents resulting from man's ignorance and transgression. In other words, man's life on earth did not start with ignorance, savagery, polytheistic beliefs, rebellion against God and moral disorder whereafter reforms were gradually introduced. On the contrary, man's life began with good order and was later corrupted because of man's perversity and folly. God sent Prophets from time to time in order to eradicate the disorder that had set in and to restore the original, good order. These Prophets constantly exhorted people to refrain from disrupting the original order and creating mischief.

Thus the Qur'ānic view on this question is altogether different from that of the proponents of the false doctrine of evolution, who postulate that man has gradually come out of darkness into light; that life has advanced in a unilinear fashion, towards increasingly better conditions. The Qur'ān rather postulates that human life began in the full light of Divine Guidance, that the original state of affairs was in accord with the Right Way prescribed by God. The blame for corruption goes to man who, falling victim to Satan's allurements, veered towards darkness and corrupted the right order of human life again and again. As for God, He continually sent Prophets in order to summon men from darkness to light, and to ask them to eschew

(57) And it is He Who sends forth winds as glad tidings in advance of His Mercy, and when they have carried a heavy-laden cloud We drive it to a dead land, then We send down rain from it and bring forth therewith fruits of every kind. In this manner do We raise the dead that you may take heed. (58) As for the good land, vegetation comes forth in abundance by the command of its Lord, whereas from the bad land, only poor vegetation comes forth.[46] Thus do We expound Our signs in diverse ways for a people who are grateful.

وَهُوَ ٱلَّذِى يُرْسِلُ ٱلرِّيَٰحَ بُشْرًۢا
بَيْنَ يَدَىْ رَحْمَتِهِۦ ۖ حَتَّىٰٓ إِذَآ أَقَلَّتْ
سَحَابًا ثِقَالًا سُقْنَٰهُ لِبَلَدٍ مَّيِّتٍ فَأَنزَلْنَا
بِهِ ٱلْمَآءَ فَأَخْرَجْنَا بِهِۦ مِن كُلِّ ٱلثَّمَرَٰتِ ۚ
كَذَٰلِكَ نُخْرِجُ ٱلْمَوْتَىٰ لَعَلَّكُمْ
تَذَكَّرُونَ ﴿٥٧﴾ وَٱلْبَلَدُ ٱلطَّيِّبُ
يَخْرُجُ نَبَاتُهُۥ بِإِذْنِ رَبِّهِۦ ۖ وَٱلَّذِى خَبُثَ
لَا يَخْرُجُ إِلَّا نَكِدًا ۚ كَذَٰلِكَ نُصَرِّفُ
ٱلْءَايَٰتِ لِقَوْمٍ يَشْكُرُونَ ﴿٥٨﴾

---

evil and wickedness. (See *Towards Understanding the Qur'ān, al-Baqarah* 2, n. 230, pp. 165–6 – Ed.)

45. This clearly shows what the expression 'mischief-making' in the verse signifies. It consists of man's turning to others than God as his guardian, patron and helper, and calling them to his aid and support. To bring about reform, therefore, consists of man's turning exclusively to God as his guardian and helper.

'Calling upon Allah with fear and longing' conveys the idea that man should fear God alone, and to Him alone he should look for the fulfilment of his wishes. While calling upon God man should realize that he is totally dependent on God's favour and that he can attain success only if God helps and guides him to it. Similarly, man should also bear in mind that once he is deprived of God's support, he is doomed to utter failure and undoing.

46. It is necessary to grasp the subtle point made here in order to appreciate the full purport of what is being said. The reference to rain and its advantages is intended to bring into focus God's power, and to affirm life after death. Moreover, it is also intended to draw attention in

(59) Indeed We sent forth Noah to his people,[47] and he said: 'O my people! Serve Allah, you have no other god than Him.[48] Indeed I fear for you the chastisement of an awesome Day.' (60) The leading men of his people replied: 'We see that you are in palpable error.' (61) He said: 'O my people! There is no error in me, but I am a Messenger from the Lord of the universe. ▶

لَقَدْ أَرْسَلْنَا نُوحًا إِلَىٰ قَوْمِهِۦ فَقَالَ يَٰقَوْمِ
ٱعْبُدُوا۟ ٱللَّهَ مَا لَكُم مِّنْ إِلَٰهٍ غَيْرُهُۥٓ إِنِّىٓ
أَخَافُ عَلَيْكُمْ عَذَابَ يَوْمٍ عَظِيمٍ ﴿٥٩﴾
قَالَ ٱلْمَلَأُ مِن قَوْمِهِۦٓ إِنَّا لَنَرَىٰكَ فِى ضَلَٰلٍ
مُّبِينٍ ﴿٦٠﴾ قَالَ يَٰقَوْمِ لَيْسَ بِى
ضَلَٰلَةٌ وَلَٰكِنِّى رَسُولٌ مِّن رَّبِّ
ٱلْعَٰلَمِينَ ﴿٦١﴾

allegorical, albeit graphic, terms to the blessings of prophethood, and how it helps men to distinguish between good and evil, between pure and impure. The intimation of Divine Guidance through the Prophets is compared to the movement of winds, the appearance of rain-laden clouds, and the fall of life-sustaining raindrops. In the same way as rainfall causes dead earth to be revived and makes the hidden treasures of life burst forth from its womb, so the impact of the teachings of the Prophets also brings dead humanity back to life, causing the hidden goodness in men to burst forth.

This allegory also hints at another important fact. In the same way that only fertile soil profits from rainfall, so only men of a righteous nature can profit from the blessings of prophethood. As for the wicked, they are like wasteland. Rainfall can cause such a land to bring forth only thorny bushes and cacti. Similarly, when the wicked come into contact with the teaching of the Prophets, the hidden evils of their nature come into full play.

This allegory is followed by a well-sustained account with illustrations from history showing that whenever the Prophets preach their Message, men split into two camps. The righteous receive the blessings of prophethood and flourish, bringing forth the fruit of their goodness. As for the wicked, once the criterion provided by the Prophets is applied their impurities are fully exposed. This enables human society to purge itself of impurities in the same way as the goldsmith purges precious metals of alloy.

47. This historical narrative opens with an account of the Prophet Noah and his people. For the people of Noah were the first to drift away from the right way of life which was followed by the Prophet Adam and his

(62) I convey to you the messages of my Lord, give you sincere advice, and I know from Allah that which you do not know. (63) Do you wonder that admonition should come to you from your Lord through a man from amongst yourselves that he may warn you, that you may avoid evil and that mercy may be shown to you?'[49] ▶

أُبَلِّغُكُمْ رِسَٰلَٰتِ رَبِّي وَأَنصَحُ لَكُمْ
وَأَعْلَمُ مِنَ ٱللَّهِ مَا لَا تَعْلَمُونَ ﴿٦٢﴾
أَوَعَجِبْتُمْ أَن جَآءَكُمْ ذِكْرٌ مِّن رَّبِّكُمْ عَلَىٰ
رَجُلٍ مِّنكُمْ لِيُنذِرَكُمْ وَلِتَتَّقُوا وَلَعَلَّكُمْ
تُرْحَمُونَ ﴿٦٣﴾

descendants. God, therefore, sent Noah to guide and reform them.

In light of the Qur'ānic allusions and Biblical statements it seems certain the people of Noah inhabited the land presently known as Iraq. This view is also supported by inscriptions of pre-Biblical times discovered in the course of archaeological excavations in Babylonia. Those inscriptions contain almost the same account which is recounted in the Qur'ān and the Torah. The locale of the event is the vicinity of Mosul. Kurdish and Armenian traditions also corroborate this account insofar as they mention that it was in this area that Noah's Ark anchored. Some relics ascribed to Noah are still found in Jazīrat Ibn 'Umar, situated to the north of Mosul and on the frontiers of Armenia in the vicinity of the Ararat mountain mass. The inhabitants of Nakhichevan believe to this day that their town was founded by Noah.

Traditions similar to the story of Noah are also found in classical Greek, Egyptian, Indian and Chinese literature. Moreover, stories of identical import have been popular since time immemorial in Burma, Malaya, the East Indies, Australia, New Guinea and various parts of Europe and America. This shows clearly that the event took place at some point in the dim past when men lived together in one region and it was after Noah's Flood that they dispersed to different parts of the world. This is why traditions of all nations mention the Flood of the early time. This is notwithstanding the fact that the actual event has increasingly been shrouded in mystery, and the authentic elements of the event overlaid with myth and legend.

48. It is evident from the above verse and from other Qur'ānic descriptions of the people of Noah that they were neither ignorant of, nor denied the existence of God, nor were they opposed to the idea of worshipping

(64) But they charged him with falsehood. Thereupon We delivered Noah and those who were with him in the Ark, and caused those who rejected Our signs as false to be drowned.[50] Surely they were a blind folk.

فَكَذَّبُوهُ فَأَنجَيْنَٰهُ وَٱلَّذِينَ مَعَهُۥ فِى ٱلْفُلْكِ وَأَغْرَقْنَا ٱلَّذِينَ كَذَّبُوا۟ بِـَٔايَٰتِنَآ ۚ إِنَّهُمْ كَانُوا۟ قَوْمًا عَمِينَ ﴿٦٤﴾

Him. Their real malady was polytheism. They had associated others with God in His godhead, and considered them akin to God in their claim that human beings should worship them as well. This basic error gave rise to a number of evils among them. There had arisen among them a class of people representing the false gods they themselves had contrived. Gradually this class of people virtually monopolized all religious, economic and political authority. This class also introduced a hierarchical structure of society which led to immense corruption and injustice. The moral degeneration which this system promoted sapped the roots of mankind's higher characteristics. When corruption reached a high peak, God sent Noah to improve the state of affairs. For long, Noah strove with patience and wisdom to bring about reform. All his efforts, however, were thwarted by the clergy which craftily kept people under its powerful hold. Eventually Noah prayed to God not to spare even a single unbeliever on the face of the earth, for they would go about misguiding human beings, and their progeny would likewise be wicked and ungrateful. (For a detailed discussion see *Hūd* 11: 25–48, *al-Shu'arā'* 26: 105–22 and *Nūḥ* 71: 1–28.)

49. There were striking similarities between Muḥammad and Noah (peace be on them). The Prophet Muḥammad (peace be on him) received the same treatment from his people as did Noah from his. The message that each of them sought to preach was also the same. Likewise, the doubts and objections raised by the people of Muḥammad (peace be on him) with regard to his prophethood were the same as those raised by Noah's people several thousand years ago. Again, what Muḥammad (peace be on him) said in response to the doubts and objections raised against him were exactly the same as what Noah had said.

The Qur'ānic narration of the stories of the Prophets makes it amply clear that the attitude of the nations to whom the Prophets were sent had always been the same as that of the Makkans towards the Message of Muḥammad (peace be on him). Apart from this, the accounts of the various Prophets and their people, display the same striking resemblances. Likewise, the Prophet Muḥammad's (peace be on him) vindication of his teaching in response to the Makkans is identical with similar attempts by

(65) And to 'Ād[51] We sent forth their brother Hūd. He said: 'O my people! Serve Allah; you have no other god than Him. Will you, then, not avoid evil?' (66) The unbelievers among the leading men of his people said: 'Indeed we see you in folly, and consider you to be liars.' ▶

۞ وَإِلَىٰ عَادٍ أَخَاهُمْ هُودًا ۗ قَالَ يَٰقَوْمِ
ٱعْبُدُوا۟ ٱللَّهَ مَا لَكُم مِّنْ إِلَٰهٍ غَيْرُهُۥٓ ۚ
أَفَلَا تَتَّقُونَ ﴿٦٥﴾ قَالَ ٱلْمَلَأُ ٱلَّذِينَ
كَفَرُوا۟ مِن قَوْمِهِۦٓ إِنَّا لَنَرَىٰكَ فِى
سَفَاهَةٍ وَإِنَّا لَنَظُنُّكَ مِنَ
ٱلْكَٰذِبِينَ ﴿٦٦﴾

other Prophets to vindicate their teachings. So doing, the Qur'ān seeks to emphasize that in the same way as the error and misguidance of which men become victims have remained essentially the same throughout the ages, the Message of God's Messengers has also been the same in all places and at all times. Again, there is a striking resemblance in the ultimate fate of all those peoples who reject the message of the Prophets and who persist in their erroneous and evil ways. This too has also been the same, namely utter destruction.

50. An uninitiated reader of the Qur'ān may mistakenly conceive that the mission of each Prophet – to call his people to God – would have finished after the few attempts they made in that connection. Some people might even entertain a rather simplistic image of their mission. It might be thought that a Prophet would have suddenly risen and proclaimed to his people that he had been designated by God as a Prophet. This would have been followed by the raising of objections to that claim. Subsequently, the Prophet concerned would have explained the matter and might have removed their misgivings. The people would have stuck to their position, would have rejected the Prophet's claim and called him a liar, whereupon God must have visited that people with punishment.

The fact of the matter, however, is that the Qur'ān has narrated in just a few lines a story that was worked out over a long period of time. The brevity of the Qur'ānic description owes itself to the fact that the Qur'ān is not interested *per se* in story-telling; that its narration and purpose are didactic. Hence, while recounting a historical event, the Qur'ān mentions only those fragments of the event which are relevant, ignoring those details which are irrelevant to Qur'ānic purposes. Again, at different places in the Qur'ān the same event is mentioned for a variety of reasons. On every occasion only those fragments of the story which are relevant to a specific purpose are mentioned and the rest are left out. An instance in point is the above narrative about Noah. In narrating Noah's story the Qur'ān aims to point out the consequences attendant upon the rejection of the Prophet's Message. Since the total period spent on conveying the Message does not have any direct relationship with that purpose, the Qur'ān altogether ignores it here. However, in passages where the Prophet and the Companions have been asked to remain patient, the long duration of the Prophet Noah's missionary effort has been mentioned. This has been done precisely with a view to raising the morale of the believers and to prevent them from feeling low because they did not see any good results coming out of that struggle. By mentioning how Noah strove patiently for such a long period of time and in the face of discouraging circumstances is quite relevant in this context as it helps to teach the lesson which is intended. That lesson is to persist in serving the cause of the truth and to refuse to be daunted by the adversity of the circumstances. See *al-'Ankabūt* 29: 14.

It would be appropriate to remove, at this stage, a doubt which might agitate the minds of some people. For one frequently reads in the Qur'ān accounts of nations which rejected their Prophets and charged them with lying. One also reads about the Prophets warning them of God's punishment, and then about its sudden advent, scourging the nation and totally destroying it. This gives rise to the question: Why do such catastrophic incidents not take place in our own time? Nations still rise and fall, but the phenomenon of their rise and fall is of a different nature. We do not see it happen that a nation is served with a warning, and is then totally destroyed by a calamity such as an earthquake, a flood, a storm, or a thunderbolt.

In order to understand this it should be remembered that a nation which has directly received God's Message from a Prophet is treated by God in a different manner from nations which have not witnessed a Prophet. For if a nation directly witnesses a Prophet – an embodiment of righteousness – and receives God's Message from his tongue, it has no valid excuse left for rejecting that Message. And if it still rejects the Message, it indeed deserves to be summarily punished. Other nations are to be placed in a different category since they received God's Message indirectly. Hence, if the nations of the present time are not visited by the devastating punishments which struck the nations of the Prophets in the past, one need not wonder since prophethood came to an end with the advent of Muḥammad (peace be on him). One should indeed have cause to wonder if one saw the opposite happen – that is, if the nations of the present were visited by punishments from God which had afflicted those nations that rejected their Prophets face to face.

This does not mean, however, that God has ceased to inflict severe punishments on nations which turn away from God and are sunk in ideological and moral error. The fact is that God's punishments still afflict different nations of the world. These punishments are both minor and major. Minor punishments are aimed at warning those nations, and the major ones are of a much more serious character and cause considerable damage. However, in the absence of the Prophets who are wont to draw

(67) He said: 'O my people! There is no folly in me; rather I am a Messenger from the Lord of the universe. (68) I convey to you the messages of my Lord, and I give you sincere advice. (69) Do you wonder that an exhortation should come to you from your Lord through a man from amongst yourselves that he may warn you? And do call to mind when He made you successors after the people of Noah and amply increased you in stature. Remember then the wondrous bounties[52] of Allah, that you may prosper. ▶

قَالَ يَٰقَوْمِ لَيْسَ بِى سَفَاهَةٌ وَلَٰكِنِّى
رَسُولٌ مِّن رَّبِّ ٱلْعَٰلَمِينَ ﴿٦٧﴾
أُبَلِّغُكُمْ رِسَٰلَٰتِ رَبِّى وَأَنَا۠ لَكُمْ
نَاصِحٌ أَمِينٌ ﴿٦٨﴾ أَوَعَجِبْتُمْ أَن جَآءَكُمْ
ذِكْرٌ مِّن رَّبِّكُمْ عَلَىٰ رَجُلٍ مِّنكُمْ
لِيُنذِرَكُمْ وَٱذْكُرُوٓا۟ إِذْ
جَعَلَكُمْ خُلَفَآءَ مِنۢ بَعْدِ قَوْمِ نُوحٍ
وَزَادَكُمْ فِى ٱلْخَلْقِ بَصْۜطَةً
فَٱذْكُرُوٓا۟ ءَالَآءَ ٱللَّهِ لَعَلَّكُمْ
تُفْلِحُونَ ﴿٦٩﴾

---

attention to moral degeneration as the basic cause of these calamities, the historians and thinkers of our time only scratch the surface and explain these in terms of physical laws or historical causes. These sophisticated explanations are of little help. On the contrary, nations so afflicted with heedlessness and moral stupor are thereby further prevented from appreciating that God has always warned evil-doing nations against following their evil ways, and that when they wilfully disregard these warnings and adamantly stick to their erroneous ways, He ultimately inflicts disastrous punishments upon them.

51. 'Ād, an ancient Arab people, were well-known throughout Arabia. They were known for their proverbial glory and grandeur. And when they were destroyed, their extinction also became proverbial. So much so that the word *'ādī* has come to be used for things ancient and the word *'ādīyāt* for archaeological remains. The land whose owner is unknown and which is lying fallow from neglect is called *'ādī al-arḍ*.

The ancient Arabic poetry is replete with references to this people. Arab genealogists consider the 'Ād as the foremost among the extinct tribes of Arabia. Once a person of the Banū Dhuhl b. Shaybān tribe, who was a resident of the 'Ād territory, called on the Prophet (peace be on him). He

(70) They said: 'Have you come to us that we should worship none other than Allah and forsake all whom our forefathers were wont to worship?[53] Then bring upon us the scourge with which you have threatened us if you are truthful?' ▶

قَالُوٓاْ أَجِئۡتَنَا لِنَعۡبُدَ ٱللَّهَ وَحۡدَهُۥ وَنَذَرَ مَا كَانَ يَعۡبُدُ ءَابَآؤُنَا فَأۡتِنَا بِمَا تَعِدُنَآ إِن كُنتَ مِنَ ٱلصَّٰدِقِينَ ٧٠

related stories to the Prophet about the people of 'Ād, stories handed down to the people of that region from generation to generation. (See Aḥmad b. Ḥanbal, *Musnad*, vol. 3, p. 482 – Ed.)

According to the Qur'ān, the people of 'Ād lived mainly in the Aḥqāf region which is situated to the south-west of the Empty Quarter (al-Rub' al-Khālī) and which lies between Ḥijāz, Yemen and Yamamah. It was from there that the people of 'Ād spread to the western coast of Yemen and established their hegemony in Oman, Ḥadramawt and Iraq. There is very little archaeological evidence about the 'Ād. Only a few ruins in South Arabia are ascribed to them. At a place in Ḥadramawt there is a grave which is considered to be that of the Prophet Hūd. James R. Wellested, a British naval officer, discovered an ancient inscription in 1837 in a place called Ḥiṣn al-Ghurāb which contains a reference to the Prophet Hūd. The contents unmistakably bear out that it had been written by those who followed the *Sharī'ah* of Hūd. (For details see *Tafhīm al-Qur'ān, al-Aḥqāf* 46, n. 25.)

52. The word *ālā'* used in the above verse stands for bounties, wondrous works of nature, and praiseworthy qualities. The purpose of the verse is to impress upon man to gratefully recognize the favours God has lavished upon him, bearing in mind that God also has the power to take them away.

53. It is worth noting that the people of 'Ād neither disbelieved in God nor refused to worship Him. They did not, however, follow the teachings of Hūd who proclaimed God alone should be worshipped, and that none other may be associated in servitude to Him.

(71) Hūd warned them: 'Surely punishment and wrath from your Lord have befallen upon you. Do you dispute with me about mere names that you and your forefathers have concocted[54] and for which Allah has sent down no sanction?[55] Wait, then, and I too am with you among those who wait.' (72) Then We delivered Hūd and his companions by Our mercy, and We utterly cut off the last remnant of those who called the lie to Our signs and would not believe.[56]

قَالَ قَدْ وَقَعَ عَلَيْكُم مِّن رَّبِّكُمْ
رِجْسٌ وَغَضَبٌ أَتُجَٰدِلُونَنِي فِي
أَسْمَآءٍ سَمَّيْتُمُوهَآ أَنتُمْ وَءَابَآؤُكُم
مَّا نَزَّلَ ٱللَّهُ بِهَا مِن سُلْطَٰنٍ فَٱنتَظِرُوٓا۟
إِنِّي مَعَكُم مِّنَ ٱلْمُنتَظِرِينَ ﴿٧١﴾
فَأَنجَيْنَٰهُ وَٱلَّذِينَ مَعَهُۥ بِرَحْمَةٍ مِّنَّا
وَقَطَعْنَا دَابِرَ ٱلَّذِينَ كَذَّبُوا۟ بِـَٔايَٰتِنَا
وَمَا كَانُوا۟ مُؤْمِنِينَ ﴿٧٢﴾

54. They looked to gods of rain, and gods of wind, wealth, and health. But none of these enjoys godhead. There are many instances in our own time of people whose beliefs are no different from the ones mentioned above. There are people who are wont to call someone *Mushkil Kushā*, 'the remover of distress' or to call someone else *Ganjbakhsh*, 'the bestower of treasures'. But God's creatures cannot remove the distresses of other creatures like themselves, nor do they have any treasure that they might give away to others. Their titles are merely empty words, bereft of the qualities attributed to them. All argumentation aimed at justifying those titles amounts to a lot of sound and fury about nothing.

55. The Makkans could produce no sanction from Allah – Whom they themselves acknowledged as the Supreme God – that He had transferred to their false gods any of His power or authority. None has any authorization from God to remove distress from, or bestow treasures on, others. It is the Makkans themselves who arbitrarily chose to confer parts of God's power on those beings.

56. The Qur'ān informs us that God brought about the total extermination of the 'Ād, a fact borne out by both Arabian historical traditions and recent archaeological discoveries. The 'Ād were so totally destroyed and their

(73) And to Thamūd[57] We sent forth their brother, Ṣāliḥ. He said to them: 'O my people! Serve Allah, you have no other god than Him. Truly there has come to you a clear proof from your Lord. This she-camel from Allah is a Divine portent for you.[58] So leave her alone to pasture on Allah's earth, and touch her with no evil lest a painful chastisement should seize you. ▶

وَإِلَىٰ ثَمُودَ أَخَاهُمْ صَٰلِحًا قَالَ يَٰقَوْمِ ٱعْبُدُوا۟ ٱللَّهَ مَا لَكُم مِّنْ إِلَٰهٍ غَيْرُهُۥ قَدْ جَآءَتْكُم بَيِّنَةٌ مِّن رَّبِّكُمْ هَٰذِهِۦ نَاقَةُ ٱللَّهِ لَكُمْ ءَايَةً فَذَرُوهَا تَأْكُلْ فِىٓ أَرْضِ ٱللَّهِ وَلَا تَمَسُّوهَا بِسُوٓءٍ فَيَأْخُذَكُمْ عَذَابٌ أَلِيمٌ ﴿٧٣﴾

monuments so completely effaced that the Arab historians refer to them as one of the *umam bā'idah* (extinct peoples) of Arabia. The Arab tradition also affirms that the only people belonging to the 'Ād who survived were the followers of the Prophet Hūd. These survivors are known as the Second 'Ād ('Ād Thāniyah). The Ḥiṣn al-Ghurāb inscriptions referred to earlier (n. 51 above) are among the remaining monuments of these people. One inscription, which is generally considered to date from the eighteenth century B.C., as deciphered by the experts, contains the following sentences:

> We have lived for a long time in this fort in full glory, free of all want. Our canals were always full to the brim with water . . . Our rulers were kings who were far removed from evil ideas, who dealt sternly with mischief-makers and governed us according to the Law of Hūd. Their edicts were recorded in a book. We believed in miracles and resurrection.

The above account fully corroborates the Qur'ānic statement that it was only the companions of Hūd who survived and inherited the glory and prosperity of the 'Ād.

57. The Thamūd are another ancient Arab people, next only to the 'Ād in fame. Legends relating to them were quite popular in pre-Islamic Arabia. In fact poetry and orations of the pre-Islamic *(Jāhilīyah)* period abound with references to them. They are also mentioned in the Assyrian inscriptions and in the Greek, Alexandrian and Roman works of history and geography. Some descendants of the Thamūd survived to a little before the birth of Jesus. The Roman historians mention that they entered into

the Roman army and fought against the Nabateans, their arch-enemy.

The Thamūd lived in the north-western part of Arabia which is still called al-Ḥijr. In the present time there is a station on the Ḥijāz railway between Madina and Tabūk. This is called Madā'in Ṣāliḥ, which was the capital town of Thamūd and was then known as al-Ḥijr, the rock-hewn city. This has survived to this day and is spread over thousands of acres. It was once inhabited by no less than half a million people. At the time of the revelation of the Qur'ān Arab trade caravans passed through the ruins of this city.

While the Prophet (peace be on him) was on his way to Tabūk, he directed the Muslims to look upon these monuments and urged them to learn the lessons which sensible persons ought to learn from the ruins of a people that had been destroyed because of their evil-doing. The Prophet (peace be on him) also pointed to the well from which the she-camel of the Prophet Ṣāliḥ used to drink. He instructed the Muslims to draw water from that well alone and to avoid all other wells. The mountain pass through which that she-camel came to drink was also indicated by the Prophet (peace be on him). The pass is still known as Fajj al-Nāqah. The Prophet (peace be on him) then gathered all the Muslims who had been directed to look around that city of rocks, and addressed them. He drew their attention to the tragic end of the Thamūd, who by their evil ways had invited God's punishment upon themselves. The Prophet (peace be on him) asked them to hastily move ahead for the place was a grim reminder of God's severe punishment and he hence called for reflection and repentance. (See Wāqidī, *al-Maghāzī,* vol. 3, pp. 1006–8. See also the comments of Ibn Kathīr on verses 73–8 – Ed.)

58. The context seems to indicate that the clear proof referred to in the verse stands for the she-camel which is also spoken of as 'a Divine portent'. In *al-Shu'arā'* 26: 154–8 it is explicitly mentioned that the Thamūd themselves had asked the Prophet Ṣāliḥ to produce some sign which would support his claim to be God's Messenger. Responding to it, Ṣāliḥ pointed to the she-camel.

This illustrates clearly that the appearance of the she-camel was a miracle. Similar miracles had been performed earlier by other Prophets with a view to fulfilling the demand of the unbelievers and thus of vindicating their claim to prophethood. The miraculous appearance of the she-camel reinforces the fact that Ṣāliḥ had presented it as a 'Divine portent' and warned his people of dire consequences if they harmed it. He explained to them that the she-camel would graze freely in their fields; that on alternate days she and other animals would drink water from their well. They were also warned that if they harmed the she-camel they would be immediately seized by a terrible chastisement from God.

Such statements could obviously only have been made about an animal which was known to be of a miraculous nature. The Thamūd observed the she-camel graze freely in their fields and she and the other camels drank

(74) And call to mind when He made you successors after 'Ād and gave you power in the earth so that you took for yourselves palaces in its plains and hewed out dwellings in the mountains.[59] Remember, then, the wondrous bounties of Allah and do not go about creating mischief in the land.'[60]

وَٱذْكُرُوٓا۟ إِذْ جَعَلَكُمْ خُلَفَآءَ مِنۢ
بَعْدِ عَادٍ وَبَوَّأَكُمْ فِى ٱلْأَرْضِ
تَتَّخِذُونَ مِن سُهُولِهَا قُصُورًا
وَتَنْحِتُونَ ٱلْجِبَالَ بُيُوتًا فَٱذْكُرُوٓا۟
ءَالَآءَ ٱللَّهِ وَلَا تَعْثَوْا۟ فِى ٱلْأَرْضِ
مُفْسِدِينَ ﴿٧٤﴾

water on alternate days from their well. The Thamūd, though unhappy with the situation, endured this for quite some time. Later, however, after prolonged deliberations, they killed her. Such lengthy deliberations demonstrate that they were afraid to kill the she-camel. It is clear that the object of their fear was none other than the she-camel as they had no reason to be afraid of Ṣāliḥ, who had no power to terrify them. Their sense of awe for the she-camel explains why they let her graze freely on their land. The Qur'ān, however, does not provide any detailed information as to what the she-camel looked like, or how she was born. The authentic *Ḥadīth* too provide no information about its miraculous birth. Hence, one need not take too seriously the statements of some of the commentators on the Qur'ān about the mode of her birth. However, as far as the fact of her miraculous birth is concerned, that is borne out by the Qur'ān itself.

59. The Thamūd were highly skilful in rock-carving, and made huge mansions by carving the mountains, as we have mentioned earlier (see n. 57 above). In this regard the works of the Thamūd resemble the rock-carvings in the Ajanta and Ellora caves in India and several other places. A few buildings erected by the Thamūd are still intact in Madā'in Ṣāliḥ and speak of their tremendous skills in civil engineering and architecture.

60. The Qur'ān asks people to draw a lesson from the tragic end of the 'Ād. For just as God destroyed that wicked people and established Muslims in positions of power and influence previously occupied by them, He can also destroy the Muslims and replace them by others if they should become wicked and mischievous. (For further elaboration see n. 52 above.)

(75) The haughty elders of his people said to those believers who had been oppressed: 'Do you know that Ṣāliḥ is one sent forth with a message from his Lord?' They replied: 'Surely we believe in the message with which he has been sent.' (76) The haughty ones remarked: 'Most certainly we disbelieve in that which you believe.'

(77) Then they hamstrung the she-camel,[61] disdainfully disobeyed the commandment of their Lord, and said: 'O Ṣāliḥ! Bring upon us the scourge with which you threatened us if you are truly a Messenger [of Allah].' (78) Thereupon a shocking catastrophe seized them,[62] so that they lay prostrate in their dwellings. ▶

قَالَ ٱلْمَلَأُ ٱلَّذِينَ ٱسْتَكْبَرُوا۟ مِن
قَوْمِهِۦ لِلَّذِينَ ٱسْتُضْعِفُوا۟ لِمَنْ ءَامَنَ
مِنْهُمْ أَتَعْلَمُونَ أَنَّ صَٰلِحًا مُّرْسَلٌ
مِّن رَّبِّهِۦ ۚ قَالُوٓا۟ إِنَّا بِمَآ أُرْسِلَ بِهِۦ
مُؤْمِنُونَ ﴿٧٥﴾ قَالَ ٱلَّذِينَ
ٱسْتَكْبَرُوٓا۟ إِنَّا بِٱلَّذِىٓ ءَامَنتُم
بِهِۦ كَٰفِرُونَ ﴿٧٦﴾ فَعَقَرُوا۟ ٱلنَّاقَةَ
وَعَتَوْا۟ عَنْ أَمْرِ رَبِّهِمْ وَقَالُوا۟
يَٰصَٰلِحُ ٱئْتِنَا بِمَا تَعِدُنَآ إِن كُنتَ مِنَ
ٱلْمُرْسَلِينَ ﴿٧٧﴾ فَأَخَذَتْهُمُ ٱلرَّجْفَةُ
فَأَصْبَحُوا۟ فِى دَارِهِمْ جَٰثِمِينَ ﴿٧٨﴾

61. Although the she-camel was killed by an individual, as we learn also from *sūrahs al-Qamar* (54) and *al-Shams* (91), the whole nation was held guilty since it stood at the killer's back. Every sin which is committed with the approval and support of a nation, is a national crime even if it has been committed by one person. In fact the Qur'ān goes a step further and declares that a sin which is committed publicly in the midst of a gathering is considered to be the collective sin of the people who tolerate it.

62. Other Qur'ānic expressions used for the calamity are *'rājifah'* (earthquake) (*al-Nāzi'āt* 79: 6); *'ṣayḥah'* (awesome cry) (*Hūd* 11: 67); *'ṣā'iqah'* (thunderbolt) (*al-Baqarah* 2: 55); and *'ṭāghiyah'* (roaring noise) (*al-Ḥāqqah* 69: 5).

(79) And Ṣāliḥ left them, saying: 'O my people! I conveyed to you the message of my Lord and gave you good advice; but you have no liking for your well-wishers.'

(80) And remember when We sent Lot [as a Messenger] to his people and he said to them:[63] 'Do you realize you practise an indecency of which no other people in the world were guilty of before you? (81) You approach men lustfully in place of women. You are a people who exceed all bounds.'[64]

فَتَوَلَّىٰ عَنْهُمْ وَقَالَ يَٰقَوْمِ لَقَدْ
أَبْلَغْتُكُمْ رِسَالَةَ رَبِّي
وَنَصَحْتُ لَكُمْ وَلَٰكِن لَّا تُحِبُّونَ
ٱلنَّٰصِحِينَ ﴿٧٩﴾ وَلُوطًا إِذْ قَالَ
لِقَوْمِهِۦٓ أَتَأْتُونَ ٱلْفَٰحِشَةَ مَا سَبَقَكُم
بِهَا مِنْ أَحَدٍ مِّنَ ٱلْعَٰلَمِينَ ﴿٨٠﴾
إِنَّكُمْ لَتَأْتُونَ ٱلرِّجَالَ شَهْوَةً مِّن
دُونِ ٱلنِّسَآءِ بَلْ أَنتُمْ قَوْمٌ
مُّسْرِفُونَ ﴿٨١﴾

63. The land inhabited by the people of Lot, which lies between Iraq and Palestine, is known as Trans-Jordan. According to the Bible, its capital town was Sodom, which is situated either somewhere near the Dead Sea, or presently lies submerged under it. Apart from Sodom, according to the Talmud, there were four other major cities, and the land lying between these cities was dotted with such greenery and orchards that the whole area looked like one big garden enchanting any onlooker. However, the whole nation was destroyed and today we can find no trace of it. So much so that it is difficult to even locate the main cities which they inhabited. If anything remains as a reminder of this nation it is the Dead Sea which is also called the Sea of Lot. The Prophet Lot who was a nephew of the Prophet Abraham, accompanied his uncle as he moved away from Iraq. Lot sojourned to Syria, Palestine and Egypt for a while and gained practical experience of preaching his message. Later God bestowed prophethood upon him and assigned to him the mission of reforming his misguided people. The people of Sodom have been referred to as the people of Lot presumably because Lot may have established matrimonial ties with those people.

One of the many accusations recorded against Lot in the Bible – and the Bible has been tampered with extensively by the Jews – is that Lot migrated to Sodom after an argument with Abraham (*Genesis* 13: 10–12).

The Qur'ān refutes this baseless charge and affirms that Lot was designated by God to work as His Messenger among his people.*

64. The Qur'ān refers elsewhere to the many evil deeds of the people of Lot. Here the Qur'ān confines itself to mentioning that most ignominious of crimes which invited God's scourge upon them.

The hideous act of sodomy, for which the people of Lot earned notoriety, has no doubt been committed by perverts in all times. The Greek philosophers had the distinction of glorifying it as a moral virtue. It was left, however, for the modern West to vigorously propagate sodomy so much so that it was declared legal by the legislatures of a few countries. All this has been done in the face of the obvious fact that this form of sexual intercourse is patently unnatural. God created distinctions between the sexes of all living beings for the purposes of reproduction and perpetuation of the species. As far as the human species is concerned, their creation into two sexes is related to another end as well: that the two should come together in order to bring into existence the family and establish human civilization. In view of this, not only were human beings divided into two sexes, but each sex was made attractive to the other. The physical structure and psychological make-up of each sex was shaped in keeping with the purpose of forging bonds of mutual cordiality between the members of the two sexes. The sexual act, which is intensely pleasurable, is at once a factor leading to the fulfilment of nature's purposes as underlined by the sexual division of humankind as well as a reward for fulfilling these purposes.

Now, the crime of the person who commits sodomy in flagrant opposition to this scheme of things, is not limited to that act alone. In fact he commits along with it a number of other crimes. First, he wages war against his own nature, against his inherent psychological predilection. This causes a major disorder which leads to highly negative effects on the lives of both the parties involved in that unnatural act – effects which are physical, psychological as well as moral. Second, he acts dishonestly with nature since while he derives sexual pleasure he fails to fulfil the societal obligation of which this pleasure is a recompense. Third, such a person also acts dishonestly with human society. For, although he avails himself of the advantages offered by various social institutions, when he has an opportunity to act, he uses his abilities in a manner which not only fails to serve

---

*The author here refers to an argument between Abraham and Lot which he considers to be a fabrication of the Jews. The obvious basis of this opinion is that such an argument between two Prophets is inconceivable since it is unbecoming of them as Prophets. The basis of this inference is a statement in *Genesis* 13: 1–12.

It seems there has been some confusion with regard to this inference. The verses of *Genesis* in question make no reference to any strife between the two Prophets. The strife to which it refers allegedly took place between the herdsmen of the two Prophets. In addition, when the two Prophets parted company it was on a pleasant note for Abraham had suggested that since there was an abundance of land, Lot should choose that part of the land he preferred so as to exclude all possibilities of strife between their herdsmen. (See *Genesis* 13: 5–10 – Ed.)

(82) Their only answer was: 'Banish them from your town. They are a people who pretend to be pure.'[65] (83) Then We delivered Lot and his household save his wife who stayed behind,[66] (84) and We let loose a shower [of stones] upon them.[67] Observe, then, the end of the evil-doers.[68]

وَمَا كَانَ جَوَابَ قَوْمِهِۦٓ إِلَّآ أَن
قَالُوٓاْ أَخْرِجُوهُم مِّن قَرْيَتِكُمْۖ
إِنَّهُمْ أُنَاسٌ يَتَطَهَّرُونَ ﴿٨٢﴾ فَأَنجَيْنَٰهُ
وَأَهْلَهُۥٓ إِلَّا ٱمْرَأَتَهُۥ كَانَتْ مِنَ
ٱلْغَٰبِرِينَ ﴿٨٣﴾ وَأَمْطَرْنَا عَلَيْهِم
مَّطَرًاۖ فَٱنظُرْ كَيْفَ كَانَ عَٰقِبَةُ
ٱلْمُجْرِمِينَ ﴿٨٤﴾

that society but which positively harms it. Apart from neglecting the obligations he owes to society, he renders himself incapable of serving the human race and his own family. He also produces effeminacy in at least one male and potentially pushes at least two females towards sexual corruption and moral depravity.

65. It is evident from the present verse that the people of Lot were not only shameless and corrupt, but were also a people who had sunk in moral depravity to such a degree that even the presence of a few righteous persons had become intolerable to them. Their moral degradation left them with no patience for anyone who sought to bring about any moral reform. Even the slightest element of purity found in their society was too much for them, and they simply wished to have their society purged of it.

When these people reached such a low point of wickedness and hostility to good, God decreed that they be wiped out altogether. When the collective life of a people becomes totally bereft of goodness and purity, it forfeits the right to exist on earth. Their example is like that of a basket of fruit. As long as some fruit remains firm, there is some justification to keep that basket. But the basket has to be thrown away when the fruit becomes rotten.

66. As the Qur'ān mentions elsewhere, Lot's wife supported her disbelieving relatives to the last.* Hence, when God directed Lot and his followers to migrate from that corrupt land, He ordained that Lot's wife be left behind.

67. The 'rainfall' in the verse does not refer to the descent of water from the sky. It refers rather to the volley of stones. The Qur'ān itself mentions that their habitations were turned upside down and ruined. (See verse 85; also *Hūd* 11: 82–3; *al-Ḥijr* 15: 74 – Ed.)

*This seems to be an inference from *al-Taḥrīm* 66: 10 – Ed.

(85) And to Midian[69] We sent forth their brother Shu'ayb He exhorted them: 'O my people! Serve Allah, you have no god but Him. Indeeu a clear proof has come to you from your Lord. So give just weight and measure and diminish not to men their things,[70] and make no mischief on the earth after it has been set in good order.[71] That is to your own good, if you truly believe.[72] ▶

وَإِلَىٰ مَدْيَنَ أَخَاهُمْ شُعَيْبًا قَالَ
يَٰقَوْمِ ٱعْبُدُوا۟ ٱللَّهَ مَا لَكُم
مِّنْ إِلَٰهٍ غَيْرُهُۥ قَدْ جَآءَتْكُم بَيِّنَةٌ
مِّن رَّبِّكُمْ فَأَوْفُوا۟ ٱلْكَيْلَ
وَٱلْمِيزَانَ وَلَا تَبْخَسُوا۟ ٱلنَّاسَ
أَشْيَآءَهُمْ وَلَا تُفْسِدُوا۟ فِى
ٱلْأَرْضِ بَعْدَ إِصْلَٰحِهَا ذَٰلِكُمْ
خَيْرٌ لَّكُمْ إِن كُنتُم مُّؤْمِنِينَ ﴿٨٥﴾

68. In light of this verse and other references in the Qur'ān, sodomy is established as one of the deadliest sins; and that it incurred God's scourge on those who indulged in it. We also know from the teachings of the Prophet (peace be on him) that the Islamic state should purge society of this crime and severely punish those guilty of it. There are several traditions from the Prophet (peace be on him) which mention that very severe punishments were inflicted on both partners of this act. According to one tradition, the Prophet (peace be on him) ordered that both partners be put to death. (See Ibn Mājah, *Kitāb al-Ḥudūd, 'Bab man 'amila 'Amal Qawm Lūṭ'* – Ed.) In another tradition it has been added that the culprits should be put to death whether they are married or un-married. (Ibn Mājah, *Kitāb al-Ḥudūd* – Ed.) In another tradition it has been said that both parties should be stoned (to death). (Ibn Mājah, *Kitāb al-Ḥudūd, 'Bab man 'amila 'Amal Qawm Lūṭ'* – Ed.) However, since no case of sodomy was reported in the lifetime of the Prophet (peace be on him), the punishment did not acquire a very clear and definitive shape. Among the Companions, 'Alī is of the view that such sinners should be beheaded and instead of being buried should be cremated. Abū Bakr also held the same view. However, 'Umar and 'Uthmān suggest that the sinners be made to stand under the roof of a dilapidated building, which should then be pulled down upon them. Ibn 'Abbās holds the view that those guilty of such a sinful act should be thrown from the top of the tallest building of the habitation and then pelted with stones. (See *al-Fiqh 'alá al-Madhāhib al-Arba'ah,* vol. 5, pp. 141–2 – Ed.) As for the jurists, Shāfi'ī pronounces the punishment of death on both partners to sodomy irrespective of their marital status, and of their role whether it be active or passive. According

to Sha'bī, Zuhrī, Mālik and Aḥmad b. Ḥanbal, they should be stoned to death. Sa'īd b. al-Musayyib, 'Aṭā', Ḥasan Baṣrī, Ibrāhīm Nakha'ī, Sufyān Thawrī and Awzā'ī believe that such sinners deserve the same punishment as laid down for unlawful sexual-intercourse: that unmarried ones should be lashed a hundred times and exiled, and that married ones should be stoned to death. Abū Ḥanīfah, however, does not recommend any specific punishment. For him, the sinner should be awarded, depending on the circumstances of each case, some deterrent punishment. According to one of the reports, the same was the view of Shāfi'ī. (See Ibn Qudāmah, *al-Mughnī,* vol. 8, pp. 187–8 – Ed.)

It should also be made clear that it is altogether unlawful for the husband to perpetrate this act on his wife. The Prophet (peace be on him), according to a tradition in Abū Dā'ūd, said: 'Cursed be he who commits this act with a woman.' (Abū Dā'ūd, *Kitāb al-Nikāḥ, 'Bāb fī Jāmi' al-Nikāḥ'* – Ed.) In other collections of *Ḥadīth* such as *Sunan* of Ibn Mājah and *Musnad* of Aḥmad b. Ḥanbal, we find the following saying of the Prophet (peace be on him): 'God will not even look at him who commits this act of sodomy with his wife in her rectum.' (Ibn Mājah, *'Kitāb al-Nikāḥ', 'Bāb al-Nahy 'an Ityān al-Nisā' fī Adbārihinn',* Aḥmad b. Ḥanbal, *Musnad,* vol. 2, p. 344 – Ed.) Likewise the following saying of the Prophet (peace be on him) is mentioned in Tirmidhī: 'He who makes sexual intercourse with a menstruating woman, or indulges in sodomy with a woman, or calls on a soothsayer, believing him to be true, denies the faith sent down to Muḥammad (peace be on him).' (Ibn Mājah, *Kitāb al-Ṭahārah, 'Bāb al-Nahy 'an Ityān al-Ḥā'iḍ'* – Ed.)

69. The territory of Madyan (Midian) lay to the north-west of Ḥijāz and south of Palestine on the coast of the Red Sea and the Gulf of Aqaba, and part of the territory stretched to the northern border of the Sinai Peninsula. The Midianites and their towns were situated at the crossroads of the trade routes from Yemen through Makka and Yanbu' to Syria along the Red Sea coast, and from Iraq to Egypt. Midian was, therefore, quite well known to the Arabs. In fact it persisted in their memory long after its destruction for the Arab trade caravans *en route* to Syria and Egypt passed through territories which were full of the ruins of their monuments.

Another point worth noting about the people of Midian is that they were reckoned to be descendants of Midyan, a son of the Prophet Abraham born of his third wife, Qaṭūrā'. According to a custom of the time, persons who attached themselves to a notable family were gradually counted as members of that family, as the descendants of that family's ancestor. It is for this reason that a large majority of Arabs were called the descendants of Ismā'īl. Likewise those who embraced faith at the hands of Ya'qūb's sons bore the general name 'the People of Israel'. Now, since the inhabitants of Midian owed allegiance to Midyan, son of Abraham, they were referred to as the descendants of Midyan and their territory was called Midian.

(86) And do not lie in ambush by every path [of life] seeking to overawe or to hinder from the path of Allah those who believe, nor seek to make the path crooked. Remember, how you were once few, and then He multiplied you, and keep in mind what was the end of mischief-makers. (87) And if there are some among you who believe in the message that I bear while some do not believe, have patience till Allah shall judge between us. He is the best of those who judge.'

وَلَا تَقْعُدُوا بِكُلِّ صِرَٰطٍ تُوعِدُونَ
وَتَصُدُّونَ عَن سَبِيلِ ٱللَّهِ مَنْ
ءَامَنَ بِهِۦ وَتَبْغُونَهَا عِوَجًا ۚ
وَٱذْكُرُوٓا۟ إِذْ كُنتُمْ قَلِيلًا
فَكَثَّرَكُمْ ۖ وَٱنظُرُوا۟ كَيْفَ كَانَ
عَٰقِبَةُ ٱلْمُفْسِدِينَ ﴿٨٦﴾ وَإِن كَانَ
طَآئِفَةٌ مِّنكُمْ ءَامَنُوا۟ بِٱلَّذِىٓ
أُرْسِلْتُ بِهِۦ وَطَآئِفَةٌ لَّمْ يُؤْمِنُوا۟
فَٱصْبِرُوا۟ حَتَّىٰ يَحْكُمَ ٱللَّهُ بَيْنَنَا ۚ وَهُوَ
خَيْرُ ٱلْحَٰكِمِينَ ﴿٨٧﴾

In view of this it should not be thought that the Prophet Shu'ayb invited them, for the first time, to follow Divine Guidance. At the time of the advent of Shu'ayb their state was no different from that of the Israelites at the time of the advent of Moses. They too were originally a Muslim people who had subsequently moved far away from Islam. For six to seven centuries they lived amongst a people who were steeped in polytheism and moral corruption, and this led to their contamination with polytheism and moral corruption. Despite their deviation and corruption, however, they claimed to be the followers of the true faith, and were proud of their religious identification.

70. This shows that the people of Midian suffered from two major ailments – polytheism and dishonesty in business. Shu'ayb devoted his efforts to purging them of those evils.

71. The import of this statement has been explained earlier in notes 44–5 above. In his exhortations to his people, Shu'ayb emphasized that they should not allow the order of life, established by the previous Prophets on the foundations of true faith and sound morals, to be corrupted by false beliefs and moral depravity.

72. This clearly shows that the people concerned claimed to be believers, as we have already pointed out. In fact, they were originally Muslims who

(88) The haughty elders of his people said: 'O Shu'ayb! We shall certainly banish you and your companions-in-faith from our town, or else you shall return to our faith.' Shu'ayb said: 'What! Even though we abhor [your faith]? (89) If we return to your faith after Allah has delivered us from it we would be fabricating a lie against Allah; nor can we return to it again unless it be by the will of Allah, our Lord.[73] Our Lord has knowledge of all things, and in Allah we put our trust. Our Lord! Judge rightly between us and our people, for You are the best of those who judge.'

۞ قَالَ ٱلۡمَلَأُ ٱلَّذِينَ ٱسۡتَكۡبَرُواْ مِن قَوۡمِهِۦ
لَنُخۡرِجَنَّكَ يَٰشُعَيۡبُ وَٱلَّذِينَ ءَامَنُواْ مَعَكَ
مِن قَرۡيَتِنَآ أَوۡ لَتَعُودُنَّ فِي مِلَّتِنَاۚ قَالَ أَوَلَوۡ
كُنَّا كَٰرِهِينَ ٨٨ قَدِ ٱفۡتَرَيۡنَا عَلَى ٱللَّهِ كَذِبًا
إِنۡ عُدۡنَا فِي مِلَّتِكُم بَعۡدَ إِذۡ نَجَّىٰنَا ٱللَّهُ
مِنۡهَاۚ وَمَا يَكُونُ لَنَآ أَن نَّعُودَ فِيهَآ إِلَّآ أَن
يَشَآءَ ٱللَّهُ رَبُّنَاۚ وَسِعَ رَبُّنَا كُلَّ شَيۡءٍ عِلۡمًاۚ
عَلَى ٱللَّهِ تَوَكَّلۡنَاۚ رَبَّنَا ٱفۡتَحۡ بَيۡنَنَا وَبَيۡنَ
قَوۡمِنَا بِٱلۡحَقِّ وَأَنتَ خَيۡرُ ٱلۡفَٰتِحِينَ ٨٩

had drifted away from Islam, who had become enmeshed in a range of evils. They not only professed to be believers, but took great pride in being so. (See n. 69 above – Ed.) Shu'ayb made this fact the starting-point of his preaching. He told them that if they indeed were believers they should live up to that fact; they should consider their salvation to lie in practising goodness and virtue, honesty and integrity; and they should distinguish between good and evil on the basis of the standards followed by righteous people rather than of those who believed neither in God nor in the Hereafter.

73. This phrase signifies substantively what is meant by the commonly-used Islamic formula *In-shā' Allāh* ('If Allah so wills'). Its meaning is evident from *al-Kahf* 18: 23–4, in which the believers are directed not to make definitive statements about what they will do without making such actions contingent on God's will. This is understandable since a believer firmly believes in God's power and is ever conscious that his destiny is inalienably tied to God's will. It is impossible for such a person to make foolish statements about what he will do and what he will not do. He is bound to make it clear that he will accomplish what he intends only if 'God so wills'.

(90) The elders of his people who disbelieved said: 'Should you follow Shu'ayb, you will be utter losers.'[74] (91) Thereupon a shocking catastrophe seized them, and they remained prostrate in their dwellings. (92) Those who had charged Shu'ayb with lying became as though they had never lived there; it is they who became utter losers.[75] (93) Shu'ayb then departed from his people, and said: 'O my people! Surely I conveyed to you the message of my Lord, and gave you sincere advice. How, then, can I mourn for a people who refuse to accept the truth?'[76]

وَقَالَ ٱلْمَلَأُ ٱلَّذِينَ كَفَرُوا۟ مِن قَوْمِهِۦ لَئِنِ
ٱتَّبَعْتُمْ شُعَيْبًا إِنَّكُمْ إِذًا لَّخَٰسِرُونَ
﴿٩٠﴾ فَأَخَذَتْهُمُ ٱلرَّجْفَةُ فَأَصْبَحُوا۟ فِى
دَارِهِمْ جَٰثِمِينَ ﴿٩١﴾ ٱلَّذِينَ كَذَّبُوا۟
شُعَيْبًا كَأَن لَّمْ يَغْنَوْا۟ فِيهَا ٱلَّذِينَ كَذَّبُوا۟
شُعَيْبًا كَانُوا۟ هُمُ ٱلْخَٰسِرِينَ ﴿٩٢﴾
فَتَوَلَّىٰ عَنْهُمْ وَقَالَ يَٰقَوْمِ لَقَدْ
أَبْلَغْتُكُمْ رِسَٰلَٰتِ رَبِّى وَنَصَحْتُ
لَكُمْ فَكَيْفَ ءَاسَىٰ عَلَىٰ قَوْمٍ
كَٰفِرِينَ ﴿٩٣﴾

74. One should not pass cursorily over this short sentence; instead one must reflect upon it. What the leaders of Midian in effect told their people was that Shu'ayb's exhortations to practise honesty and righteousness, and to strictly adhere to moral values, would spell their disaster. They implied that they could not succeed in the business carried on by the people of Midian if they were totally honest and straightforward in their dealings. Were they to let trading caravans pass by unmolested, they would lose all the advantages of being located at the crossroads of the major trade routes and by their proximity to the civilized and prosperous countries such as Egypt and Iraq. Also, if they were to become peaceful and to cease their attacks upon the trade caravans, they would no longer be held in awe by neighbouring countries.

Such attitudes have not, however, been confined to the tribal chiefs of Shu'ayb. People who stray away from truth, honesty and righteousness, regardless of their age and clime, have always found in honesty a means of great loss. People of warped mentalities in every age have always believed that trade, politics, and other worldly pursuits can never flourish unless they resort to dishonest and immoral practices. The main objection against the Message of truth in all ages has been that the pursuit of truth spells material doom.

75. The destruction of the people of Midian remained proverbial in Arabia for a long time. As such the following lines in *Psalms* are significant:

> Yea, they conspire with one accord;
> against thee they make a covenant –
> the tents of Edom and the Ish'maelites,
> Moab and the Hagrites,
> Gebal and Ammon and Am'alek,
> Philistia with the inhabitants of Tyre;
> Assyria also has joined them;
> they are the strong arms of the children of Lot.
> Do to them as thou didst to Mid'ian (*Psalms* 83: 5–9).

Note also the following statement in *Isaiah*:

> A remnant will return, the remnant of Jacob, to the mighty God. For though your people Israel be as the sand of the sea, only a remnant of them will return. Destruction is decreed, overflowing with righteousness. For the Lord, the Lord of hosts, will make a full end, as decreed, in the midst of all the earth. Therefore, thus says the Lord, the Lord of hosts: 'O my people, who dwell in Zion be not afraid of the Assyrians when they smite you with their rod and lift up their staff against you as the Egyptians did. For in a very little while my indignation will come to an end, and my anger will be directed to their destruction. And the Lord of hosts will wield against them a scourge, as when he smote Mid'ian at the rock of Oreb . . . ' (*Isaiah* 10: 21–6).

76. The stories narrated here have a definite didactic purpose and were narrated with a view to highlighting their relevance to the time of the Prophet (peace be on him). In each of these stories one of the parties is a Prophet who in respect of his teachings greatly resembles Muḥammad (peace be on him), in summoning his people to the right way, in admonishing them, in sincerely seeking their welfare. At the other end of the scale in each narrative are the unbelieving nations who greatly resembled the Quraysh in the time of the Prophet (peace be on him) with regard to their disbelief and moral degeneration.

By recounting the tragic end of each of these unrighteous nations of the past, the Quraysh are reminded of the moral purpose of these stories. Through the stories they are told that if, because of their stubbornness they fail to follow the Messenger of God during the term of respite granted to them, they will be subjected to the same destruction which befell those past nations who persisted in wrong-doing and error.

MAP NO. 1: THE LANDS OF THE ANCIENT TRIBES MENTIONED IN *SŪRAH AL-A'RĀF*

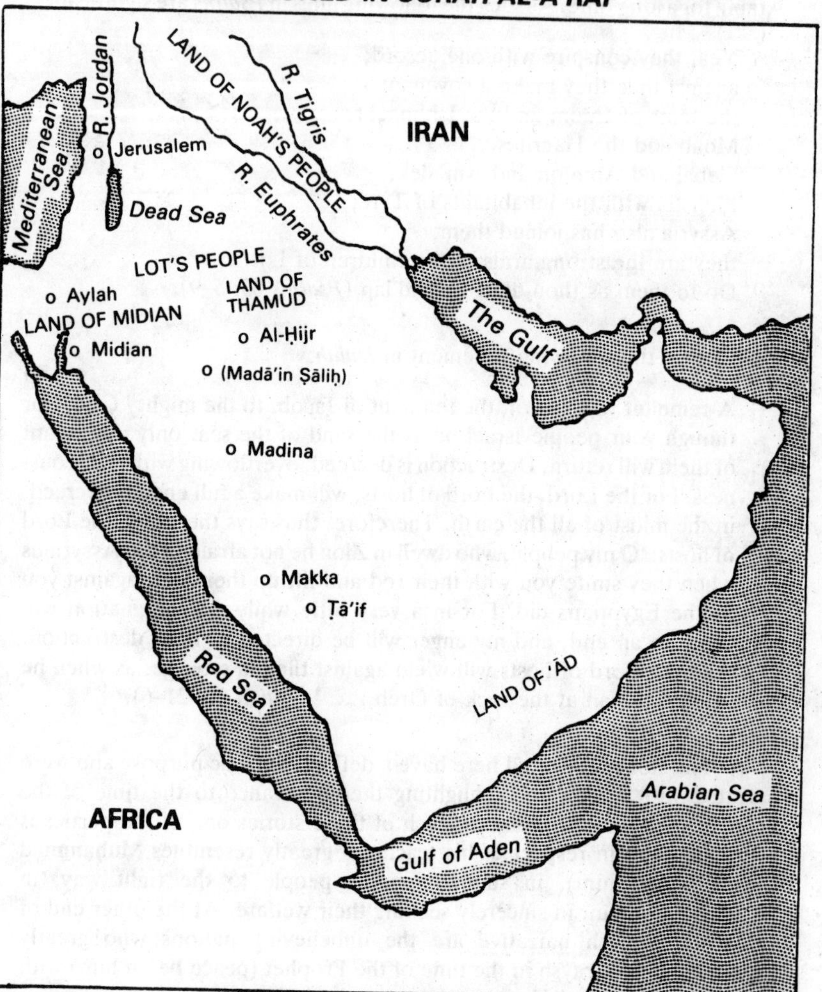

(94) Never have We sent a Prophet to a place without trying its people with adversity and hardship that they may humble themselves. (95) Then We changed adversity into ease until they throve and said: 'Our forefathers had also seen both adversity and prosperity.' So We suddenly seized them without their even perceiving it.[77] (96) Had the people of those towns believed and been God-fearing, We would certainly have opened up to them blessings from the heavens and the earth; but they gave the lie [to their Prophets] and so We seized them for their deeds. ▶

وَمَآ أَرْسَلْنَا فِى قَرْيَةٍ مِّن نَّبِىٍّ إِلَّآ
أَخَذْنَآ أَهْلَهَا بِٱلْبَأْسَآءِ وَٱلضَّرَّآءِ
لَعَلَّهُمْ يَضَّرَّعُونَ ﴿٩٤﴾ ثُمَّ بَدَّلْنَا مَكَانَ
ٱلسَّيِّئَةِ ٱلْحَسَنَةَ حَتَّىٰ عَفَوا۟ وَّقَالُوا۟ قَدْ
مَسَّ ءَابَآءَنَا ٱلضَّرَّآءُ وَٱلسَّرَّآءُ
فَأَخَذْنَٰهُم بَغْتَةً وَهُمْ لَا يَشْعُرُونَ ﴿٩٥﴾
وَلَوْ أَنَّ أَهْلَ ٱلْقُرَىٰٓ ءَامَنُوا۟ وَٱتَّقَوْا۟
لَفَتَحْنَا عَلَيْهِم بَرَكَٰتٍ مِّنَ ٱلسَّمَآءِ
وَٱلْأَرْضِ وَلَٰكِن كَذَّبُوا۟ فَأَخَذْنَٰهُم
بِمَا كَانُوا۟ يَكْسِبُونَ ﴿٩٦﴾

77. After narrating individually the stories of how various nations responded to the Message of their Prophets, the Qur'ān now spells out the general rule which has been operative throughout the ages. First, before the appearance of a Prophet in any nation, conditions that would conduce to the acceptance of his Message were created. This was usually done by subjecting the nations concerned to a variety of afflictions and punishments. They were made to suffer miseries such as famine, epidemics, colossal losses in trade and business, defeat in war. Such events usually have a healthy impact on people. They lead to a softening in their hearts. They generate humility and modesty. They enable people to shake off their pride and shatter their reliance on wealth and power and induce them to trust the One Who is all-powerful and fully controls their destiny. Above all, such events incline people to heed the words of warning and to turn to God in humility.

But if the people continue to refrain from embracing the truth they are subjected to another kind of test – that of affluence. This last test signals the beginning of their destruction. Rolling in abundant wealth and luxury, people are inclined to forget the hard times they have experienced. Their foolish leaders also inculcate in their minds an altogether preposterous concept of history. They explain the rise and fall of nations and the alternation of prosperity and adversity among human beings by reference to blind natural forces, and in total disregard of moral values. Hence if a nation is seized by an affliction or scourge, such people see no reason why it should be explained in terms of moral failure. They are rather inclined to consider that a person's readiness to heed moral admonition or to turn humbly towards God, is a sign of psychological infirmity.

This foolish mentality has been portrayed all too well by the Prophet (peace be on him): 'A believer continually faces adversity until he comes out of it purified of his sins. As for the hypocrite, his likeness in adversity is that of a donkey who does not know why his master had tied him and why he later released him.' (Cited by Ibn Kathīr in his comments on the verse – Ed.) Hence, when a people become so hard of heart that they neither turn to God in suffering, nor thank Him for His bounties in prosperity, they are liable to be destroyed at any moment.

It should be noted that the above rule which was applied to the nations of the previous Prophets, was also applied in the time of the Prophet Muḥammad (peace be on him). When this *sūrah* was revealed the Quraysh displayed exactly the same characteristics and attitudes as those nations which had earlier been destroyed. According to a tradition narrated by both 'Abd Allāh b. Mas'ūd and 'Abd Allāh b. 'Abbās, as the Quraysh grew in defiance to the Prophet's call, he prayed to God that he might be assisted by inflicting famine on the Quraysh, as in the days of the Prophet Joseph. Accordingly, God subjected the Quraysh to such a severe famine that they took to subsisting on carcasses, the skins of animals, bones, and wool. Unnerved by this the Quraysh, led by Abū Sufyān, implored the Prophet (peace be on him) to pray to God on their behalf. But when the Prophet's prayer helped to improve the situation somewhat, the Quraysh reverted to their arrogant and ignorant ways. (Bukhārī, *Kitāb al-Ṭahārah, Bāb idhā istashfa'a al-Mushrikūn bi al-Muslim'* – Ed.) The wicked ones among them tried to dissuade from God those who had derived some lesson from the famine. They argued that famines take place in course of operation of natural laws, that they are merely a recurrent physical phenomenon. They emphasized that the occurrence of famine should not mislead people into believing in Muḥammad (peace be on him). It was during this time that the *sūrah* under discussion was revealed. The above verses were thus quite relevant and it is against this backdrop that one appreciates their full significance. (For details see *Yūnus* 10: 21; *al-Naḥl* 16: 112; *al-Mu'minūn* 23: 75–6; and *al-Dukhān* 44: 9–16.)

(97) Do the people of those towns feel secure that Our punishment will not come to them at night while they are asleep? (98) Or, do the people of those towns feel secure that Our punishment will not come to them by daylight while they are at play? (99) Do they feel secure against the design of Allah?[78] None can feel secure against the design of Allah except the utter losers.

(100) Has it not, then, become plain to those who have inherited the earth in the wake of the former generations that, had We so willed, We could have afflicted them for their sins,[79] (they, however, are heedless to basic facts and so) We seal their hearts so that they hear nothing.[80] ▶

أَفَأَمِنَ أَهْلُ الْقُرَىٰ أَن يَأْتِيَهُم بَأْسُنَا
بَيَاتًا وَهُمْ نَائِمُونَ ﴿٩٧﴾ أَوَأَمِنَ أَهْلُ
الْقُرَىٰ أَن يَأْتِيَهُم بَأْسُنَا ضُحًى
وَهُمْ يَلْعَبُونَ ﴿٩٨﴾ أَفَأَمِنُوا مَكْرَ
اللَّهِ فَلَا يَأْمَنُ مَكْرَ اللَّهِ إِلَّا الْقَوْمُ
الْخَاسِرُونَ ﴿٩٩﴾ أَوَلَمْ يَهْدِ لِلَّذِينَ
يَرِثُونَ الْأَرْضَ مِن بَعْدِ أَهْلِهَا
أَن لَّوْ نَشَاءُ أَصَبْنَاهُم بِذُنُوبِهِمْ
وَنَطْبَعُ عَلَىٰ قُلُوبِهِمْ فَهُمْ لَا
يَسْمَعُونَ ﴿١٠٠﴾

78. The expression *makr* signifies a secret strategy of which the victim has no inkling until the decisive blow is struck. Until then, the victim is under the illusion that everything is in good order.

79. Every nation which rises in place of one that falls, can perceive the misdeeds which brought about the preceding nation's fall. Were such a people to make use of their reason, to appreciate the false ideas and misdeeds which led to the undoing of those who once strutted abroad in vainglory, they would have realized that the Supreme Being Who had once punished them for their misdeeds and deprived them of power and glory had not ceased to exist. Nor has that Supreme Being been deprived of the power to inflict a punishment on the people of the present times, a power with which He smote the nations of the past. Nor has God become bereft of the capacity to dislodge the wicked nations of today in the manner He did in the past.

(101) To those [earlier] communities – some of whose stories We relate to you – there had indeed come Messengers with clear proofs, but they would not believe what they had once rejected as false. Thus it is that Allah seals the hearts of those who deny the truth.[81] (102) We did not find most of them true to their covenants; indeed We found most of them to be transgressors.[82]

تِلْكَ ٱلْقُرَىٰ نَقُصُّ عَلَيْكَ مِنْ أَنۢبَآئِهَا ۚ وَلَقَدْ جَآءَتْهُمْ رُسُلُهُم بِٱلْبَيِّنَٰتِ فَمَا كَانُوا۟ لِيُؤْمِنُوا۟ بِمَا كَذَّبُوا۟ مِن قَبْلُ ۚ كَذَٰلِكَ يَطْبَعُ ٱللَّهُ عَلَىٰ قُلُوبِ ٱلْكَٰفِرِينَ ﴿١٠١﴾ وَمَا وَجَدْنَا لِأَكْثَرِهِم مِّنْ عَهْدٍ ۖ وَإِن وَجَدْنَآ أَكْثَرَهُمْ لَفَٰسِقِينَ ﴿١٠٢﴾

80. Those people who derive no lesson from history, who thoughtlessly pass over the ruins of the past, remaining engrossed in heedlessness, are deprived by God of the capacity to think correctly and to pay due attention to the counsel of well-wishers. Such is the God-made law of nature that if someone closes his eyes, not even a single ray of sun-light will reach his sight. Similarly, if someone is bent upon closing his ears none can make him hear even a word.

81. The purpose behind the 'sealing of hearts' mentioned in the preceding verse is also explained in the present verse. It is clear from the two verses that the 'sealing of hearts' means that man's capacity to hear and understand the truth is seriously impaired because of the operation of natural, psychological laws. Because of these laws, once a person turns away from the truth because of his irrational prejudices and the dominance of lust, he becomes enmeshed in his own obstinacy and adamance. With the passage of time this adamance is compounded to such an extent that despite all rational and empirical evidence in support of the truth, he continues to reject it.

82. The statement that 'We did not find most of them true to their covenants' signifies the general propensity of people not to honour their commitments. They are neither faithful to the primordial covenant which they made with God (see *al-A'rāf* 7: 172) which is binding on every mortal as God's servant and creature, nor faithful to the collective covenant which is binding on every human being as a member of the human fraternity. Nor are men generally faithful to the commitments which they make to God in hours of distress or in moments when their moral instincts are awake and astir. Violation of any of these covenants has been termed *fisq* (transgression).

(103) After those We sent forth Moses with Our signs to Pharaoh and his nobles,[83] but they dealt with Our signs unjustly.[84] Observe, then, what happened to the mischief-makers.

(104) And Moses said: 'O Pharaoh![85] I am a Messenger from the Lord of the universe. (105) And it behoves me to say nothing about Allah except what is true. I have come to you with a clear sign of having been sent from your Lord. So let the Children of Israel go with me.'[86]

ثُمَّ بَعَثْنَا مِنۢ بَعْدِهِم مُّوسَىٰ بِـَٔايَٰتِنَآ
إِلَىٰ فِرْعَوْنَ وَمَلَإِي۟هِۦ فَظَلَمُوا۟ بِهَا
فَٱنظُرْ كَيْفَ كَانَ عَٰقِبَةُ
ٱلْمُفْسِدِينَ ﴿١٠٣﴾ وَقَالَ مُوسَىٰ
يَٰفِرْعَوْنُ إِنِّى رَسُولٌ مِّن رَّبِّ
ٱلْعَٰلَمِينَ ﴿١٠٤﴾ حَقِيقٌ عَلَىٰٓ
أَن لَّآ أَقُولَ عَلَى ٱللَّهِ إِلَّا ٱلْحَقَّ قَدْ
جِئْتُكُم بِبَيِّنَةٍ مِّن رَّبِّكُمْ
فَأَرْسِلْ مَعِىَ بَنِىٓ إِسْرَٰٓءِيلَ ﴿١٠٥﴾

---

83. The stories narrated in the Qur'ān bring home unmistakenly the point that people who reject God's Message are not spared; rather they are destroyed. In narrating at length the story of Moses, Pharaoh and the Israelites, the Qur'ān provides some important lessons for the unbelieving Quraysh, the Jews, and also the believers.

The Quraysh are advised that the apparently large differences in the numerical strength of the forces of truth and falsehood in the early phase of the Islamic movement should not lead them to entertain any kind of illusion. History provides ample testimony that the Message of truth has always had a very humble beginning. That its proponent, initially, is in the hopelessly small minority of one; in fact, one in the whole world. He then proceeds, despite his resourcelessness, to challenge the hegemony of falsehood, to declare war against it, despite the fact that falsehood is backed by powerful states and empires. And ultimately the truth triumphs. The Quraysh are also reminded that all conspiracies hatched against the Prophets and all the means employed to suppress the Message of truth are ultimately foiled. They are further told that God grants long terms of respite to the evil-doing nations so that they might mend their ways and reform themselves. But when they persistently disregard all warnings and learn no lesson from instructive events, He smites them with an exemplary punishment.

Some further lessons are meant to be conveyed to those who believed in the Prophet (peace be on him). First, that they should not feel disheartened by the paucity of resources, nor be overawed by the impressive numerical strength, pomp and grandeur of their enemies. Nor should they lose heart if they find that God's help does not come at the expected hour. Second, that those who follow in the footsteps of the Jews are bound, ultimately, to be seized by the same curse which afflicted the Jews.

As for the Israelites, they are warned against the evil effects of clinging to falsehood. Illustrations of this were provided by important events in their own history. They are also asked to purge the Message of the earlier Prophets of all accretions and distortions and to restore it to its original purity.

84. 'They dealt with Our signs unjustly' refers to their rejection of God's signs and to the fact that they dismissed them as sheer sorcery. If a person scoffs at a beautiful couplet, and dubs it as amateurish rhyming, this amounts to committing an offence against poetry itself. Likewise, to brand those extraordinary acts of God as sorcery and magic – even though magicians declared that those acts were beyond their ability – constitutes a serious offence not only against God's signs but also against common sense and truth.

85. 'Pharaoh' literally means 'the offspring of the sun-god'. The ancient Egyptians called the sun 'Ra', worshipped it as their supreme deity, and Pharaoh – Ra's physical manifestation and representative – was named after it. It was for this reason that all Egyptian rulers claimed their authority on the basis of their association with Ra, and every ruler who mounted the Egyptian throne called himself Pharaoh, trying thereby to assure his people that he was their supreme deity.

It may be noted that the Qur'ānic narrative regarding Moses refers to two Pharaohs. The first of these was one during whose reign Moses was born and in whose palace he was brought up. The second Pharaoh to whom reference is made is the one whom Moses invited to Islam and who was asked to liberate the Israelites. It is this latter Pharaoh who was finally drowned. Modern scholarship is inclined to the view that the first Pharaoh was Rameses II who ruled over Egypt from 1292 B.C. to 1225 B.C. while the second Pharaoh was Minpetah, his son, who had become a co-sharer in his father's authority during the latter's lifetime and who, after his death, became the fully-fledged ruler of Egypt. This, however, is not fully established since Moses, according to the Egyptian calendar, died in 1272 B.C. In any case these are merely historical conjectures. It is quite difficult to establish a clear chronological framework owing to discrepancies in the Egyptian, Israeli and Christian calendars.

86. Moses was sent to Pharaoh to invite him to two things; first, to surrender himself to God (i.e. *Islam*); and second, to release the Israelites

(106) Pharaoh said: 'If you have brought a sign, then bring it forth if you are truthful.' (107) Thereupon Moses threw his rod, and suddenly it was a veritable serpent. (108) Then he drew out his hand, and it appeared luminous to all beholders.[87]

قَالَ إِن كُنتَ جِئْتَ بِـَٔايَةٍ فَأْتِ بِهَآ إِن
كُنتَ مِنَ ٱلصَّٰدِقِينَ ﴿١٠٦﴾ فَأَلْقَىٰ
عَصَاهُ فَإِذَا هِىَ ثُعْبَانٌ مُّبِينٌ ﴿١٠٧﴾
وَنَزَعَ يَدَهُۥ فَإِذَا هِىَ بَيْضَآءُ
لِلنَّٰظِرِينَ ﴿١٠٨﴾

– who were already Muslims – from his oppressive bondage. The Qur'ān refers occasionally to both these objectives, and occasionally confines itself to mentioning either of the two.

87. Moses was granted these two miraculous signs in order to provide testimony to his being a Messenger of God, the creator and sovereign of the universe. As we have mentioned earlier, whenever the Prophets introduced themselves as God's Message-bearers, people asked them to produce some miraculous sign, to perform something supernatural. In response to those demands the Prophets produced what the Qur'ān terms as 'signs', and which are called 'miracles' by theologians.

Those who tend to play down the supernatural character of such signs or miracles, and who try to explain them in terms of natural laws of causation, in fact attempt to build a mid-way house between believing and disbelieving in the statements of the Qur'ān. Such an approach can hardly be considered reasonable. What it does demonstrate, however, is how such people can be pulled in two opposite directions. On the one hand, they are not inclined to believe in a Book which abounds in narrations of a supernatural kind. On the other hand, being born followers of their ancestral religion, they are not inclined to reject the Book which carries supernatural narrations.

With regard to miracles, there are two basic questions that people should ask themselves. Did God, after creating the universe and establishing a system of natural causations therein, suspend Himself such that it is no longer possible for Him to interfere in the workings of the universe? Or does He still hold the reins to His realm in His owns Hands so that His command is enforced every moment, and He does retain the power to alter the shape of things and the normal course of events – either partially or fully – as and when He wills?

It is impossible for those who respond in the affirmative to the first question to accept the idea of miracles. For clearly miracles do not fit in with their concept of God and the universe. Honesty demands that instead

(109) The elders of Pharaoh's people said: 'Surely this man is a skilful magician (110) who seeks to drive you out from your land.[88] What would you have us do?' (111) Then they advised Pharaoh: 'Put off Moses and his brother for a while, and send forth heralds to your cities (112) to summon every skilful magician to your presence.'[89] ▶

قَالَ ٱلْمَلَأُ مِن قَوْمِ فِرْعَوْنَ إِنَّ هَٰذَا
لَسَٰحِرٌ عَلِيمٌ ﴿١٠٩﴾ يُرِيدُ أَن يُخْرِجَكُم مِّنْ
أَرْضِكُمْ فَمَاذَا تَأْمُرُونَ ﴿١١٠﴾ قَالُوٓا۟
أَرْجِهْ وَأَخَاهُ وَأَرْسِلْ فِى ٱلْمَدَآئِنِ
حَٰشِرِينَ ﴿١١١﴾ يَأْتُوكَ بِكُلِّ سَٰحِرٍ
عَلِيمٍ ﴿١١٢﴾

of indulging in far-fetched explanations of Qur'ānic statements on miracles, such people should clearly declare that they do not believe in the Qur'ān. For quite obviously the Qur'ān is explicit, even quite emphatic in affirming the former concept of God.

As for those who, being convinced by Qur'ānic arguments, respond in the affirmative to the second question regarding God and the universe, for them there is no difficulty in accepting miracles. Let us take the instance mentioned in verse 107, namely that the rod of Moses turned into a serpent. Now, there are those who believe that serpents can come into being only through one process – the known biological process. Such people are bound to reject the statement that Moses' rod changed into a serpent and later reverted to its original shape. On the contrary, if you are fully convinced that it is God's command alone which causes life to arise from lifeless matter, and that God has full power to confer whichever kind of life He wills, the transformation of the rod into a serpent and its subsequent reversion to its original state is no stranger than the transformation of any other lifeless matter into a living entity. The fact that the latter happens virtually every day whereas the former took place only a few times in history is not enough to declare the first as incredibly strange and the second as 'natural'.

88. The above account raises the question as to how a destitute member of the slave Israeli nation could pose such a serious threat to an emperor as mighty as Pharaoh. This is especially so when one considers that Pharaoh was not only an absolute ruler over territory which stretched in one direction from Syria to Libya and in the other from the Mediterranean coast to Ethiopia, but was even considered a deity deserving of worship.

One might also wonder how the transformation of Moses' rod into a serpent could be considered an event of such magnitude as to give rise to the fear that Moses would overthrow the entrenched empire and unseat the royal family as well as the entire ruling class. It might further seem strange that the mere declaration of prophethood and the demand to liberate the people of Israel caused such a furore even though no other political question had been touched upon.

The answer here lies in the fact that Moses' claim to prophethood implied the call to total change, obviously including political change. For if a person lays claim to be God's Messenger, it implies that people obey him unreservedly. For God's Messengers are not sent to the world to obey other human beings and live in subordination to them; they rather ask others to accept them as their leaders and rulers. It is this which explains why Pharaoh and his coterie felt threatened by an all-out revolution – political, economic and social – when Moses came forth with his call.

There remains the question as to why the claim to prophethood was considered such a potential threat when Moses enjoyed the support of none except his brother, Aaron, and his claim was reinforced by only two miracles – those of the shining hand and the rod which turned into a serpent. This can be explained by two things. First, that Pharaoh and his courtiers knew very well about Moses. All were aware of his extraordinary abilities and his inherent calibre as a leader of men. Also, according to the traditions of the Talmud and Josephus – provided they are authentic – Moses had also learnt the martial arts and other skills which were available only exclusively to royalty and which were required in connection with their political and military leadership. Moreover, he had proved his mettle as a good general during the expedition to Ethiopia. Furthermore, during the course of his eight years of life in Midian – rigorous years in the desert working as a shepherd – he had purged himself of all his weaknesses because of his association with the Pharaonic system. Hence, when the Pharaonic court was confronted by a mature, serene and pious man who came forth with the claim of prophethood, it was obviously impossible for them to give short shrift to his claim. Second, the miracles of the rod and the shining hand overawed Pharaoh and his courtiers to such an extent they were almost convinced that Moses did indeed enjoy the support of some supernatural power. That they were unnerved by the very first proof of his prophethood is borne out by the contradictions in their charges against Moses. On the one hand they dubbed Moses a sorcerer, and on the other hand they accused him of plotting to banish them from their own land. It is clear that had they taken Moses for a mere sorcerer, they would not have expressed fears of political upheaval. For sorcery has never brought about any political change in the world.

89. The plan of Pharaoh's courtiers clearly suggests that they knew the difference between mere sorcery and a miracle. They were well aware that

(113) And the magicians came to Pharaoh and said: 'Shall we have a reward if we win?' (114) Pharaoh replied: 'Certainly, and you shall be among those who are near to me.' (115) Then they said: 'O Moses, will you [first] throw your rod, or shall we throw?' (116) Moses said: 'You throw.' So when they threw [their rods], they enchanted the eyes of the people, and struck them with awe, and produced a mighty sorcery. (117) Then We directed Moses: 'Now you throw your rod.' And lo! it swallowed up all their false devices.[90]

وَجَآءَ ٱلسَّحَرَةُ فِرۡعَوۡنَ قَالُوٓاْ إِنَّ
لَنَا لَأَجۡرًا إِن كُنَّا نَحۡنُ ٱلۡغَٰلِبِينَ ﴿١١٣﴾
قَالَ نَعَمۡ وَإِنَّكُمۡ لَمِنَ ٱلۡمُقَرَّبِينَ ﴿١١٤﴾
قَالُواْ يَٰمُوسَىٰٓ إِمَّآ أَن تُلۡقِيَ وَإِمَّآ
أَن نَّكُونَ نَحۡنُ ٱلۡمُلۡقِينَ ﴿١١٥﴾ قَالَ
أَلۡقُواْۖ فَلَمَّآ أَلۡقَوۡاْ سَحَرُوٓاْ أَعۡيُنَ
ٱلنَّاسِ وَٱسۡتَرۡهَبُوهُمۡ وَجَآءُو بِسِحۡرٍ
عَظِيمٖ ﴿١١٦﴾ ۞ وَأَوۡحَيۡنَآ إِلَىٰ مُوسَىٰٓ
أَنۡ أَلۡقِ عَصَاكَۖ فَإِذَا هِيَ تَلۡقَفُ مَا
يَأۡفِكُونَ ﴿١١٧﴾

miracles are effective and have the capacity to bring about actual transformation whereas sorcery results merely in optic illusion. Hence, they dubbed Moses a sorcerer so as to refute his claim to prophethood. They claimed instead that the transformation of the rod into a serpent was not a miracle; that it was rather a magical performance which could be undertaken by any sorcerer. Therefore, they asked all the sorcerers of the land to come together and display how rods could be magically transformed into serpents. They believed that such a magical show would remove the awesome effect created by Moses' miracles on the people, or at least sow doubts in their minds about those miracles.

90. It would be a mistake to believe that the rod of Moses swallowed up the rods and ropes cast by the other sorcerers and which had looked like serpents. The Qur'ānic statement means that the rod of Moses swallowed up the falsehood faked by them. This clearly shows that wherever Moses' rod moved, it destroyed the magical effect which had caused the transformation of their ropes and rods. One blow of Moses' rod caused every other rod to revert to a rod, and every rope to revert to a rope. (For further elaboration see *Tafhīm al-Qur'ān, Ṭā Hā* 20, n. 42.)

(118) Thus was the truth established, and their doings proved in vain. (119) Pharaoh and his men were defeated and put to shame, (120) and the magicians flung themselves prostrate, (121) saying: 'We believe in the Lord of the universe, (122) the Lord of Moses and Aaron.'[91]

(123) Pharaoh said: 'What! Do you believe before you have my permission? Surely this is a plot you have contrived to drive out the rulers from the capital. So you shall see, (124) I shall cut off your hands and feet on the opposite sides, and then crucify you all.'

(125) They replied: 'We shall surely return to our Lord. (126) Will you punish us just because we believed in the signs of our Lord when they came to us? Our Lord! Shower us with perseverance and cause us to die as those who have submitted [to You].'[92]

فَوَقَعَ ٱلْحَقُّ وَبَطَلَ مَا كَانُوا۟ يَعْمَلُونَ ﴿١١٨﴾
فَغُلِبُوا۟ هُنَالِكَ وَٱنقَلَبُوا۟ صَٰغِرِينَ ﴿١١٩﴾
وَأُلْقِىَ ٱلسَّحَرَةُ سَٰجِدِينَ ﴿١٢٠﴾ قَالُوٓا۟
ءَامَنَّا بِرَبِّ ٱلْعَٰلَمِينَ ﴿١٢١﴾ رَبِّ مُوسَىٰ
وَهَٰرُونَ ﴿١٢٢﴾ قَالَ فِرْعَوْنُ ءَامَنتُم
بِهِۦ قَبْلَ أَنْ ءَاذَنَ لَكُمْ إِنَّ هَٰذَا لَمَكْرٌ
مَّكَرْتُمُوهُ فِى ٱلْمَدِينَةِ لِتُخْرِجُوا۟ مِنْهَآ
أَهْلَهَا فَسَوْفَ تَعْلَمُونَ ﴿١٢٣﴾ لَأُقَطِّعَنَّ
أَيْدِيَكُمْ وَأَرْجُلَكُم مِّنْ خِلَٰفٍ ثُمَّ
لَأُصَلِّبَنَّكُمْ أَجْمَعِينَ ﴿١٢٤﴾ قَالُوٓا۟
إِنَّآ إِلَىٰ رَبِّنَا مُنقَلِبُونَ ﴿١٢٥﴾ وَمَا تَنقِمُ
مِنَّآ إِلَّآ أَنْ ءَامَنَّا بِـَٔايَٰتِ رَبِّنَا لَمَّا
جَآءَتْنَا رَبَّنَآ أَفْرِغْ عَلَيْنَا صَبْرًا وَتَوَفَّنَا
مُسْلِمِينَ ﴿١٢٦﴾

91. Thus God turned the tables on Pharaoh and his courtiers. They had arranged the magic show in the hope that it would convince the people that Moses was just a sorcerer, and thus make them sceptical about his claim to prophethood. But the actual outcome was quite the opposite. The sorcerers who had been assembled were defeated. Not only that, it was also unanimously acknowledged that the signs displayed by Moses in

(127) The elders of Pharaoh's people said: 'Will you leave alone Moses and his people to spread mischief in the land, and forsake you and your gods?' Pharaoh replied: 'We will kill their male children and spare their female ones.[93] For indeed we hold irresistible sway over them.'

(128) Moses said to his people: 'Seek help from Allah and be steadfast. The earth is Allah's, He bestows it on those of His servants He chooses. The end of things belongs to the God-fearing.' (129) The people of Moses replied: 'We were oppressed before your coming to us and after it.' Moses said: 'Your Lord will soon destroy your enemy and make you rulers in the land. Then He will see how you act.'

وَقَالَ ٱلْمَلَأُ مِن قَوْمِ فِرْعَوْنَ أَتَذَرُ مُوسَىٰ
وَقَوْمَهُۥ لِيُفْسِدُوا۟ فِى ٱلْأَرْضِ وَيَذَرَكَ
وَءَالِهَتَكَ ۚ قَالَ سَنُقَتِّلُ أَبْنَآءَهُمْ
وَنَسْتَحْىِۦ نِسَآءَهُمْ وَإِنَّا فَوْقَهُمْ
قَٰهِرُونَ ﴿١٢٧﴾ قَالَ مُوسَىٰ لِقَوْمِهِ
ٱسْتَعِينُوا۟ بِٱللَّهِ وَٱصْبِرُوٓا۟ ۖ إِنَّ
ٱلْأَرْضَ لِلَّهِ يُورِثُهَا مَن يَشَآءُ مِنْ
عِبَادِهِۦ ۖ وَٱلْعَٰقِبَةُ لِلْمُتَّقِينَ ﴿١٢٨﴾
قَالُوٓا۟ أُوذِينَا مِن قَبْلِ أَن تَأْتِيَنَا
وَمِنۢ بَعْدِ مَا جِئْتَنَا ۚ قَالَ عَسَىٰ
رَبُّكُمْ أَن يُهْلِكَ عَدُوَّكُمْ
وَيَسْتَخْلِفَكُمْ فِى ٱلْأَرْضِ
فَيَنظُرَ كَيْفَ تَعْمَلُونَ ﴿١٢٩﴾

---

support of his claim were not feats of magic. Rather, his signs rather manifested the might of God, the Lord of the universe, and hence could not be overcome by magic.

92. Faced with utter failure Pharaoh finally resorted to branding the whole magic tournament as a conspiracy concocted by Moses and his accomplice sorcerers. Under threat of death and physical torture he asked the sorcerers to confess that they had acted in collusion with Moses. This last move by Pharaoh was ineffectual. For the sorcerers readily agreed to endure every torture, clearly proving thereby that their decision to accept Moses' message reflected their sincere conviction and that no conspiracy

(130) We afflicted the people of Pharaoh with hard times and with poor harvest that they may heed. (131) But whenever prosperity came their way, they said: 'This is our due.' And whatever hardship befell them, they attributed it to the misfortune of Moses and those who followed him. Surely, their misfortune had been decreed by Allah – but most of them do not know that.

وَلَقَدْ أَخَذْنَا آلَ فِرْعَوْنَ بِالسِّنِينَ
وَنَقْصٍ مِنَ الثَّمَرَاتِ لَعَلَّهُمْ
يَذَّكَّرُونَ ﴿١٣٠﴾ فَإِذَا جَاءَتْهُمُ
الْحَسَنَةُ قَالُوا لَنَا هَٰذِهِ ۖ وَإِنْ تُصِبْهُمْ
سَيِّئَةٌ يَطَّيَّرُوا بِمُوسَىٰ وَمَنْ مَعَهُ ۗ
أَلَا إِنَّمَا طَائِرُهُمْ عِنْدَ اللَّهِ وَلَٰكِنَّ
أَكْثَرَهُمْ لَا يَعْلَمُونَ ﴿١٣١﴾

---

was involved. Pharaoh was hardly left with any choice. He, therefore, gave up all pretence to follow truth and justice, and brazenly resorted to persecution instead.

The tremendous and instantaneous change which took place in the characters of the sorcerers is also of significance. The sorcerers had come all the way from their homes with the purpose of vindicating their ancestral faith and receiving pecuniary reward from Pharaoh for overcoming Moses. However, the moment true faith illumined their hearts, they displayed such resoluteness of will and love for the truth that they contemptuously turned down Pharaoh's offer, and demonstrated their full readiness to endure even the worst punishments for the sake of the truth that had dawned upon them.

93. There were two periods of persecution. The first was during the reign of Rameses II and took place before Moses' birth, whereas the second period of persecution started after Moses' assumption to the office of prophethood. Common to both periods is the killing of the male issue of Israelites while the female was spared. It was a calculated design to rob the Israelites of their identity and to bring about their forcible assimilation. An inscription discovered during the archaeological excavations of 1896 probably belongs to this period. According to this inscription, Pharaoh Minpetah rounds off the narration of his achievements and victories in these words: 'The Israel have been exterminated, and no seed of them is left.' (For further explanation see *al-Mu'min* 40: 25.)

(132) And they said to Moses: 'Whatever sign you might produce before us in order to enchant us, we are not going to believe you.'[94] (133) Then We afflicted them with a great flood[95] and locusts, and the lice,[96] and the frogs, and the blood. All these were distinct signs and yet they remained haughty. They were a wicked people. (134) Each time a scourge struck them they said: 'O Moses! Pray for us to your Lord on the strength of the prophethood He has bestowed upon you. Surely, if you remove this scourge from us, we will truly believe in you, and will let the Children of Israel go with you.'

وَقَالُوا مَهْمَا تَأْتِنَا بِهِ مِنْ ءَايَةٍ لِتَسْحَرَنَا
بِهَا فَمَا نَحْنُ لَكَ بِمُؤْمِنِينَ ﴿١٣٢﴾
فَأَرْسَلْنَا عَلَيْهِمُ الطُّوفَانَ وَالْجَرَادَ
وَالْقُمَّلَ وَالضَّفَادِعَ وَالدَّمَ ءَايَٰتٍ
مُفَصَّلَٰتٍ فَاسْتَكْبَرُوا وَكَانُوا قَوْمًا
مُجْرِمِينَ ﴿١٣٣﴾ وَلَمَّا وَقَعَ عَلَيْهِمُ
الرِّجْزُ قَالُوا يَٰمُوسَى ادْعُ لَنَا رَبَّكَ
بِمَا عَهِدَ عِنْدَكَ لَئِن كَشَفْتَ
عَنَّا الرِّجْزَ لَنُؤْمِنَنَّ لَكَ وَلَنُرْسِلَنَّ
مَعَكَ بَنِي إِسْرَٰءِيلَ ﴿١٣٤﴾

94. Pharaoh's courtiers obstinately persisted in branding Moses' signs as sorcery although they knew well that sorcery had nothing in common with the miraculous signs granted to Moses. Even a fool would not be ready to believe that the country-wide famine and the consistent decrease in agricultural output could have been caused by magic. It is for this reason that the Qur'ān says:

> But when Our signs, which should have opened their eyes, came to them they said: 'This is clear sorcery! And they rejected those signs out of iniquity and arrogance even though they were inwardly convinced of it' (*al-Naml* 27: 13–14).

95. This probably refers to the torrential rain accompanied by hailstorm. While we do not totally exclude the possibility of other kinds of storms, we are inclined to the view that it probably signifies hailstorm since the Bible specifically mentions that. (See *Exodus* 9: 23–4 – Ed.)

(135) But when We removed the scourge from them until a term – a term which they were bound to reach – they at once broke their promise. (136) So We inflicted Our retribution on them, and caused them to drown in the sea because they gave the lie to Our signs and were heedless of them. (137) And We made those who had been persecuted inherit the eastern and western lands which We had blessed.[97] Thus your Lord's gracious promise was fulfilled to the Children of Israel, for they had endured with patience; and We destroyed all that Pharaoh and his people had wrought, and all that they had built.

فَلَمَّا كَشَفْنَا عَنْهُمُ ٱلرِّجْزَ إِلَىٰٓ
أَجَلٍ هُم بَٰلِغُوهُ إِذَا هُمْ يَنكُثُونَ
﴿١٣٥﴾ فَٱنتَقَمْنَا مِنْهُمْ فَأَغْرَقْنَٰهُمْ فِى
ٱلْيَمِّ بِأَنَّهُمْ كَذَّبُوا۟ بِـَٔايَٰتِنَا وَكَانُوا۟
عَنْهَا غَٰفِلِينَ ﴿١٣٦﴾ وَأَوْرَثْنَا ٱلْقَوْمَ
ٱلَّذِينَ كَانُوا۟ يُسْتَضْعَفُونَ
مَشَٰرِقَ ٱلْأَرْضِ وَمَغَٰرِبَهَا
ٱلَّتِى بَٰرَكْنَا فِيهَا ۖ وَتَمَّتْ كَلِمَتُ رَبِّكَ
ٱلْحُسْنَىٰ عَلَىٰ بَنِىٓ إِسْرَٰٓءِيلَ بِمَا صَبَرُوا۟ ۖ
وَدَمَّرْنَا مَا كَانَ يَصْنَعُ
فِرْعَوْنُ وَقَوْمُهُۥ وَمَا كَانُوا۟
يَعْرِشُونَ ﴿١٣٧﴾

96. The word used in the text – *qummal* – denotes lice, fleas, small locusts, mosquitoes, and weevil. This rather general term has been used in the Qur'ān probably to suggest that while men were afflicted with lice and fleas, weevil destroyed the barns. (Cf. *Exodus* 7–12. See also *Tafhīm al-Qur'ān, al-Zukhruf* 43, n. 43.)

97. The Israelites were made the inheritors of Palestine. This has been interpreted by some commentators of the Qur'ān to mean that the Israelites were made the rulers of Egypt as well. This view, however, is neither supported by the Qur'ān nor by any other historical and archaeological evidence. We have, therefore, serious reservations about the correctness of this opinion. (See *Tafhīm al-Qur'ān, al-Kahf* 18, n. 57, and *al-Shu'arā'* 26, n. 45.)

(138) And We led the Children of Israel across the sea; and then they came upon a people who were devoted to the worship of their idols. They said: 'O Moses, make for us a god even as they have gods.'[98] Moses said: 'You are indeed an ignorant people.' (139) The way these people follow is bound to lead to destruction; and all their works are vain. ▶

وَجَٰوَزْنَا بِبَنِىٓ إِسْرَٰٓءِيلَ ٱلْبَحْرَ فَأَتَوْا۟
عَلَىٰ قَوْمٍ يَعْكُفُونَ عَلَىٰٓ أَصْنَامٍ لَّهُمْ ۚ
قَالُوا۟ يَٰمُوسَى ٱجْعَل لَّنَآ إِلَٰهًا كَمَا لَهُمْ
ءَالِهَةٌ ۚ قَالَ إِنَّكُمْ قَوْمٌ تَجْهَلُونَ ﴿١٣٨﴾ إِنَّ
هَٰٓؤُلَآءِ مُتَبَّرٌ مَّا هُمْ فِيهِ وَبَٰطِلٌ مَّا كَانُوا۟
يَعْمَلُونَ ﴿١٣٩﴾

98. The point at which the Israelites probably crossed the Red Sea lies somewhere between the present Suez and Ismailia. After that they headed towards the south of the Sinai peninsula along the coastal route. The western and northern regions of the Sinai peninsula were then included in the Egyptian empire. In the southern part of the peninsula, in the area lying between the present towns of Ṭūr and Abū Zanīmah, there were copper and turquoise mines. Since these were of immense value to the Egyptians, a number of garrisons had been set up to ensure their security. One such garrison was located at a place known as Mafqah, which also housed a big temple. The ruins of this temple can still be found in the south-western part of the peninsula. In its vicinity there was an ancient temple, dedicated to the moon-god of the Semites. Passing by these places the people of Israel, who had been subservient to the Egyptians for a long time and were thus considerably Egyptianized in their outlook, felt the desire to indulge in idol-worship.

The extent to which the Israelites had become degenerated as a result of their slavery may be gauged by Joshua's last address to the Israelites delivered seventy years after their exodus from Egypt:

> Now therefore fear the Lord, and serve him in sincerity and in faithfulness; put away the gods which your fathers served beyond the River, and in Egypt, and serve the Lord. And if you are unwilling to serve the Lord, choose this day whom you will serve; whether the gods which your fathers served in the region beyond the River, or the gods of the Amorites in whose land you dwell; but as for me and my house, we will serve the Lord (*Joshua* 24: 14–15).

(140) Moses said: 'Should I seek any god for you other than Allah although it is He who has exalted you above all?' (141) And call to mind when We delivered you from Pharaoh's people who perpetrated on you a terrible torment, putting your males to death and sparing your females. Surely in it there was an awesome trial for you from your Lord.

(142) And We appointed for Moses thirty nights, to which We added ten, whereby the term of forty nights set by his Lord was fulfilled.[99] ▶

قَالَ أَغَيْرَ ٱللَّهِ أَبْغِيكُمْ إِلَٰهًا
وَهُوَ فَضَّلَكُمْ عَلَى ٱلْعَٰلَمِينَ
﴿١٤٠﴾ وَإِذْ أَنجَيْنَٰكُم مِّنْ ءَالِ
فِرْعَوْنَ يَسُومُونَكُمْ سُوٓءَ
ٱلْعَذَابِ يُقَتِّلُونَ أَبْنَآءَكُمْ
وَيَسْتَحْيُونَ نِسَآءَكُمْ وَفِى
ذَٰلِكُم بَلَآءٌ مِّن رَّبِّكُمْ
عَظِيمٌ ﴿١٤١﴾ ۞ وَوَٰعَدْنَا مُوسَىٰ
ثَلَٰثِينَ لَيْلَةً وَأَتْمَمْنَٰهَا بِعَشْرٍ
فَتَمَّ مِيقَٰتُ رَبِّهِۦٓ أَرْبَعِينَ لَيْلَةً

This shows that even though the Israelites had been taught and trained by Moses for forty years and by Joshua for twenty-eight years, they had still been unable to purge their minds of those influences which had warped their outlook and mentality during their period of bondage under Pharaoh. These Muslims had begun to look upon idol-worship as natural. Even after their exodus, the sight of a temple would incline them to indulge in the idolatrous practices which they had observed among their former masters.

99. After the exodus of the Israelites from Egypt which marks, on the one hand, the end of the constraints of slavery and, on the other, the beginning of their life as an independent nation, Moses was summoned by God to Mount Sinai in order that he might receive the Law for Israel. He was initially summoned for a period of forty days so that he might single-mindedly devote himself to worshipping, fasting, meditation and reflection and thus develop the ability to receive the revelation which was to put a very heavy burden upon him.

In compliance with God's command, Moses left the Israelites at the place now known as the Wādī al-Shaykh which lies between Nabī Ṣāliḥ and Mount Sinai. The place where the Israelites had camped is presently called

MAP NO. 2: EXODUS OF ISRAEL

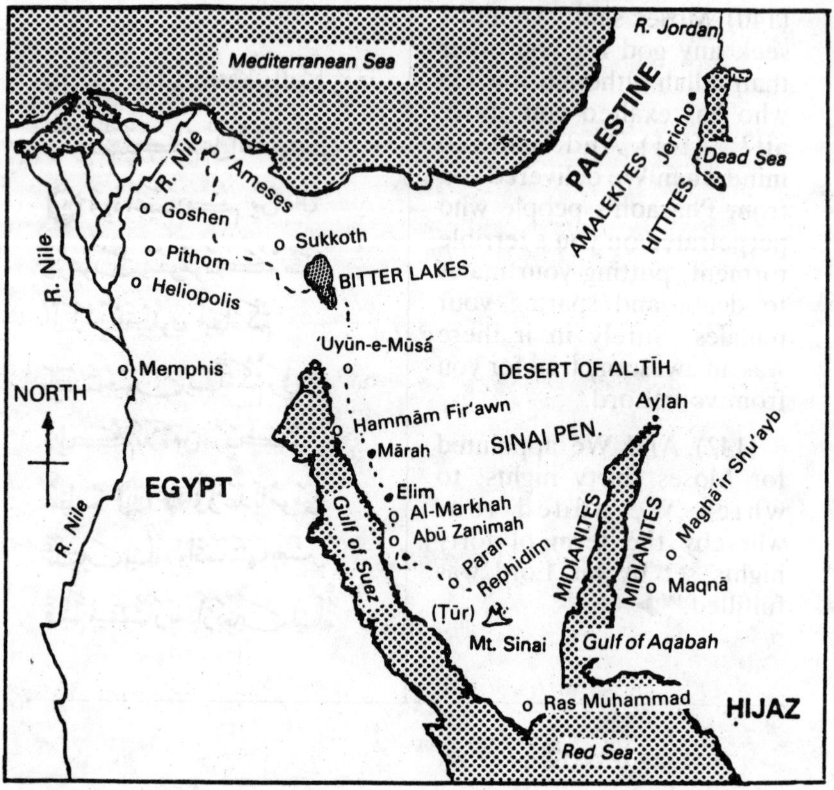

Explanation

1. *Goshen is the area in Egypt where the Prophet Joseph had settled the Israelites.*
2. *Memphis was the capital of Egypt in the time of the Prophet Moses.*
3. *Bitter Lakes are presently located at quite a distance from the Gulf of Suez but in ancient times they were connected to the sea.*
4. *The Prophet Moses set out from 'Ameses with the Israelites and they joined and followed him on the way from all sides. He probably wanted to bring them safely through the wilderness to Sinai, but the fear of the Egyptian military camps on the one hand and the hot pursuit by Pharaoh on the other, took them on to Baal Zephon, where they crossed the Bitter Lakes at some point and it was here that Pharaoh and all his hosts were drowned.*
5. *The Prophet Moses and the Israelites travelled through Mārah, Elim, al-Markhah and Paran Rephidim and came to the place now called Jabal Mūsa (Sinai of the Old Testament) and also Ṭūr. The valley around here has been mentioned as the Holy Valley of Ṭuwā in the Qur'ān (Sūrah Ṭā Hā 20: 12).*
6. *Ḥammām Fir'awn is the place where, according to the local tradition in the Sinai Peninsula, the body of Pharaoh was found floating in the water.*
7. *Ṭūr on this map shows the present sea-port of Ṭūr rather than Mount Ṭūr.*
8. *Al-Markhah is situated at the edge of the Wilderness of Sin of the Old Testament, where manna and salwā had begun to be sent down.*
9. *Near Paran Rephidim is found the famous rock in Mount Horeb, which was smitten by the Prophet Moses causing twelve springs of water to gush forth.*
10. *Al-Tīh is the desert in which the Israelites remained wandering homeless for forty years. Tīh is derived from yatihūn (Sūrah al-Mā'idah 5: 26) and means 'wandering homelessly'.*
11. *'Aqabuh or Aylah' which was Ezion-geber in ancient times, is the place where, according to the popular tradition, the well-known incident of the Sabbath-breakers took place.*

And Moses said to Aaron, his brother: 'Take my place among my people, act righteously, and do not follow the path of those who create mischief.'[100] (143) And when Moses came at Our appointment, and his Lord spoke to him, he said: 'O my Lord! Reveal Yourself to me, that I may look upon You!' He replied: 'Never can you see Me. However, behold this mount; if it remains firm in its place, only then you will be able to see Me.' And as soon as his Lord unveiled His glory to the mount, He crushed it into fine dust, and Moses fell down in a swoon. And when he recovered, he said: 'Glory be to You! To You I turn in repentance, and I am the foremost among those who believe.' ►

وَقَالَ مُوسَىٰ لِأَخِيهِ هَـٰرُونَ
ٱخْلُفْنِى فِى قَوْمِى وَأَصْلِحْ وَلَا تَتَّبِعْ
سَبِيلَ ٱلْمُفْسِدِينَ ﴿١٤٢﴾ وَلَمَّا جَآءَ
مُوسَىٰ لِمِيقَـٰتِنَا وَكَلَّمَهُۥ رَبُّهُۥ قَالَ
رَبِّ أَرِنِىٓ أَنظُرْ إِلَيْكَ ۚ قَالَ لَن تَرَىٰنِى
وَلَـٰكِنِ ٱنظُرْ إِلَى ٱلْجَبَلِ فَإِنِ ٱسْتَقَرَّ
مَكَانَهُۥ فَسَوْفَ تَرَىٰنِى ۚ فَلَمَّا تَجَلَّىٰ
رَبُّهُۥ لِلْجَبَلِ جَعَلَهُۥ دَكًّا وَخَرَّ
مُوسَىٰ صَعِقًا ۚ فَلَمَّآ أَفَاقَ قَالَ
سُبْحَـٰنَكَ تُبْتُ إِلَيْكَ وَأَنَا۠ أَوَّلُ
ٱلْمُؤْمِنِينَ ﴿١٤٣﴾

Maydān al-Rāḥah. At one end of the valley is a hillock where, according to local tradition, the Prophet Ṣāliḥ pitched his tent after his migration from the land of Thamūd. A mosque built as a monument to the Prophet Ṣāliḥ still adorns the landscape. Mount Hārūn is located at the other end of the valley where, again, according to local tradition, the Prophet Hārūn (Aaron) stayed after his exasperation with the Israelites because of their cow-worship. The top of the towering Mount Sinai, standing 7,359 feet high, is mostly enveloped by clouds. The cave to which Moses retired for forty days to devote himself to worship and meditation is situated at the top of the mountain, and still attracts many pilgrims. Close to the cave are a mosque and a church. Moreover, a monastery built in the Justinian period stands even today at the foot of the mountain. (See *Tafhīm al-Qur'ān, al-Naml* 27: nn. 9–10.)

(144) He said: 'O Moses! I have indeed preferred you to all others by virtue of the Message I have entrusted to you and by virtue of My speaking to you. Hold fast, therefore, to whatever I have granted you, and give thanks.'

(145) And We ordained for Moses in the Tablets all manner of admonition, and instruction concerning all things,[101] and said to him:

Hold to these, with all your strength, and bid your people to follow them in accord with their best understanding.[102] I shall soon show you the habitation of the wicked.[103] ▶

قَالَ يَٰمُوسَىٰٓ إِنِّى ٱصْطَفَيْتُكَ عَلَى
ٱلنَّاسِ بِرِسَٰلَٰتِى وَبِكَلَٰمِى فَخُذْ مَآ
ءَاتَيْتُكَ وَكُن مِّنَ ٱلشَّٰكِرِينَ ﴿١٤٤﴾
وَكَتَبْنَا لَهُۥ فِى ٱلْأَلْوَاحِ مِن
كُلِّ شَىْءٍ مَّوْعِظَةً وَتَفْصِيلًا
لِّكُلِّ شَىْءٍ فَخُذْهَا بِقُوَّةٍ وَأْمُرْ
قَوْمَكَ يَأْخُذُوا۟ بِأَحْسَنِهَا ۚ سَأُو۟رِيكُمْ
دَارَ ٱلْفَٰسِقِينَ ﴿١٤٥﴾

100. Although Aaron was senior to Moses in age by three years, he was placed under the direction of the Prophet Moses and was required to assist him in connection with his mission. As explained elsewhere in the Qur'ān, Aaron was not assigned independent prophethood; he was rather appointed a Prophet by God in response to Moses' prayer that he be appointed as his assistant. (See *Ṭā Hā* 20: 29–31 – Ed.)

101. The Bible categorically mentions that the tablets were of stone. The act of writing on these tablets is attributed, in both the Qur'ān and the Bible, to God. Nonetheless, it is not possible to ascertain whether the actual act of writing was performed by God exercising His power directly, or by God in the sense of His assignment of the task to some angel or to Moses (cf. *Exodus* 31: 18, 32: 15–16; and *Deuteronomy* 5: 6–22).

102. The Israelites were asked to hold fast to the Law; to follow it in its plain meaning, a meaning which can be grasped by an ordinary man of

(146) I shall turn away from My signs those who, without any right, behaved haughtily in the earth,[104] even if they may witness each and every sign, they shall not believe therein. And even if they see the right path, they shall still not follow it; but if they see the path of error, they shall choose it for their path. This is because they rejected Our signs as false and were heedless to them. (147) Vain are the deeds of those who reject Our signs as false and to the meeting of the Hereafter.[105] Shall they be recompensed, except according to their deeds?'

سَأَصْرِفُ عَنْ ءَايَٰتِيَ ٱلَّذِينَ يَتَكَبَّرُونَ
فِي ٱلْأَرْضِ بِغَيْرِ ٱلْحَقِّ وَإِن يَرَوْا۟
كُلَّ ءَايَةٍ لَّا يُؤْمِنُوا۟ بِهَا وَإِن
يَرَوْا۟ سَبِيلَ ٱلرُّشْدِ لَا يَتَّخِذُوهُ سَبِيلًا
وَإِن يَرَوْا۟ سَبِيلَ ٱلْغَيِّ يَتَّخِذُوهُ
سَبِيلًا ۚ ذَٰلِكَ بِأَنَّهُمْ كَذَّبُوا۟ بِـَٔايَٰتِنَا
وَكَانُوا۟ عَنْهَا غَٰفِلِينَ ﴿١٤٦﴾ وَٱلَّذِينَ
كَذَّبُوا۟ بِـَٔايَٰتِنَا وَلِقَآءِ ٱلْءَاخِرَةِ
حَبِطَتْ أَعْمَٰلُهُمْ ۚ هَلْ يُجْزَوْنَ
إِلَّا مَا كَانُوا۟ يَعْمَلُونَ ﴿١٤٧﴾

---

sound heart and good intent with the help of his common sense. This stipulation was added in order to discourage the chicanery and hair-splitting to which lawyers resort in order to accommodate the crooked aims of the people. The warning was necessary to emphasize that holding fast to the Law was not to be equated with following the chicanery of the lawyers.

103. The Israelites were told that on their way they would come across the ruins of earlier nations who had refused to turn to God and who had persisted in their evil ways. Observing those ruins would be instructive insofar as they eloquently spoke of the tragic end that meets those who indulge in such iniquity.

(148) And in the absence of Moses[106] his people made the image of a calf from their ornaments, which lowed. Did they not observe that it could neither speak nor give them any guidance? And still they made it an object of worship. They were indeed wrong-doing.[107] ▶

وَاتَّخَذَ قَوْمُ مُوسَىٰ مِنۢ بَعْدِهِۦ مِنْ
حُلِيِّهِمْ عِجْلًا جَسَدًا لَّهُۥ خُوَارٌ ۚ
أَلَمْ يَرَوْا أَنَّهُۥ لَا يُكَلِّمُهُمْ وَلَا يَهْدِيهِمْ
سَبِيلًا ۘ ٱتَّخَذُوهُ وَكَانُوا۟
ظَٰلِمِينَ ﴿١٤٨﴾

104. It is God's law that evil-doers do not and cannot take any lesson from the otherwise instructive events which they observe. The arrogance mentioned here refers to man's delusion that he is on a higher plane than God's creatures and servants. It is this which prompts him to disregard God's command and to adopt an attitude which suggests that he neither considers himself God's servant, nor God his Lord. Such egotism has no basis in fact; it is sheer vanity. For as long as man lives on God's earth, what can justify his living as a servant of anyone other than the Lord of the universe? It is for this reason that the Qur'ān declares this arrogance to be 'without any right'.

105. That the acts of such persons are vain and fruitless is evident from the fact that the acceptance of man's acts by God is subject to two conditions. First, one's acts should conform to the Law laid down by God. Second, man should be prompted by the desire to achieve success in the Hereafter rather than merely in this world. If these conditions are not fulfilled, a person's acts will be of no consequence. He who performs an act in defiance of God's guidance, is guilty of rebellion and is undeserving of God's reward. He who acts only to obtain worldly success, is neither entitled to nor should expect any reward from God in the Hereafter. If someone uses another person's land contrary to his wish, what else can he expect from him than punishment? The same holds true for he who deliberately uses someone's land, knowing well that he is not entitled to any produce after the restoration of that land to its owner. There is no justification for him to expect any share of the produce of that land.

106. Here reference is made to the forty days which Moses spent on Mount Sinai in compliance with God's command when his people remained in the plain at the foot of the mountain called Maydān al-Rāḥah.

(149) And when they were afflicted with remorse and realized that they had fallen into error, they said: 'If our Lord does not have mercy on us and does not pardon us, we shall be among the losers.' (150) And when Moses returned to his people, full of wrath and sorrow, he said: 'Vile is the course you have followed in my absence. Could you not patiently wait for the decree of your Lord?' And he threw down the Tablets [of the Law] and took hold of his brother's head, dragging him to himself. Aaron said: 'My mother's son, the people overpowered me and almost killed me. So let not my enemies gloat over me, and do not number me among the wrong-doing folk.'[108] ▶

وَلَمَّا سُقِطَ فِىٓ أَيْدِيهِمْ وَرَأَوْا۟ أَنَّهُمْ
قَدْ ضَلُّوا۟ قَالُوا۟ لَئِن لَّمْ يَرْحَمْنَا رَبُّنَا
وَيَغْفِرْ لَنَا لَنَكُونَنَّ مِنَ
ٱلْخَٰسِرِينَ ﴿١٤٩﴾ وَلَمَّا رَجَعَ مُوسَىٰٓ إِلَىٰ
قَوْمِهِۦ غَضْبَٰنَ أَسِفًا قَالَ بِئْسَمَا خَلَفْتُمُونِى
مِنۢ بَعْدِىٓ ۖ أَعَجِلْتُمْ أَمْرَ رَبِّكُمْ ۖ وَأَلْقَى
ٱلْأَلْوَاحَ وَأَخَذَ بِرَأْسِ أَخِيهِ يَجُرُّهُۥٓ إِلَيْهِ ۚ
قَالَ ٱبْنَ أُمَّ إِنَّ ٱلْقَوْمَ ٱسْتَضْعَفُونِى
وَكَادُوا۟ يَقْتُلُونَنِى فَلَا تُشْمِتْ بِىَ
ٱلْأَعْدَآءَ وَلَا تَجْعَلْنِى مَعَ ٱلْقَوْمِ
ٱلظَّٰلِمِينَ ﴿١٥٠﴾

---

107. Their cow-worship was another manifestation of the Israelites' slavish attachment to the Egyptian traditions at the time of the Exodus. It is well-known that cow-worship was widespread in Egypt and it was during their stay there that the Israelites developed this strange infatuation. The Qur'ān also refers to their inclination to cow-worship: 'Their hearts were overflowing with love for the calf because of their unbelief' (*al-Baqarah* 2: 93). What is more surprising about their turn to idolatry is that it took place just three months after their escape from Egypt. During that time they had witnessed the parting of the sea, the drowning of Pharaoh, and their own deliverance from what otherwise seemed inescapable slavery to the Egyptians. They knew well that all those events had taken place owing to the unmistakable and direct interference of the all-powerful God. Yet they had the audacity to demand that their Prophet should make for them

(151) Thereupon Moses said: 'O Lord! Grant forgiveness upon me and my brother and admit us to Your Mercy, for You are most merciful of the merciful.' (152) In reply they were told: 'Verily those who worshipped the calf will certainly incur indignation from their Lord, and will be abased in the life of this world. Thus do We reward those who fabricate lies. ►

قَالَ رَبِّ ٱغْفِرْ لِى وَلِأَخِى وَأَدْخِلْنَا
فِى رَحْمَتِكَ ۖ وَأَنتَ أَرْحَمُ
ٱلرَّٰحِمِينَ ﴿١٥١﴾ إِنَّ ٱلَّذِينَ ٱتَّخَذُوا۟
ٱلْعِجْلَ سَيَنَالُهُمْ غَضَبٌ مِّن
رَّبِّهِمْ وَذِلَّةٌ فِى ٱلْحَيَوٰةِ ٱلدُّنْيَا ۚ
وَكَذَٰلِكَ نَجْزِى ٱلْمُفْتَرِينَ ﴿١٥٢﴾

a false god that they might worship. Not only that, soon after Moses left them for Mount Sinai, they themselves contrived a false god. Disgusted with such conduct on the part of the Israelites, some Prophets have likened their people to a nymphomaniac who loves all save her husband and who is unfaithful to him even on their nuptial night.

108. The above Qur'ānic verse absolves Aaron of the charge levelled against him by the Jews. According to the Biblical version of the story of calf-worship, however, it was Aaron who had made the golden calf for the people of Israel. To quote:

> When the people saw that Moses delayed to come down from the mountain, the people gathered themselves together to Aaron, and said to him, 'Up, make up gods who shall go before us; as for this Moses, the man who brought us up out of the land of Egypt, we do not know what has become of him.' And Aaron said to them, 'Take off the rings of gold which are in the ears of your wives, your sons, and your daughters, and bring them to me.' So all the people took off the rings of gold which were in their ears, and brought them to Aaron. And he received the gold at their hand, and fashioned it with a graving tool, and made a molten calf; and they said, 'These are your gods, O Israel, who brought you up out of the land of Egypt.' When Aaron saw this, he built an altar before it; and Aaron made proclamation and said, 'Tomorrow shall be a feast to the Lord.' And they rose up early on the morrow, and offered burnt offerings and brought peace offerings; and the people sat down to eat and drink, and rose up to play (*Exodus* 32: 1–6).

(153) As for those who do evil, and later repent and have faith, such shall find their Lord All-Forgiving, All-Compassionate after (they repent and believe).

(154) And when the anger of Moses was stilled, he took up the Tablets again, the text of which comprised guidance and mercy to those who fear their Lord. ▶

وَالَّذِينَ عَمِلُوا السَّيِّئَاتِ ثُمَّ تَابُوا مِن
بَعْدِهَا وَآمَنُوا إِنَّ رَبَّكَ مِن بَعْدِهَا
لَغَفُورٌ رَّحِيمٌ ﴿١٥٣﴾ وَلَمَّا سَكَتَ عَن
مُّوسَى الْغَضَبُ أَخَذَ الْأَلْوَاحَ وَفِي
نُسْخَتِهَا هُدًى وَرَحْمَةٌ لِّلَّذِينَ هُمْ لِرَبِّهِمْ
يَرْهَبُونَ ﴿١٥٤﴾

The Qur'ān, however, refutes the above account at many places and points out that it was Sāmirī the rebel of God rather than Aaron the Prophet who committed that heinous sin. (For details see *Ṭā Hā* 20: 90 ff.)

Strange though it may appear, the Israelites maligned the characters of those very people whom they believed to be the Messengers of God. The accusations they hurled at them included such heinous sins as polytheism, sorcery, fornication, deceit and treachery. Needless to say, indulgence in any of these sins is disgraceful for even an ordinary believer and decent human being, let alone Prophets. In the light of the history of Israeli morals, however, it is quite understandable why they maligned their own Prophets. In times of religious and moral degeneration when both the clergy and laity were steeped in sin and immorality, they tried to seek justification for their misdeeds. In order to sedate their own consciences they ascribed the very sins of which they were guilty to their Prophets and then their own inability to refrain from sins on the grounds that not even the Prophets could refrain.

The same characteristic is evident in Hinduism. When the Hindus reached the lowest point in their moral degeneration, they produced a literature which presents a very perverted image of Hindu ideals. This literature portrayed their gods, hermits and monks as crass sinners. In doing so, they suggested that since such noble people could not refrain from indulging in grave sins, ordinary mortals are inevitably bound to commit them. Moreover, a person's indulgence in immoral acts should not make him remorseful for the same acts were committed earlier by their monks and hermits.

(155) And out of his people Moses singled out seventy men for Our appointment.[109] Then, when violent shaking seized them, he addressed his Lord: 'Had You willed, O my Lord, You could have destroyed them and me long ago. Will You destroy us for what the fools amongst us did? That was nothing but a trial from You whereby You mislead whom You will and guide whom You will.[110] You alone are our guardian. Forgive us, then, and have mercy upon us. You are the best of those who forgive. (156) And ordain for us what is good in this world and in the World to Come for to You have we turned.' He replied: 'I afflict whomsoever I wish with My chastisement. As for My mercy, it encompasses everything.[111] I will show mercy to those who abstain from evil, pay *Zakāh*, and have faith in Our signs.'

وَٱخْتَارَ مُوسَىٰ قَوْمَهُۥ سَبْعِينَ رَجُلًا
لِّمِيقَٰتِنَا فَلَمَّآ أَخَذَتْهُمُ ٱلرَّجْفَةُ
قَالَ رَبِّ لَوْ شِئْتَ أَهْلَكْتَهُم مِّن قَبْلُ
وَإِيَّٰىَ أَتُهْلِكُنَا بِمَا فَعَلَ ٱلسُّفَهَآءُ مِنَّآ
إِنْ هِىَ إِلَّا فِتْنَتُكَ تُضِلُّ بِهَا مَن تَشَآءُ
وَتَهْدِى مَن تَشَآءُ أَنتَ وَلِيُّنَا فَٱغْفِرْ
لَنَا وَٱرْحَمْنَا وَأَنتَ خَيْرُ ٱلْغَٰفِرِينَ ١٥٥
وَٱكْتُبْ لَنَا فِى هَٰذِهِ ٱلدُّنْيَا
حَسَنَةً وَفِى ٱلْءَاخِرَةِ إِنَّا هُدْنَآ
إِلَيْكَ قَالَ عَذَابِىٓ أُصِيبُ بِهِۦ مَنْ
أَشَآءُ وَرَحْمَتِى وَسِعَتْ كُلَّ
شَىْءٍ فَسَأَكْتُبُهَا لِلَّذِينَ يَتَّقُونَ
وَيُؤْتُونَ ٱلزَّكَوٰةَ وَٱلَّذِينَ هُم
بِـَٔايَٰتِنَا يُؤْمِنُونَ ١٥٦

---

109. Moses was summoned for the second time to Mount Sinai along with seventy chiefs of the nation in order that they might seek pardon for their calf-worship and renew their covenant with God. Reference to this event is not found in the Bible and Talmud. They simply mention that Moses was summoned to receive new tablets as replacements for the ones he had thrown down and broken. (Cf. *Exodus* 34.)

110. When a people are put to the test it is an occasion of crucial importance for it helps to distinguish the righteous from the wicked. Like

(157) [To-day this mercy is for] those who follow the *ummī* Prophet,[112] whom they find mentioned in the Torah and the Gospel with them.[113] He enjoins upon them what is good and forbids them what is evil. He makes the clean things lawful to them and prohibits all corrupt things,[114] and removes from them their burdens and the shackles that were upon them.[115] So those who believe in him and assist him, and succour him and follow the Light which has been sent down with him, it is they who shall prosper. ►

ٱلَّذِينَ يَتَّبِعُونَ ٱلرَّسُولَ ٱلنَّبِىَّ ٱلْأُمِّىَّ
ٱلَّذِى يَجِدُونَهُۥ مَكْتُوبًا عِندَهُمْ
فِى ٱلتَّوْرَىٰةِ وَٱلْإِنجِيلِ يَأْمُرُهُم
بِٱلْمَعْرُوفِ وَيَنْهَىٰهُمْ عَنِ ٱلْمُنكَرِ
وَيُحِلُّ لَهُمُ ٱلطَّيِّبَٰتِ وَيُحَرِّمُ
عَلَيْهِمُ ٱلْخَبَٰٓئِثَ وَيَضَعُ عَنْهُمْ
إِصْرَهُمْ وَٱلْأَغْلَٰلَ ٱلَّتِى كَانَتْ عَلَيْهِمْ
فَٱلَّذِينَ ءَامَنُوا۟ بِهِۦ وَعَزَّرُوهُ وَنَصَرُوهُ
وَٱتَّبَعُوا۟ ٱلنُّورَ ٱلَّذِىٓ أُنزِلَ مَعَهُۥٓ أُو۟لَٰٓئِكَ
هُمُ ٱلْمُفْلِحُونَ ﴿١٥٧﴾

---

a winnow, it separates out of the mass the useful from the useless. Hence in his wisdom God subjects people to tests. Those who successfully pass through them, owe their success to the support and guidance they receive from God. As for those who are unsuccessful, their failure is the result of their not receiving that support and guidance. This does not detract from the fact that men neither arbitrarily receive or are denied God's support and guidance. Both extending and withholding support and guidance follow a rule which is based on wisdom and justice. The fact, however, remains that man can succeed in the test to which he is put only if God supports and guides him.

111. It is false to assume that the general rule underlying God's governance of His realm is that of wrath which is occasionally tempered with mercy and benevolence. On the contrary, the general rule is that of mercy and benevolence and wrath is the exception which is aroused when man's transgression and rebellion exceed all reasonable limits.

112. The preceding verse concludes God's response to Moses' prayer. This was the appropriate moment to invite the Israelites to follow the Message preached by the Prophet Muḥammad (peace be on him). The upshot of what is being said here is that people can even now attain God's

mercy exactly as they could in the past. These conditions require that people should now follow the Prophet Muḥammad (peace be on him), since refusal to follow a Prophet after his advent amounts to gross disobedience to God. Those who do not commit themselves to follow the Prophet (peace be on him) cannot attain the essence of piety no matter how hard they try to make a pretence of it by observing the minor details of religious rituals generally associated with piety.

Likewise, the Israelites had been told that paying *Zakāh* was essential to win God's mercy. However, payment of *Zakāh* is meaningless unless one supports the struggle to establish the hegemony of truth which was being carried on under the leadership of the Prophet (peace be on him). For unless one spends money to exalt the word of God, the very foundations of *Zakāh* are lacking, even if a person spends huge amounts in the way of charity. They were also reminded that they had been told in the past that God's mercy was exclusively for those who believed in His Revelation. Now those who rejected the Revelation received by Muḥammad (peace be on him) could never be considered believers in Revelation no matter how zealously they claim to believe in the Torah.

Reference to the Prophet (peace be on him) in this verse as *ummī* is significant as the Israelites branded all other nations as Gentiles *(ummīs)*. Steeped in racial prejudice, they did not consider members of other nations as their equals, let alone accept any person not belonging to them as a Prophet. The Qur'ān also states the Jewish belief that they would not be taken to task for whatever they might do to non-Jews. (See *Āl 'Imrān* 3: 75.) Employing the same term which they themselves had used, the Qur'ān tells them that their destiny was linked with the *ummī* Prophet. By obeying him they would become deserving of God's mercy. As for disobedience to the Prophet (peace be on him), it would continue to arouse God's wrath which had been afflicted upon them for centuries.

113. Pointed and repeated reference to the coming of the Prophet Muḥammad (peace be on him) is made in the Bible. (See *Deuteronomy* 18: 15–19; *Matthew* 21: 33–46; *John* 1: 19–25; 14: 15–17, 25–30; 15: 25–6; 16: 7–15.)

114. The Prophet declares the pure things which they had forbidden as lawful, and the impure things which they had legitimized as unlawful.

115. The Israelites had fettered their lives by undue restrictions which had been placed on them by the legal hair-splitting of their jurists, the pietistic exaggerations of their spiritual leaders, the introduction of superstitions and self-contrived laws and regulations by their masses. The Prophet, by relieving them of every unnecessary burden and releasing them from every unjustified restriction, in fact liberated their shackled lives.

(158) [Say, O Muḥammad]: 'O men! I am Allah's Messenger to you all – of Him to Whom belongs the dominion of the heavens and the earth. There is no god but He. He grants life and deals death. Have faith, then, in Allah and in His Messenger, the *ummī* Prophet who believes in Allah and His words; and follow him so that you may be guided aright.'

(159) Among the people of Moses[116] there was a party who guided others in the way of the truth and established justice in its light.[117] ▶

قُلْ يَٰٓأَيُّهَا ٱلنَّاسُ إِنِّى رَسُولُ ٱللَّهِ
إِلَيْكُمْ جَمِيعًا ٱلَّذِى لَهُۥ مُلْكُ
ٱلسَّمَٰوَٰتِ وَٱلْأَرْضِ لَآ إِلَٰهَ إِلَّا هُوَ يُحْىِۦ
وَيُمِيتُ فَـَٔامِنُوا۟ بِٱللَّهِ وَرَسُولِهِ ٱلنَّبِىِّ
ٱلْأُمِّىِّ ٱلَّذِى يُؤْمِنُ بِٱللَّهِ
وَكَلِمَٰتِهِۦ وَٱتَّبِعُوهُ لَعَلَّكُمْ
تَهْتَدُونَ ﴿١٥٨﴾ وَمِن قَوْمِ
مُوسَىٰٓ أُمَّةٌ يَهْدُونَ بِٱلْحَقِّ وَبِهِۦ
يَعْدِلُونَ ﴿١٥٩﴾

116. This marks the resumption of the main theme of the discourse which had been interrupted by the parenthesis (see verses 157–8) calling people to affirm the prophethood of Muḥammad (peace be on him).

117. The translators generally render the verse as the following:

> Of the people of Moses there is a section who guide and do justice in the light of truth. (Translation by Abdullah Yusuf Ali.)

They do so because, in their view, the present verse describes the moral and intellectual state of the Israelites at the time when the Qur'ān was revealed. However, the context seems to indicate that the above account refers to the state of the Israelites at the time of the Prophet Moses. Thus, the purpose of the verse is to emphasize that even in the days of their calf-worship when God rebuked them, all members of Israel were not corrupt; that a sizeable section of them was righteous.

(160) And We divided them into twelve tribes, forming them into communities.[118] When his people asked Moses for water We directed him: 'Smite the rock with your rod.' Then twelve springs gushed forth from the rock and every people knew their drinking-places. And We caused thick clouds to provide them shade, and We sent down upon them manna and quails,[119] saying: 'Eat of the clean things that We have provided you.' They wronged not Us, but it was themselves that they wronged.

وَقَطَّعْنَٰهُمُ ٱثْنَتَىْ عَشْرَةَ أَسْبَاطًا أُمَمًا
وَأَوْحَيْنَآ إِلَىٰ مُوسَىٰٓ إِذِ ٱسْتَسْقَىٰهُ
قَوْمُهُۥٓ أَنِ ٱضْرِب بِّعَصَاكَ
ٱلْحَجَرَ فَٱنۢبَجَسَتْ مِنْهُ ٱثْنَتَا
عَشْرَةَ عَيْنًا قَدْ عَلِمَ كُلُّ أُنَاسٍ
مَّشْرَبَهُمْ وَظَلَّلْنَا عَلَيْهِمُ ٱلْغَمَٰمَ
وَأَنزَلْنَا عَلَيْهِمُ ٱلْمَنَّ وَٱلسَّلْوَىٰ
كُلُوا۟ مِن طَيِّبَٰتِ مَا رَزَقْنَٰكُمْ
وَمَا ظَلَمُونَا وَلَٰكِن كَانُوٓا۟
أَنفُسَهُمْ يَظْلِمُونَ ١٦٠

118. This refers to the organization of the people of Israel which has been mentioned in the Qur'ān in *al-Mā'idah* 5: 12 and also described, at length, in the Bible in *Numbers*. According to these sources, in compliance with God's command the Prophet Moses first conducted the census of the Israelites in the wilderness of Sinai. He registered their twelve tribes, ten of whom were descendants of the Prophet Jacob, and the remaining two descendants of the Prophet Joseph, as separate and distinct tribes. He appointed a chief for each tribe and assigned to him the duty to maintain moral, religious, social and military discipline within each tribe and to enforce the Law. The Levites, who were descendants of the Prophets Moses and Aaron, however, were organized as a distinct group entrusted with the task of providing religious guidance to all tribes.

119. This organization was one of the numerous favours which God had bestowed upon the Israelites. Mention is made of three other favours bestowed upon them. First, an extraordinary arrangement for their water supply was made in the otherwise arid Sinai peninsula. Second, the sky was covered with clouds such that they were protected from the scorching heat of the sun. Third, a unique meal, consisting of manna and quails, was sent down on them. Had this Divine arrangement, catering as it did for

(161) And recall[120] when it was said to them: 'Dwell in this town and eat plentifully of whatever you please, and say: "Repentance", and enter the gate prostrate. We shall forgive you your sins and shall bestow further favours on those who do good.' (162) Then the wrong-doers among them substituted another word in place of the one told them. So We sent upon them a scourge from the heaven as a punishment for their wrong-doing.[121]

وَإِذْ قِيلَ لَهُمُ ٱسْكُنُوا۟ هَٰذِهِ ٱلْقَرْيَةَ
وَكُلُوا۟ مِنْهَا حَيْثُ شِئْتُمْ وَقُولُوا۟
حِطَّةٌ وَٱدْخُلُوا۟ ٱلْبَابَ سُجَّدًا نَّغْفِرْ
لَكُمْ خَطِيٓـَٔـٰتِكُمْ سَنَزِيدُ
ٱلْمُحْسِنِينَ ﴿١٦١﴾ فَبَدَّلَ
ٱلَّذِينَ ظَلَمُوا۟ مِنْهُمْ قَوْلًا غَيْرَ
ٱلَّذِى قِيلَ لَهُمْ فَأَرْسَلْنَا عَلَيْهِمْ
رِجْزًا مِّنَ ٱلسَّمَآءِ بِمَا
كَانُوا۟ يَظْلِمُونَ ﴿١٦٢﴾

---

the millions of wandering Israelites' basic necessities of life, not been made, they would certainly have perished.

On visiting that land even today it is difficult to visualize how such an arrangement providing shelter, food and water for millions of people was made. The population of this peninsula stands even today at a paltry 55,000 people. (It may be noted that this statement was made in the fifties of the present century. However, the present population of the Sinai is 200,000 – Ed.) If a five or six hundred thousand strong army were to camp there today, it would be quite a task for those at the helm to provide the necessary supplies for the army. Little wonder, then, that many scholars who believe neither in the Scripture nor in miracles, rule out the historical accuracy of the event. For them, the people of Israel camped in an area lying south of Palestine and north of Arabia. In view of the physical and economic geography of the Sinai peninsula, they consider it totally incredible that such a large population could have stayed there for years. What has made these scholars even more sceptical about the event is the fact that the Israelites were not then in a position to procure supplies from either the Egyptians or the 'Amāliqah' who inhabited respectively the eastern and northern parts of the peninsula, since both groups were hostile to them. It is against this background that one may appreciate the immense importance of the favours God conferred on the Israelites. Likewise, it also gives one some idea of the blatant ingratitude of the people of Israel since they consistently defied and betrayed God even though they had

(163) And ask the people of Moses concerning the town situated along the sea[122] how its people profaned the Sabbath when fish came to them breaking the water's surface on Sabbath days,[123] and would not come to them on other than Sabbath-days. Thus did We try them because of their disobedience.[124] (164) And recall when a party of them said: 'Why do you admonish a people whom Allah is about to destroy or punish severely?' They said: 'We admonish them in order to be able to offer an excuse before Your Lord, and in the hope that they will guard against disobedience.' ▶

وَسۡـَٔلۡهُمۡ عَنِ ٱلۡقَرۡيَةِ ٱلَّتِي كَانَتۡ
حَاضِرَةَ ٱلۡبَحۡرِ إِذۡ يَعۡدُونَ فِي
ٱلسَّبۡتِ إِذۡ تَأۡتِيهِمۡ حِيتَانُهُمۡ
يَوۡمَ سَبۡتِهِمۡ شُرَّعٗا وَيَوۡمَ لَا
يَسۡبِتُونَ لَا تَأۡتِيهِمۡۚ كَذَٰلِكَ
نَبۡلُوهُم بِمَا كَانُواْ يَفۡسُقُونَ ١٦٣ وَإِذۡ
قَالَتۡ أُمَّةٞ مِّنۡهُمۡ لِمَ تَعِظُونَ قَوۡمًا ٱللَّهُ
مُهۡلِكُهُمۡ أَوۡ مُعَذِّبُهُمۡ عَذَابٗا شَدِيدٗاۖ
قَالُواْ مَعۡذِرَةً إِلَىٰ رَبِّكُمۡ وَلَعَلَّهُمۡ
يَتَّقُونَ ١٦٤

witnessed a great many divine signs. (See *Towards Understanding the Qur'ān,* vol. I, *al-Baqarah* 2: nn. 72–3 and 76, pp. 76–7 – Ed.)

120. This alludes to their constant defiance and rebellion in face of God's favours which eventually brought about their destruction.

121. For details see *Towards Understanding the Qur'ān,* vol. I, *al-Baqarah* 2: nn. 74–5, pp. 76–7.

122. Most scholars identify this place with Eilat, Eilath or Eloth. (Cf. *Encyclopaedia Britannica,* XV edition, 'Macropaedia', vol. 3, art. 'Elat' – Ed.) The seaport called Elat which has been built by the present state of Israel (which is close to the Jordanian seaport, Aqaba), stands on the same site. It lies at the end of that long inlet of the Red Sea situated between the eastern part of the Sinai peninsula and the western part of Arabia. It was a major trading centre in the time of Israelite ascendancy. The Prophet Solomon took this city as the chief port for his fleet in the Red Sea.

The event referred to in the above verse is not reported in Jewish Scriptures. Nor do historical accounts shed any light on it. Nonetheless, it appears from the way it has been mentioned in the above verse and in *al-Baqarah* that the Jews of the early days of Islam were quite familiar with the event. (See *Towards Understanding the Qur'ān,* vol. I, *al-Baqarah* 2: 65 and n. 83, pp. 81–2 – Ed.) This view is further corroborated by the fact that even the Madinan Jews who spared no opportunity to criticize the Prophet (peace be on him) did not raise any objection against this Qur'ānic account.

123. 'Sabbath', which means Saturday, was declared for the Israelites as the holy day of the week. God declared the Sabbath as a sign of the perpetual covenant between God and Israel. (*Exodus* 31: 12–16.) The Israelites were required to strictly keep the Sabbath which meant that they may not engage in any worldly activity; they may not cook, nor make their slaves or cattle serve them. Those who violated these rules were to be put to death. The Israelites, however, publicly violated these rules. In the days of the Prophet Jeremiah (between 628 and 586 B.C.), the Israelites carried their merchandise through the gates of Jerusalem on the Sabbath day itself. Jeremiah, therefore, warned them that if they persisted in their flagrant violation of the Law, Jerusalem would be set on fire. (*Jeremiah* 17: 21–7.) The same complaint is voiced in the Book of the Prophet Ezekiel (595–536 B.C.) who referred to their violation of the Sabbath rules as their major sin. (*Ezekiel* 20: 12–24.) In view of these Scriptural references it seems plausible that the event mentioned in the above Qur'ānic verse is related to the same period.

124. Men are tested by God in a variety of ways. When a person or group of people begin to turn away from God and incline themselves towards disobedience, God provides abundant opportunities for them to disobey. This is done in order that the full potential for disobedience, which had remained hidden because of lack of such an opportunity, might come to the surface.

(165) Then, when they forgot what they had been exhorted, We delivered those who forbade evil and afflicted the wrong-doers with a grievous chastisement[125] because of their evil-doing. (166) And when they persisted in pursuing that which had been forbidden We said: 'Become despised apes.'[126]

فَلَمَّا نَسُوا مَا ذُكِّرُوا بِهِۦٓ أَنجَيْنَا ٱلَّذِينَ
يَنْهَوْنَ عَنِ ٱلسُّوٓءِ وَأَخَذْنَا ٱلَّذِينَ
ظَلَمُوا بِعَذَابٍۭ بَـِٔيسٍۭ بِمَا كَانُوا
يَفْسُقُونَ ﴿١٦٥﴾ فَلَمَّا عَتَوْا عَن
مَّا نُهُوا عَنْهُ قُلْنَا لَهُمْ كُونُوا قِرَدَةً
خَـٰسِـِٔينَ ﴿١٦٦﴾

125. This shows that the people in that town were of three categories. One, those who flagrantly violated God's commands. Two, those who were silent spectators to such violations and discouraged those who admonished the criminals, pleading that their efforts were fruitless. Three, those who, moved by their religious commitment, actively enjoined good and forbade evil so that the evil-doers might make amends. In so doing, they were prompted by a sense of duty to bring back the evil-doers to the right path, and if the latter did not respond to their call, they would at least be able to establish before their Lord that for their part they had fulfilled their duty to admonish the evil-doers. So, when the town was struck by God's punishment, only the people belonging to the last category were spared for they had displayed God-consciousness and performed the duties incumbent upon them. As for the people of the other two categories, they were reckoned as transgressors and were punished in proportion to their crimes.

Some commentators on the Qur'ān are of the opinion that whereas the Qur'ān specifically describes the fate of the people belonging to the first and third categories, it is silent about the treatment meted out to the people of the second category. It cannot be said, therefore, with certainty whether they were spared or punished. It is reported that Ibn 'Abbās initially believed that God's punishment included the second category as well. It is believed that later his disciple 'Ikramah convinced him that only the people of the second category would be delivered in the same manner as the people of the third category.

A closer study of the Qur'ānic account, however, shows that Ibn 'Abbās's earlier viewpoint is sound. It is evident that the people of the town would inevitably have been grouped into two categories on the eve of God's punishment: those who were spared and those who were not. Since the Qur'ān states that the people of the third category had been spared, it may

(167) And recall when Your Lord proclaimed[127] that 'He would continually set in authority over them, till the Day of Judgement, those who would ruthlessly oppress them.'[128] Surely, your Lord is swift in chastising; and yet He is All-Forgiving, All-Merciful.

وَإِذْ تَأَذَّنَ رَبُّكَ لَيَبْعَثَنَّ عَلَيْهِمْ إِلَىٰ
يَوْمِ ٱلْقِيَـٰمَةِ مَن يَسُومُهُمْ سُوٓءَ
ٱلْعَذَابِ ۗ إِنَّ رَبَّكَ لَسَرِيعُ ٱلْعِقَابِ ۖ
وَإِنَّهُۥ لَغَفُورٌ رَّحِيمٌ ١٦٧

be legitimately assumed that the people belonging to both the first and the second categories were punished. This view is also corroborated by the preceding verse:

> Also recall when a party of them said: 'Why do you admonish a people whom Allah is about to destroy or punish severely?' They said: 'We admonish them in order to be able to offer an excuse before your Lord, and in the hope that they will guard against disobedience.' (Verse 164.)

Thus it clearly emerges from the above discussion that all the people of the place where evil deeds are publicly committed stand guilty. One cannot be absolved merely on the basis that one had not committed any evil. One may be acquitted only in the event that one made every possible effort to bring about reform and actively worked in the cause of the truth. This constitutes the divine law pertaining to collective evil as is evident from the teachings of the Qur'ān and *Ḥadīth*. The Qur'ān says:

> And guard against the mischief that will not only bring punishment to the wrong-doers among you. Know well that Allah is severe in punishment (*al-Anfāl* 8: 25).

Explaining the above verse the Prophet (peace be on him) remarked: 'God does not punish the generality of a people for the evil committed by a particular section of that people until they observe others committing evil and do not denounce it even though they are in a position to do so. And when they do that, God punishes all, the evil-doers and the people in general.' (Aḥmad b. Ḥanbal, *Musnad*, vol. 4, p. 192 – Ed.)

Moreover, the verse in question seems to suggest that God's punishment afflicted the town concerned in two stages. The first stage is referred to as 'a grievous chastisement', for in the next stage they were turned into apes. We may, therefore, hold that people belonging to both the first and the second categories were subjected to punishment. But the punishment of

(168) And We dispersed them through the earth in communities – some were righteous, others were not – and We tested them with prosperity and adversity that they may turn back (to righteousness). (169) Then others succeeded them who inherited the scriptures, and yet kept themselves occupied in acquiring the goods of this world and kept saying: 'We shall be forgiven.' And when there comes to them an opportunity for acquiring more of those goods, they seize it.[129] Was not the covenant of the Book taken from them that they would not ascribe to Allah anything but the truth? And they have read what is in the Book[130] and know that the abode of the Hereafter is better for the God-fearing.[131] Do you not understand? ▶

وَقَطَّعْنَٰهُمْ فِى ٱلْأَرْضِ أُمَمًا مِّنْهُمُ
ٱلصَّٰلِحُونَ وَمِنْهُمْ دُونَ ذَٰلِكَ
وَبَلَوْنَٰهُم بِٱلْحَسَنَٰتِ وَٱلسَّيِّـَٔاتِ
لَعَلَّهُمْ يَرْجِعُونَ ﴿١٦٨﴾ فَخَلَفَ مِنۢ بَعْدِهِمْ
خَلْفٌ وَرِثُوا۟ ٱلْكِتَٰبَ يَأْخُذُونَ عَرَضَ
هَٰذَا ٱلْأَدْنَىٰ وَيَقُولُونَ سَيُغْفَرُ لَنَا وَإِن
يَأْتِهِمْ عَرَضٌ مِّثْلُهُۥ يَأْخُذُوهُ أَلَمْ يُؤْخَذْ عَلَيْهِم
مِّيثَٰقُ ٱلْكِتَٰبِ أَن لَّا يَقُولُوا۟ عَلَى ٱللَّهِ
إِلَّا ٱلْحَقَّ وَدَرَسُوا۟ مَا فِيهِ وَٱلدَّارُ ٱلْءَاخِرَةُ
خَيْرٌ لِّلَّذِينَ يَتَّقُونَ أَفَلَا تَعْقِلُونَ ﴿١٦٩﴾

---

transforming the persistent evil-doers into apes was confined only to the people of the second category. (God knows best. If I am right, that is from God. If I err, that is from me alone. God is All-Forgiving, All-Merciful.)

126. For details see *Towards Understanding the Qur'ān*, vol. I, *al-Baqarah* 2: n. 83, pp. 81–2.

127. The Qur'ānic expression *'ta'adhdhana'* means almost the same as 'he warned; he proclaimed'.

128. Since the 8th century B.C. the Israelites were warned consistently. This is borne out by the contents of the Books of the Prophets Isaiah,

Jeremiah, and their successors. Jesus too administered the same warning which is borne out by many of his orations in the New Testament. This was also later confirmed by the Qur'ān. History bears out the veracity of the statement made both in the Qur'ān and the earlier scriptures. For throughout history, since the time the Jews were warned, they have continually been subjected to abject persecution in one part of the world or another.

129. The Jews knowingly commit sins in the belief that being God's chosen people they will necessarily be pardoned and spared God's punishment. As a result of this misconception, they neither repent nor refrain from committing sins. How unfortunate the Jews are! They received the Scriptures which could have made them leaders of all mankind. But they were so petty-minded that they aspired to nothing higher than paltry worldly benefits. Thus even though they had the potential of becoming the upholders of justice and righteousness across the world they ended up merely as worshippers of this world.

130. The people of Israel know well that the Torah does not unconditionally assure them salvation. They have never been promised by God or any of His Prophets that they will attain deliverance no matter what they do. Therefore they have absolutely no right to ascribe to God something which He never told them. What makes their crime even worse is that their claim to unconditional salvation constitutes a sacrilege of their covenant with God whereby they pledged never to attribute any false statement to God.

131. The above verse has two renderings. It may be either translated as above or it may be rendered thus: 'For the righteous, only the home in the Hereafter is the best.' Going by the first rendering, the verse means that salvation is not the exclusive privilege of a particular person or a family. It is absolutely out of the question that one will attain deliverance even if one commits sins, simply on account of being a Jew. A little reflection will help one realize that only the righteous and God-fearing will be rewarded in the Hereafter. In the light of the second rendering, only the unrighteous prefer worldly gains to reward in the Hereafter. As for the righteous, they are conscious of the importance of the Hereafter and hence forego worldly benefits for the sake of reward in the Next World.

(170) Those who hold fast to the Book and establish Prayer – We shall not allow the reward of such righteous men to go to waste. (171) And recall when We shook the mountain over them as though it were a canopy, and they thought that it was going to fall over them; and We said: 'Hold firmly to that which We have given you, and remember what is in it, that you may guard against evil.'[132]

وَالَّذِينَ يُمَسِّكُونَ بِالْكِتَٰبِ وَأَقَامُوا
الصَّلَوٰةَ إِنَّا لَا نُضِيعُ أَجْرَ الْمُصْلِحِينَ
﴿١٧٠﴾ ۞ وَإِذْ نَتَقْنَا الْجَبَلَ فَوْقَهُمْ كَأَنَّهُ
ظُلَّةٌ وَظَنُّوا أَنَّهُ وَاقِعٌ بِهِمْ خُذُوا مَا
ءَاتَيْنَٰكُم بِقُوَّةٍ وَاذْكُرُوا مَا فِيهِ لَعَلَّكُمْ
تَتَّقُونَ ﴿١٧١﴾

---

132. The allusion here is to the event which took place when Moses proclaimed God's Divine Law at the foot of Mount Sinai.

> Then Moses brought the people out of the camp to meet God; and they took their stand at the foot of the mountain. And Mount Sinai was wrapped in smoke, because the Lord descended upon it in fire; and the smoke of it went up like the smoke of a kiln, and the whole mountain quaked greatly. (*Exodus* 19: 17–18.)

This awesome atmosphere was created by God at the time when He made the people of Israel enter into a covenant with Him in order to impress upon them the gravity of the event and the supreme importance of the covenant. It should not be mistakenly assumed, however, that the people of Israel, who were reluctant to make the covenant, were forced to enter into it. In fact they were all believers and had gone to the Mount merely to make the covenant. The extraordinary conditions which God created were such as to make the Israelites realize that making a covenant with God was not an ordinary matter. They were rather made to feel that they were entering into a covenant with none other than Almighty God and that violating it could spell their disaster.

This concludes the discourse especially addressed to the Israelites. From here on the discourse is directed to all mankind, and particularly to the people whom the Prophet (peace be on him) addressed directly.

(172) And recall (O Prophet)[133] when your Lord brought forth descendants from the loins of the sons of Adam, and made them witnesses against their own selves, asking them: 'Am I not your Lord?' They said: 'Yes, we do testify.'[134] We did so lest you claim on the Day of Resurrection: 'We were unaware of this.'

وَإِذْ أَخَذَ رَبُّكَ مِنۢ بَنِىٓ ءَادَمَ مِن ظُهُورِهِمْ ذُرِّيَّتَهُمْ وَأَشْهَدَهُمْ عَلَىٰٓ أَنفُسِهِمْ أَلَسْتُ بِرَبِّكُمْ قَالُوا۟ بَلَىٰ شَهِدْنَآ أَن تَقُولُوا۟ يَوْمَ ٱلْقِيَـٰمَةِ إِنَّا كُنَّا عَنْ هَـٰذَا غَـٰفِلِينَ ﴿١٧٢﴾

133. The preceding discourse concluded with the note that God made the Israelites enter into a covenant with their Lord. In the following passages all men are told that a covenant with God is not the exclusive privilege of Israel. In fact all human beings are bound in a covenant with God and a Day will come when they will be made to answer how well they were able to observe that covenant.

134. This event, according to several traditions, took place at the time of the creation of Adam. Apart from the prostration of the angels before Adam and the proclamation that man would be God's vicegerent on earth, all the future progeny of Adam were gathered, and were endowed with both existence and consciousness in order to bear witness to God's lordship. The best interpretation of this event is found in a statement by 'Ubayy b. Ka'b, who has probably given the substance of what he had heard from the Prophet (peace be on him):

> God gathered all human beings, divided them into different groups, granted them human form and the faculty of speech, made them enter into a covenant, and then making them witnesses against themselves He asked them: 'Am I not your Lord?' They replied: 'Assuredly you are Our Lord.' Then God told them: 'I call upon the sky and the earth and your own progenitor, Adam, to be witness against you lest you should say on the Day of Judgement that you were ignorant of this. Know well that no one other than Me deserves to be worshipped and no one other than Me is your Lord. So do not ascribe any partner to Me. I shall send to you My Messengers who will remind you of this covenant which you made with Me. I shall send down to you My Books.' In reply all said: 'We witness that You are Our Lord and our Deity. We have no lord or deity other than You.' (Aḥmad b. Ḥanbal, *Musnad*, vol. 5, p. 135 – Ed.)

(173) Or say: 'Our forefathers before us who associated others with Allah in His divinity; we were merely their offspring who followed them. And would You destroy us for that which the unrighteous did?'[135] ▶

أَوۡ تَقُولُوٓاْ إِنَّمَآ أَشۡرَكَ ءَابَآؤُنَا مِن قَبۡلُ وَكُنَّا ذُرِّيَّةٗ مِّنۢ بَعۡدِهِمۡۖ أَفَتُهۡلِكُنَا بِمَا فَعَلَ ٱلۡمُبۡطِلُونَ ١٧٣

This event has also been interpreted by some commentators in a purely allegorical sense. They are of the opinion that the purpose of the Qur'ān is merely to emphasize that the acceptance of God's lordship is innate in human nature. However, this was narrated in such a way as to suggest that the event did actually take place. We do not subscribe to this allegorical interpretation of the primordial covenant of man with God. For both the Qur'ān and *Ḥadīth* recount it not only as an actual happening, but also affirm that the covenant would be adduced as an argument against man on the Day of Judgement. There remains, therefore, no ground whatsoever to interpret the event in terms of mere allegory.

In our own view the event did take place. God caused all human beings whom He intended to create until the Last Day to come into existence. He endowed upon them life, consciousness and the faculty of speech, and brought home to them that there is no god or lord besides Him, and that Islam alone is the right way to serve Him.

If someone considers calling all human beings together in one assembly impossible, that shows, more than anything else the woeful paucity of his imagination. For if someone accepts that God has the power to create countless human beings in succession, there is no reason to suppose that He did not have the power to create them all at some given moment prior to the creation of the universe, or that He will be unable to resurrect them all at some given moment in the future. Again, it stands to reason that at a time when God wanted to designate man as His vicegerent on earth after endowing him with reason and understanding, He took from him an oath of allegiance. All this is so reasonable that the actual occurrence of the covenant should not cause any wonder. On the contrary, one should wonder if the event did not take place.

135. The verse describes the purpose of the primordial covenant. The purpose is to make every person responsible for his deeds so that if he rebels against God he will be held fully accountable for that rebellion. Because of the covenant, no one will be able either to plead for acquittal

on grounds of ignorance, or blame his misdeeds on his ancestors. In other words, this primordial covenant has been mentioned as the reason for the inherent awareness in every single person that God is the only Lord and Deity. Thus, none can totally absolve himself of his responsibility on the plea that he was altogether ignorant, or transfer the blame for his error to the corrupt environment in which he was brought up.

Now, it can be argued that even if the covenant did take place, no human being remembers its occurrence. No human being is aware that a long time ago, at the time of creation, he had affirmed, in response to God's query, that God indeed was his Lord. This being the case, it can be further argued that no charge can be legitimately brought against man on the ground of a covenant with God which he no longer remembers to have made.

In response to this it can be said that had the covenant been made fully in man's conscious memory, it would be meaningless for God to put man to the test in this world. Hence, there can be no denying that the covenant is not preserved in man's conscious memory. But it has doubtlessly been preserved in man's sub-conscious mind. In this respect the primordial covenant is no different from other pieces of knowledge in man's sub-conscious mind. Whatever man has so far achieved in the way of culture and civilization can be attributed to his latent potentialities. All external factors and internal motivations simply account for helping the actualization of those potentialities. Neither education nor training nor environmental factors can bring out anything which is not potentially found in the human mind. Likewise, external factors have no power to root out man's latent potentialities. External factors may, at the most, cause a person to deflect from the course dictated by sound human nature. However, man's sound nature is inclined to resist the pressure of external forces and exert itself in order to find an outlet. As we have said earlier, this is not peculiar to man's religious propensity alone, but is equally true of all his mental potentialities. In this regard the following points are particularly noteworthy:

(1) All man's potentialities exist in the sub-conscious mind and prove their existence when they manifest themselves in the form of human action.

(2) The external manifestation of these potentialities requires external stimuli such as instruction, upbringing, and attitudinal orientation. In other words, our actions consist of the responses of our inherent potentialities to external stimuli.

(3) Man's inner potentialities can be suppressed both by false urges within him as well as external influences by trying to pervert and distort those latent potentialities. The potentialities themselves, however, cannot be totally rooted out.

The same holds true of man's intuitive knowledge regarding his position in the universe and his relationship with his Creator. In this connection the following points should be borne in mind:

(1) That man has always had such intuitive knowledge is evident from the fact that this knowledge has surfaced throughout history in every period and in every part of the world, and which no power has so far been able to extirpate.

(2) That this intuitive knowledge conforms to objective reality is borne out by the fact that whenever this knowledge has influenced human life, it has had beneficial results.

(3) That in order to manifest itself in his practical life, man's intuitive knowledge has always required external stimuli. The stimuli have consisted of the advent of the Prophets (peace be on them), the revelation of the Heavenly Books, and the striving of those who have tried to follow them and invite others to do the same. It is for this reason that the Qur'ān has been designated as *mudhakkir* (the reminder); *dhikr* (remembrance); *tadhkirah* (admonition), and the function of the Qur'ān has been characterized as *tadhkīr* (reminding). What this suggests is that the Prophets, the Heavenly Books and those who invite people to the truth do not seek to provide human beings with something new, something which exists outside of them. Their task rather consists of bringing to the surface and rejuvenating what is latent, though dormant, in man himself.

Throughout the ages man has always positively responded to this 'Reminder'. This itself is testimony to the fact that it is embodied in a knowledge which has always been recognized by man's soul.

Forces arising from ignorance and obscurantism, lust and bigotry, and the erroneous teachings and promptings of devils – human as well as *jinn* – have always attempted to suppress, conceal, and distort the fact that the truth preached by the Prophets is embedded in man's soul. These attempts gave rise to polytheism, atheism, religious misdirection and moral corruption. Despite the combined efforts of the forces of falsehood, however, this knowledge has always had an imprint on the human heart. Hence, whenever any effort was made to revive that knowledge, it has proved successful.

Doubtlessly, those who are bent on denying the truth can resort to a great deal of sophistry in order to deny or at least create doubt and confusion about the existence of this knowledge. However, on the Day of Resurrection the Creator will revive in man the memory of the first assembly when man made his covenant with God and accepted Him as his Only Lord. On that occasion God will provide evidence to the effect that the covenant always remained imprinted on man's soul. He will also show how from time to time man tried to suppress his inner voice which urged

(174) And thus do We expound the signs[136] that they may turn back (to the right path).[137] (175) And recite to them [O Muḥammad] the story of the man to whom We gave Our signs[138] and who turned away from them; then ultimately Satan caught up with him and he was led astray. ▶

وَكَذَٰلِكَ نُفَصِّلُ ٱلْآيَٰتِ وَلَعَلَّهُمْ
يَرْجِعُونَ ﴿١٧٤﴾ وَٱتْلُ عَلَيْهِمْ نَبَأَ
ٱلَّذِىٓ ءَاتَيْنَٰهُ ءَايَٰتِنَا فَٱنسَلَخَ
مِنْهَا فَأَتْبَعَهُ ٱلشَّيْطَٰنُ فَكَانَ
مِنَ ٱلْغَاوِينَ ﴿١٧٥﴾

him to respond to the call of the covenant; how again and again his heart pressed him to affirm the truth; how his intuition induced him to denounce the errors of belief and practice; how the truth ingrained in his soul tried to express itself and respond to those who called to it; and how on each occasion he lulled his inner self to sleep because of his lust and bigotry.

However a Day will come when man will no longer be in a position to put forth specious arguments to justify his false claims. That will be the Day when man will have no option but to confess his error. It will then be impossible for people to say that they were ignorant, or negligent. In the words of the Qur'ān: '. . . and they will bear witness against themselves that they had disbelieved' (*al-An'ām* 6: 130).

136. 'Signs' here refer to the imprints made by knowledge of the truth on the human heart which help towards cognition of the truth.

137. 'To return' here signifies giving up rebellion, and reverting to obedience to God.

138. The words of the text seem to indicate that the person mentioned must indeed be a specific rather than an imaginary figure mentioned for the sake of parable. It may be borne in mind that God and His Messenger (peace be on him) usually mention evil without specific references to any individual. This is obviously in keeping with their dignity. Only examples of evil are mentioned since those examples are meant for didactic purposes, and this is done without smearing anyone's reputation.

Some commentators on the Qur'ān, however, have applied the statement made here to some persons who lived in the time of the Prophet (peace be on him) as well as before him. Some of them mention the name of Bal'am b. Bā'ūrā', others that of Umayyah b. Abī al-Ṣalt, and still others that of Ṣayfī b. al-Rāhib. (See the comments of Qurṭubī on verses 175 and

(176) Now had We so willed We could indeed have exalted him through those signs, but he clung to earthly life and followed his carnal desires. Thus his parable is that of the dog who lolls out his tongue whether you attack him or leave him alone.[139] Such is the parable of those who reject Our signs as false. Narrate to them these parables that they may reflect.

(177) Evil is the example of the people who reject Our signs as false and perpetrate wrong against their own selves. (178) He whom Allah guides, he alone is rightly guided; and he whom Allah lets go astray – it is they who are the loser.'

وَلَوْ شِئْنَا لَرَفَعْنَٰهُ بِهَا وَلَٰكِنَّهُۥٓ أَخْلَدَ
إِلَى ٱلْأَرْضِ وَٱتَّبَعَ هَوَىٰهُ فَمَثَلُهُۥ
كَمَثَلِ ٱلْكَلْبِ إِن تَحْمِلْ عَلَيْهِ
يَلْهَثْ أَوْ تَتْرُكْهُ يَلْهَث ذَّٰلِكَ
مَثَلُ ٱلْقَوْمِ ٱلَّذِينَ كَذَّبُوا۟ بِـَٔايَٰتِنَا
فَٱقْصُصِ ٱلْقَصَصَ لَعَلَّهُمْ
يَتَفَكَّرُونَ ﴿١٧٦﴾ سَآءَ مَثَلًا ٱلْقَوْمُ
ٱلَّذِينَ كَذَّبُوا۟ بِـَٔايَٰتِنَا وَأَنفُسَهُمْ
كَانُوا۟ يَظْلِمُونَ ﴿١٧٧﴾ مَن يَهْدِ ٱللَّهُ
فَهُوَ ٱلْمُهْتَدِى وَمَن يُضْلِلْ
فَأُو۟لَٰٓئِكَ هُمُ ٱلْخَٰسِرُونَ ﴿١٧٨﴾

176 – Ed.) Nonetheless, in the absence of any authentic information about the identity of the persons under discussion, we might as well consider the description made here to fit a certain type of person.

139. Since the statement here embodies a very significant point, it needs to be carefully examined. The person mentioned in the verse as the representative of the evil type possessed knowledge of God's signs, and hence of the truth. This should have helped him to give up an attitude which he knew to be wrong, and to act in a manner which he knew to be right. Had he followed the truth and acted righteously God would have enabled him to rise to higher levels of humanity. He, however, overly occupied himself with the advantages, pleasures, and embellishments of the worldly life. Instead of resisting worldly temptations, he totally succumbed to them so much so that he abandoned altogether his lofty spiritual ambitions and became indifferent to the possibilities of intellectual and moral growth. He even brazenly violated all those limits which, according to his knowledge, should have been observed. Hence when he

(179) And certainly We have created for Hell many of the *jinn* and mankind;[140] they have hearts with which they fail to understand; and they have eyes with which they fail to see; and they have ears with which they fail to hear. They are like cattle – indeed, even more astray. Such are utterly heedless.

وَلَقَدْ ذَرَأْنَا لِجَهَنَّمَ كَثِيرًا مِّنَ
ٱلْجِنِّ وَٱلْإِنسِ ۖ لَهُمْ قُلُوبٌ لَّا يَفْقَهُونَ
بِهَا وَلَهُمْ أَعْيُنٌ لَّا يُبْصِرُونَ بِهَا وَلَهُمْ
ءَاذَانٌ لَّا يَسْمَعُونَ بِهَآ ۚ أُو۟لَٰٓئِكَ كَٱلْأَنْعَٰمِ
بَلْ هُمْ أَضَلُّ ۚ أُو۟لَٰٓئِكَ هُمُ ٱلْغَٰفِلُونَ ﴿١٧٩﴾

deliberately turned away from the truth merely because of his moral weakness, he was misled by Satan who is ever ready to beguile and mislead man. Satan continually led him from one act of depravity to another until he landed him in the company of those who are totally under Satan's control and who have lost all capacity for rational judgement.

This is followed by a statement in which God likens the person in question to a dog. A dog's protruding tongue and the unceasing flow of saliva from his mouth symbolize unquenchable greed and avarice. The reason for likening the human character described above to a dog is because of his excessive worldliness. It is known that in several languages of the world it is common to call people overly devoted to worldliness as 'dogs of the world'. For what, after all, is the characteristic of a dog? It is nothing else but greed and avarice. Just look at the dog! As he moves around, he continuously sniffs the earth. Even if a rock is hurled at him he runs at it in the hope that it might be a piece of bone or bread. Before he discovers it to be a rock, he hastens to seize it in his mouth. Even a person's indifference does not deter a dog from waiting expectantly for food – panting for breath, his tongue spread out and drooping, and a whole world from one perspective alone – that of his belly! Even if he discovers a large carcass, he would not be content with his portion of it, but would try to make it exclusively his and would not let any other dog even come close. It seems that if any urge other than appetite tickles him, it is the sexual urge. This metaphor of the dog, highlights the fate of the worldly man who breaks loose from his faith and knowledge, who entrusts his reins to blind lust and who ends up as one wholly devoted to gratifying his own appetite.

140. This does not mean that God has created some people for the specific purpose of fuelling Hell. What it does mean is that even though

(180) Allah has the most excellent names.[141] So call on Him by His names and shun those who distort them. They shall soon be requited for their deeds.[142] (181) And of those whom We have created there is a party who guide men through the truth and act justly according to it. (182) As for those who reject Our signs as false, We shall lead them, step by step, to their ruin without their even perceiving it. (183) And (for this purpose) I will grant them respite. My design is incontrovertible.

وَلِلَّهِ الْأَسْمَاءُ الْحُسْنَىٰ فَادْعُوهُ بِهَا وَذَرُوا
الَّذِينَ يُلْحِدُونَ فِي أَسْمَائِهِ
سَيُجْزَوْنَ مَا كَانُوا يَعْمَلُونَ ﴿١٨٠﴾ وَمِمَّنْ
خَلَقْنَا أُمَّةٌ يَهْدُونَ بِالْحَقِّ وَبِهِ
يَعْدِلُونَ ﴿١٨١﴾ وَالَّذِينَ كَذَّبُوا
بِآيَاتِنَا سَنَسْتَدْرِجُهُمْ مِنْ حَيْثُ
لَا يَعْلَمُونَ ﴿١٨٢﴾ وَأُمْلِي لَهُمْ إِنَّ
كَيْدِي مَتِينٌ ﴿١٨٣﴾

God has bestowed upon men faculties of observation, hearing and reasoning, some people do not use them properly. Thus, because of their own failings, they end up in Hell.

The words employed to give expression to the idea are ones which reflect deep grief and sorrow. This can perhaps be grasped by the occasional outbursts of sorrow by human beings. If a mother is struck by the sudden death of her sons in a war, she is prone to exclaim: 'I had brought up my sons that they might serve as cannon fodder!' Her exclamatory utterance does not mean that that was the real purpose of the upbringing. What she intends to convey by such an utterance is a strong condemnation of those criminals because of whom all her painful efforts to bring up her sons have gone to waste.

141. Here the present discourse is nearing its end. Before concluding, people are warned in a style which combines admonition with censure against some basic wrongs. People are here being warned particularly against denial combined with mockery which they had adopted towards the teachings of the Prophet (peace be on him).

142. The name of a thing reflects how it is conceptualized. Hence, inappropriate concepts are reflected in inappropriate names, and vice versa. Moreover, the attitude a man adopts towards different things is also

(184) Have they not pondered that their companion [i.e. the Prophet Muḥammad] is not afflicted with insanity? He is only a plain warner. (185) Have they not observed the kingdom of the heavens and the earth, and all that Allah has created[143] and that their term of life might have drawn near?[144] After this warning from the Prophet, what will it be that will make them believe? (186) For those whom Allah lets go astray, there is no guide; and He will leave them in their transgression to stumble blindly.

أَوَلَمْ يَتَفَكَّرُوا مَا بِصَاحِبِهِم مِّن جِنَّةٍ إِنْ
هُوَ إِلَّا نَذِيرٌ مُّبِينٌ ﴿١٨٤﴾ أَوَلَمْ يَنظُرُوا فِي
مَلَكُوتِ السَّمَاوَاتِ وَالْأَرْضِ وَمَا خَلَقَ
اللَّهُ مِن شَيْءٍ وَأَنْ عَسَىٰ أَن يَكُونَ قَدِ اقْتَرَبَ
أَجَلُهُمْ فَبِأَيِّ حَدِيثٍ بَعْدَهُ يُؤْمِنُونَ ﴿١٨٥﴾
مَن يُضْلِلِ اللَّهُ فَلَا هَادِيَ لَهُ وَيَذَرُهُمْ
فِي طُغْيَانِهِمْ يَعْمَهُونَ ﴿١٨٦﴾

based on the concepts he entertains of those things. If a concept about a thing is erroneous, so will be man's relationship with it. On the other hand, a right concept about a thing will lead to establishing the right relationship with it. In the same way as this applies to relationships with worldly objects, so it applies to relationships with God. If a man is mistaken about God – be it about His person or attributes – he will choose false words for God. And the falsity of concepts about God affects man's whole ethical attitude. This is understandable since man's whole ethical attitude is directly related to man's concept of God and God's relationship with the universe and man. It is for this reason that the Qur'ān asks man to shun profanity in naming God. Only the most beautiful names befit God, and hence man should invoke Him by them. Any profanity in this respect will lead to evil consequences.

The 'most excellent names' used of God express His greatness and paramountcy, holiness, purity, and the perfection and absoluteness of all His attributes. The opposite trend has been termed *ilḥād* in this verse. The word *ilḥād* literally means 'to veer away from the straight direction'. The word is used, for instance, when an arrow misses the mark and strikes elsewhere. (See Rāghib al-Iṣfahānī, *al-Mufradāt,* q.v. *ilḥād* – Ed.) The commitment of *ilḥād* in naming God mentioned in the verse consists of choosing names which are below His majestic dignity and which are inconsistent with the reverence due to Him; names which ascribe evil or defect to God, or reflect false notions about Him. Equally blasphemous is the act of calling some creature by a name which befits God alone. The Qur'ānic exhortation in the above verse to 'shun those who distort God's names' implies that if misguided people fail to see reason, the righteous should not engross themselves in unnecessary argumentation with them. For such men will themselves suffer dire consequences.

143. The word 'companion' here refers to the Prophet (peace be on him), who was born, brought up, grew into youth, in short, spent his whole life including his old age in their midst. Before the advent of his prophethood, Muḥammad (peace be on him) was known to all the Quraysh as good natured and of sound mind. However, as he started calling people to accept the Message of God, they immediately dubbed him insane. Now it is obvious that they were not attributing insanity to him as regards his pre-prophetic life, for they had nothing evil to say about that period of his life. The charge of insanity, therefore, was levelled against the Message he began to preach when he was designated a Prophet.

The Qur'ān, therefore, asks them to give serious thought to the teachings of the Prophet (peace be on him) and to see if there is anything that is inconsistent with sanity, or is meaningless and irrational. Had people reflected on the order of the universe, or carefully considered even one single creation of God, they would have been convinced of the truth of the teachings of the Prophet (peace be on him). They would have realized that whatever he said to refute polytheism, or to establish God's unity or the accountability of man in the Hereafter, or about the necessity of man's surrender to God, was corroborated by the entire order of the universe and every single atom of God's creation.

144. The unbelievers, feeble-minded as they are, fail to understand that no one knows when he will die. For death overtakes man totally unawares. This being the case, what will be the end of those who waste the time at their disposal until death overtakes them and fail to find the direction to their salvation?

(187) They ask you concerning the Hour, when will its coming be? Say: 'The knowledge of it is with my Lord alone: none but He will disclose it at its time. That will weigh heavily on the heavens and the earth; and it shall not come to you other than all of a sudden.' They ask you – as if you are eagerly inquisitive about it – concerning it. Say to them: 'The knowledge of it is with none except Allah. But most people are unaware of this reality.' (188) Tell them [O Muḥammad]: 'I have no power to benefit or harm myself except as Allah may please. And had I knowledge of the unseen, I should have amassed all kinds of good, and no evil would have ever touched me.[145] I am merely a warner and the herald of glad tidings to those who have faith.'

يَسْـَٔلُونَكَ عَنِ ٱلسَّاعَةِ أَيَّانَ مُرْسَىٰهَا ۖ قُلْ
إِنَّمَا عِلْمُهَا عِندَ رَبِّى ۖ لَا يُجَلِّيهَا لِوَقْتِهَآ إِلَّا
هُوَ ۚ ثَقُلَتْ فِى ٱلسَّمَـٰوَٰتِ وَٱلْأَرْضِ ۚ لَا
تَأْتِيكُمْ إِلَّا بَغْتَةً ۗ يَسْـَٔلُونَكَ كَأَنَّكَ حَفِىٌّ
عَنْهَا ۖ قُلْ إِنَّمَا عِلْمُهَا عِندَ ٱللَّهِ وَلَـٰكِنَّ
أَكْثَرَ ٱلنَّاسِ لَا يَعْلَمُونَ ﴿١٨٧﴾ قُل لَّآ أَمْلِكُ
لِنَفْسِى نَفْعًا وَلَا ضَرًّا إِلَّا مَا شَآءَ ٱللَّهُ ۚ وَلَوْ
كُنتُ أَعْلَمُ ٱلْغَيْبَ لَٱسْتَكْثَرْتُ
مِنَ ٱلْخَيْرِ وَمَا مَسَّنِىَ ٱلسُّوٓءُ ۚ إِنْ أَنَا۠ إِلَّا
نَذِيرٌ وَبَشِيرٌ لِّقَوْمٍ يُؤْمِنُونَ ﴿١٨٨﴾

145. The time of the advent of the Last Day is known to God alone Who knows the Unseen which, in fact, is not known even to the Prophet (peace be on him). Being human, he is not aware what the morrow has in store for him and his family. Had his knowledge encompassed everything – even things that lie beyond the ken of sense-perception and events that lie hidden in the future – he would have accumulated immense benefit and would have been able to avoid a great deal of loss owing to such foreknowledge. That being the case, it is sheer naivety to ask the Prophet about the actual time for the advent of the Last Day.

(189) It is He – Allah – Who created you from a single being, and out of it He made its mate, that he may find comfort in her. And when he covers her, she bears a light burden and goes about with it. Then, when she grows heavy, they pray to their Lord: 'If You bestow upon us a healthy child, we will surely give thanks.' (190) But when He vouchsafes them a healthy child, they attribute to Him partners regarding what Allah had bestowed upon them. Subliminally exalted is Allah above that which they associate with Him.[146]

هُوَ ٱلَّذِي خَلَقَكُم مِّن نَّفْسٍ وَٰحِدَةٍ
وَجَعَلَ مِنْهَا زَوْجَهَا لِيَسْكُنَ إِلَيْهَا ۖ فَلَمَّا
تَغَشَّىٰهَا حَمَلَتْ حَمْلًا خَفِيفًا فَمَرَّتْ
بِهِۦ ۖ فَلَمَّآ أَثْقَلَت دَّعَوَا ٱللَّهَ رَبَّهُمَا لَئِنْ
ءَاتَيْتَنَا صَٰلِحًا لَّنَكُونَنَّ مِنَ ٱلشَّٰكِرِينَ
﴿١٨٩﴾ فَلَمَّآ ءَاتَىٰهُمَا صَٰلِحًا جَعَلَا لَهُۥ
شُرَكَآءَ فِيمَآ ءَاتَىٰهُمَا ۚ فَتَعَٰلَى ٱللَّهُ عَمَّا
يُشْرِكُونَ ﴿١٩٠﴾

146. The present and succeeding verses (190–8) seek to refute polytheism. These verses are devoted to highlighting the implications of the postulate which even the polytheists affirmed – that it is God Who originally created the human species. They also acknowledge that every human being owes his existence to God. God also holds absolute power over the entire process leading to man's birth, right from the fertilization of the ovum in the uterus to its onward development in the form of a living being, then investing it with numerous faculties and ensuring its birth as a sound, healthy baby. No one has the power to prevent God, if He so willed, from causing a woman to give birth to an animal or to some odd creature, or to a physically or mentally handicapped baby. This fact is also equally acknowledged by monotheists and polytheists. It is for this reason that in the final stage of pregnancy, people are inclined to turn to God and pray for the birth of a sound and healthy baby.

It is, however, the very height of man's ignorance and folly that after a sound and healthy baby has been born as a result of God's will, man makes offerings at the altars of false gods, goddesses, or saints. Occasionally the names given to the child (e.g., *'abd al-Rasūl*, *'abd al-'Uzzá*, *'abd Shams*, etc.) also indicate that man feels grateful to others than God and regards

(191) Do they associate (with Allah in His divinity) those who can create nothing; rather, they are themselves created? (192) They have no power to help others, nor can they help themselves. (193) And if you call them to true guidance, they will not follow you. It is all the same for you whether you call them to true guidance or keep silent.[147]

أَيُشْرِكُونَ مَا لَا يَخْلُقُ شَيْـًٔا وَهُمْ يُخْلَقُونَ ﴿١٩١﴾ وَلَا يَسْتَطِيعُونَ لَهُمْ نَصْرًا وَلَآ أَنفُسَهُمْ يَنصُرُونَ ﴿١٩٢﴾ وَإِن تَدْعُوهُمْ إِلَى ٱلْهُدَىٰ لَا يَتَّبِعُوكُمْ سَوَآءٌ عَلَيْكُمْ أَدَعَوْتُمُوهُمْ أَمْ أَنتُمْ صَـٰمِتُونَ ﴿١٩٣﴾

the child as a gift either of some Prophet, some noted Companion of the Prophet (peace be on him), or some other noted personality such as his spiritual mentor rather than a gift from God.

There has been some misunderstanding with regard to the point emphasized here. This misunderstanding has been further reinforced by traditions of doubtful authenticity. The Qur'ān mentions that human beings are created from a single person, and obviously here that person means Adam (peace be on him). Now this reference to one person is soon followed by reference to his spouse, and that both prayed to God for the birth of a sound and healthy baby. And when that prayer was accepted, the couple are mentioned as having associated others with God in the granting of His favour.

The misunderstanding consists in considering this couple, who fell prey to polytheism, to be Adam and Eve. People resorted to unauthentic traditions to explain the above verse and the story which thus gained acceptance was the following. It was claimed that Eve suffered several mishaps since her offspring would die after birth. Satan seized this opportunity to mislead her into naming her baby 'Abd al-Ḥārith (the slave of Satan). (See the comments of Ibn Kathīr on verse 190. Cf. Aḥmad b. Ḥanbal, *Musnad,* vol. 5, p. 11 – Ed.) What is most shocking is that some of these unsubstantiated traditions have been ascribed to the Prophet (peace be on him). The fact, however, is that the above account does not have even an iota of truth. Nor is it, in any way, corroborated by the Qur'ān itself. The only point brought home by the Qur'ān is that it is God alone, to the total exclusion of everyone else, Who brought the first human couple into being. And again it is God alone Who causes the birth of each baby born out of the intercourse between a man and a woman. The Qur'ān also points out that the acknowledgement of this truth is innate in human nature which is evident from the fact that in states of distress and crisis man turns prayerfully to God alone. Ironically, however, after God blesses those prayers with acceptance, a number of people associate others with God in His divinity. The fact is that the present verses do not refer to any particular man and woman. The allusion is in fact to every man and woman enmeshed in polytheism.

Here another point deserves attention. These verses condemn the Arabian polytheists on account of the fact that when God granted them sound children in response to their prayers they associated others with God in offering thanks. But what is the situation of many Muslims of today who strongly believe in the unity of God? Their situation seems even worse. It is not uncommon for them to ask others than God to grant children. They make vows during pregnancy to others than God, and make offerings to others than God after child-birth. Yet they are satisfied that they have a full guarantee of Paradise since they are believers in the One True God whereas the Arabian polytheists would inevitably be consigned to Hell. It is only the doctrinal errors of the pre-Islamic Arabian polytheists which may be condemned. The doctrinal errors of Muslims are beyond all criticism and censure.

147. As to the false gods set up by the polytheists, what is the extent of their power? Not only do they not have the power to guide others, they do not even have the power to follow others or even to answer the call of their devotees.

(194) Those whom you invoke other than Allah are creatures like you. So invoke them and see if they answer your call, if what you claim is true. (195) Have they feet on which they can walk? Have they hands with which they can grasp? Have they eyes with which they can see? Have they ears with which they can hear?[148] Say [O Muḥammad]: 'Invoke all those to whom you ascribe a share in Allah's divinity, then scheme against me and grant me no respite. (196) My guardian is Allah Who has revealed the Book, and it is He Who protects the righteous.[149] (197) And those whom you invoke other than Allah, they can neither help themselves nor you. (198) And if you were to call them to true guidance, they will not hear; and you observe them looking at you whereas they have no power to see.'

إِنَّ ٱلَّذِينَ تَدْعُونَ مِن دُونِ ٱللَّهِ عِبَادٌ
أَمْثَالُكُمْ فَٱدْعُوهُمْ فَلْيَسْتَجِيبُوا۟
لَكُمْ إِن كُنتُمْ صَٰدِقِينَ ﴿١٩٤﴾
أَلَهُمْ أَرْجُلٌ يَمْشُونَ بِهَآ أَمْ لَهُمْ أَيْدٍ
يَبْطِشُونَ بِهَآ أَمْ لَهُمْ أَعْيُنٌ يُبْصِرُونَ
بِهَآ أَمْ لَهُمْ ءَاذَانٌ يَسْمَعُونَ بِهَا قُلِ
ٱدْعُوا۟ شُرَكَآءَكُمْ ثُمَّ كِيدُونِ فَلَا تُنظِرُونِ
﴿١٩٥﴾ إِنَّ وَلِـِّۧىَ ٱللَّهُ ٱلَّذِى نَزَّلَ ٱلْكِتَٰبَ
وَهُوَ يَتَوَلَّى ٱلصَّٰلِحِينَ ﴿١٩٦﴾ وَٱلَّذِينَ
تَدْعُونَ مِن دُونِهِۦ لَا يَسْتَطِيعُونَ
نَصْرَكُمْ وَلَآ أَنفُسَهُمْ يَنصُرُونَ
﴿١٩٧﴾ وَإِن تَدْعُوهُمْ إِلَى ٱلْهُدَىٰ لَا يَسْمَعُوا۟
وَتَرَىٰهُمْ يَنظُرُونَ إِلَيْكَ وَهُمْ
لَا يُبْصِرُونَ ﴿١٩٨﴾

148. Polytheistic religions seem to have three characteristics: (1) idols and images that are held as objects of worship; (2) some persons and spirits that are considered deities represented in the form of idols and images, etc.; and (3) certain beliefs which underlie their polytheistic rites. The Qur'ān denounces all these. At this place, however, the attack is directed against the objects to which the polytheists directed their worship.

149. This is in response to the threats held out by the polytheists to the Prophet (peace be on him). They used to tell the Prophet (peace be on him)

(199) [O Prophet!] Show forgiveness, enjoin equity, and avoid the ignorant. (200) And if it happens that a prompting from Satan should stir you up, seek refuge with Allah. He is All-Hearing, All-Knowing. (201) If the God-fearing are instigated by any suggestion of Satan, they instantly become alert, whereafter they clearly perceive the right way. (202) As for their brethren [the Satans], they draw them deeper into error and do not relax in their efforts.[150]

خُذِ ٱلْعَفْوَ وَأْمُرْ بِٱلْعُرْفِ وَأَعْرِضْ عَنِ
ٱلْجَٰهِلِينَ ﴿١٩٩﴾ وَإِمَّا يَنزَغَنَّكَ مِنَ
ٱلشَّيْطَٰنِ نَزْغٌ فَٱسْتَعِذْ بِٱللَّهِ إِنَّهُۥ
سَمِيعٌ عَلِيمٌ ﴿٢٠٠﴾ إِنَّ ٱلَّذِينَ
ٱتَّقَوْا۟ إِذَا مَسَّهُمْ طَيْفٌ مِّنَ ٱلشَّيْطَٰنِ
تَذَكَّرُوا۟ فَإِذَا هُم مُّبْصِرُونَ ﴿٢٠١﴾
وَإِخْوَٰنُهُمْ يَمُدُّونَهُمْ فِى ٱلْغَىِّ ثُمَّ
لَا يُقْصِرُونَ ﴿٢٠٢﴾

---

that if he did not give up opposing their deities and denouncing them, he would be overwhelmed by the wrath of those deities and court utter disaster.

150. Here some important directives are addressed to the Prophet (peace be on him) regarding how he should preach the Message of Islam and how he should guide and reform people. The object of these directives is not merely to instruct the Prophet (peace be on him), but also to instruct all those who would shoulder the same responsibility after the Prophet (peace be on him) was no longer amidst them. The major directives are as follows:

(1) The most important qualities that must be cultivated by anyone who calls others to the truth are tenderness, magnanimity, and forbearing. Such a person should also have the capacity to tolerate the lapses of his companions and to patiently endure the excesses of his opponents. He should also be able to keep his cool in the face of grave provocation and gracefully connive at the offensive behaviour of others. In facing the angry words, slander, persecution and mischief of his opponents, he should exercise the utmost self-restraint. Harshness, severity, bitterness, and vindictive provocativeness on his part are bound to undermine his mission. The same point seems to have been made in a *Ḥadīth* in which the Prophet (peace be on

him) says that he has been commanded by his Lord: '. . . to say the just word whether I am angry or pleased; to maintain ties with him who severs ties with me; and to give to him who denies me (my right); and to forgive him who wrongs me.' (See the comments of Qurṭubī in his *Tafsīr* on the verse – Ed.) The Prophet (peace be on him) also instructed all those whom he deputized for preaching: 'Give good news rather than arouse revulsion; make things easy rather than hard.' (Muslim, *Kitāb al-'Ilm, 'Bāb fī al-amr bi al-Taysīr wa Tark al-Ta'sīr'* – Ed.) This distinguishing feature of the Prophet's personality has also been mentioned in the Qur'ān:

> It was thanks to Allah's mercy that you were gentle to them. Had you been rough, hard-hearted, they would surely have scattered away from you (*Āl 'Imrān* 3: 159).

(2) The second key to the success in *da'wah* work is to stay away from excessive theorizing and intellectual hair-splitting. One should rather call people in clear and simple terms to those virtues which are recognized as such by the generality of mankind and appeal to common sense. The great advantage of this method is that the Message of Islam finds its way right to the hearts of people at all levels of understanding. Those who then seek to oppose the Message are soon exposed and end up antagonizing the common people. For when the common people observe on the one hand decent and righteous people being opposed for the simple reason that they are inviting people to universally-known virtues, and on the other hand observe those opponents resorting to all kinds of immoral and inhuman means, they are bound to incline to support the standard-bearers of truth and righteousness. This process goes on until a point where the only opponents left are those whose self-interest is inextricably linked with the prevailing unrighteous system, or those who have been totally blinded by their bigoted adherence to ancestral tradition or by their irrational biases.

The wisdom underlying the Prophet's method accounts for his phenomenal success and for the speedy spread of Islam in and around Arabia within a short span of time. People flocked to Islam in vast numbers so much so that in some lands eighty and ninety per cent of the population embraced Islam. In fact there are even instances of a hundred per cent of the population embracing Islam.

(3) The interest of the Islamic mission requires, on the one hand, that righteousness should be enjoined on those who have the propensity to become righteous. On the other hand, it also requires that those who are overly insistent in their adherence to falsehood, should be left alone, and that their acts of provocation be ignored. Those who seek to spread Islam should confine their efforts to persuading only those who are prepared to consider the Message of Islam in a

reasonable manner. When someone becomes altogether unreasonable and quarrelsome, and resorts to indecent methods of taunting and reviling Islam, Muslims should simply refuse to become adversative. For all the time and effort devoted to reforming such people will be totally wasted.

(4) The moment the proponent of the Islamic Message feels that he is being provoked by the excesses, mischief, and uncalled-for objections and accusation, he should realize that he is being influenced by Satan. In such a situation he should immediately seek refuge with God, and restrain himself lest his impulsiveness damage his cause. The cause of Islam can be served only by those who act cool-headedly. Only those steps are appropriate which have been taken after due consideration rather than under the influence of impulse and emotion. Satan, however, is ever on the look-out for opportunities to sabotage the efforts made in the cause of Islam. He, therefore, ensures that those who are working for the Islamic cause are subjected to unjust and mischievous attacks from their opponents. The purpose underlying this is to provoke the workers for the cause of Islam to engage in the senseless and harmful task of mounting counter-attacks against their opponents.

The appeal that Satan makes to those well-meaning, religious people is often couched in religious phraseology and is backed up by religious argument. But the fact is that those counter-attacks are undertaken merely under the impulse of man's lower self. The last two verses, therefore, make it clear that those who are God-fearing are always very sensitive to provocations under the impulse of Satan, and as soon as they become aware of such a provocation, they promote the best interests of the cause of truth rather than satisfy their vengeful feelings. As for those who are driven by egotistical impulses, they succumb to the promptings of Satan and are eventually set on an erroneous path. They fall victim to Satan, act virtually as his puppet, and subsequently their degradation knows no limit. They pay their opponents back in the same coin, tit for tat.

What has been said above also has another import. It seeks to remind the God-fearing that their ways should be perceptibly different from the ways of those who do not fear God. The God-fearing not only avoid evil, but the very idea of committing it pricks their conscience and rankles their hearts. They have an instinctive revulsion against evil, a revulsion similar to what a cleanliness-loving man feels at the sight of a big stain or a splash of filth on his clothes. This feeling causes the God-fearing to remove every stain of evil. Quite contrary are those who have no fear of God, who have no desire to stay away from evil and who are in harmony with the ways of Satan. Such people are always given to evil thoughts and wrong-doing.

(203) [O Prophet!] When you do not produce before them any miracle, they say: 'Why do you not choose for yourself a miracle?'[151] Say to them: 'I follow only what is revealed to me by my Lord. This is nothing but a means of insight into the truth, and guidance and mercy from your Lord to the people who believe.[152] (204) So when the Qur'ān is recited, listen carefully to it, and keep silent so that you may be shown mercy.'[153]

وَإِذَا لَمْ تَأْتِهِم بِآيَةٍ قَالُوا لَوْلَا
اجْتَبَيْتَهَا ۚ قُلْ إِنَّمَا أَتَّبِعُ مَا يُوحَىٰ
إِلَيَّ مِن رَّبِّي ۚ هَٰذَا بَصَائِرُ مِن رَّبِّكُمْ
وَهُدًى وَرَحْمَةٌ لِّقَوْمٍ يُؤْمِنُونَ ﴿٢٠٣﴾
وَإِذَا قُرِئَ الْقُرْآنُ فَاسْتَمِعُوا
لَهُ وَأَنصِتُوا لَعَلَّكُمْ تُرْحَمُونَ ﴿٢٠٤﴾

151. This question is a taunt rather than a simple query. What the utterance implies is that if the claim to prophethood is genuine, it should have been supported by some miracle. The next verse contains a fitting rejoinder to the taunt.

152. The Prophet (peace be on him) is being made to tell his opponents in clear terms that he has no power to get whatever he wants. Being God's Messenger, he is required to follow the directives of the One Who has sent him and has granted him the Qur'ān which has the light of guidance. The major characteristic of this Book is that those who seek guidance from it do indeed find the right way. The moral excellence visible in the lives of those people who accept the Qur'ān is testimony to the fact that they have been blessed with God's mercy.

153. The unbelievers are asked to shed their prejudice and to abandon their deliberate indifference to the Qur'ān. Whenever the Qur'ān is recited to them, they stuff their fingers into their ears and make a lot of noise lest they or any others hear the Qur'ān. They should better behave more maturely and make an effort to grasp the teachings of the Qur'ān. It is quite likely that their study of the Book would ultimately make them share with Muslims the blessings of the Qur'ān. This is an excellent, subtle and heart-winning approach which simply cannot be over-praised. Those who are interested in learning the art of effective preaching can benefit immensely by pondering over this Qur'ānic verse.

(205) And remember [O Prophet] your Lord in your mind, with humility and fear, and without raising your voice; remember Him in the morning and evening, and do not become of those who are negligent.[154] (206) [The angels] who are near to your Lord, never turn away from His service out of arrogance;[155] they rather glorify Him[156] and prostrate themselves before Him.[157]

وَٱذْكُر رَّبَّكَ فِى نَفْسِكَ تَضَرُّعًا
وَخِيفَةً وَدُونَ ٱلْجَهْرِ مِنَ ٱلْقَوْلِ
بِٱلْغُدُوِّ وَٱلْآصَالِ وَلَا تَكُن مِّنَ
ٱلْغَٰفِلِينَ ﴿٢٠٥﴾ إِنَّ ٱلَّذِينَ عِندَ رَبِّكَ
لَا يَسْتَكْبِرُونَ عَنْ عِبَادَتِهِۦ وَيُسَبِّحُونَهُۥ
وَلَهُۥ يَسْجُدُونَ ۩ ﴿٢٠٦﴾

The main purpose of the verse has also been explained. By implication, however, the verse also enjoins people to be silent and to listen attentively to the Qur'ān when it is being recited. The verse also provides the basis of the rule that when the leader *(imām)* is reciting verses of the Qur'ān in Prayer, the followers in the congregation should (refrain from reciting and) listen to the recitation in silence. There is some disagreement among scholars on this issue. Abū Ḥanīfah and his disciples are of the view that the followers in the congregation should remain silent, irrespective of whether the *imām* is reciting the Qur'ān aloud or silently in his mind. On the other hand, Mālik and Aḥmad b. Ḥanbal are of the opinion that the followers in the congregation should listen silently only when the Qur'ān is being recited aloud. According to Shāfi'ī, the followers in the congregation should also recite the Qur'ān regardless of whether the *imām* is reciting the Qur'ān aloud or silently. His view is based on the *Ḥadīth* that Prayer without recitation of *al-Fātiḥah* is void. (See Ibn Rushd, *Bidāyat al-Mujtahid*, vol. 1, pp. 149–50; Ibn Qudāmah, *al-Mughnī*, vol. 1, pp. 562–9 – Ed.)

154. The command to remember the Lord signifies remembrance in Prayer as well as otherwise, be it verbally or in one's mind. Again the directive to remember God in the morning and in the evening refers to Prayer at those times as well as remembering God at all times. The purpose of so saying is to emphasize constant remembrance of God. This admonition – that man ought to remember God always – constitutes the conclusion of the discourse lest man becomes heedless of God. For every error and corruption stems from the fact that man tends to forget that God is his

Lord and that in his own part he is merely a servant of God who is being tested in the world; that he will be made to render, after his death, a full account to his Lord of all his deeds. All those who care to follow righteousness would, therefore, be ill-advised not to let these basic facts slip out of their minds. Hence Prayer, remembrance of God and keeping one's attention ever focused on God are frequently stressed in the Qur'ān.

155. It is Satan who behaves arrogantly and disdains to worship God, and such an attitude naturally brings about degradation and abasement. But an attitude marked by consistent surrender to God characterizes angels and leads people to spiritual elevation and proximity to God. Those interested in attaining this state should emulate the angels and refrain from following the ways of Satan.

156. To celebrate God's praise signifies that the angels acknowledge and constantly affirm that God is beyond any flaw, free from every defect, error and weakness; that He has no partner or peer; that none is like Him.

157. Whoever recites or hears this verse should fall in prostration so as to emulate the practice of angels. In addition, prostration also proves that one has no shred of pride, nor is one averse to the duty of being subservient to God.

In all, there are fourteen verses in the Qur'ān the recitation of which requires one to prostrate. That one should prostrate on reading or hearing these verses is, in principle, an incontrovertible point. There is, however, some disagreement about it being obligatory *(wājib)*. Abū Ḥanīfah regards it as obligatory while other authorities consider it to be recommended (Ibn Qudāmah, *al-Mughnī*, vol. 1, p. 663; Al-Jazīrī, *Kitāb al-Fiqh 'alá al-Madhāhib al-Arba'ah*, vol. 1, p. 464 – Ed.) According to traditions, while reciting the Qur'ān in large gatherings, when the Prophet (peace be on him) came upon a verse the recitation of which calls for prostration, he prostrated, and the whole gathering followed suit. The traditions mention that sometimes some people did not have room to prostrate. Such people prostrated on the backs of others. (See Bukhārī, *Abwāb Sujūd al-Qur'ān, 'Bāb Izdiḥām al-Nās idhá qara'a al-Imām al-Sajdah'* – Ed.) It is reported in connection with the conquest of Makka that in the course of the Qur'ān-recitation, as the Prophet (peace be on him) read such a verse, those standing fell into prostration while those who were mounted on horses and camels performed prostration in that very state. It is also on record that while delivering a sermon from the pulpit the Prophet (peace be on him) came down from the pulpit to offer prostration, and resumed his sermon thereafter. (Abū Dā'ūd, *Kitāb al-Ṣalāh, 'Bāb al-Sujūd fī Ṣād'* – Ed.)

It is generally believed that the conditions for this kind of prostration are exactly the same as required for offering Prayer – that one should be in a state of ritual purity, that one should be facing the Ka'bah, and that the prostration should be performed as in the state of Prayer. However, the traditions we have been able to find in the relevant sections of the *Ḥadīth* collection do not specifically mention these conditions. It thus appears that one may perform prostration, irrespective of whether one fulfils these conditions or not. This view is corroborated by the practice of some of the early authorities. Bukhārī, for instance, reports about 'Abd Allāh b. 'Umar that he used to perform prostration even though he would have required ablution if he wanted to perform Prayer. (See Bukhārī, *Abwāb Sujūd al-Qur'ān, 'Bāb Sujūd al-Muslimīn ma' al-Mushrikīn'* – Ed.) Likewise, it has been mentioned in *Fatḥ al-Bārī* about 'Abd al-Raḥmān al-Sulamī that if he was reciting the Qur'ān while moving, and he recited a verse calling for prostration, he would simply bow his head (rather than make full prostration). And he would do that even when he was required to make ablution for Prayer, and regardless of whether he was facing the Ka'bah or not.

In our view, therefore, while it is preferable to follow the general opinion of the scholars on the question, it would not be blameworthy if someone deviates from that opinion. The reason for this is that the general opinion of the scholars on this question is not supported by well-established *Sunnah*, and there are instances of deviation from it on the part of the early authorities.

Sūrah 8

Al-Anfāl

(Madinan Period)

Period of Revelation

Sūrah al-Anfāl was revealed after the Battle of Badr in 2 A.H./624 C.E., and provides a full-length critique of the first major armed conflict between the forces of Islam and those of Unbelief. Given that the contents comprise a single discourse, it would seem that the entire *sūrah* was revealed in one piece rather than in fragments. However, it cannot be altogether ruled out that certain comments relating to problems which arose as a result of the Battle of Badr were revealed later and were subsequently incorporated into the main body of the *sūrah* without impairing the continuity and coherence of its narrative. Be that as it may, the *sūrah* is too well-organized and too neatly integrated for it to be considered the collection of several independent and disparate discourses.

Historical Background

It would seem appropriate before commenting on the substantive questions discussed in the *sūrah,* to look from an historical angle, at the Battle of Badr and the events relating to it.

Towards the end of the Makkan period of the Prophet's life (i.e. towards the end of the twelve years of his ministry as a Prophet in Makka), it was already clear that the Message of Islam stood on firm ground. This was so not only because the Prophet (peace be on him) was a man of superb moral character, a man distinguished for his magnanimity and wisdom, but also because he was totally dedicated to the cause of Islam. He had also given sufficient evidence of his being possessed of unrelenting determination to carry out his mission to a successful conclusion and of being ever prepared to brave whatever dangers and hardships which might confront him. Moreover, the Message preached by the Prophet (peace be on him) had such an intrinsic merit that the minds and hearts of the people around him were irresistibly drawn to it. As a result walls of ignorance and bigotry and barriers of inherited prejudice were gradually crumbling and proving ineffective to prevent the spread of Islam. Initially, the standard-bearers of the age-old *Jāhilīyah* (Ignorance) of Arabia had dismissed Islam as trivial and frivolous. But as Islam won an increasing number of converts during the last phase of the Prophet's life in Makka, the enemies began to look upon it as a force to reckon with, and busied themselves with strategies for its total obliteration.

However, no matter how promising the achievements of the Muslims might have been, a few gaps had yet to be filled before the movement of the Prophet (peace be on him) could attain success. First, it was yet to be established that the Message of the Prophet (peace be on him) had won a sufficiently large following of those who not only believed in it, but who were fired with an intense love for and devotion to it. Nor had it been established that the followers of the Prophet (peace be on him) were ready to exert all their energies and resources in pursuit of their cause. It was also yet to be seen whether they would sacrifice their possessions and incur the hostility of the rest of the world and even go so far as to sever their ties with even their closest relatives if their cause would so demand. The early Muslims had doubtlessly proved their mettle by bravely putting up with the persecution of the Makkans, a fact which reflected the sincerity of their faith and the firmness of their commitment to Islam. Nevertheless, they had yet to pass through many more trials before it could be incontestably established that the Message of Islam was being championed by a band of truly devoted adherents who cherished nothing more than the cause which they had set out to promote.

Second, even though the Message of Islam had begun to reverberate throughout the Arabian peninsula, its influence was diffused. Its supporters were scattered throughout the length and breadth of the land. These scattered supporters had not as yet been knit together into a collective force which would be needed for a decisive encounter with the entrenched un-Islamic way of life.

Third, the influence of Islam had not yet permeated itself over any one particular region to the extent whereby it could hold sway over it. In no region was Islam powerful enough for a base to be established for it to consolidate its position and thereafter to reach out to others. Having a tenuous grounding, the situation of Islam was comparable to that of chloroquine in an empty stomach whereby the latter is ever prone to throw it out.

Fourth, the Message of Islam had yet to make its full impact on human life insofar as the Muslims had neither had the opportunity to shape a collective order according to their vision nor to develop distinctive economic, social and political institutions consistent with those norms and values. Nor had they as yet had any serious interaction with other powers that would lead them either to engage in armed conflict or conclude agreements of peace. Hence the ideals which, according to Islam, ought to guide and regulate the day-to-day life of man had not yet come into sharp focus. Nor had it yet been fully established how earnest the Muslims and their Prophet (peace be on him) were in putting into practice the principles which they espoused. The events that followed, however, enabled the Muslims to overcome these deficiencies.

During the last three or four years of the Makkan period of the Prophet's life, Islam had begun to radiate towards Yathrib (later called Madina) and the Yathribites seemed much more receptive to Islam than the people of other areas. In the twelfth year of Prophethood, 622 C.E., and during *Ḥajj,* a delegation comprising seventy-five people from Yathrib called on the Prophet (peace be on him) in the darkness of the night. Not only did they embrace Islam but also expressed their desire that the Prophet (peace be on him) and his followers should move to and settle down in their home town. This invitation to the Muslims, which must be regarded as the favour of God to them, was readily welcomed by the Prophet (peace be on him).

This seemingly modest event, however, changed the whole course of events. For the people of Yathrib had invited the Prophet (peace be on him) not just to live in security amongst them as a refugee but rather because they wished to welcome him in their midst in his capacity as the Messenger of God and hence as their leader and ruler. (See, for instance, the pledge of 'Ubādah b. al-Ṣāmit in which he promised not to disobey the Prophet in *ma'rūf.* Ibn Hishām, vol. 2, pp. 433–4. See also the documents commonly known as the

'Constitution of Madina' in which obedience to the Prophet (peace be on him) has been prominently envisaged in the newly established body-politic. See Ibn Hishām, vol. 2, pp. 501–4 – Ed.) It is obvious that the people of Yathrib (Madina) had not asked the Makkan Muslims to migrate to their town merely to enjoy a life of peace and security. They had rather invited them so that the entire body of Muslims might concentrate at one place and establish a collective Islamic entity. Yathrib thus offered itself as the City of Islam and the Prophet's acceptance of the offer ensured that it became the first *Dār al-Islām* (Domain of Islam) in Arabia.

The people of Yathrib were well aware of the implications of inviting the Prophet (peace be on him) into their midst. It was abundantly clear to them that their small town would be exposed to social and cultural boycott, and even to the active hostility of the entire Arabian peninsula. It was with a full awareness of the risks involved that those erstwhile supporters of Islam – the *Anṣār* – made their pledge of fealty to the Prophet (peace be on him) in that eventful meeting on the occasion of *Bay'at al-'Aqabah*. While the pledge of fealty was being concluded, Asad b. Zurārah, the youngest member of the Yathribite delegation, rose and said:

> Do not hasten, O people of Yathrib! We made our way to this man only because we firmly believe that he is the Messenger of God. We know that taking him away from here means that the whole of Arabia will be aroused to hostility, that some of the best of you will get killed, and swords will fall upon you. If you can put up with these dangers, take him [i.e. the Prophet (peace be on him)], and you will be rewarded by God. But if you feel afraid of yourselves (that you will not be able to live up to your commitments) then leave him alone and let that be clearly known. Such is more likely to be condoned by God [than your betrayal of the Prophet (peace be on him) later]. (See Aḥmad b. Ḥanbal, *Musnad,* vol. 3, pp. 322 and 340 – Ed.)

Almost the same point was reiterated by another member of the delegation of Yathrib, 'Abbās b. 'Ubādah b. Naḍlah:

> Do you realize what pledge you are making to this person? (They said: 'Yes'.) By making a pledge of fealty to this person you are in fact pledging to fight against the whole world. If you feel that in case your properties are destroyed or your nobles killed, you will surrender him [to his enemies], it is better that you forsake him today. For, by God, this will humiliate you in

this world and the Next. However, if you are determined to stand by him whom you are now inviting to your home, and would do so even if your properties are destroyed and your nobles killed, then take him with you. For, by God, that is best for you in this world and the Next. (Ibn Hishām, vol. 1, p. 446 – Ed.)

By way of response, all the members of the delegation unanimously exclaimed: 'We are prepared to support him even if our wealth is destroyed and our nobles killed.' (Ibn Hishām, vol. 1, p. 446.) Thereafter the famous pledge, known as *Bay'at al-'Aqabah al-Thāniyah,* was made.

On the other hand, the implications of this pledge of fealty were not lost on the Makkans. Quite obviously the pledge meant not just providing a haven of refuge but also an operational base to the Prophet (peace be on him). This constituted no ordinary threat to the Makkans who were fully aware of the Prophet's dynamic personality and his outstanding leadership qualities. In addition, the determination and devotion of the Muslims had already been tested by the Makkans, and thanks to the pledge of 'Aqabah, they were well on their way to proper organization under the Prophet's leadership in Madina. The event, therefore, seemed to sound a death-knell to the entrenched old order of Arabia.

Moreover, the concentration of the Muslims in such a strategic place as Madina, which made the trade route from Yemen to Syria along the shores of the Red Sea vulnerable to hostile action from the Muslims, alarmed the Quraysh. This trade route was of crucial importance for the economic well-being not only of the Quraysh but also of many other polytheistic tribes of Arabia. Making good use of Madina's strategic location, the Muslims could disrupt the whole economy of the existing un-Islamic order. The importance of this trade route can be ascertained by the fact that it yielded the Makkan merchants an annual income of up to 250,000 guineas. In addition there were the sizeable profits made by the merchants of Ṭā'if and other places in Arabia from the traders passing along the route. (For detailed information about the value of the merchandise of this trading caravan see al-Wāqidī, vol. 1, pp. 27–8 – Ed.)

The Quraysh were fully cognizant of the importance of the pledge of fealty made by the people of Yathrib. The very night when the Pledge of 'Aqabah was to be concluded, the Makkans got wind of it and it caused a furore among them. First, they tried to dissuade the Yathribites from making the pledge to the Prophet (peace be on him). However, when the Muslims began migrating in twos and threes to Yathrib, the Quraysh realized that at some point the Prophet (peace be on him) would also move there.

Fully aware of the dangers to them implicit in the Prophet's migration to Madina, the Makkans resorted to extreme measures to prevent him from doing so. A council of the Quraysh was held in order to discuss the matter just a few days before the Prophet (peace be on him) actually migrated. After prolonged arguments and counter-arguments it was finally resolved that one person should be taken from each clan of the Quraysh except Banū Hāshim, and they should join hands in putting the Prophet (peace be on him) to the sword. They opted for this course of action because the involvement of all the Quraysh would make it virtually impossible for Banū Hāshim to take revenge. They would rather find themselves in a situation in which the only option available to them would be to accept blood-money. However, thanks to God's help and owing to the Prophet's total trust in God and his own wise tactical moves, the plan of the Quraysh was frustrated and the Prophet (peace be on him) was able to reach Madina safely. (See Ibn Hishām, vol. 1, p. 482 – Ed.)

With the failure of their scheme, the Quraysh thought up another scheme and accordingly wrote to 'Abd Allāh b. Ubayy*: 'You have granted shelter in your town to one of our men. We swear by God that either you should fight against him, or expel him, or else we will attack you and kill your males and enslave your females.' (Abū Dā'ūd, K. al-Kharāj wa al-Fay' wa al-Imarāh, 'Bāb fī Khabar al-Naḍīr' – Ed.) On receiving this letter 'Abd Allāh b. 'Ubayy felt inclined to cause mischief. The Prophet (peace be on him), however, put a timely end to it. Later, when Sa'd b. Mu'ādh a Madinan chief went to Makka to perform *'Umrah,* Abū Jahl stopped him at the entrance of the Ka'bah and told him: 'Do you think we will let you perform circumambulation *(ṭawāf)* in Makka while you provide help and support to the renegades of our faith? Had you not been with Abū Ṣafwān [i.e. Umayyah ibn al-Khalaf], you would not have returned to your folks alive.' To this Sa'd's reply was: 'By God, if you prevent me from that (viz. performing the rites of Pilgrimage) I will prevent you from something that will cause you greater hurt – (i.e. carrying on trade along the route to Syria). (Al-Bukhārī,

*It may be recalled that the Madinans had decided to confer on 'Abd Allāh b. Ubayy the kingship of Madina before the Prophet's migration. But the arrival of the Prophet (peace be on him) in Madina and the spread of Islam among the tribes of Aws and Khazraj threw cold water on his ambitions. (See al-Wāqidī, vol. 2, pp. 419 and 421 – Ed.)

'Al-Maghāzī', 'Bāb Dhikr al-Nabī . . . man Yuqtal bi Badr' – Ed.)

Thus the Makkans threatened to prevent the Muslims from making Pilgrimage to Makka, and the Madinans returned the threat by making it known that if they did that the route to Syria could be rendered perilous for the Makkans.

In fact the Muslims had no other choice but to gain and consolidate their control over that trade route so that the Quraysh and other tribes inimical to the Muslims might reconsider their hostile policy. It is not surprising, therefore, that after reaching Madina the first problem to which the Prophet (peace be on him) addressed his attention after setting up the rudiments of the administration of the nascent Islamic society and concluding treaties with neighbouring Jewish tribes was precisely that of the trade route to Syria. In grappling with that problem the Prophet (peace be on him) adopted two measures in particular.

First, he embarked upon negotiations with the tribes inhabiting the area close to the trade route so as to conclude treaties of alliance or at least of neutrality. In this respect his efforts were crowned with success. He also concluded a pact of neutrality with the Juhaynah, the tribe living in the mountainous region adjacent to the Red Sea coast. Then in 1 A.H./623 C.E. he concluded a mutual defence alliance with Banū Ḍamrah, who lived in the area close to Yanbu' and Dhu al-'Ushayrah. In the middle of 2 A.H./623 or 624 C.E. another tribe, Banū Mudlij, the neighbours and allies of Banū Ḍamrah, joined the alliance. Above all, his missionary efforts also bore fruit and there came into being a sizeable group of those who had either converted to Islam or at least sympathized with it.

Second, the Prophet (peace be on him) sent a series of small expeditions in quick succession along the trade route to scare the trading caravans of the Quraysh. On several occasions the Prophet (peace be on him) himself joined these expeditions. In the first year of *Hijrah,* 624 C.E., four such expeditions were dispatched. In the accounts narrated in the *Maghāzī* works these expeditions are known as *Sarīyah* Ḥamzah, *Sarīyah* 'Ubaydah b. Ḥārith, *Sarīyah* Sa'd b. Abī Waqqāṣ, and *Ghazwat* al-Abwā'.* In the beginning of the following year similar expeditions were undertaken and are known as *Ghazwat* Buwāṭ and *Ghazwah* Dhu al-'Ushayrah.

These expeditions are noteworthy for two reasons. First, no blood was shed, nor any caravan looted. This clearly shows that the

*In Islamic terminology, *Sarīyah* refers to the expedition dispatched by the Prophet (peace be on him) under the leadership of any of his Companions whereas *Ghazwah* refers to the expeditions led by the Prophet (peace be on him) himself.

MAP NO. 3: THE TRADE ROUTES OF THE QURAYSH

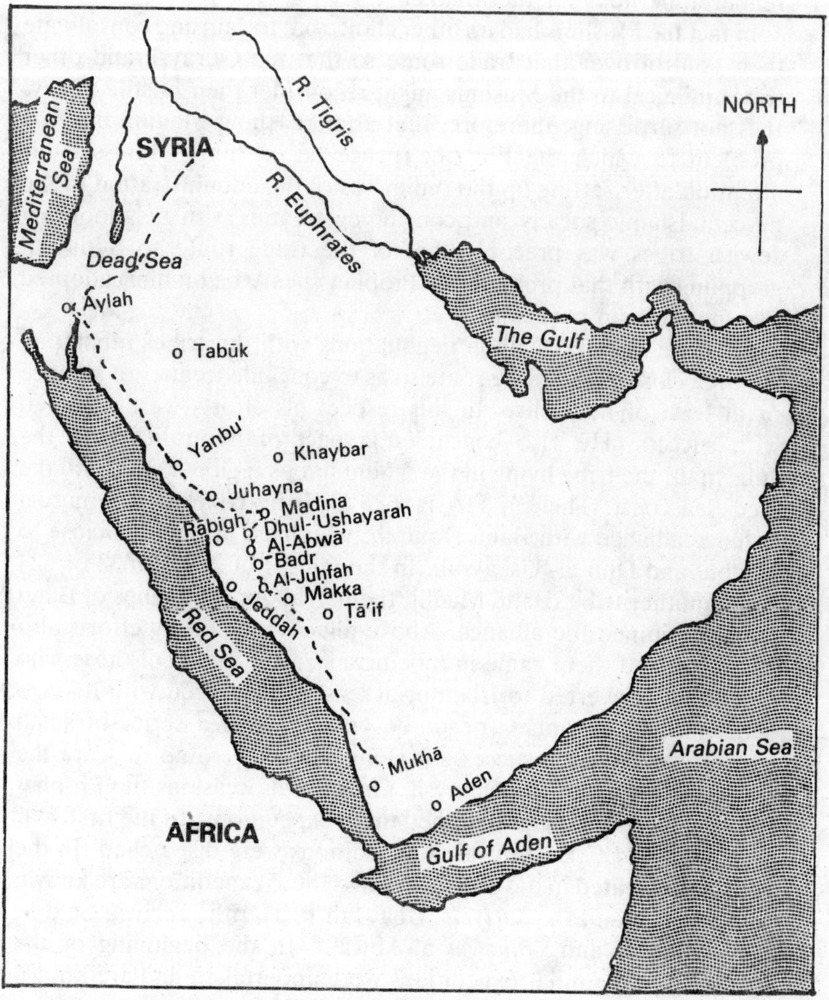

purpose of the expeditions was to give a warning to the Quraysh. The second noteworthy feature of these expeditions was that not a single Madinan took part in them. The expeditions were manned solely by Makkan Emigrants. This was done deliberately so as to keep the conflict confined among the Quraysh and to avoid any escalation that would have ensued as a result of other tribes being involved. On the other hand, the Makkans quite regularly sent invading parties. In one such expedition under the leadership of Kurz b. Jābir al-Fihrī, the Makkans carried out a raid in the vicinity of Madina itself and carried away the cattle of the inhabitants. The Quraysh also tried their best to drag other tribes into the fray. Moreover, they did not confine their military manoeuvres to warnings or threats but engaged in real acts of plunder and bloodshed. (See Ibn Sa'd, *Ṭabaqāt,* vol. 2, p. 9 – Ed.)

It was against this background that the Muslims came to find out in Sha'bān 2 A.H./February or March 624 C.E. that a large caravan of the Quraysh, carrying goods worth 50,000 guineas, and escorted by no more than 30 or 40 security guards *en route* to Makka from Syria, had arrived at a place within the reach of the Madinans. Since the number of guards was disproportionately small to the value of the merchandise, and the Makkans well remembered the earlier expeditions of the Muslims, they feared that the Muslims would attack their caravan. Abū Sufyān, the leader of the caravan, therefore, rushed a messenger to Makka and sought help and reinforcements. Following the Arab custom of the time, when the messenger approached Makka he chopped off the ears and slit the nose of the camel, turned the saddle upside down, tore his cloak and yelled: 'O people of Quraysh! Rush to your trading caravan. Muḥammad and his followers are out to seize your goods with Abū Sufyān. I don't think you will be able to get them. Help! Help!' (Al-Wāqidī, vol. 1, p. 31 – Ed.)

This caused an uproar throughout Makka, with the leading Quraysh chiefs deciding to go to war. About 1000 fighters, including 600 soldiers in coats of mail, and 100 cavalry, moved out of Makka with much pomp and show. (Al-Wāqidī, vol. 1, p. 31; al-Ṭabarī, *Ta'rīkh,* vol. 2, p. 430 – Ed.) They wanted not only to rescue the caravan but also to nip in the bud the threat posed by the Muslims. They had made up their minds to deal a crushing blow to the rising power of the Muslims. They also wanted to terrorize the neighbouring tribes so as to ensure the safety of their trading caravans in the future.

The Prophet (peace be on him), who always kept himself abreast of developments which had any bearing on his mission, realized that the time to take a decisive step had come. He felt that if a bold and effective step was not taken right then, the Islamic movement might be enervated and suffer a blow from which it might never be able to recover. The situation at the time was such that the *Muhājirūn* (Emigrants) had not fully settled for they had spent barely two years in their new habitat. Among the major components of the Muslim community in Madina the Emigrants were resourceless and the local Helpers *(Anṣār)* lacked experience in fighting. Not only that, the neighbouring Jewish tribes were bent on hostility. Also within the ranks of the Muslims in Madina there existed other hostile elements such as a powerful group of hypocrites *(Munāfiqūn)* and the polytheists. Furthermore, the tribes living in the neighbourhood of Madina were not only overawed by the Quraysh, but also held a religious affinity with them.

In such circumstances had the Quraysh taken the initiative and launched an attack on Madina, it might well have led to the obliteration of the small community of Muslims in that town. But the situation was such that even if the Quraysh abstained from attacking the Muslims and merely took their caravan back to Makka by dint of their military strength without any interception from the Muslims, this would have adversely affected the political and military prestige of the Muslims. It was quite likely that in such a case the Muslims would have been considered too feeble to be granted any quarter in any part of Arabia. It might also have encouraged the formation of a powerful alliance between the Quraysh and other tribes. Moreover, the axis of the Madinan Jews, the hypocrites, the polytheists and the Quraysh might have openly risen and so placed the Muslims in an exceedingly difficult situation. For once their prestige had been undermined, their lives, property and honour would have been jeopardized. In view of these facts, the Prophet (peace be on him) decided to use all the resources available to him and marched to the battleground in order that it might be resolved once and for all as to which of the contending parties had the right to live.

Having made up his mind, the Prophet (peace be on him) gathered together both the *Anṣār* and *Muhājirūn* and informed them of the situation. He told them unequivocally that the Quraysh trading caravan was in the north whereas the invading Quraysh army was in the south and moving towards Madina. He also informed them that God had promised the Muslims that they would be able to seize any of the two parties they wished. (*al-Anfāl* 8: 7 – Ed.) Now it was for them to make the choice: did they wish to attack the trading caravan or the approaching army? A number of Muslims preferred to attack the caravan. However, since the Prophet (peace be on him) had something else in mind, he repeated his question. To this Miqdād b. 'Amr, one of the *Muhājirūn* responded in the following words:

> O Messenger of God! Proceed as God has commanded you to. We are with you, regardless of what you decide. We shall not say as the Children of Israel said to Moses: 'Go forth, you and your Lord, and fight. As for us, we shall remain here sitting' (*al-Mā'idah* 5: 24). We rather say: 'Go forth, you and your Lord, and fight, and we shall fight on your side as long as the eyelid of any one of us keeps moving.' (See Ibn Hishām, vol. 1, p. 615; al-Wāqidī, vol. 1, p. 48 – Ed.)

However, the decision to attack the Quraysh army could not be taken without ascertaining the views of the *Anṣār*. So far no help had been sought from them in military expeditions. This was thus the first occasion when it would be determined as to how far the *Anṣār* would go in order to fulfil the commitment to support Islam which they had made at the time of pledging their fealty to the Prophet (peace be on him). Without addressing the *Anṣār* directly, the Prophet (peace be on him) again put the two alternatives before his audience. (See Ibn Hishām, vol. 1, p. 615 – Ed.) Realizing that what the Prophet (peace be on him) was really aiming at was to ascertain the opinion of the *Anṣār* on the question, Sa'd b. Mu'ādh rose and inquired whether the Prophet's question was directed to the *Anṣār*. When the Prophet (peace be on him) replied in the affirmative, he said:

> We decided to believe in you. We affirmed the veracity of your claim [to be the Messenger of God] and we bore witness to the truth of your teachings. We have also given you our pledge and concluded with you a firm covenant to hear and to obey. O Messenger of God! Do as you wish. By the One Who has sent you with the truth, if you were to take us to the sea and plunge into it, and none of us shall remain behind. We shall not mind if you confront the enemy with us tomorrow. We shall persevere in battle, shall remain faithful in the encounter with the enemy, and possibly God will enable us to achieve what will soothe your eyes. So take us along to the battlefield with God's blessing. (Al-Wāqidī, vol. 1, pp. 48–9 – Ed.)

MAP NO. 4: THE CARAVAN ROUTES FROM MAKKA TO SYRIA VIA BADR AND FROM MADINA TO BADR

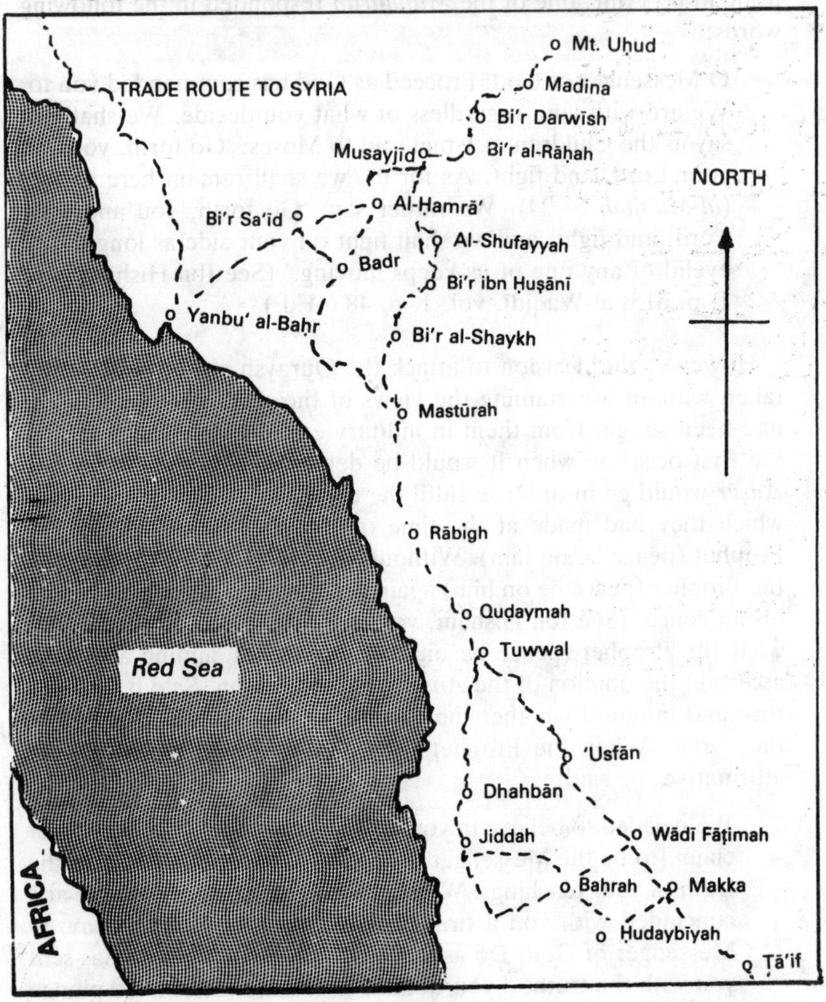

After these deliberations it was decided that the Muslims should go forth and confront the Quraysh army rather than take on the trading caravan. This was no ordinary decision. Although the Muslims had made up their minds to fight, their number hardly exceeded 300. Of these, 86 were *Muhājirūn* and of the rest, 61 belonged to the Aws and 170 to the Khazraj, the two main clans of Madina. Such was the scarcity of resources that only two or three Muslims had horses. The number of camels too was no more than 70 so that three or four persons took turns on each camel. There was also an acute paucity of weapons. Only 60 Muslims had coats of mail.

No wonder, leaving aside the devoted ones who were fired with the zeal to sacrifice their lives for Islam, a number of them feared their destruction at the Battle of Badr. Naturally those who had embraced Islam under the impression that it would bring them material advantage began to have second thoughts. They looked upon the decision to take on the Quraysh army as an aberrant act prompted by religious fanaticism. However, the Prophet (peace be on him) and the true believers were convinced that the time had come for them to stake their lives for their cause. Trusting God, they set off straight along the south-western route, towards the approaching Quraysh army. It is obvious that had the decision of the Prophet (peace be on him) been to intercept the trading caravan, they would have proceeded in the north-western direction.*

On 17th Ramaḍān the two armies – those of the Quraysh and the Muslims – encountered each other at a place called Badr. As they stood face to face, the Prophet (peace be on him) noted that the Quraysh outnumbered the Muslims by three to one. Moreover, the Muslims were scantily equipped. Observing this, the Prophet (peace

*It is noteworthy that while narrating the Battle of Badr both the historians and biographers of the Prophet (peace be on him) have placed their reliance on traditions embodied in the works of *Ḥadīth* and *Maghāzī*. But a good many of these traditions are opposed to the statements made by the Qur'ān and are therefore not to be relied upon. It is not just on grounds of religious faith that we consider the Qur'ānic version more trustworthy. We are of the view that even from an historical point of view the most trustworthy version is the one embodied in this *sūrah* – *al-Anfāl*. This is so because the *sūrah* was revealed immediately after the Battle of Badr, and its statements were in the knowledge of those who had participated in the battle itself from both the sides. Had there been any discrepancy between the Qur'ānic statements and the facts of the battle, that would have been pointed out and repudiated by innumerable people. It may be noted that the author believes that the Qur'ānic verses clearly indicate what the Prophet (peace be on him) intended when he proceeded from Madina to confront the Quraysh army. (See *al-Anfāl* 8: 5–8; cf. Shiblī Nu'mānī, *Sīrat al-Nabī*, 6th edition, vol. 1, pp. 343 ff. – Ed.) On the contrary, the earlier Muslim historians and biographers are inclined to the view that the original intent of the Prophet (peace be on him) was to attack the trading caravan. (See Ibn Hishām, vol. 1, pp. 606 f.; Ibn Sa'd, vol. 2, pp. 11 f.; and al-Wāqidī, vol. 1, pp. 20, 21 – Ed.)

be on him) outstretched his arms and prayed with great earnestness and humility:

> O God! Here are the Quraysh who in their vain glory seek to call the lie to Your Messenger. O God! Support us with the help You promised me. O God! Were this group [of Muslims] to perish, none in the whole earth shall worship You. (Ibn Hishām, vol. 1, p. 621 – Ed.)

The Battle of Badr was a severe test for all Muslims. The faith of the *Muhājirūn* was truly tested in the battle for they were lined up against their own kith and kin, some having to cross swords with their father, son, uncle, or brother if the latter happened to be in the Quraysh army. To have to fight against one's near and dear ones because they sought to obliterate Islam was a very serious test indeed and only those who had decided to support the truth with total single-mindedness and were fully willing to sever all ties with falsehood could come o. successfully.

The test through which the *Anṣār* had to pass was no less severe. They had already antagonized the most powerful Arabian tribes – the Quraysh and their allies – by providing shelter to the Muslims. But now they were going to commit an act of much greater daring and provocation. They were going to engage the Quraysh in battle. This meant that their small town, inhabited by a few thousand souls, would virtually invite the hostility of the whole of Arabia. Such a step could have been taken only by those committed devotees of the truth who had become totally impervious to personal interests. Ultimately, however, the sincerity of the Muslims won them God's help. The Quraysh, who had exulted in their power, suffered defeat at the hands of the ill-equipped Muslims. Seventy of the Quraysh were killed. Another 70 were taken as captives and their possessions seized by the Muslims as booty. The leading members of the Quraysh, those who had stood in the vanguard of hostility towards Islam, were cut down during the course of the battle.

This decisive victory made Islam a force to reckon with across all of Arabia. As a Western scholar has pointed out: 'Prior to the battle of Badr, Islam was merely a religion. After Badr, it became the religion of the state, or the state itself.'

Subject Matter

The *sūrah* under discussion offers a critique of this great battle. However, the tenor of this critique is radically different from those

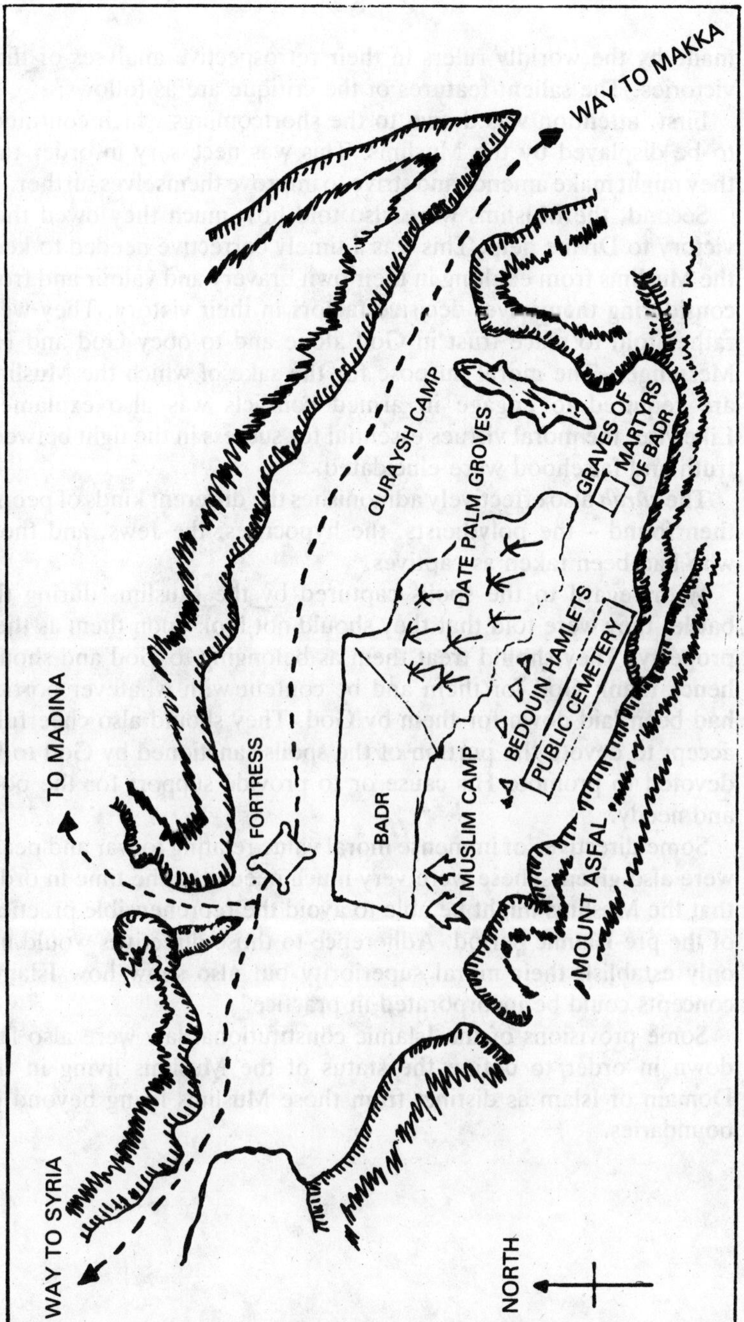

MAP NO. 5: THE BATTLEFIELD OF BADR

made by the worldly rulers in their retrospective analyses of their victories. The salient features of the critique are as follows:

First, attention was drawn to the shortcomings which continued to be displayed by the Muslims. This was necessary in order that they might make amends and strive to improve themselves further.

Second, the Muslims were also told how much they owed their victory to Divine help. This was a timely corrective needed to keep the Muslims from exulting in their own bravery and valour and from considering themselves decisive factors in their victory. They were rather told to place trust in God alone and to obey God and His Messenger. The moral purpose for the sake of which the Muslims are required to engage in armed conflicts was also explained. Likewise, the moral virtues essential for success in the fight between truth and falsehood were elucidated.

The *sūrah* also effectively admonishes the different kinds of people then found – the polytheists, the hypocrites, the Jews, and those who had been taken as captives.

With regard to the spoils captured by the Muslims during the battle, they were told that they should not look upon them as their property. They should treat them as belonging to God and should hence thank God for them and be content with whatever portion had been laid down for them by God. They should also cheerfully accept to devote the portion of the spoils sanctioned by God to be devoted to promote His cause or to provide support for the poor and needy.

Some directives of immense moral value relating to war and peace were also given. These were very much needed at the time in order that the Muslims might be able to avoid the reprehensible practices of the pre-Islamic period. Adherence to those directives would not only establish their moral superiority but also show how Islamic concepts could be incorporated in practice.

Some provisions of the Islamic constitutional law were also laid down in order to define the status of the Muslims living in the Domain of Islam as distinct from those Muslims living beyond its boundaries.

In the name of Allah, the Compassionate, the Merciful.

بِسۡمِ ٱللَّهِ ٱلرَّحۡمَٰنِ ٱلرَّحِيمِ

(1) They ask you concerning the spoils of war? Tell them: 'The spoils of war belong to Allah and the Messenger. So fear Allah, and set things right between you, and obey Allah and His Messenger if you are true believers.[1] ▶

يَسۡـَٔلُونَكَ عَنِ ٱلۡأَنفَالِۖ قُلِ ٱلۡأَنفَالُ لِلَّهِ وَٱلرَّسُولِۖ فَٱتَّقُواْ ٱللَّهَ وَأَصۡلِحُواْ ذَاتَ بَيۡنِكُمۡۖ وَأَطِيعُواْ ٱللَّهَ وَرَسُولَهُۥٓ إِن كُنتُم مُّؤۡمِنِينَ ١

1. The critique of the battle opens with this unusual note. Some disagreements had arisen among the Muslims with regard to sharing the spoils of war. As it was their first experience of fighting under the banner of Islam, the Muslim soldiers had scarcely any notion of the regulations they were required to follow on the battlefield and for settling problems arising from warfare.

Doubtlessly some preliminary instructions had been laid down for them in *Sūrah al-Baqarah* 2 and *Sūrah Muḥammad* 47. (See 2: 190 ff. and 47: 4 ff. – Ed.) However, the full set of regulations that could contribute to civilizing the conduct of warfare had yet to be laid down. Hence, when it came to war as with several other societal matters, the Muslims were still under the influence of pre-Islamic ideas and concepts. Going by the age-old Arab customs, those who had seized the spoils of war considered themselves their sole and legitimate owners. On the other hand, the Muslims who had concentrated on driving away the enemy rather than on collecting the spoils, claimed that they deserved an equal share of the spoils. They contended that had they slackened in their duty of pursuing the enemy, the latter might have struck back, turning the Muslim victory into a defeat. Similarly, another group of Muslims who had escorted the Prophet (peace be on him) on the battlefield, also laid claim to an equal share. For, they believed, it was they who had rendered an invaluable service insofar as neglect of duty on their part might have resulted in endangering the precious life of the Prophet (peace be on him), in which case the possibility of victory and its attendant spoils and their distribution would all have been totally out of the question. Nonetheless, the group of Muslims who already possessed the spoils saw no merit in these claims. Arguments and counter-arguments gave rise to bitterness and bad blood. (For disagreements among Muslims on the question of distribution of spoils of war see

Ibn Hishām, vol. 1, pp. 641–2; al-Wāqidī, vol. 1, p. 78. See also the comments on the verse in Qurṭubī and Ibn Kathīr – Ed.)

It was at this juncture that God revealed the present *sūrah*. The opening verse takes up this issue. 'They ask you concerning *anfāl*' is the query with which the *sūrah* opens. The very use of the word *anfāl* instead of *ghanā'im* in the query implies the answer. For the word *anfāl*, which is the plural of *nafl*, stands for that which is extra, that which is over and above what is obligatory. If this extra is from the servant, it denotes that additional service which he voluntarily renders over and above what is obligatory. On the other hand, when this extra is from the master, it denotes the additional reward which the master awards his servant over and above what he is entitled to. What is being conveyed here by using the word *anfāl* is, in fact, that all wrangling about spoils is out of place since it concerns not their rights, but the additional rewards they might receive from God. Any and all heated discussion in which they engaged was irrelevant since it was entirely for God to decide whether He should grant any extra reward or not; and if He should grant it, then how much, and to whom. In short, it was not for men to say who should and who should not receive any part of the spoils.

This was a major conceptual reform. The war that a Muslim wages is not in order to accumulate worldly benefits. He resorts to it for the moral and social reform of the world and does so when the opposing forces make it impossible to bring about reform by means of persuasion and preaching. Being reformers, the Muslims should focus their attentions on their goal – the reform of the world – rather than on the material benefits which accrue to them incidentally by way of God's additional reward in lieu of their strivings. If the attention of Muslims is not diverted from material benefits to their true mission, it is likely that material benefits would become an end in themselves.

Moreover, the concept introduced by the Qur'ān (see the verse above) also brought about a major administrative reform pertaining to war and the spoils of war. Before the advent of Islam, a soldier used to appropriate all that he could lay his hands on, claiming to be its rightful owner, or else spoils were seized either by the king or the commander of the army. In the former case, mutual conflicts ensued among soldiers of the victorious army, with the frequent result that their victory turned into defeat. On the other hand, if the spoils were seized by the commander of the army or the ruler, soldiers often concealed and stole the spoils. By declaring that the spoils belong to God and His Messenger, the Qur'ān made it obligatory on all soldiers to commit all the spoils of war to the custody of the commander, concealing not even something as trivial as a sewing needle. Subsequently the Qur'ān laid down an elaborate set of laws to distribute the spoils of war. According to it, one-fifth of the spoils is to be deposited in the public treasury for public welfare and to provide support for the poor, while four-fifths is to be distributed among the soldiers. (*al-Anfāl* 8: 41 – Ed.) It thus put an end to the evils inherent in the old system.

(2) The true believers are those who, when Allah's name is mentioned, their hearts quake, and when His verses are recited to them their faith grows,[2] and who put their trust in their Lord; (3) who establish Prayer and spend out of what We have provided them. (4) Such people are indeed true believers. They have high ranks with their Lord, and forgiveness for their sins[3] and an honourable sustenance. ▶

إِنَّمَا ٱلْمُؤْمِنُونَ ٱلَّذِينَ إِذَا ذُكِرَ ٱللَّهُ
وَجِلَتْ قُلُوبُهُمْ وَإِذَا تُلِيَتْ عَلَيْهِمْ
ءَايَٰتُهُۥ زَادَتْهُمْ إِيمَٰنًا وَعَلَىٰ رَبِّهِمْ
يَتَوَكَّلُونَ ﴿٢﴾ ٱلَّذِينَ يُقِيمُونَ
ٱلصَّلَوٰةَ وَمِمَّا رَزَقْنَٰهُمْ يُنفِقُونَ ﴿٣﴾
أُو۟لَٰٓئِكَ هُمُ ٱلْمُؤْمِنُونَ حَقًّا لَّهُمْ دَرَجَٰتٌ
عِندَ رَبِّهِمْ وَمَغْفِرَةٌ وَرِزْقٌ
كَرِيمٌ ﴿٤﴾

A subtle point implicit in the above verse should not be overlooked. In the opening verse of the *sūrah* nothing has been said beyond affirming the principle that the spoils belong to God and His Messenger. The problem as to how the spoils should be distributed was not touched upon. The Qur'ān does however subsequently treat the question of distribution (see verse 41 below). It is significant that in this second instance the word used is a verbal derivative of *ghanīmah* (spoils, booty) (see verse 41 below) whereas in the opening verse the word used is *anfāl*.

2. A man's faith grows as he is able to confirm and submit to the command of God which he comes across. This is especially so where he submits to commands which go against his own personal predilections. A man's faith attains great heights if instead of trying to twist and distort the commands of God and the Prophet (peace be on him), he develops the habit of accepting and submitting to all the commands of God and the Prophet (peace be on him); if he strives to shape his conduct to the teachings which go against his personal opinions and conceptions, which are contrary to his habits, interests and convenience, which are not in consonance with his loyalties and friendships. For, if he hesitates to respond positively to God's command, his faith is diminished. One thus learns that faith is not a static, immobile object. Nor is every act of belief, or unbelief, of the same quality. An act of belief may be better or worse than another act of belief. Likewise, an act of unbelief may differ in quality from another act of unbelief. For both, belief and unbelief, are capable of growth and decline.

All this concerns the essence of belief and unbelief. However, when

(5) (Now with regard to the spoils the same situation exists as when) your Lord brought you forth from your home in a righteous cause while a party among the believers were much averse to it. (6) They disputed with you about the truth after that had become evident, as if they were being driven to death with their eyes wide open.[4]

كَمَآ أَخۡرَجَكَ رَبُّكَ مِنۢ بَيۡتِكَ بِٱلۡحَقِّ
وَإِنَّ فَرِيقٗا مِّنَ ٱلۡمُؤۡمِنِينَ لَكَٰرِهُونَ
٥ يُجَٰدِلُونَكَ فِي ٱلۡحَقِّ بَعۡدَ مَا تَبَيَّنَ
كَأَنَّمَا يُسَاقُونَ إِلَى ٱلۡمَوۡتِ وَهُمۡ
يَنظُرُونَ ٦

belief and unbelief are mentioned as a basis for membership of the Muslim community or in connection with legal rights and responsibilities as necessary corollaries of that membership, a clear line of demarcation has to be drawn between those who believe and those who do not. In this respect the determination of who is a believer and who is not will depend on the basic minimum of belief regardless of quality of belief. In an Islamic society all those who believe will be entitled to the same legal rights and will be required to fulfil the same duties regardless of the differences in the quality of their faith. Likewise, all unbelievers – regardless of the differences in the quality of their unbelief – will be placed in the category of unbelievers disregarding the question whether their unbelief is of an ordinary quality or an extremely serious one.

3. Even the best and the most devoted believers are liable to commit lapses. As long as man is man, it is impossible for his record to be filled exclusively with righteousness of the highest order and to be free from all lapses, shortcomings and weaknesses. Out of His infinite mercy, however, God overlooks man's shortcomings as long as he fulfils the basic duties incumbent upon him as God's servant, and favours him with a reward far greater than that warranted by his good works. Had it been a rule that man would be judged strictly on the basis of his deeds, that he would be punished for every evil deed and rewarded for every good deed, no man, howsoever righteous, would have escaped punishment.

4. When the people in question were required to fight, they were disinclined to do so for they felt that they were being driven to death and destruction. Their condition is somewhat similar for they are now required

(7) And recall when Allah promised you that one of the two hosts would fall to you,[5] and you wished that the one without arms should fall into your hands.[6] But Allah sought to prove by His words the truth to be true and to annihilate the unbelievers to the last remnant (8) that He might prove the truth to be true and the false to be false, however averse the evil-doers might be to it.[7]

وَإِذْ يَعِدُكُمُ ٱللَّهُ إِحْدَى ٱلطَّآئِفَتَيْنِ
أَنَّهَا لَكُمْ وَتَوَدُّونَ أَنَّ غَيْرَ ذَاتِ
ٱلشَّوْكَةِ تَكُونُ لَكُمْ وَيُرِيدُ
ٱللَّهُ أَن يُحِقَّ ٱلْحَقَّ بِكَلِمَٰتِهِۦ وَيَقْطَعَ
دَابِرَ ٱلْكَٰفِرِينَ ﴿٧﴾ لِيُحِقَّ ٱلْحَقَّ
وَيُبْطِلَ ٱلْبَٰطِلَ وَلَوْ كَرِهَ ٱلْمُجْرِمُونَ
﴿٨﴾

---

not to contend about spoils of war and wait for God's command as to how the spoils of war should be distributed.

This verse could also mean that if Muslims obeyed God and followed the Prophet (peace be on him) rather than their own desires, they would witness as good a result as they witnessed on the occasion of the Battle of Badr. On this occasion too many were reluctant to take on the Quraysh and considered it nothing short of suicide (see verse 6). But when they obeyed the command of God and His Prophet (peace be on him), it proved to be a source of life and survival.

Incidentally, this statement in the Qur'ān implicitly negates reports usually mentioned in the works of *Sīrah* and *Maghāzī* and which suggest that the Prophet (peace be on him) and his Companions had initially set out from Madina in order to raid the trading caravan of the Quraysh, and that it was only when they came to know that the Quraysh army was advancing to provide protection to the trading caravan that the Muslims were faced with the option of either attacking the caravan or the Quraysh army. The Qur'ānic version is quite contrary. Accordingly, from the moment when the Prophet (peace be on him) set out from his house, he was intent upon a decisive battle with the Quraysh. In addition, the decision as to whether the Muslims should confront the trading caravan or the army was taken at the very beginning rather than later on. It is also evident that even though it was quite clear that it was essential to confront the Quraysh army, a group of Muslims tried to avoid it and kept pleading for their viewpoint. Even when a firm decision had been taken that the Muslims would attack the Quraysh army rather than the caravan, this group set out for the encounter with the view that they were being driven to death and

(9) And recall when you implored your Lord for help and He responded to you: 'I will indeed reinforce you with a thousand angels, coming host after host.' (10) Allah meant this as glad tidings and that your hearts may be set at rest. For every help comes from Allah alone. Surely Allah is All-Mighty, All-Wise.

(11) And recall when Allah brought on you drowsiness,[8] giving you a feeling of peace and security from Him, and He sent down rain upon you from the sky that He might cleanse you through it and take away from you the pollution of Satan and strengthen your hearts, and steady your feet through it.[9]

إِذْ تَسْتَغِيثُونَ رَبَّكُمْ فَاسْتَجَابَ
لَكُمْ أَنِّي مُمِدُّكُم بِأَلْفٍ مِّنَ
الْمَلَٰٓئِكَةِ مُرْدِفِينَ ﴿٩﴾ وَمَا
جَعَلَهُ اللَّهُ إِلَّا بُشْرَىٰ وَلِتَطْمَئِنَّ
بِهِۦ قُلُوبُكُمْ وَمَا النَّصْرُ إِلَّا مِنْ عِندِ
اللَّهِ إِنَّ اللَّهَ عَزِيزٌ حَكِيمٌ ﴿١٠﴾ إِذْ
يُغَشِّيكُمُ النُّعَاسَ أَمَنَةً مِّنْهُ وَيُنَزِّلُ
عَلَيْكُم مِّنَ السَّمَآءِ مَآءً لِّيُطَهِّرَكُم
بِهِۦ وَيُذْهِبَ عَنكُمْ رِجْزَ الشَّيْطَٰنِ
وَلِيَرْبِطَ عَلَىٰ قُلُوبِكُمْ وَيُثَبِّتَ بِهِ
الْأَقْدَامَ ﴿١١﴾

---

destruction. (See verses 5–8. Cf. al-Wāqidī, vol. 1, pp. 19–21; Ibn Sa'd, vol. 2, pp. 11–14 – Ed.)

5. God's promise was that the Muslims would be able to overcome whichever of the two parties they wished to attack – the trading caravan or the Quraysh army.

6. This refers to the trading caravan which had some 30 to 40 armed guards for protection.

7. This gives some idea of the prevalent situation at the time. As we have said earlier (see above, p. 128), the march of the Quraysh towards Madina meant that only one of the two would survive in Arabia – either Islam or the entrenched system of *Jāhilīyah* (Ignorance). Had the Muslims not taken up the challenge, the very survival of Islam would have been

(12) And recall when your Lord inspired the angels: 'I am certainly with you. So make firm the feet of those who believe. I will cast terror into the hearts of those who disbelieve. So strike at their necks and strike at every pore and tip.'[10] (13) This is because they defied Allah and His Messenger. Whoever defies Allah and His Messenger must know that Allah is severe in punishment.[11] (14) That is your punishment (from Allah). So taste this punishment,[12] and know that for the unbelievers is the punishment of the Fire.

إِذْ يُوحِي رَبُّكَ إِلَى ٱلْمَلَٰٓئِكَةِ أَنِّي مَعَكُمْ
فَثَبِّتُوا۟ ٱلَّذِينَ ءَامَنُوا۟ سَأُلْقِى فِى قُلُوبِ
ٱلَّذِينَ كَفَرُوا۟ ٱلرُّعْبَ فَٱضْرِبُوا۟
فَوْقَ ٱلْأَعْنَاقِ وَٱضْرِبُوا۟ مِنْهُمْ
كُلَّ بَنَانٍ ﴿١٢﴾ ذَٰلِكَ بِأَنَّهُمْ
شَآقُّوا۟ ٱللَّهَ وَرَسُولَهُۥ وَمَن يُشَاقِقِ ٱللَّهَ
وَرَسُولَهُۥ فَإِنَّ ٱللَّهَ شَدِيدُ ٱلْعِقَابِ
﴿١٣﴾ ذَٰلِكُمْ فَذُوقُوهُ وَأَنَّ
لِلْكَٰفِرِينَ عَذَابَ ٱلنَّارِ ﴿١٤﴾

---

imperilled. But since the Muslims took the initiative and dealt a severe blow to the military strength of the Quraysh it became possible for Islam to consolidate itself and subsequently the forces of Ignorance suffered a succession of humiliating reverses.

8. In the Battle of Uḥud the Muslims passed through a similar experience (see *Āl 'Imrān* 3: 154 above). On both occasions, when prevalent conditions should have produced intense fear and panic among them, God filled their hearts with such peace and tranquillity that they were overpowered with drowsiness.

9. This refers to the heavy downpour on the night preceding the Battle of Badr. It helped the Muslims in three ways. First, it provided them with an abundant water supply which they quickly stored in large reservoirs. Second, rain compacted the loose sand in the upper part of the valley where the Muslims had pitched their tents. This helped the Muslims plant their feet firmly and facilitated their movement. Third, where the Quraysh army was stationed in the lower part of the valley, the ground turned marshy.

The defilement caused by Satan which occurs in the verse refers to the fear and panic which initially afflicted the Muslims.

(15) Believers, whenever you encounter a hostile force of unbelievers, do not turn your backs to them in flight. (16) For he who turns his back on them on such an occasion – except that it be for tactical reasons, or turning to join another company – he shall incur the wrath of Allah and Hell shall be his abode. It is an evil destination.[13]

يَٰٓأَيُّهَا ٱلَّذِينَ ءَامَنُوٓا۟ إِذَا لَقِيتُمُ ٱلَّذِينَ
كَفَرُوا۟ زَحْفًا فَلَا تُوَلُّوهُمُ ٱلْأَدْبَارَ ﴿١٥﴾
وَمَن يُوَلِّهِمْ يَوْمَئِذٍ دُبُرَهُۥٓ إِلَّا مُتَحَرِّفًا
لِّقِتَالٍ أَوْ مُتَحَيِّزًا إِلَىٰ فِئَةٍ فَقَدْ بَآءَ
بِغَضَبٍ مِّنَ ٱللَّهِ وَمَأْوَىٰهُ جَهَنَّمُ
وَبِئْسَ ٱلْمَصِيرُ ﴿١٦﴾

---

10. In view of the general principle propounded in the Qur'ān we presume that the angels did not take part in the actual fighting. What we may suggest is that the angels helped the Muslims and as a result their blows became more accurate and effective.

11. In recounting the events of the Battle of Badr, the Qur'ān aims to explain the significance of the word *al-anfāl* (spoils of war). In the opening verse of the *sūrah* the Muslims were told that they should not deem the spoils to be a reward for their toil. Rather, the spoils should constitute a special reward granted to the Muslims by God, to Whom the spoils rightfully belong. The events recounted here support this. The Muslims could reflect on the course of events and see for themselves to what extent the victory they had achieved was due to God's favour, and to what extent it was due to their own efforts.

12. Here the discourse is suddenly directed to the unbelievers who were mentioned (in verse 13) as deserving of God's punishment.

13. The Qur'ān does not forbid orderly retreat under strong pressure from the enemy provided it is resorted to as a stratagem of war, for example seeking reinforcements or joining another party in the rear. What the Qur'ān does forbid is disorderly flight produced by sheer cowardice and defeatism. Such a retreat takes place because the deserter holds his life dearer than his cause. Such cowardice has been characterized as one of those three major sins which, if committed, can be atoned for by no other good deed whatsoever. These three sins are: ascription of divinity to anyone or anything other than God, violation of the rights of parents, and flight

(17) So the fact is that it was not you, but it was Allah Who killed them; and it was not you when you threw [sand at them], but it was Allah Who threw it,[14] (and the believers were employed for the task) that He might cause the believers to successfully pass through this test. Allah is All-Hearing, All-Knowing. (18) This is His manner of dealing with you. As for the unbelievers, Allah will surely undermine their designs. ▶

فَلَمْ تَقْتُلُوهُمْ وَلَٰكِنَّ ٱللَّهَ قَتَلَهُمْ ۚ
وَمَا رَمَيْتَ إِذْ رَمَيْتَ وَلَٰكِنَّ
ٱللَّهَ رَمَىٰ ۚ وَلِيُبْلِىَ ٱلْمُؤْمِنِينَ مِنْهُ
بَلَآءً حَسَنًا ۚ إِنَّ ٱللَّهَ سَمِيعٌ
عَلِيمٌ ﴿١٧﴾ ذَٰلِكُمْ وَأَنَّ ٱللَّهَ
مُوهِنُ كَيْدِ ٱلْكَٰفِرِينَ ﴿١٨﴾

from the battlefield during fighting in the way of God. (See al-Mundhirī, 'Kitāb al-Jihād', 'Bāb al-Tarhīb min al-Firār min al-Zaḥf' – Ed.) In another tradition the Prophet (peace be on him) has mentioned seven deadly sins which totally ruin a man's Next Life. One of these is flight from the battlefield in an encounter between Islam and Unbelief. (Muslim, 'K. al-Īmān', 'Bāb al-Kabā'ir wa Akbaruhā'; Bukhārī, 'K. al-Waṣāyā', 'Bāb fī Qawl Allāh Ta'ālá: inna al-ladhīna Ya'kulūna Amwāl al-Yatāmá Ẓulman' – Ed.) This has been declared a deadly sin because in addition to being an act of sheer cowardice, it demoralizes others and can generate demoralization which can have disastrous consequences. An individual soldier's desertion might cause a whole platoon, or even a whole regiment, and ultimately the whole army, to take flight. For once a soldier flees in panic, it is hard to control the others.

14. This refers to the occasion when the armies of the Muslims and the unbelievers stood face to face in the Battle of Badr and were on the verge of actual fighting. At that moment, the Prophet (peace be on him) threw a handful of dust at the enemy saying: 'May their faces be scorched.' So saying the Prophet (peace be on him) made a gesture and the Muslims started their charge. (See Aḥmad b. Ḥanbal, *Musnad,* vol. 1, p. 368; Ibn Hishām, vol. 1, p. 668; Ibn Kathīr, comments on the verse – Ed.)

(19) (Tell the unbelievers:) 'If you have sought a judgement, then surely a judgement has come to you.[15] And if you desist from disobedience, it is all the better for you. But if you revert to your mischief, We will again chastise you; and your host, howsoever numerous, will never be of any avail to you. Know well, Allah is with the believers.'

(20) Believers! Obey Allah and His Messenger and do not turn away from him after you hear his command. (21) And do not be like those who say: 'We hear', though they do not hearken.[16] (22) Indeed the worst kind of all beasts in the sight of Allah are the people that are deaf and dumb,[17] and do not understand.

إِن تَسْتَفْتِحُوا فَقَدْ جَاءَكُمُ
الْفَتْحُ وَإِن تَنتَهُوا فَهُوَ خَيْرٌ
لَّكُمْ وَإِن تَعُودُوا نَعُدْ وَلَن تُغْنِيَ
عَنكُمْ فِئَتُكُمْ شَيْئًا وَلَوْ كَثُرَتْ
وَأَنَّ اللَّهَ مَعَ الْمُؤْمِنِينَ ﴿١٩﴾ يَا أَيُّهَا
الَّذِينَ آمَنُوا أَطِيعُوا اللَّهَ وَرَسُولَهُ
وَلَا تَوَلَّوْا عَنْهُ وَأَنتُمْ تَسْمَعُونَ ﴿٢٠﴾
وَلَا تَكُونُوا كَالَّذِينَ قَالُوا سَمِعْنَا
وَهُمْ لَا يَسْمَعُونَ ﴿٢١﴾ ۞ إِنَّ شَرَّ
الدَّوَابِّ عِندَ اللَّهِ الصُّمُّ الْبُكْمُ
الَّذِينَ لَا يَعْقِلُونَ ﴿٢٢﴾

---

15. Before marching out from Makka the unbelievers held the covering of the Ka'bah and prayed: 'O God! Grant victory to the better of the two parties.' Abū Jahl, in particular invoked God's judgement: 'O God! Grant victory to the one who is in the right and cause humiliation to the wrong-doer.' God answered these prayers fully and the outcome of the battle clearly pointed to the party which was in the right.

16. In the present context, 'hearing' means taking heed with a view to obey. The verse alludes to those hypocrites who professed to believe and yet were not willing to carry out the commands of God.

17. These are the ones who neither hear nor speak the truth. So far as truth is concerned, their ears are deaf and their mouths dumb.

(23) And had Allah known in them any good He would surely have made them hear; but (being as they are) even if He made them hear, they would have surely turned away in aversion.[18]

(24) Believers! Respond to Allah, and respond to the Messenger when he calls you to that which gives you life. Know well that Allah stands between a man and his heart, and it is to Him that all of you shall be mustered.[19]

وَلَوْ عَلِمَ ٱللَّهُ فِيهِمْ خَيْرًا لَّأَسْمَعَهُمْ ۖ وَلَوْ
أَسْمَعَهُمْ لَتَوَلَّوا۟ وَّهُم مُّعْرِضُونَ
﴿٢٣﴾ يَٰٓأَيُّهَا ٱلَّذِينَ ءَامَنُوا۟ ٱسْتَجِيبُوا۟
لِلَّهِ وَلِلرَّسُولِ إِذَا دَعَاكُمْ لِمَا يُحْيِيكُمْ ۖ
وَٱعْلَمُوٓا۟ أَنَّ ٱللَّهَ يَحُولُ بَيْنَ ٱلْمَرْءِ
وَقَلْبِهِۦ وَأَنَّهُۥٓ إِلَيْهِ تُحْشَرُونَ ﴿٢٤﴾

18. Such people have neither any love for the truth nor any desire to strive for it. Hence even if they were enabled by God to go forth to the battlefield, they would have turned on their heels at the very first sight of danger. That such people should be a part of the Muslim army might have led to greater harm than good.

19. The most effective means of preventing man from falling prey to hypocrisy is to implant two ideas in his mind. First, that he will have to face the reckoning and judgement of God Who knows what is in the deep recesses of his heart. Even man's intentions and desires, the purposes which he seeks to achieve, the ideas that he seeks to keep hidden in his heart, are all well known to God. Second, that ultimately every man will be mustered to God; that He is so powerful that none can escape His judgement. The deeper the roots of these convictions, the further is man removed from hypocrisy. Hence, while admonishing Muslims against hypocrisy, the Qur'ān frequently resorts to emphasizing these two articles of belief.

(25) And guard against the mischief that will not only bring punishment to the wrong-doers among you.[20] Know well that Allah is severe in punishment. (26) And recall when you were few in numbers and deemed weak in the land, fearful lest people do away with you. Then He provided you refuge, strengthened you with His help, and provided you sustenance with good things that you may be grateful.[21]

وَٱتَّقُوا۟ فِتْنَةً لَّا تُصِيبَنَّ ٱلَّذِينَ ظَلَمُوا۟
مِنكُمْ خَآصَّةً ۖ وَٱعْلَمُوٓا۟ أَنَّ ٱللَّهَ
شَدِيدُ ٱلْعِقَابِ ﴿٢٥﴾ وَٱذْكُرُوٓا۟ إِذْ
أَنتُمْ قَلِيلٌ مُّسْتَضْعَفُونَ فِى ٱلْأَرْضِ
تَخَافُونَ أَن يَتَخَطَّفَكُمُ ٱلنَّاسُ
فَـَٔاوَىٰكُمْ وَأَيَّدَكُم بِنَصْرِهِۦ وَرَزَقَكُم
مِّنَ ٱلطَّيِّبَٰتِ لَعَلَّكُمْ تَشْكُرُونَ ﴿٢٦﴾

---

20. This refers to those widespread social evils whose baneful effects are not confined only to those addicted to them, but which affect even those who, although they might not be addicted to those sins, are a part of that society. For example, if filth is found at just a few places in a locality it will possibly affect only those who have not kept themselves or their houses clean. However, if it becomes widespread and no one is concerned with removing uncleanliness and maintaining sanitary conditions, then everything including water and soil will become contaminated. As a result, if epidemics break out, they will not only afflict those who were responsible for spreading filth and themselves lived in unsanitary conditions, but virtually all the residents of that locality.

What is true of unsanitary conditions in a physical sense, also holds true for filth and uncleanliness in a moral sense. If immoral practices remain confined to a few people here and there but the overall moral concern of the society prevents those practices from becoming widespread and public, their harmful effects remain limited. But when the collective conscience of the society is weakened to a point whereby immoral practices are not suppressed, when people indulge in evils without any sense of shame and even go around vaunting their immoral deeds, when good people adopt a passive attitude and are content with being righteous merely in their own lives and are unconcerned with or silent about collective evils, then the entire society invites its doom. Such a society then becomes the victim of a scourge that does not distinguish between the grain and the chaff.

What God's directive seeks to impress upon people is that the reformatory mission of the Prophet (peace be on him) and the cause he was inviting

(27) Believers! Do not be unfaithful to Allah and the Messenger, nor be knowingly unfaithful to your trusts.[22] (28) Know well that your belongings and your children are but a trial,[23] and that with Allah there is a mighty reward. (29) Believers! If you fear Allah He will grant you a criterion[24] and will cleanse you of your sins and forgive you. Allah is Lord of abounding bounty.

يَٰٓأَيُّهَا ٱلَّذِينَ ءَامَنُوا۟ لَا تَخُونُوا۟ ٱللَّهَ
وَٱلرَّسُولَ وَتَخُونُوٓا۟ أَمَٰنَٰتِكُمْ وَأَنتُمْ
تَعْلَمُونَ ﴿٢٧﴾ وَٱعْلَمُوٓا۟ أَنَّمَآ
أَمْوَٰلُكُمْ وَأَوْلَٰدُكُمْ فِتْنَةٌ وَأَنَّ
ٱللَّهَ عِندَهُۥٓ أَجْرٌ عَظِيمٌ ﴿٢٨﴾ يَٰٓأَيُّهَا
ٱلَّذِينَ ءَامَنُوٓا۟ إِن تَتَّقُوا۟ ٱللَّهَ يَجْعَل
لَّكُمْ فُرْقَانًا وَيُكَفِّرْ عَنكُمْ
سَيِّـَٔاتِكُمْ وَيَغْفِرْ لَكُمْ ۗ وَٱللَّهُ ذُو
ٱلْفَضْلِ ٱلْعَظِيمِ ﴿٢٩﴾

people to was the source of life and well-being for them both individually and collectively. People should bear in mind that if they fail to participate wholeheartedly in the task to which they were invited and remain silent spectators to rampant evils, that would invite a scourge that would embrace all. It would afflict even those individuals who neither themselves committed evils nor were instrumental in spreading them and who might in fact have been righteous in their personal conduct. This point was emphasized earlier (see *al-A'rāf* 7: 163–6) and was illustrated by reference to the Sabbath-breakers, and constitutes the underlying Islamic philosophy for waging war for purposes of reform.

21. The reference to gratefulness in the verse is worthy of reflection. Bearing in mind the subject under discussion, it appears that gratefulness does not simply mean that Muslims should acknowledge God's favour to them insofar as He rescued them from their state of abject weakness. God had not only salvaged them from an insecure life in Makka and provided them with a haven of security in Madina where they enjoyed an abundance of livelihood. Gratefulness does not simply require all that. Apart from acknowledging God's favour, gratefulness also demands that Muslims should faithfully obey God and His Messenger out of a consciousness of God's munificence, out of loyalty and devotion to the Prophet's mission, and should cast aside all dangers, hardships and misfortunes that might confront them. In their struggle for God's cause Muslims should have complete trust in God Who has helped them on earlier occasions and Who has delivered them from dangers. The Muslims should also have faith that if they work sincerely in God's cause He will certainly help and protect

them. Hence, the gratefulness expected of the Muslims does not simply consist of a verbal acknowledgement of God's benefaction. Gratefulness to God should manifest itself in actual deeds as well. If someone were to acknowledge the favour of his Lord, and yet is slack in seeking His good pleasure, lacks sincerity in serving Him, and entertains doubts that God's benefaction will continue in the future, then that can hardly be characterized as gratitude.

22. 'Trusts' embrace all the responsibilities which are imparted to someone because he is trusted. These might consist of obligations arising out of an agreement or collective covenant. It might also consist of the secrets of a group. It might also consist of personal or collective property, or any office or position which might be bestowed upon a person by the group. (For further explanation see *Towards Understanding the Qur'ān*, vol. II, *al-Nisā'* 4, n. 88, pp. 49 f – Ed.)

23. Excessive love of money and one's children often impair the sincerity of a person's faith and often lead man to hypocrisy, treachery and dishonesty. The Qur'ān, therefore, clearly points out that since love of wealth or children drives people off the right path, it constitutes a considerable test for them. One's property, one's business and one's offspring constitute a test for man since they have been in his custody so as to judge to what extent he observes the limits of propriety laid down by God and adequately performs his responsibilities. What is tested is how far man is able to control his animal self – which is strongly attached to worldly purposes – so that he is able to act as God's servant and render all the rights of worldly life in the manner laid down by God.

24. 'Criterion' signifies that which enables one to distinguish between true and false; between real and fake. This is the shade of meaning conveyed by the Qur'ānic term *'furqān'*. If a man is God-fearing and tries his best to refrain from acts which displease God, God will create in him the ability to discern for himself at every step which actions are proper and which are not; which attitude conduces to God's good pleasure and which is likely to incur His wrath. This inner light will serve as a pointer at every turn and crossing, at every up and down in life, guiding him as to when he should proceed and when he should refrain, telling him which is the path of truth and leads to God, and which is false and leads to Satan.

(30) And recall how those who disbelieved schemed against you to take you captive, or kill you, or drive you away.[25] They schemed and Allah did also scheme. Allah is the best of those who scheme. (31) And when Our verses are recited to them, they say: 'We have heard. We could, if we willed, compose the like of it. They are nothing but fables of the ancient times.' ▶

وَإِذْ يَمْكُرُ بِكَ ٱلَّذِينَ كَفَرُوا۟ لِيُثْبِتُوكَ
أَوْ يَقْتُلُوكَ أَوْ يُخْرِجُوكَ وَيَمْكُرُونَ
وَيَمْكُرُ ٱللَّهُ وَٱللَّهُ خَيْرُ ٱلْمَٰكِرِينَ
﴿٣٠﴾ وَإِذَا تُتْلَىٰ عَلَيْهِمْ ءَايَٰتُنَا قَالُوا۟
قَدْ سَمِعْنَا لَوْ نَشَآءُ لَقُلْنَا مِثْلَ هَٰذَآ
إِنْ هَٰذَآ إِلَّآ أَسَٰطِيرُ ٱلْأَوَّلِينَ ﴿٣١﴾

---

25. Apprehending the Prophet's migration to Madina, the Quraysh convened a high-level council attended by all the tribal chiefs at *Dār al-Nadwah* (Council House) to decide on a decisive course of action against the Prophet (peace be on him). They realized that once the Prophet (peace be on him) left Makka, he would be beyond their reach, rendering them helpless in face of a formidable threat. A group of them was of the view that the Prophet (peace be on him) should be imprisoned for life and kept in chains. This proposal was, however, turned down on the ground that the Prophet's detention would not deter his followers from preaching Islam and that they would seize the first opportunity to release the Prophet (peace be on him) even at the risk to their own lives. Another group suggested that the Prophet (peace be on him) should be exiled, for this would remove the mischief and subversion far from Makka, and it would not matter where he spent his days nor what he did, for Makka would be immune from his influence. This proposal, too, was discarded for fear of the Prophet's persuasiveness and eloquence, and his ability to win the hearts of the people of other tribes and thus pose a greater threat in the future. Finally, Abū Jahl suggested that a band of young men drawn from all the different clans of the Quraysh should jointly pounce upon the Prophet (peace be on him) and kill him. In such a case the responsibility for his blood would rest upon all the clans of the Quraysh. It would thus become impossible for 'Abd Manāf, the Prophet's clan, to take revenge on any one particular clan. Such a move would compel the Prophet's relatives to drop their claims for retaliation and force them to settle for blood-money. Accordingly, the young men charged with the execution of this plan were selected, and were advised of the exact place and time at which they were expected to carry

(32) And also recall when they said: 'O Allah! If this indeed be the truth from You, then rain down stones upon us from heaven, or bring upon us a painful chastisement.'[26] (33) But Allah was not to chastise them while you are in their midst; nor was Allah going to chastise them while they sought His forgiveness.[27] ▶

وَإِذْ قَالُوا۟ ٱللَّهُمَّ إِن كَانَ هَٰذَا هُوَ ٱلْحَقَّ مِنْ عِندِكَ فَأَمْطِرْ عَلَيْنَا حِجَارَةً مِّنَ ٱلسَّمَآءِ أَوِ ٱئْتِنَا بِعَذَابٍ أَلِيمٍ ﴿٣٢﴾ وَمَا كَانَ ٱللَّهُ لِيُعَذِّبَهُمْ وَأَنتَ فِيهِمْ ۚ وَمَا كَانَ ٱللَّهُ مُعَذِّبَهُمْ وَهُمْ يَسْتَغْفِرُونَ ﴿٣٣﴾

out the crime. Not only that, the would-be assassins did indeed arrive at the appointed place at the appointed time. However, before they could harm him the Prophet (peace be on him) managed to escape safely. The Quraysh plot was thus frustrated at the eleventh hour. (See Ibn Hishām, vol. 1, pp. 480–2. See also Ibn Kathīr's comments on the verse – Ed.)

26. These words were uttered by way of challenge rather than a prayer to God. What they meant was that had the message of the Prophet (peace be on him) been true, and from God, its rejection would have entailed a heavy scourge, and stones would have fallen on them from heaven. Since nothing of the sort happened, it was evident that the message was neither true nor from God.

27. This is a rejoinder to the challenge implicit in the above-mentioned remark of the unbelievers. In response it was explained why people were spared heavenly scourge during the Makkan period of the Prophet's life. The first reason being that God does not punish a people as long as the Prophet is in their midst, busy inviting them to the truth. Such people are rather granted respite and are not deprived of the opportunity to reform themselves by sending a scourge all too quickly. Second, if there are a good number of people in a land who recognize that they have been negligent and heedless and have been guilty of iniquity, who seek God's forgiveness and strive to reform themselves, there remains no legitimate ground for subjecting them to a heavenly scourge. The time for such a scourge comes when a Prophet who has spared no efforts to reform his people feels that he has exhausted all his efforts, and concludes that his people have no justification to persist in their iniquity, and departs from

(34) But what prevents Allah from chastising them now when they are hindering people from the Holy Mosque, even though they are not even its true guardians. For its true guardians are none but the God-fearing, though most of them do not know that. (35) Their Prayer at the House is nothing but whistling and hand-clapping.[28] Taste, then, this chastisement for your denying the truth.[29] ▶

وَمَا لَهُمْ أَلَّا يُعَذِّبَهُمُ ٱللَّهُ وَهُمْ
يَصُدُّونَ عَنِ ٱلْمَسْجِدِ ٱلْحَرَامِ
وَمَا كَانُوٓا۟ أَوْلِيَآءَهُۥٓ ۚ إِنْ أَوْلِيَآؤُهُۥٓ
إِلَّا ٱلْمُتَّقُونَ وَلَٰكِنَّ أَكْثَرَهُمْ
لَا يَعْلَمُونَ ﴿٣٤﴾ وَمَا كَانَ صَلَاتُهُمْ
عِندَ ٱلْبَيْتِ إِلَّا مُكَآءً
وَتَصْدِيَةً ۚ فَذُوقُوا۟ ٱلْعَذَابَ
بِمَا كُنتُمْ تَكْفُرُونَ ﴿٣٥﴾

---

that land or is banished from it by its people or is murdered by them. A scourge from on high then becomes imminent since the people of that land have proven by their deeds their inability to tolerate any righteous element in their midst.

28. This is to dispel a misconception common among the Arabs of those days. They were generally inclined to assume that since the Quraysh were the guardians and keepers of the Ka'bah and were also engaged in worship at that holy spot, they were recipients of God's special favours. Here people are told that the *de facto* guardianship of the Ka'bah should not be confused with its *de jure* guardianship. For only the God-fearing and pious are the rightful guardians of the Ka'bah. As for the Quraysh, far from behaving in a manner becoming of the guardians of the Ka'bah, they had virtually installed themselves as its masters, and were guilty of preventing people from worshipping there at will. This attitude blatantly betrayed their impiety and unrighteousness. As for their worship in the Ka'bah, it was altogether devoid of religious devotion and sincerity. They neither turned earnestly to God, nor displayed any genuine submission or humility, nor engaged in worshipfully remembering Him. Their worship consisted of meaningless noise and clamour, of acts which seemed closer to play and jest than acts of religious devotion. How could such a guardianship of the Ka'bah and such non-serious acts in the name of worship win God's favour for them, or secure for them immunity from God's scourge?

(36) Surely those who deny the truth spend their wealth to hinder people from the way of Allah, and will continue to so spend until their efforts become a source of intense regret for them, and then they will be vanquished, and then these deniers of the truth will be driven to Hell, (37) so that Allah may separate the bad from the good, and join together all those who are bad into a pile one upon another, and cast them into Hell. They, it is they who are the losers.[30]

(38) [O Prophet!] Tell the unbelievers that if they desist from evil, their past shall be forgiven and if they revert to their past ways, then it is well known what happened with the people of the past.

إِنَّ ٱلَّذِينَ كَفَرُوا يُنفِقُونَ أَمْوَٰلَهُمْ
لِيَصُدُّوا عَن سَبِيلِ ٱللَّهِ ۚ فَسَيُنفِقُونَهَا
ثُمَّ تَكُونُ عَلَيْهِمْ حَسْرَةً ثُمَّ
يُغْلَبُونَ ۗ وَٱلَّذِينَ كَفَرُوٓا إِلَىٰ جَهَنَّمَ
يُحْشَرُونَ ﴿٣٦﴾ لِيَمِيزَ ٱللَّهُ ٱلْخَبِيثَ
مِنَ ٱلطَّيِّبِ وَيَجْعَلَ ٱلْخَبِيثَ بَعْضَهُۥ
عَلَىٰ بَعْضٍ فَيَرْكُمَهُۥ جَمِيعًا فَيَجْعَلَهُۥ
فِى جَهَنَّمَ ۚ أُو۟لَـٰٓئِكَ هُمُ ٱلْخَـٰسِرُونَ
﴿٣٧﴾ قُل لِّلَّذِينَ كَفَرُوٓا إِن يَنتَهُوا
يُغْفَرْ لَهُم مَّا قَدْ سَلَفَ وَإِن يَعُودُوا
فَقَدْ مَضَتْ سُنَّتُ ٱلْأَوَّلِينَ ﴿٣٨﴾

---

29. The Quraysh believed that God's punishment necessarily takes the form of some natural calamity or a rain of stones from the sky. They are, however, told that their decisive defeat in the Battle of Badr, which ensured the survival of Islam and spelled death for their much-cherished *Jāhilīyah* was a form of God's punishment for them.

30. What can be more calamitous than a person's discovery at the end of the road that all the time, energy, ability and the very quintessence of his life which he has devoted has driven him straight to his utter ruin; that his investments far from yielding any interest or dividend will require from him the payment of a grievous penalty instead.

(39) And fight against them until the mischief ends and the way prescribed by Allah – the whole of it – prevails.[31] Then, if they give up mischief, surely Allah sees what they do. (40) But if they turn away, then know well that Allah is your Protector – an excellent Protector and an excellent Helper.

(41) Know that one fifth of the spoils that you obtain belongs to Allah, to the Messenger, to the near of kin, to the orphans, and the needy, and the wayfarer.[32] This you must observe if you truly believe in Allah and in what We sent down on Our servant[33] on the day when the true was distinguished from the false, the day on which the two armies met in battle. Allah has power over all things.

وَقَٰتِلُوهُمْ حَتَّىٰ لَا تَكُونَ فِتْنَةٌ
وَيَكُونَ ٱلدِّينُ كُلُّهُۥ لِلَّهِ ۚ فَإِنِ
ٱنتَهَوْا۟ فَإِنَّ ٱللَّهَ بِمَا يَعْمَلُونَ
بَصِيرٌ ﴿٣٩﴾ وَإِن تَوَلَّوْا۟ فَٱعْلَمُوٓا۟ أَنَّ
ٱللَّهَ مَوْلَىٰكُمْ ۚ نِعْمَ ٱلْمَوْلَىٰ وَنِعْمَ
ٱلنَّصِيرُ ﴿٤٠﴾ ۞ وَٱعْلَمُوٓا۟ أَنَّمَا
غَنِمْتُم مِّن شَىْءٍ فَأَنَّ لِلَّهِ خُمُسَهُۥ
وَلِلرَّسُولِ وَلِذِى ٱلْقُرْبَىٰ
وَٱلْيَتَٰمَىٰ وَٱلْمَسَٰكِينِ وَٱبْنِ
ٱلسَّبِيلِ إِن كُنتُمْ ءَامَنتُم بِٱللَّهِ
وَمَآ أَنزَلْنَا عَلَىٰ عَبْدِنَا يَوْمَ
ٱلْفُرْقَانِ يَوْمَ ٱلْتَقَى ٱلْجَمْعَانِ ۗ
وَٱللَّهُ عَلَىٰ كُلِّ شَىْءٍ قَدِيرٌ ﴿٤١﴾

31. This is a reiteration of the purpose, mentioned earlier in *al-Baqarah* 2: 193, for which Muslims are required to wage war. The purpose is two-fold. Negatively speaking, the purpose is to eradicate 'mischief'. The positive purpose consists of establishing a state of affairs wherein all obedience is rendered to God alone. This alone is the purpose for which the believers may, rather should, fight. Fighting for any other purpose is not lawful. Nor does it behove men of faith to take part in wars for worldly purposes. (For further explanation see *Towards Understanding the Qur'ān*, vol. I, *al-Baqarah* 2, nn. 204 and 205, pp. 152–3 – Ed.)

32. This verse lays down the law for distributing the spoils of war. Spoils of war, as mentioned earlier, essentially belong to God and His Messenger. They alone have the right to dispose of them. As for the soldiers who fight, they are not the rightful owners of the spoils; whatever they do receive should be considered an extra reward from God rather than their legitimate right.

Here it is stated how God and His Messenger decided to dispose of the spoils. The prescribed rule is that the soldiers should deposit all the spoils with the ruler or the commander without making any effort to conceal anything. One-fifth of the spoils thus deposited would be assigned for the purposes mentioned in the present verse and four-fifths would be distributed among the soldiers who had taken part in the fighting. In keeping with the directive contained in the present verse, after every battle the Prophet (peace be on him) used to proclaim: 'These are your spoils. My own share in them is no more than one-fifth and even that fifth is spent on you. Bring everything, even if it be a piece of thread or a needle, or anything bigger or smaller, and take nothing by stealth *(ghulūl),* for taking by stealth is a shameful deed, and would lead to Hell.' (Aḥmad b. Ḥanbal, *Musnad,* vol. 5, p. 316 – Ed.)

It is pertinent to remember that the share of God and His Messenger (peace be on him) in the spoils signifies that a part of the spoils should be earmarked for the struggle to exalt the Word of God and to establish Islam as an operational system of life.

As to the word 'kinsmen' in the verse, during the Prophet's lifetime, it stood for his relatives. Since the Prophet (peace be on him) devoted all his time to the cause of Islam, he was not in a position to earn his own living. Hence, some arrangement had to be made for the maintenance of the Prophet (peace be on him) as well as for his family and the relatives dependent upon him for financial support. Hence a part of *khums* (one-fifth of the spoils of war) was specified for that purpose. There is, however, some disagreement among jurists as to whom this share should go to after the Prophet's death. Some jurists are of the view that after the Prophet's death the rule stands repealed. According to other jurists, this part should go to relatives of those who succeeded him to Caliphate. Other jurists are of the view that this share should be distributed among the poor members of the Prophet's family. To the best of my knowledge, the Rightly-Guided Caliphs followed the last practice. (See the comments of Qurṭubī, Ibn Kathīr and Jaṣṣāṣ on the verse. See also Ibn Rushd, *Bidāyat al-Mujtahid,* vol. 1, pp. 377–8 – Ed.)

33. This refers to the support and help from God which brought about victory for the Muslims.

(42) And recall when you were encamped at the nearer end of the valley (of Badr) and they were at the farther end and the caravan below you (along the seaside). Had you made a mutual appointment to meet in encounter, you would have declined. But encounter was brought about so that Allah might accomplish what He had decreed, and that he who was to perish should perish through a clear proof, and who was to survive might survive through a clear proof.[34] Surely Allah is All-Hearing, All-Knowing.[35]

(43) And recall when Allah showed them to you in your dream to be few in number.[36] And had He showed them to you to be numerous, you would have flagged and disagreed with one another about fighting them. But Allah saved you. Surely Allah knows what is hidden in the breasts.

إِذْ أَنتُم بِالْعُدْوَةِ الدُّنْيَا وَهُم
بِالْعُدْوَةِ الْقُصْوَىٰ وَالرَّكْبُ
أَسْفَلَ مِنكُمْ ۚ وَلَوْ تَوَاعَدتُّمْ
لَاخْتَلَفْتُمْ فِي الْمِيعَادِ ۙ وَلَٰكِن
لِّيَقْضِيَ اللَّهُ أَمْرًا كَانَ مَفْعُولًا
لِّيَهْلِكَ مَنْ هَلَكَ عَن بَيِّنَةٍ
وَيَحْيَىٰ مَنْ حَيَّ عَن بَيِّنَةٍ ۗ وَإِنَّ
اللَّهَ لَسَمِيعٌ عَلِيمٌ ﴿٤٢﴾ إِذْ
يُرِيكَهُمُ اللَّهُ فِي مَنَامِكَ قَلِيلًا ۖ
وَلَوْ أَرَاكَهُمْ كَثِيرًا لَّفَشِلْتُمْ
وَلَتَنَازَعْتُمْ فِي الْأَمْرِ وَلَٰكِنَّ
اللَّهَ سَلَّمَ ۗ إِنَّهُ عَلِيمٌ بِذَاتِ
الصُّدُورِ ﴿٤٣﴾

34. The living and the dead spoken of in the above verse do not signify the individuals who survived the battle or those killed during it. The reference here is to the ideological entities of Islam and *Jāhilīyah*.

35. God is neither blind nor deaf nor ignorant. On the contrary, He is All-Knowing, All-Seeing, All-Wise. Hence, we find reflection of God's knowledge, wisdom and justice in history.

(44) And recall when He made them appear as few in your eyes when you met them in the battle just as He lessened you in their eyes so that Allah might accomplish what had been decreed. To Allah are all matters referred for decision.

(45) Believers! When you encounter a host in battle, stand firm and remember Allah much that you may triumph. (46) And obey Allah and His Messenger, and do not quarrel with one another lest you should lose courage and your power depart. Be steadfast, surely Allah is with those who remain steadfast.[37] ▶

وَإِذْ يُرِيكُمُوهُمْ إِذِ الْتَقَيْتُمْ فِيٓ
أَعْيُنِكُمْ قَلِيلًا وَيُقَلِّلُكُمْ فِيٓ
أَعْيُنِهِمْ لِيَقْضِيَ اللَّهُ أَمْرًا كَانَ
مَفْعُولًا وَإِلَى اللَّهِ تُرْجَعُ الْأُمُورُ ﴿٤٤﴾
يَٰٓأَيُّهَا الَّذِينَ ءَامَنُوٓا إِذَا لَقِيتُمْ
فِئَةً فَاثْبُتُوا وَاذْكُرُوا اللَّهَ
كَثِيرًا لَّعَلَّكُمْ تُفْلِحُونَ ﴿٤٥﴾
وَأَطِيعُوا اللَّهَ وَرَسُولَهُۥ وَلَا تَنَٰزَعُوا
فَتَفْشَلُوا وَتَذْهَبَ رِيحُكُمْ وَاصْبِرُوٓا
إِنَّ اللَّهَ مَعَ الصَّٰبِرِينَ ﴿٤٦﴾

---

36. This refers to the time when the Prophet (peace be on him) was leaving Madina along with the Muslims, or was on his way to Badr for the encounter with the Quraysh and did not have any definite information about the strength of the enemy. In a dream, however, the Prophet (peace be on him) had a vision of the enemy. On the basis of that vision, the Prophet (peace be on him) estimated that the enemy was not too powerful. Later when the Prophet (peace be on him) narrated his dream to the Muslims, they were also encouraged and boldly went ahead to confront the enemy.

37. The believers were asked to exercise self-restraint. They were required to refrain from haste, panic, consternation, greed and uncalled-for enthusiasm. They were counselled to proceed cool-headedly and to take well-considered decisions. They were also asked not to relent an inch even in the face of grave dangers; refrain from acting rashly under provocation; to desist from taking hasty action out of impatience. They were also asked to exercise control over themselves lest they were tempted by worldly

(47) And be not like those who came forth from their homes exulting, with a desire to be seen of men, and hindering others from the way of Allah.[38] Allah encompasses all that they do.

وَلَا تَكُونُوا كَالَّذِينَ خَرَجُوا مِن دِيَـٰرِهِم بَطَرًا وَرِئَآءَ ٱلنَّاسِ وَيَصُدُّونَ عَن سَبِيلِ ٱللَّهِ ۚ وَٱللَّهُ بِمَا يَعْمَلُونَ مُحِيطٌ ﴿٤٧﴾

gains. All these instructions are implicit in the Qur'ānic directive of 'patience' given to the Muslims. God extends all help and support to those who exercise 'patience' *(ṣabr)* in the above sense.

38. This alludes to the army of the disbelieving Quraysh, which, when it proceeded on a military expedition against the Muslims, was accompanied by singing and dancing minstrels. (See Ibn Sa'd, vol. 2, p. 13 – Ed.) Whenever the army halted, dancing and drinking parties were held. Also the army arrogantly vaunted its military power and numerical strength before the tribes and localities which fell on the way, and boasted of its invincibility. (See al-Wāqidī, vol. 1, p. 39 – Ed.) This much is about the moral state of the Quraysh army. What was even worse was the object of their fighting. They were not fighting for any lofty ideal. What they aimed at was merely to defeat the forces of truth and justice, to suppress and obliterate the only group which sought to uphold the truth. They simply did not want anyone to champion the cause of truth and justice.

This occasion was considered appropriate to warn the Muslims not to let themselves degenerate into a group like the Quraysh. God had favoured them with faith and devotion to the truth, and gratitude to God for this favour required that they should purify both their conduct and their reason for fighting.

This directive was not meant just for the time in which it was revealed. It is equally applicable today, and will remain applicable in all times to come. The forces of Unbelief today are no different from those in the time of the Prophet (peace be on him) for the moral state of the present-day armies is no better than of armies in the past. Arrangements for prostitution and drinking are as much a part of the present-day armies of unbelievers as ever before. The soldiers in these armies feel no shame in openly demanding the maximum amount of alcoholic drinks and as many call-girls as possible. Without any sense of shame the soldiers virtually ask their compatriots to make available to them their daughters and sisters for the gratification of their lust. That being the case, how can one expect that the soldiers of today would not go about committing debauchery and

(48) And recall when Satan made their works seem fair to them and said: 'None shall overcome you today, and I am your supporter.' But when the two armies faced each other, he turned on his heels, and said: 'Surely I am quit of you for I behold that which you do not. Indeed I fear Allah, and Allah is stern in punishment.' (49) And recall when the hypocrites and those whose hearts were diseased said: 'Their faith has deluded these (believers).[39] But he who puts his trust in Allah shall find Allah All-Mighty, All-Wise.' (50) And if you could only see when the angels took away the souls of the unbelievers, striking them on their faces and backs, saying: 'Taste the torment of burning. (51) This is your punishment for what your hands wrought. Allah is not unjust in the least to His creatures.' ▶

وَإِذْ زَيَّنَ لَهُمُ ٱلشَّيْطَٰنُ أَعْمَٰلَهُمْ
وَقَالَ لَا غَالِبَ لَكُمُ ٱلْيَوْمَ مِنَ
ٱلنَّاسِ وَإِنِّي جَارٌ لَّكُمْ فَلَمَّا
تَرَآءَتِ ٱلْفِئَتَانِ نَكَصَ عَلَىٰ عَقِبَيْهِ
وَقَالَ إِنِّي بَرِيٓءٌ مِّنكُمْ إِنِّيٓ أَرَىٰ
مَا لَا تَرَوْنَ إِنِّيٓ أَخَافُ ٱللَّهَ وَٱللَّهُ
شَدِيدُ ٱلْعِقَابِ ﴿٤٨﴾ إِذْ يَقُولُ
ٱلْمُنَٰفِقُونَ وَٱلَّذِينَ فِي قُلُوبِهِم
مَّرَضٌ غَرَّ هَٰٓؤُلَآءِ دِينُهُمْ وَمَن
يَتَوَكَّلْ عَلَى ٱللَّهِ فَإِنَّ ٱللَّهَ عَزِيزٌ
حَكِيمٌ ﴿٤٩﴾ وَلَوْ تَرَىٰٓ إِذْ يَتَوَفَّى
ٱلَّذِينَ كَفَرُوا۟ ٱلْمَلَٰٓئِكَةُ يَضْرِبُونَ
وُجُوهَهُمْ وَأَدْبَٰرَهُمْ وَذُوقُوا۟ عَذَابَ
ٱلْحَرِيقِ ﴿٥٠﴾ ذَٰلِكَ بِمَا قَدَّمَتْ
أَيْدِيكُمْ وَأَنَّ ٱللَّهَ لَيْسَ بِظَلَّٰمٍ
لِّلْعَبِيدِ ﴿٥١﴾

---

polluting the life of the people in the lands which they happen to conquer?

Apart from moral corruption, the soldiers of the present-day armies are known for their arrogance and affrontery to the conquered peoples. Their gestures and conversation – both of ordinary soldiers and officers – bespeak of their arrogance. Arrogance is also reflected in the statements made by the statesmen of the militarily-strong and triumphant nations who in effect boastfully say to their people, in the words of the Qur'ān: 'No one shall overcome you today' (*al-Anfāl* 8: 48) and challenging the whole world in their vainglory: 'Who is greater than us in strength?' (*Fuṣṣilat* 41: 15).

(52) Their case is like that of the people of Pharaoh and those before them. They denied the signs of Allah and so Allah seized them for their sins. Surely Allah is All-Powerful, Stern in retribution. (53) This happened because Allah is not one to change the favour which He has bestowed upon a people until they have changed their attitude.[40] Surely Allah is All-Hearing, All-Knowing. ▶

كَدَأْبِ ءَالِ فِرْعَوْنَ وَٱلَّذِينَ مِن
قَبْلِهِمْ كَفَرُوا۟ بِـَٔايَٰتِ ٱللَّهِ فَأَخَذَهُمُ
ٱللَّهُ بِذُنُوبِهِمْ إِنَّ ٱللَّهَ قَوِىٌّ شَدِيدُ
ٱلْعِقَابِ ﴿٥٢﴾ ذَٰلِكَ بِأَنَّ ٱللَّهَ لَمْ يَكُ
مُغَيِّرًا نِّعْمَةً أَنْعَمَهَا عَلَىٰ قَوْمٍ حَتَّىٰ يُغَيِّرُوا۟
مَا بِأَنفُسِهِمْ وَأَنَّ ٱللَّهَ سَمِيعٌ
عَلِيمٌ ﴿٥٣﴾

These powers are evidently wicked, but the purposes for which they wage war are even more so. These powers are keen, out of sheer trickery, to assure the rest of the world that in waging war they are prompted only by the welfare of mankind. In actual fact, they might have either one motive for waging war or another, but it is absolutely certain that the motive is not the welfare of mankind. Their purpose is to establish their exclusive control and to exploit the resources created by God for all mankind. Their goal is to reduce other nations to the position of hewers of wood and drawers of water and to subject them to thraldom and servitude. Here Muslims are being told, in effect, that they should eschew the ways of non-Muslims and desist from devoting their lives, energy and resources to the evil purposes for which non-Muslims engage in warfare.

39. Observing that a small band of resourceless Muslims was getting ready to confront the powerful Quraysh, the hypocrites as well as those who were heedless of God and cared only for worldly interests, often tended to say to one another that the religious passion of the Muslims had driven them to utter fanaticism and zealotry. They were sure that the Muslims would face a total rout on the battlefield. They were puzzled by how the Prophet (peace be on him), in whom the Muslims believed, had cast such a spell over them that they were altogether incapable of rational calculation and were hence rushing straight into the very mouth of death.

40. Unless a nation renders itself totally unworthy of God's favour, it is not deprived of it.

(54) Their case is like that of the people of Pharaoh and those before them: they rejected the signs of their Lord as false and so We destroyed them for their sins, and caused the people of Pharaoh to drown. For they were wrong-doers all.

(55) Surely the worst moving creatures in the sight of Allah are those who definitively denied the truth and are therefore in no way prepared to accept it; (56) (especially) those with whom you entered into a covenant and then they broke their covenant time after time, and who do not fear Allah.[41]

كَدَأْبِ ءَالِ فِرْعَوْنَ وَالَّذِينَ مِن
قَبْلِهِمْ كَذَّبُوا بِـَٔايَٰتِ رَبِّهِمْ فَأَهْلَكْنَٰهُم
بِذُنُوبِهِمْ وَأَغْرَقْنَآ ءَالَ فِرْعَوْنَ وَكُلٌّ
كَانُوا ظَٰلِمِينَ ﴿٥٤﴾ إِنَّ شَرَّ الدَّوَآبِّ
عِندَ اللَّهِ الَّذِينَ كَفَرُوا فَهُمْ لَا يُؤْمِنُونَ
﴿٥٥﴾ الَّذِينَ عَٰهَدتَّ مِنْهُمْ ثُمَّ
يَنقُضُونَ عَهْدَهُمْ فِي كُلِّ مَرَّةٍ
وَهُمْ لَا يَتَّقُونَ ﴿٥٦﴾

41. This refers especially to the Jews. After arriving in Madina, the Prophet (peace be on him) concluded a treaty of mutual co-operation and good neighbourliness with them. Not only did the Prophet (peace be on him) take the initiative in this connection, he also tried his best to maintain pleasant relations with them. The Prophet (peace be on him) also felt greater affinity with the Jews than with the polytheists of Makka. As a rule he always showed preference to the customs and practices of the People of the Book over those of the polytheists. But somehow the Jewish rabbis and scholars were irked by the Prophet's preaching of pure monotheism and moral uprightness, let alone his scathing criticism of the deviations which appeared in Jewish belief and conduct. They were constantly engaged, therefore, in efforts to sabotage the new religious movement. In this respect, they left no stone unturned. They collaborated with the hypocrites who were apparently an integral part of the Muslim body-politic. To serve the same end they fanned flames to rejuvenate the old animosities between the Aws and Khazraj which had brought about bloodshed and fratricide in pre-Islamic times. They attempted to hatch conspiracies against Islam in collaboration with the Quraysh and other

(57) So if you meet them in war, make of them a fearsome example for those who follow them[42] that they may be admonished. (58) And if you fear treachery from any people (with whom you have a covenant) then publicly throw their covenant at them.[43] Allah does not love the treacherous. (59) Let not the deniers of the truth be deluded that they will gain any advantage. Surely they can never overcome Us!	فَإِمَّا تَثْقَفَنَّهُمْ فِي ٱلْحَرْبِ فَشَرِّدْ بِهِم مَّنْ خَلْفَهُمْ لَعَلَّهُمْ يَذَّكَّرُونَ ﴿٥٧﴾ وَإِمَّا تَخَافَنَّ مِن قَوْمٍ خِيَانَةً فَٱنۢبِذْ إِلَيْهِمْ عَلَىٰ سَوَآءٍ ۚ إِنَّ ٱللَّهَ لَا يُحِبُّ ٱلْخَآئِنِينَ ﴿٥٨﴾ وَلَا يَحْسَبَنَّ ٱلَّذِينَ كَفَرُوا۟ سَبَقُوٓا۟ ۚ إِنَّهُمْ لَا يُعْجِزُونَ ﴿٥٩﴾

tribes. What was all the more deplorable was that they indulged in these nefarious activities despite their treaty of friendship and co-operation with the Prophet (peace be on him).

When the Battle of Badr took place, they took it for granted that the Muslims would not be able to survive the very first attack of the Quraysh. However, when the outcome of the battle dashed their hopes, they became all the more spiteful. Apprehending that the victory in the Battle of Badr would help the Muslims consolidate their position, they carried out their hostile activities against Islam even more vigorously. Ka'b b. Ashraf, a Jewish chief, went to Makka personally and recited stirring elegies for their dead warriors with a view to provoking the Quraysh into hostile action against the Muslims. It was the same Ka'b b. Ashraf who considered the Muslim victory in the Battle of Badr such a catastrophe that he regarded death to be better than life. In his own words: 'The belly of the earth has become preferable to us than its back.' (Ibn Hishām, vol. 2, p. 51 – Ed.) Banū Qaynuqā', a Jewish tribe, in brazen violation of their agreement of friendship and alliance with the Muslims, took to indecent molestation and teasing the Muslim women who passed through their quarters. When the Prophet (peace be on him) reproached them for this shameful conduct, they threatened the Prophet (peace be on him), saying: 'Do not be deluded by your encounter with a people who had no knowledge of warfare, and so you had good luck with them. By God, if we were to wage war against you, you will know that we are the men.' (Ibn Hishām, vol. 2, p. 47 – Ed.)

42. The verse makes it lawful for Muslims to feel absolved of the obligations of a treaty with a people who, despite that alliance, threw the

obligations of the treaty overboard and engaged in hostile actions against the Muslims. It would even be lawful for the Muslims to engage in hostilities against them. Likewise, if the Muslims are engaged in hostilities against a people and the non-Muslims who are bound in treaties of alliance or friendship with the Muslims, array themselves on the side of the enemy and fight against the Muslims, it would be lawful for the Muslims to treat them as enemies and kill them. For by their brazen violation of the obligations of the treaty concluded with their people, they had made it absolutely lawful for Muslims to disregard the terms of that treaty concerning the inviolability of the lives and properties of at least those individuals.

43. According to the above verse, it is not lawful for Muslims to decide unilaterally that their treaty with an ally is annulled either because of their grievance that their ally did not fully observe the terms of the treaty in the past or on ground of the fear that he would treacherously breach it in the future. There is no justification for Muslims to make such a decision nor to behave as if no treaty bound the two parties. On the contrary, whenever the Muslims are forced into such a situation they are required to inform the other party, before embarking on any hostile action, that the treaty was terminated. This step is necessary in order that both parties are clear in their minds as to where things stand. Guided by this principle, the Prophet (peace be on him) laid down a basic rule of Islamic international law in the following words: 'Whoever is bound in treaty with a people may not dissolve it until either its term expires, or he flings it at them (i.e. publicly declares that it had been annulled).' (Abū Dā'ūd, 'Jihād', Bāb fī al-Imām yakūn baynahā wa bayn al-'Adūw 'Ahd, vol. 2, p. 75; Aḥmad b. Ḥanbal, *Musnad,* vol. 4, pp. 111 and 113 – Ed.) The Prophet (peace be on him) further elucidated this by saying: 'Do not be treacherous even to him who is treacherous to you' (Abū Dā'ūd, 'Kitāb al-Būyū'', 'Bāb fī al-Rajul Ya'khudh Ḥaqqahū man taḥt Yadih', vol. 2, p. 260 – Ed.)

These directives were not given merely in order that preachers might preach them from the pulpit or embellish them in religious books. On the contrary, Muslims were required to follow these directives in their everyday lives, and they did in fact do so. Once Mu'āwiyah, during his reign, concentrated his troops on the borders of the Roman Empire in order to carry out a sudden attack immediately after the expiry of the treaty. 'Amr b. 'Anbasah, a Companion, strongly opposed this manoeuvre. He supported his opposition by reference to a tradition from the Prophet (peace be on him) in which he condemned such an act of treachery. Ultimately Mu'āwiyah had to yield and call off his troops. (See the comments on the verse by Qurṭubī and Ibn Kathīr. See also Aḥmad b. Ḥanbal, *Musnad,* vol. 4, pp. 113 and 389 – Ed.)

To annul a treaty unilaterally and to launch an armed attack without any warning was common practice in the time of ancient *Jāhilīyah* (Ignorance). That practice remains in vogue in the 'civilized' *Jāhilīyah* of the present day as well. Recent instances in point are the Russian invasion of Germany and the Russian and British military action against Iran during the Second World War. Such actions are usually justified on the ground that a previous warning would have put the enemy on the alert and would have enabled him to put up even stiffer resistance. It is also justified by saying that a military initiative has the effect of pre-empting a similar military initiative by the enemy. If such pleading can absolve people of their moral obligations, then every offence is justifiable. In such a case even those who commit theft, robbery, illegitimate sexual intercourse, homicide, or forgery can proffer either one pretext or the other for so doing. It is also amazing that acts which are deemed unlawful for individuals are deemed perfectly lawful when they are committed by nations.

It should also be pointed out that an unannounced attack, according to Islamic law, is lawful in one situation: when the ally has clearly violated the treaty and has blatantly indulged in hostile action. Only in such an eventuality it is not binding on Muslims to first declare the dissolution of the treaty. Not only that, in such a circumstance it is also lawful to launch an unannounced military action. In deriving this legal rule, Muslim jurists have drawn on the Prophet's own conduct in regard to the Quraysh who had breached the Ḥudaybīyah Treaty in dealing with Banū Khuzā'ah. In this instance the Prophet (peace be on him) did not notify them that the treaty had been annulled. On the contrary, he invaded Makka without warning. (See Qurṭubī's comments on the verse – Ed.) Nonetheless, while acting on this exceptional provision one should be cautious and take into account the totality of circumstances in which the Prophet (peace be on him) took this step. That alone will help one to properly follow the Prophet's example. For one should try to imitate the Prophet's example in its totality rather than just one or other aspect of it depending on one's whim. What we know from the *Sīrah* and *Ḥadīth* with regard to this is the following:

First, that the Quraysh had so openly violated the treaty that its annulment had become absolutely clear. Even men of the Quraysh themselves acknowledged that the treaty was no longer in operation. It is because of this realization that the Quraysh had deputed Abū Sufyān to Madina to negotiate for its renewal (Al-Ṭabarī, *Ta'rīkh,* vol. 3, p. 46 – Ed.) This fact clearly indicates that the Quraysh were in no doubt that the treaty stood dissolved. It is immaterial whether the party which annulled the treaty verbally declared so or not for it had been violated so blatantly that no room for doubt was left.

Second, after the annulment of the treaty the Prophet (peace be on him) did not say anything, either in clear or ambiguous terms, which could justify the impression that he still regarded the Quraysh to be his allies or that the treaty relations with them were still intact. All relevant reports, on the contrary, suggest that when Abū Sufyān pleaded for the renewal of the treaty, the Prophet (peace be on him) did not accede to that request. (Ibn Hishām, vol. 2, p. 395 – Ed.)

(60) Make ready for an encounter against them all the forces and well-readied horses you can muster[44] that you may overawe the enemies of Allah and your own enemies and others besides them of whom you are unaware but of whom Allah is aware. Whatever you may spend in the cause of Allah shall be fully repaid to you, and you shall not be wronged.	وَأَعِدُّوا۟ لَهُم مَّا ٱسْتَطَعْتُم مِّن قُوَّةٍ وَمِن رِّبَاطِ ٱلْخَيْلِ تُرْهِبُونَ بِهِۦ عَدُوَّ ٱللَّهِ وَعَدُوَّكُمْ وَءَاخَرِينَ مِن دُونِهِمْ لَا تَعْلَمُونَهُمُ ٱللَّهُ يَعْلَمُهُمْ وَمَا تُنفِقُوا۟ مِن شَىْءٍ فِى سَبِيلِ ٱللَّهِ يُوَفَّ إِلَيْكُمْ وَأَنتُمْ لَا تُظْلَمُونَ ٦٠

Third, the Prophet (peace be on him) himself initiated military action against the Quraysh and he did so openly. There was no element of duplicity or fraud in the Prophet's behaviour; there was no trace of pretence to be at peace while secretly engaging in belligerent activities.

This is the full picture of the Prophet's attitude on the occasion. Hence the directive of flinging the treaty in the face of the other party as embodied in the above verse (i.e. informing the other party that the treaty had been terminated) may only be disregarded in very special circumstances such as those existing then. And should it be disregarded then this should be done in the straightforward and graceful manner adopted by the Prophet (peace be on him).

Moreover, if some dispute arises with a people with whom the Muslims have a treaty and the dispute remains unresolved even after direct negotiations or international mediation; or if the other party appears bent upon forcing a military solution to the problem, it would be lawful for Muslims to resort to force. However, according to the above verse, force may be used by Muslims after making a clear proclamation of the annulment of the treaty, and that the action taken should be overt. To carry out military action by stealth is an immoral act and can nowhere be found among the teachings of Islam.

44. Muslims should be equipped with military resources and should have a standing army in a state of preparedness, in order that it may be used when needed. Never should it happen that the Muslims are caught unawares and have to hurriedly look around right and left to build up their defences

(61) If they incline to peace, incline you as well to it, and trust in Allah. Surely He is All-Hearing, All-Knowing.

(62) And should they seek to deceive you, Allah is sufficient for you.[45] He it is Who strengthened you with His succour and the believers (63) and joined their hearts. Had you given away all the riches of the earth you could not have joined their hearts, but it is Allah Who joined their hearts.[46] Indeed He is All-Mighty, All-Wise. (64) O Prophet! Allah is sufficient for you and the believers who follow you.

۞ وَإِن جَنَحُوا لِلسَّلْمِ فَاجْنَحْ لَهَا
وَتَوَكَّلْ عَلَى اللَّهِ ۚ إِنَّهُ هُوَ السَّمِيعُ الْعَلِيمُ
٦١ وَإِن يُرِيدُوا أَن يَخْدَعُوكَ فَإِنَّ
حَسْبَكَ اللَّهُ ۚ هُوَ الَّذِي أَيَّدَكَ بِنَصْرِهِ
وَبِالْمُؤْمِنِينَ ٦٢ وَأَلَّفَ بَيْنَ
قُلُوبِهِمْ ۚ لَوْ أَنفَقْتَ مَا فِي الْأَرْضِ
جَمِيعًا مَّا أَلَّفْتَ بَيْنَ قُلُوبِهِمْ
وَلَٰكِنَّ اللَّهَ أَلَّفَ بَيْنَهُمْ ۚ إِنَّهُ
عَزِيزٌ حَكِيمٌ ٦٣ يَا أَيُّهَا النَّبِيُّ
حَسْبُكَ اللَّهُ وَمَنِ اتَّبَعَكَ مِنَ
الْمُؤْمِنِينَ ٦٤

---

and collect arms and supplies in order to meet the challenge of the enemy. For then it might be too late and the enemy might have accomplished its purpose.

45. In international dealings Muslims should not act with timidity. They should rather have faith in God and should act with courage and bravery. However, as soon as the enemy is inclined to reconciliation, they should welcome the move and should not be reluctant to make peace even if they are unsure whether or not the enemy is sincere about peace, and whether or not he intends to use the settlement as a ruse to commit later treachery. Since it is impossible to know the true intention of others, allowance should be made for their words. If the enemy is sincere in his offer of reconciliation, the Muslims should not continue bloodshed because his sincerity, in their eyes, is suspect. On the contrary, if the enemy is insincere, the Muslims should have courage, thanks to their trust in God, and should go forth for reconciliation. They should stretch out the hand of peace in answer to the enemy's outstretched hand, for that is an index of their moral superiority. As for the hand of friendship which has been hypocritically stretched out in enmity, Muslims should have the strength to smash that hand to pieces.

(65) O Prophet! Rouse the believers to fighting. If there be twenty of you who persevere, they shall vanquish two hundred; and if there be of you a hundred, they shall vanquish a thousand of those who disbelieve, for they are a people who lack understanding.[47]

يَٰٓأَيُّهَا ٱلنَّبِيُّ حَرِّضِ ٱلْمُؤْمِنِينَ عَلَى ٱلْقِتَالِ ۚ إِن يَكُن مِّنكُمْ عِشْرُونَ صَٰبِرُونَ يَغْلِبُوا۟ مِا۟ئَتَيْنِ ۚ وَإِن يَكُن مِّنكُم مِّا۟ئَةٌ يَغْلِبُوٓا۟ أَلْفًا مِّنَ ٱلَّذِينَ كَفَرُوا۟ بِأَنَّهُمْ قَوْمٌ لَّا يَفْقَهُونَ ﴿٦٥﴾

46. Here the allusion is to that strong bond of love and brotherhood that developed among the Arabs who embraced Islam and whose conversion brought them solidarity. This strong solidarity existed despite the fact that they came from a variety of tribes which had long-standing traditions of mutual enmity. This was a special favour of God on the Muslims, especially evident in the case of the Aws and the Khazraj. It was barely a couple of years before their acceptance of Islam that the two clans virtually thirsted for each other's blood. During the Battle of Buʿāth both seemed set to totally exterminate each other. (Ibn Hishām, vol. 1, pp. 427–8 – Ed.) To turn such severe enmity into deep cordiality and brotherhood within a span of two or three years and to join together mutually repellent elements into a unity as firm as that of a solid wall as was witnessed in regard to the Muslim community during the life of the Prophet (peace be on him) was doubtlessly beyond the power of any mortal. Were anyone to depend on worldly factors alone, it would have been impossible to bring about such an achievement. God's support was the deciding factor in this development and this only serves to emphasize that Muslims should always seek and depend on God's support and favour rather than on worldly factors.

47. What is nowadays called morale has been described as 'understanding' in the Qur'ān. The Qur'ānic expression is more scientific than the currently used word 'morale'. For the word in this context refers to the one who is fully cognizant of his objective, who is quite clear in his mind that the cause for which he has staked his life is much more valuable than his own life, and hence if that cause is left unrealized, his life will lose all its worth and meaning. Such a conscious, committed person actually becomes many times more powerful than he who fights without any consciousness of his cause, even though the two might be comparable in physical strength. Above all, he who has a clear understanding of the reality

(66) Allah has now lightened your burden for He found weakness in you. So if there be a hundred of you who persevere, they shall vanquish two hundred; and if there be a thousand of you they shall, by the leave of Allah, vanquish two thousand.[48] Allah is with those who persevere.

ٱلْـَٔـٰنَ خَفَّفَ ٱللَّهُ عَنكُمْ وَعَلِمَ أَنَّ
فِيكُمْ ضَعْفًا ۚ فَإِن يَكُن مِّنكُم مِّا۟ئَةٌ
صَابِرَةٌ يَغْلِبُوا۟ مِا۟ئَتَيْنِ ۚ وَإِن يَكُن مِّنكُمْ
أَلْفٌ يَغْلِبُوٓا۟ أَلْفَيْنِ بِإِذْنِ ٱللَّهِ ۗ وَٱللَّهُ
مَعَ ٱلصَّـٰبِرِينَ ﴿٦٦﴾

of his own being, of God, of his relationship with God, of the reality of life and death, and of life after death, who is also well aware of the difference between truth and falsehood, and of the consequences of the victory of falsehood over truth, his strength surpasses by far the strength of others for whom, even though they 'understand', their consciousness is related to nationalism or patriotism or class conflict. It is for this reason that the Qur'ān declares that a believer with understanding is ten times stronger than an unbeliever. For the believer understands the truth and a non-believer does not. It may be remembered, however, that the verse also mentions another important factor in addition to 'understanding' which makes a believer much stronger than an unbeliever, and that is 'patience'.

48. This does not mean that since the faith of Muslims had declined, their ten times superiority over the unbelievers had been reduced to twice only. What it means is that ideally a Muslim is ten times stronger than an unbeliever. However, since the Muslims had not as yet been thoroughly trained and had not reached the desired level of maturity in their understanding, they are asked not to feel uneasy at least of challenging an enemy which is twice as strong. It should be borne in mind that the Qur'ānic directive was given in 2 A.H./624 C.E. when most of the Muslims, being recent converts to Islam, had undergone little training. As they gained maturity under the Prophet's guidance, the desired ratio of one to ten between the Muslims and the unbelievers was established. That Muslims are ten times stronger than unbelievers is a fact witnessed frequently in the battles during the life of the Prophet (peace be on him) and of the Rightly-Guided Caliphs.

(67) It behoves not a Prophet to take captives until he has sufficiently suppressed the enemies in the land. You merely seek the gains of the world whereas Allah desires (for you the good) of the Hereafter. Allah is All-Mighty, All-Wise. (68) Had there not been a previous decree from Allah, a stern punishment would have afflicted you for what you have taken. (69) So eat that which you have obtained – for it is lawful and clean – and fear Allah.[49] Surely Allah is Ever-Forgiving, Most Merciful.

مَا كَانَ لِنَبِيٍّ أَن يَكُونَ لَهُۥٓ أَسْرَىٰ حَتَّىٰ
يُثْخِنَ فِى ٱلْأَرْضِ ۚ تُرِيدُونَ عَرَضَ
ٱلدُّنْيَا وَٱللَّهُ يُرِيدُ ٱلْءَاخِرَةَ ۗ وَٱللَّهُ عَزِيزٌ
حَكِيمٌ ﴿٦٧﴾ لَّوْلَا كِتَـٰبٌ مِّنَ ٱللَّهِ سَبَقَ
لَمَسَّكُمْ فِيمَآ أَخَذْتُمْ عَذَابٌ عَظِيمٌ ﴿٦٨﴾
فَكُلُوا۟ مِمَّا غَنِمْتُمْ حَلَـٰلًا طَيِّبًا ۚ وَٱتَّقُوا۟
ٱللَّهَ ۚ إِنَّ ٱللَّهَ غَفُورٌ رَّحِيمٌ ﴿٦٩﴾

49. In attempting to explain the circumstantial background of the above verse, some commentators on the Qur'ān have referred to the deliberations for deciding the fate of the Quraysh captives after the Battle of Badr. In that council Abū Bakr pleaded to release the captives in return for ransom while 'Umar suggested that they should be put to the sword. Preferring Abū Bakr's suggestion, the Prophet (peace be on him) set all the captives free in return for ransom. However, God disapproved the decision as is evident from the above-quoted verse. (See Muslim, 'Jihād', 'Bāb al-Imdād bi al-Malā'ikah fī Ghazwah Badr'; and the comments on verses 67 and 68 by Ibn Kathīr; and on verse 67 by Jaṣṣāṣ and Qurṭubī – Ed.) The viewpoint of the commentators can be faulted on the grounds that they failed to offer any persuasive explanation of this part of the same Qur'ānic verse: 'Had it not been for a previous decree from Allah.' This could mean either the Divine decree in eternity which determines all that will happen, or, God's decree in eternity to make the spoils of war lawful for the Muslims. Now, it is evident that it is unlawful to take anything from someone unless it has been declared lawful according to Revealed Law. Hence, were the above view to be accepted, it would mean that all, including the Prophet (peace be on him), had committed a sin. Such an interpretation can hardly be

(70) O Prophet! Say to the captives in your hands: 'If Allah finds any goodness in your hearts He will give you that which is better than what has been taken away from you, and He will forgive you. Allah is Ever-Forgiving, Most Merciful.' (71) But if they seek to betray you, know that they had already betrayed Allah. Therefore He made you prevail over them. Allah is All-Knowing, All-Wise.

يَٰٓأَيُّهَا ٱلنَّبِيُّ قُل لِّمَن فِيٓ أَيۡدِيكُم مِّنَ
ٱلۡأَسۡرَىٰٓ إِن يَعۡلَمِ ٱللَّهُ فِي قُلُوبِكُمۡ
خَيۡرٗا يُؤۡتِكُمۡ خَيۡرٗا مِّمَّآ أُخِذَ مِنكُمۡ
وَيَغۡفِرۡ لَكُمۡۚ وَٱللَّهُ غَفُورٞ رَّحِيمٞ ٧٠
وَإِن يُرِيدُواْ خِيَانَتَكَ فَقَدۡ خَانُواْ
ٱللَّهَ مِن قَبۡلُ فَأَمۡكَنَ مِنۡهُمۡۗ وَٱللَّهُ عَلِيمٌ
حَكِيمٌ ٧١

entertained especially since this view is dependent on the authority of isolated *(āḥād)* traditions.

In my opinion, in order to understand the above verse it should be borne in mind that preliminary instructions about war had already been given in *Sūrah Muḥammad* which was revealed before the Battle of Badr:

> Therefore, when you meet, the Unbelievers (in fight), smite at their necks. At length, when you have thoroughly subdued them, bind a bond firmly (on them). Thereafter, either resort to generosity or to ransom until the war lays down its burden (*Muḥammad* 47: 4).

This verse had already made it lawful for the Muslims to hold the enemy in captivity or to accept ransom contingent on the total suppression of the enemy. The Muslims had, therefore, acted in accordance with the permission granted by God to accept ransom. However, in so doing they had neglected the stipulation that the enemy should be fully subdued before the acceptance of ransom. (See the comments of Jaṣṣāṣ on verses 67–9 – Ed.) While the Quraysh army was retreating, many Muslims took to collecting the spoils and taking the unbelievers as captives. It was only a few Muslims who chased the fleeing enemy. Had the Muslims made a concerted pursuit, a death-blow could have been struck at the Quraysh power, once and for all. God, therefore expressed His disapproval of this manner of dealing with the situation as the above-quoted verse suggests. It is obvious that it is not the Prophet (peace be on him) but the generality of Muslims at whom the reproach is directed.

(72) Surely those who believed and migrated and strove hard in the way of Allah with their possessions and their lives, and those that sheltered and helped them – they alone are the true allies of one another.	إِنَّ ٱلَّذِينَ ءَامَنُواْ وَهَاجَرُواْ وَجَٰهَدُواْ بِأَمْوَٰلِهِمْ وَأَنفُسِهِمْ فِى سَبِيلِ ٱللَّهِ وَٱلَّذِينَ ءَاوَواْ وَّنَصَرُوٓاْ أُوْلَٰٓئِكَ بَعْضُهُمْ أَوْلِيَآءُ بَعْضٍ

The purpose of the verse is to impress upon the Muslims that they had not yet imbibed the mission of the Prophet (peace be on him). Prophets are not concerned with filling their coffers with spoils and ransom money. Rather their mission is to crush the power of the unbelievers. This was not the first instance when the Muslims had showed their worldliness. They had earlier expressed their preference to raid the trade caravan to fighting against the Quraysh army. Then, rather than try to crush the enemy, they turned to collecting spoils and taking captives, and later remonstrated about the distribution of booty. Had it not been that God had granted them permission to accept ransom (see *Muḥammad* 47: 4), He would have severely punished them on that count. God, however, was merciful to them and permitted them to enjoy whatever they had seized. They should, therefore, refrain from behaviour which might be displeasing to God. It is pertinent to point out that Jaṣṣāṣ in his *Aḥkām al-Qur'ān*, considers the above view a plausible interpretation of the verse. (See the comments of Jaṣṣāṣ on this verse, vol. 3, pp. 72–3 – Ed.) Ibn Hishām also contains a report which supports the view. The report mentions that while the Muslims were engaged in seizing captives of war and collecting booty, the Prophet (peace be on him) observed signs of disapproval on the face of Sa'd b. Mu'ādh. The Prophet (peace be on him) asked him: 'O Sa'd! It appears that you do not approve of the behaviour of these people.' He replied: 'Yes, O Messenger of God! It is the first encounter in which God has caused the rout of the unbelievers. This opportunity should have been better utilized for crushing the unbelievers thoroughly rather than for amassing captives of war.' (Ibn Hishām, vol. 1, p. 628 – Ed.)

And those who believed but did not migrate (to *Dār al-Islām*), you are under no obligation of alliance unless they migrate.[50] And should they seek help from you in the matter of religion, it is incumbent on you to provide help unless it be against a people with whom you have a pact.[51] Allah is cognizant of all that you do. ▶

وَالَّذِينَ ءَامَنُوا وَلَمْ يُهَاجِرُوا مَا لَكُم
مِّن وَلَٰيَتِهِم مِّن شَيْءٍ حَتَّىٰ يُهَاجِرُوا
وَإِنِ اسْتَنصَرُوكُمْ فِي الدِّينِ
فَعَلَيْكُمُ النَّصْرُ إِلَّا عَلَىٰ قَوْمٍ
بَيْنَكُمْ وَبَيْنَهُم مِّيثَٰقٌ وَاللَّهُ بِمَا
تَعْمَلُونَ بَصِيرٌ ﴿٧٢﴾

50. The above verse is an important provision in Islamic constitutional law. For it prescribes that any agreement on guardianship would be applicable exclusively to Muslims who are either the original inhabitants of the territory which has become *Dār al-Islām* (the Domain of Islam) or Muslims who have migrated to the *Dār al-Islām.* As to Muslims living outside the jurisdiction of the Islamic state, the bond of religious brotherhood would doubtlessly exist between them and Muslim residents of the Islamic state. The two groups, however, would not have the relationship of *walāyah* (mutual alliance). Likewise, a *walāyah* relationship would not exist between Muslims who do not migrate to *Dār al-Islām* but come to it as Muslim subjects of a non-Muslim state.

The Arabic word *walāyah* denotes the relationship of kinship, support, succour, protection, friendship, and guardianship. In the context of the present verse the word signifies the relationship of mutual support between the Islamic state and its citizens, and between the citizens themselves. Thus, this verse lays down that in a political and constitutional sense, only those Muslims who live within the territorial boundaries of the Islamic state will enjoy the privileges of *walāyah* (guardianship) of the Islamic state. As for Muslims who are settled in a non-Islamic state, they are excluded from its political and constitutional guardianship.

It is difficult to spell out in detail the implications of this rule. Just to give some idea of it, it should be pointed out that because they lack guardianship the Muslims of *Dār al-Kufr* (the Domain of Unbelief) cannot inherit the property of a deceased Muslim in the Islamic state. Nor may they act as guardians of Muslim citizens of an Islamic state. Nor is it lawful for a matrimonial contract to be made between Muslims, one of whom is living in an Islamic state and the other outside of it. Likewise, the Islamic state may not appoint to an office of authority those who have not surrendered their citizenship of the non-Islamic state. Above all, these

(73) And those who disbelieve, they are allies of one another; and unless you act likewise, there will be oppression in the world and great corruption.[52]	وَٱلَّذِينَ كَفَرُواْ بَعْضُهُمْ أَوْلِيَآءُ بَعْضٍ إِلَّا تَفْعَلُوهُ تَكُن فِتْنَةٌ فِى ٱلْأَرْضِ وَفَسَادٌ كَبِيرٌ ﴿٧٣﴾

provisions of Islamic law determine the foreign policy of the Islamic state. (Cf. Ibn Qudāmah, *al-Mughnī*, vol. 8, pp. 456–8 – Ed.) Since this clause restricts the role and control of the Islamic state over Muslims living within that state, the Islamic state is not obliged to look after the Muslims outside its domain. The following tradition embodies this point: 'I am acquit of every Muslim living among the polytheists.' (Abū Dā'ūd, 'Jihād', 'Bāb al-Nahy 'an Qatl man i'taṣama bi al-Sujūd – Ed.) Islamic law, therefore, strikes at the root cause of the conflict which bedevils the relationship between different nations. For, whenever a state tries to champion the cause of the minority living outside its territory, it gives rise to intricate problems which cannot be resolved even by a succession of wars.

51. The above verse makes it clear that the Muslims living outside the Islamic state have no political bond with the Islamic state. This verse, however, does emphasize that those Muslims are not free of the bond of religious brotherhood. If Muslims living in a non-Islamic state are persecuted and seek help from the Islamic state or its citizens, it is incumbent upon the latter to help the persecuted Muslims.

While helping one's brethren-in-faith the Muslims are expected to act scrupulously. This help should be rendered without violating international obligations and with due regard to the requirements of moral propriety. If the Islamic state happens to be bound in a treaty relationship with a nation which inflicts wrong on Muslims, the oppressed Muslims will not be helped in a manner which is inconsistent with the moral obligations incumbent on the Islamic state as a result of that treaty.

The Qur'ān uses the word *mīthāq* for treaty. This expression is a derivative of an Arabic word which stands for trust and confidence. The expression, therefore, implies that the two parties trust each other, that there is no difference between them irrespective of whether a no-war agreement has been formally concluded or not.

The actual words of the verse بينكم وبينهم ميثاق ('[unless there be] a pact between you and them') make it plain that the treaty concluded by the Islamic state with a non-Muslim state does not merely bind the two governments. The moral obligations arising from that treaty are binding

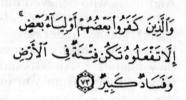

(74) Those who believe and have migrated and strove in the way of Allah, and those who gave them refuge and help – it is they who are the true believers. Theirs shall be forgiveness and honourable sustenance. (75) And those who believed afterwards and migrated and strove along with you: they belong to you. But those related by blood are nearer to one another according to the Book of Allah.[53] Allah has knowledge of everything.

وَالَّذِينَ ءَامَنُوا وَهَاجَرُوا وَجَٰهَدُوا
فِي سَبِيلِ اللَّهِ وَالَّذِينَ ءَاوَوا وَّنَصَرُوٓا
أُوْلَٰٓئِكَ هُمُ الْمُؤْمِنُونَ حَقًّا لَّهُم مَّغْفِرَةٌ
وَرِزْقٌ كَرِيمٌ ﴿٧٤﴾ وَالَّذِينَ ءَامَنُوا مِنۢ
بَعْدُ وَهَاجَرُوا وَجَٰهَدُوا مَعَكُمْ فَأُوْلَٰٓئِكَ
مِنكُمْ وَأُوْلُوا الْأَرْحَامِ بَعْضُهُمْ أَوْلَىٰ
بِبَعْضٍ فِي كِتَٰبِ اللَّهِ إِنَّ اللَّهَ بِكُلِّ شَيْءٍ
عَلِيمٌ ﴿٧٥﴾

---

upon the Muslim nation as a whole including its individuals not to violate the obligations of the treaty into which an Islamic state has entered with some other state. However, it is only the Muslims of the Islamic state who are bound by the agreement signed by the Islamic state. Muslims living outside the Islamic state have no such obligations. This accounts for the fact that Abū Baṣīr and Abū Jandal were not bound by the Ḥudaybīyah treaty concluded between the Prophet (peace be on him) and the Makkan unbelievers.

52. If the words 'unless you also help one another' in the verse are regarded as a continuation of the preceding verse, they would mean that if Muslims do not support each other in the way unbelievers do, this would give rise to much mischief and disorder in the world. However, if these words are considered to be connected with the directives embodied in verse 72 onwards, their purpose would be to emphasize that the world would become full of mischief and disorder if the Muslims of *Dār al-Islām* (a) failed to help one another; (b) failed to provide political support and protection to the Muslims who have settled down in non-Islamic states and have not migrated to *Dār al-Islām*; (c) failed to help the Muslims living under oppression in territories outside *Dār al-Islām* when they ask for it; and (d) failed to sever their friendly ties with the unbelievers.

53. The purpose of the verse is to make it clear that the basis of inheritance is blood relationship and marriage rather than the mere bond of Islamic brotherhood. What occasioned this statement was the misunderstanding which had arisen after migration to Madina, when the Prophet (peace be on him) establisned fraternal relations between the *Anṣār* and the *Muhājirūn* and made pairs of them declaring that they were 'brothers' of each other. (See Ibn Hishām, vol. 1, pp. 504–6 – Ed.)

Sūrah 9

Al-Tawbah

(Madinan Period)

Title

This *sūrah* has two titles, *al-Tawbah* and *al-Barā'ah*. The former title owes its origin to the reference in the *sūrah* to God's pardoning of lapses committed by some believers (see verse 117); and the latter title to the public dissolution of all treaty obligations with the Polytheists mentioned in the opening verse of the *sūrah*.

It is noteworthy that the usual opening formula, *Bi ism Allāh al-Raḥmān al-Raḥīm* ('In the name of Allah, the Compassionate, the Merciful') is not prefixed to this *sūrah*. Commentators on the Qur'ān have attributed a number of different reasons for this. Of these the explanation given by Fakhr al-Dīn al-Rāzī seems to be the most plausible: as the Prophet (peace be on him) did not direct his scribes to prefix the formula, his Companions and Successors also omitted it. Succeeding generations similarly adhered to the omission. (See Rāzī's introductory remarks to this *sūrah* in his *Tafsīr* – Ed.) This demonstrates how the Muslims painstakingly sought to receive the Qur'ānic text from the Prophet (peace be on him) exactly as it was revealed, and the care which they took to preserve it in its pristine form.

Period of Revelation and Contents

The *sūrah* comprises three discourses.

The first discourse runs from the opening verse to the fifth section of the *sūrah* (i.e. verses 1–37 – Ed.) It was revealed in or around Dhu al-Qa'dah 9 A.H./631 C.E., soon after the Prophet (peace be on him) dispatched Abū Bakr as the leader of the Pilgrims to Makka. After the verses had been revealed, the Prophet (peace be on him) instructed 'Alī to follow Abū Bakr and to recite the same verses proclaiming the new directives embodied in them before a representative gathering of Arabs who had gone there for Pilgrimage.

The second discourse covers sections six to nine of the *sūrah* (i.e. verses 38–72 – Ed.) It was revealed in or around Rajab 9 A.H./631 C.E. when the Prophet (peace be on him) was busy making his preparations for an expedition to Tabūk. The discourse seeks to arouse the believers to wage *jihād*, and reproaches severely those who, out of hypocrisy or infirmity of their faith, or out of sheer sloth and laziness, were reluctant to risk their lives and wealth in God's cause.

Beginning with section ten (verse 73 ff.), the third discourse runs up to the end of the *sūrah*. Revealed upon the Prophet's return from the Tabūk expedition, it consists of several fragments which were revealed on different occasions during that period, and which, under God's own instruction, were arranged by the Prophet (peace be on him) in the form of a coherent discourse. Since all these fragments centre around a common subject, and are related to the same set of events, any incongruity does not arise. The third discourse warns the hypocrites about their misdeeds and strongly censures those who, on the occasion of the expedition to Tabūk, had stayed behind. The verses also embody a combination of reproach and pardon for the believers who, even though they were sincere in their faith, had abstained from waging *jihād* in God's cause.

Chronologically, the first discourse should have come at the end of the *sūrah*. However, in view of the significance of its contents, the Prophet (peace be on him) in arranging the Qur'ānic text placed it at the beginning of the *sūrah*.

Historical Background

Having discussed the *sūrah*'s period of the revelation, let us now look at its historical setting.

The contents of the *sūrah* are related to events arising from the Treaty of Ḥudaybīyah (6 A.H./628 C.E). By the time this treaty was concluded, the struggle which had carried on for six long years had begun to bear fruit and Islam had emerged as the basis of an organized society, the inspiring force of a distinct cultural entity, and the guiding principle of a fully-fledged, sovereign state. The relatively peaceful atmosphere created by the Treaty of Ḥudaybīyah enabled Islam to propagate its teachings far and wide. (For a more detailed treatment of this, see the introductory remarks to *sūrahs al-Mā'idah* 5 and *al-Fatḥ* 48.) The subsequent course of events followed two quite different directions but led to dire consequences. One of these concerned Arabia, and the other the Byzantine Empire.

A number of effective measures were taken by the Muslims after the conclusion of the Treaty to propagate Islam and consolidate and reinforce Muslim power. The result was that within a period of two years Islam had spread considerably and had become so immensely powerful that in comparison to Islam the age-old *Jāhilīyah* of Arabia was reduced to an utterly ineffectual position. Eventually, when the more zealous members of the Quraysh found themselves on the verge of defeat, they lost all patience and broke the Treaty of Ḥudaybīyah. By so doing they wanted to free themselves from the constraints of the Treaty and prepare for a decisive encounter with Islam. The Prophet (peace be on him), however, did not allow the Quraysh to seize the initiative. Launching a sudden attack on Makka in Ramaḍān 8 A.H./629 C.E. he was able to seize it. (See *sūrah* 8, n. 43 above.) Later, the ancient *Jāhilīyah* of Arabia resorted to desperate acts of belligerency. On the occasion of the Battle of Ḥunayn other tribes loyal to *Jāhilīyah* mustered their military forces together in a bid to prevent the spread of Islam's reformative revolution which, after the capture of Makka, had almost reached its zenith. Their efforts, however, came to naught and their defeat made it abundantly evident that Arabia was destined to become and remain *Dār al-Islām*. Hardly one year had passed after the Battle of Ḥunayn than the greater part of Arabia entered the fold of Islam. The power of *Jāhilīyah* lay shattered. Only a few opponents remained in the arena, and the ones that could still be found lay scattered across the peninsula, unable to wield any mentionable influence.

Events which took place on the borders of the Byzantine Empire in the north contributed to this trend. The Prophet (peace be on him) showed exceptional courage when he led a thirty thousand-strong force against the Byzantine army. By contrast, the Byzantine forces demonstrated timidity insofar as they chose to avoid armed conflict with the Muslims. As a result both the Prophet (peace be on him) and his faith were held in awe throughout Arabia. Upon the Prophet's return from Tabūk, delegation after delegation poured into Madina from every corner of the peninsula, embracing Islam and committing themselves to obey the Prophet (peace be on him).* This development has been portrayed in the Qur'ān in the following words:

> When there comes to you help from Allah, and victory, and you see people enter the religion of Allah in crowds . . . (*al-Naṣr* 110: 1–2).

Conflict with the Byzantine Empire had begun even before the conquest of Makka. After the Treaty of Ḥudaybīyah the Prophet (peace be on him) sent many delegations to different parts of Arabia calling people to Islam. One such delegation went to the tribes inhabiting land close to the Syrian border in the north. These tribes were mainly Christians and were largely under the influence of the Byzantine Empire. They put fifteen members of the delegation to the sword at a place called Dhāt al-Ṭalaḥ (or Dhāt Aṭlāḥ). Only the leader of the delegation, Ka'b ibn 'Umayr al-Ghifārī, managed to return home safely. (See Wāqidī, vol. 2, pp. 752–3; Ibn Sa'd, vol. 2, pp. 127–8 – Ed.) Around the same period the Prophet (peace be on him) sent an envoy, Ḥārith ibn 'Umayr, to Shuraḥbīl ibn 'Amr, the chief of Buṣrá, in order to communicate to him the message of Islam. Shuraḥbīl, who was both a tribal chief and a satrap of the Byzantine Empire, was responsible for the assassination of the Prophet's envoy, Ḥārith. (See Ibn Sa'd, vol. 2, p. 128 – Ed.)

In these circumstances the Prophet (peace be on him) sent a three thousand-strong army of devotees towards the Syrian border in Jumād al-Awwal 8 A.H./629 C.E. This action was intended to secure the area for the Muslims and to deter the opponents of Islam from committing excesses against them should they mistakenly consider that the Muslims lacked strength.

When the army approached Ma'ān, reports were received that Shuraḥbīl was advancing towards them with a hundred thousand-strong army. Reports were also received that the Caesar of Rome was himself present at Ḥims, and that he had dispatched reinforcements to the tune of another hundred thousand under the command of his younger brother, Theodore. Against all odds the three thousand-strong Muslim contingent continued to advance and clashed with Shuraḥbīl's army, a hundred thousand strong, at Mu'tah. (For details of the expedition of Mu'tah see Ibn Sa'd, vol. 2, pp. 128–30; Wāqidī, vol. 2, pp. 755–79; and Ibn Hishām, vol. 2, pp. 373–89 – Ed.)

*The traditionists have mentioned here seventy delegations comprised of ordinary tribesmen, chiefs and princes from all areas of Arabia.

MAP NO. 6: ARABIA AT THE TIME OF TABŪK EXPEDITION

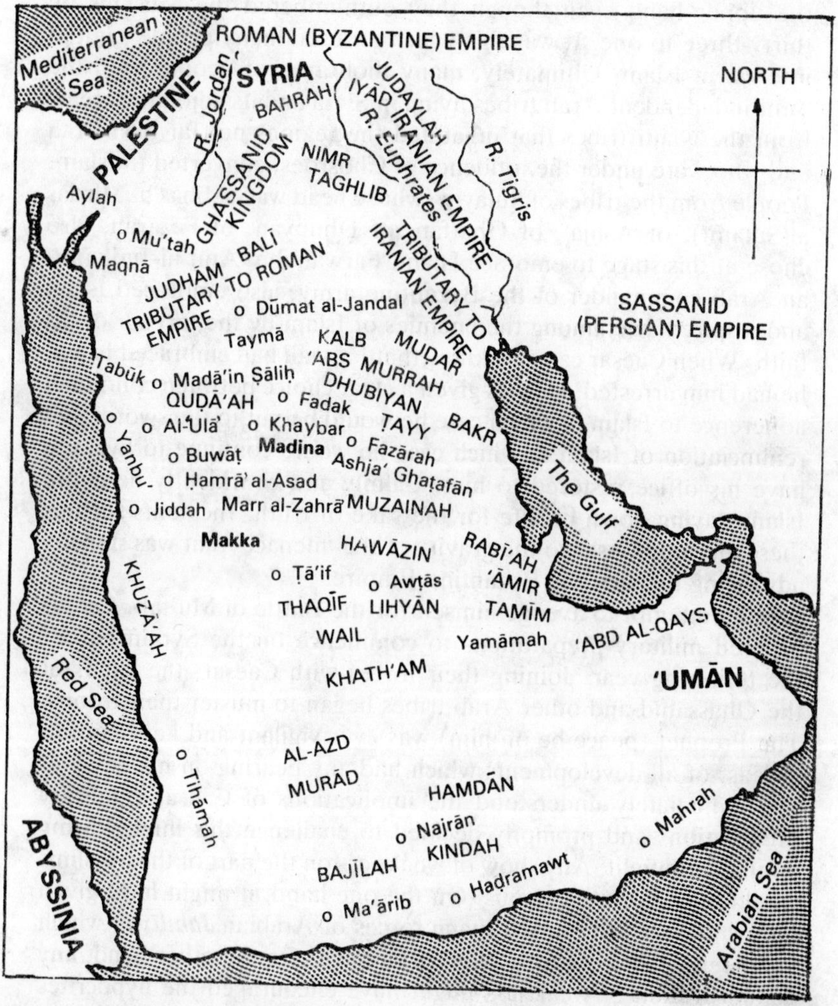

KEY: Names of tribes in capital letters.
o denotes towns.

The expected outcome of such an encounter was not hard to imagine – the total extermination of the Muslim force. What happened, however, was quite different. It came as a shock to the whole of Arabia and the Middle East that the Romans failed to gain the upper hand even though they outnumbered the Muslims by thirty-three to one. It was this which aroused many people's initial interest in Islam. Ultimately, many thousands of people from the semi-independent Arab tribes living in Syria and its adjoining areas, from the Najdī tribes that inhabited the regions not far from Iraq and who were under the influence of Chosroes, converted to Islam. People from the tribes of Sulaym (whose head was 'Abbās b. Mirdās al-Sulamī), of Ashja', of Ghaṭfān, of Dhubyān, of Fazārah, also chose at this stage to embrace Islam. Farwah ibn 'Amr al-Judhamī, an Arab commander of the Byzantine army, also embraced Islam and inspired awe among the enemies of Islam by the fervour of his faith. When Caesar came to know that Farwah had embraced Islām, he had him arrested. He was given a clear choice between continued adherence to Islam in which case he would be put to the sword, and renunciation of Islam in which case he would continue to live and have his office restored to him. Calmly and confidently he chose Islam, laying down his life for the sake of truth. Incidents such as these alerted Caesar to the gravity of the 'menace' that was steadily advancing towards the Byzantine Empire.

In an attempt to avenge himself for the Battle of Mu'tah, Caesar ordered military preparations to commence on the Syrian border the following year. Joining their forces with Caesar, the chiefs of the Ghassanid and other Arab tribes began to muster their troops. The Prophet (peace be on him) was ever vigilant and kept himself abreast of all developments which had any bearing on his mission. He immediately understood the implications of Caesar's military preparations and promptly decided to challenge this mighty army on the battlefield. Any show of weakness on the part of the Muslims would have been disastrous. On the one hand, it might have given a fresh lease of life to the dying forces of Arabian *Jāhilīyah* which had been dealt a crushing blow at Ḥunayn. On the other hand, any demonstration of weakness might have encouraged the hypocrites to cause serious damage to Islam from within. For the hypocrites were in touch with the Ghassanid Christian prince and with Caesar himself through Abū 'Āmir. Under the garb of religious piety they actively worked to achieve their sinister purposes and had even built a mosque – the Mosque of Ḍirār – in the vicinity of Madina which served as their operational base. Also Caesar himself, whose morale was also high at the time for he had just then defeated the Persians, could have been prompted to mount an attack.

If these three forces were to join hands and unitedly attack the Muslims they could well turn the tables against them; the Muslims could lose what then seemed to be a winning battle. Alive to these facts and realizing the gravity of the situation, the Prophet (peace be on him) publicly appealed to the Muslims to prepare for war against one of the two superpowers. He did so even though there prevailed near famine conditions in Arabia. The scorching heat of summer was at its peak, the harvest season had just about arrived, and there was a conspicuous shortage of material resources needed to wage a war. On similar previous occasions, the usual practice of the Prophet (peace be on him) had been not to disclose such strategic information beforehand, i.e. the direction in which he would move and the enemy with whom he would engage. In fact whenever he left Madina on a military expedition it was his practice to conceal his intent by following an unusual route to the battlefield. On this occasion, however, he did not conceal his intent, and declared that the Romans were his target, and that he would advance towards Syria.

The gravity of the situation was felt by everyone in Arabia. For the remaining devotees of *Jāhilīyah* the encounter between Islam and the Byzantine Empire offered them a last ray of hope and they looked forward to its outcome eagerly. The hypocrites also fully expected the Romans to strike a deadly blow against Islam. From their base, the Mosque of Ḍirār, they looked forward to the future eagerly, hoping that the outcome of the battle would afford them an opportunity to play their sinister game with impunity. Hence they spared no effort in their attempts to undermine the Muslim military plans.

Sincere Muslims also realized that the cause for which they had been striving for the last twenty-two years was at stake. They knew well that valiant action could open the door to Islam's ascendancy over the whole world. Conversely, any lapse on their part might seal Islam's fate even in Arabia. Moved by such thoughts, they responded fervently to the Prophet's call and commenced their war preparations, each Muslim contributing much more than his financial means warranted. Huge amounts of money were donated by 'Uthmān b. 'Affān and 'Abd al-Raḥmān b. 'Awf. 'Umar contributed half of all his belongings whereas Abū Bakr placed all that he possessed at the feet of the Prophet (peace be on him). In the same spirit, Companions with low incomes brought their hard-earned wages and donated them to the Prophet (peace be on him). Women generously donated their jewellery to the war fund. Moved by the zeal to fight in God's cause, thousands of Muslims flocked to Madina from far and wide and expressed their readiness to sacrifice their lives. Those who could not be included in the Muslim army because of the acute paucity of cavalry and other war provisions wept bitterly, and lamented their exclusion so pathetically that the Prophet (peace be on him) was moved. The occasion, in fact, served as a touchstone for distinguishing the sincere from the insincere, the true men of faith from the hypocrites. The moment was so crucial for Islam that not going to the battle-front revealed the hollowness of a man's claim to believe in Islam. Accordingly, whenever the Prophet (peace be on him) was informed during his journey to Tabūk that someone had decided to stay behind, he spontaneously said: 'Let him alone. If there is any good in him, God will re-unite him with you. And if it is otherwise, then [thank God that] He relieved you of him.' (Ibn Hishām, vol. 2, p. 523 – Ed.)

In the month of Rajab 9 A.H./631 C.E. the Prophet (peace be on him) along with thirty thousand soldiers of whom only one thousand were mounted marched towards Syria. Camels were so few that the soldiers had to take turns to ride them. The blazing heat of the summer and the scarcity of water added to their hardship. On this occasion the Muslims displayed a singular firmness of mind in enduring all hardships, for which they were amply rewarded upon their arrival at Tabūk. When the Muslims reached their destination they learned that Caesar and his tributaries had moved their troops away from the borders and that there was consequently no enemy with whom they could fight. The writers of the *Sīrah* works (biographies of the Prophet) mention this incident in a manner which suggests that upon reaching Tabūk it was found that the reports which the Prophet (peace be on him) had received about the concentration of troops on the Syrian-Arabian border were false. The fact, however, is that Caesar had indeed begun amassing his troops on the border. He had to abandon the idea of an encounter and withdrew his army because the Prophet (peace be on him) arrived ahead of the anticipated time and well before the planned concentration of troops had been completed. Caesar had not forgotten that the Muslims had given a very good account of themselves earlier on the battlefield at Mu'tah, and despite the overwhelming odds against them. Hence Caesar did not dare confront the thirty thousand-strong army of Muslims especially when it was led by the Prophet (peace be on him) himself. He would probably have still been reluctant to engage in battle even if he had mustered a hundred thousand or two hundred thousand-strong army. (For the expedition to Tabūk see Ibn Hishām, vol. 2, pp. 515–29; Wāqidī, vol. 3, pp. 989–1025; Ibn Sa'd, vol. 2, pp. 165–8; Ṭabarī, *Ta'rīkh*, vol. 3, pp. 100–11 – Ed.)

The Prophet (peace be on him) was satisfied with the advantages accruing from this moral victory. Instead of pushing on any further, he chose to derive maximum political and strategic advantage from the incident. He stayed in Tabūk for twenty days and by exerting military pressure was able to make several buffer states, which had so far been under the hegemony of the Byzantine Empire, agree to become tributaries of the Islamic state and so resign themselves to vassal status. In this connection, mention should be made of some notable chiefs – Ukaydir b. 'Abd al-Malik al-Kindī of Du'mat al-Jandal, Yūḥannā b. Ru'bah of Eilah, and of the Christian chiefs of Maqnā, Jarbā', and Adhruḥ who agreed to pay the poll tax and accepted to live under the hegemony of Madina. The result was that the Islamic state now extended to the borders of the Byzantine Empire. In addition, a good number of Arab tribes whom successive Caesars had exploited against other Arabs crossed over to the Islamic side offering their support to the Muslims as opposed to the Romans.

This proved highly advantageous insofar as it enabled the Muslims to consolidate their position in Arabia before launching upon a prolonged conflict with the Romans. This bloodless victory at Tabūk shattered the power of both the unbelievers and the hypocrites who had looked forward to a revival of the ancient *Jāhilīyah* of Arabia. In sheer desperation, a great number of them saw that the only reasonable course left open to them was to enter the fold of Islam. Even though some of them lacked inner conviction, their entrance into the fold of Islam ensured the assimilation of their forthcoming generations to Islam. The few die-hard unbelievers that remained loyal to polytheism and *Jāhilīyah* were so enfeebled that they no longer constituted a serious obstacle to the completion of the reformatory revolution for which God had raised His Messenger (peace be on him).

Subject Matter

If we bear this background in mind it will help us appreciate more fully the major issues of the hour which the *sūrah* seeks to treat:

1. Since the believers had by then gained full control over Arabia

and the forces against Islam lay crushed, it was necessary to proclaim the transformation of Arabia into a fully-fledged *Dār al-Islām*. The following represent the salient features of that strategy:

(a) Polytheism and all its offshoots should be absolutely obliterated from Arabia in order to ensure that that land would always remain the exclusive base of Islam; a land where no extraneous ideologies would be allowed to impair the purity of Islamic belief and practice, nor any non-Islamic elements allowed to create subversion. It was for this reason that a proclamation of total dissociation from the unbelievers was made and all agreements and treaties previously concluded with them were publicly annulled.

(b) Since the believers were now in control of the Ka'bah it was considered altogether inappropriate to allow polytheistic practices to continue in the shrine which was originally consecrated for the worship of the One True God. It was, therefore, proclaimed that the Ka'bah should henceforth be placed under the exclusive charge of the believers and all practices rooted in polytheism and *Jāhilīyah* should be forcibly extirpated from the precincts of the House of God. It was also proclaimed that the polytheists should no longer even be permitted to approach the Ka'bah. This was done to rule out the possibility of any further sacrilege of God's House built by the Prophet Abraham (peace be on him).

(c) It was also considered highly inappropriate for any vestige of pre-Islamic polytheistic custom to be allowed to continue under the new Islamic dispensation. Attention was, therefore, drawn to their eradication. Of these, the hideous practice of *nasī'* (the transposing of a prohibited month) was forthwith forbidden. This was to serve as an example for Muslims to do away with all vestiges of *Jāhilīyah*.

2. Once the objectives of the mission of Islam had been fulfilled within the peninsula, the next step was to spread the message outside Arabia. The Byzantine and Sassanid empires, the two mighty powers of the day, would be the major obstacles. A confrontation was, therefore, inevitable. Similar encounters with other non-Islamic political and social systems of the day

would also be imminent at a later stage. In pursuit of their goal, the Muslims were directed, if necessary by force, to put an end to all sovereign political entities which refused to submit to the truth, and to force non-Muslims to live under the suzerainty of Islam. Muslims were taught to recognize the right of non-Muslims either to embrace Islam or reject it. The Muslims did not, however, recognize that non-Muslims had the right to enforce the laws of their choice in opposition to the Divine Law of God on earth as it is created by God, and to thrust their errors and wrong-doings upon generation after generation by keeping the reins of power in their hands. At the most they may be allowed to persist in their ignorance, if they so wished. They could do so, however, only if they paid *jizyah* (poll tax) and remained subservient to the Islamic state.

3. The third serious problem was presented by the hypocrites who so far had been treated leniently. However, since pressure from hostile forces from without had considerably relaxed, in some instances ceased altogether, the Qur'ān declared that henceforth no leniency ought to be shown them. These hidden enemies of Islam should be treated with the same severity as the open deniers of Islam. In line with this policy and during the preparations for the Tabūk expedition, the Prophet (peace be on him) arranged for Suwaylim's house, where a group of hypocrites had assembled to discuss their plans for dissuading the Muslims from joining the expedition to Tabūk, to be set ablaze. (See Ibn Hishām, vol. 2, p. 517 – Ed.) Again, it was in keeping with the same policy that as soon as the Prophet (peace be on him) returned from Tabūk he demolished and set ablaze Masjid Ḍirār (the hypocrites' mosque in Madina). (See Ibn Hiṣhām, vol. 2, pp. 529–30 – Ed.)

4. It also seemed necessary to strengthen the faith of the true believers in order that any weakness in their determination might be eradicated. This was essential as the mission of Islam was about to enter its universal phase in which one single entity, Muslim Arabia, would be arrayed against the entire non-Muslim world. At such a stage in its development there could be no greater menace to Islam than the weakness of the faith of its followers. Accordingly, anyone who on the eve of the Tabūk expedition had either neglected or slackened off in his duty was severely reproached. Any lagging behind without legitimate cause was considered, beyond any doubt, evidence

of hypocrisy, a sign of not having true faith. It was stated, therefore, unequivocally that participation in the struggle to exalt the Word of Allah and in the conflict between Islam and unbelief would henceforth be considered the basic criterion of a person's faith. Whoever was found to be slack in his efforts to sacrifice his life, wealth and resources in Islam's cause would no longer be regarded as genuine and none of his acts, no matter how pious he might otherwise be, would compensate for this slackness.

(1) This is a declaration of disavowal[1] by Allah and His Messenger to those who associate others with Allah in His divinity and with whom you have made treaties:[2] (2) 'You may go about freely in the land, for four months,[3] but know well that you will not be able to frustrate Allah, and that Allah will bring disgrace upon those who deny the truth.'

بَرَآءَةٌ مِّنَ ٱللَّهِ وَرَسُولِهِۦٓ إِلَى ٱلَّذِينَ
عَٰهَدتُّم مِّنَ ٱلْمُشْرِكِينَ ﴿١﴾
فَسِيحُوا۟ فِى ٱلْأَرْضِ أَرْبَعَةَ أَشْهُرٍ
وَٱعْلَمُوٓا۟ أَنَّكُمْ غَيْرُ مُعْجِزِى ٱللَّهِ وَأَنَّ
ٱللَّهَ مُخْزِى ٱلْكَٰفِرِينَ ﴿٢﴾

---

1. As we have mentioned above, the first discourse (verses 1–37) was revealed in 9 A.H./631 C.E. at a time when the Prophet (peace be on him) had already sent Abū Bakr as leader of the Pilgrims to perform *Ḥajj*. Since these verses were revealed during Abū Bakr's absence, the Companions in Madina asked the Prophet (peace be on him) to have them conveyed to Abū Bakr with the instruction that they may be recited publicly during the *Ḥajj*. The Prophet (peace be on him), however, decided that the verses should be recited on his behalf by someone from his own family. Accordingly, he entrusted the task to 'Alī and directed him that not only should he publicly recite the verses concerned, but should also make the following proclamation on that occasion: (i) that no one who refuses to accept Islam would enter Paradise; (ii) that no polytheist would henceforth be allowed to perform *Ḥajj*; (iii) that naked circumambulation around the Ka'bah – a pre-Islamic Arabian practice – would henceforth be forbidden; (iv) that the treaties concluded between the Prophet (peace be on him) and the unbelievers which were still in force since the other party had not broken them, would be honoured until the expiry of their terms. (See Qurṭubī's comments on verses 1–2 quoting Tirmidhī and Ibn Kathīr's comments on verses 1–3.)

It is worth noting that the first *Ḥajj* of the Islamic era after the conquest of Makka in 8 A.H./630 C.E. was performed largely in accordance with the then prevalent practices. However, in 9 A.H./631 C.E. the Muslims performed the second *Ḥajj* according to the rules prescribed by Islam whereas the polytheists performed it according to their own customs. It was in 10 A.H./632 C.E. that the third *Ḥajj*, more commonly known as the *Ḥajjat al-Wādā'* (The Farewell Pilgrimage) was performed in a purely Islamic manner. The Prophet (peace be on him) did not perform the first two Pilgrimages. He did, however, lead the third *Ḥajj* when polytheism had been fully extirpated.

2. The Qur'ān had already laid down the rule: 'If you fear treachery from any group, then publicly throw their covenant at them, for Allah does not love the treacherous' (8: 58). Thus the Muslims were required to publicly terminate their treaties before they engaged in hostilities with groups whom they feared would violate those agreements. To take up arms against a people with whom one is bound by a treaty without its annulment is tantamount to treachery and as such does not become the Muslims. This Qur'ānic principle also applied to those tribes that, despite their treaties, had constantly conspired against and were openly hostile to Islam whenever the opportunity presented itself. This was very much the attitude of all the polytheistic tribes with the notable exception of the Banū Kinānah and the Banū Ḍamrah, and perhaps of a couple of other lesser known tribes.

This public dissociation with polytheism and its adherents by the Qur'ān amounted to the outlawing of polytheism and polytheists in Arabia. The polytheists thereafter had no shelter in the land since the greater part of Arabia had come under Islam's sway. The polytheists looked ever for an opportunity (such as the threat of the invasion of the Islamic state by the Byzantines or the Sassanids, or of the possible death of the Prophet (peace be on him)) to violate their treaties and to fling the Islamic realm into civil war and anarchy. However, God and His Messenger had turned the tables on them before they had the chance. The public annulment of the treaties presented the polytheists with three alternatives. They could either come out into the open and engage in conflict with the Islamic state which would have led to their total extinction. They could flee from Arabia or they could embrace Islam and submit themselves and the lands which they controlled to the Islamic state.

The wisdom of this action can be better appreciated if one considers the level of denunciation which broke out in different parts of Arabia in less than two years after the Prophet's death, and which jolted the very foundation of the newly-established Islamic order. Had this declaration of 9 A.H./631 C.E. not struck a death-blow to the forces of polytheism, and had the Islamic order not been firmly entrenched, the movement of apostasy which arose in the early days of Abū Bakr's Caliphate would have surfaced earlier and been more forceful. It might also have led to a much fiercer civil war and rebellion, and the course of Islamic history might well have been different altogether.

3. This proclamation was made on the 10th of Dhū al-Ḥij'ah, 9 A.H./631 C.E. The polytheists were granted a respite of four months concluding on the 10th Rabī' al-Awwal, 10 A.H./631 C.E. They were thus offered the opportunity to take stock of their situation. If they decided that they should fight it out, they could do so. Similarly, they could choose either to leave the land, or after careful consideration embrace Islam.

(3) This is a public proclamation by Allah and His Messenger to all men on the day of the Great Pilgrimage:[4] 'Allah is free from all obligation to those who associate others with Allah in His divinity; and so is His Messenger. If you repent, it shall be for your own good; but if you turn away, then know well that you will not be able to frustrate Allah. So give glad tidings of a painful chastisement to those who disbelieve. (4) In exception to those who associate others with Allah in His divinity are those with whom you have made treaties and who have not violated their treaties nor have backed up anyone against you. Fulfil your treaties with them till the end of their term. Surely Allah loves the pious.'[5]

وَأَذَٰنٌ مِّنَ ٱللَّهِ وَرَسُولِهِۦٓ إِلَى ٱلنَّاسِ
يَوْمَ ٱلْحَجِّ ٱلْأَكْبَرِ أَنَّ ٱللَّهَ بَرِىٓءٌ
مِّنَ ٱلْمُشْرِكِينَ ۙ وَرَسُولُهُۥ ۚ فَإِن تُبْتُمْ
فَهُوَ خَيْرٌ لَّكُمْ ۖ وَإِن تَوَلَّيْتُمْ
فَٱعْلَمُوٓا۟ أَنَّكُمْ غَيْرُ مُعْجِزِى ٱللَّهِ ۗ
وَبَشِّرِ ٱلَّذِينَ كَفَرُوا۟ بِعَذَابٍ أَلِيمٍ
٣ إِلَّا ٱلَّذِينَ عَٰهَدتُّم مِّنَ
ٱلْمُشْرِكِينَ ثُمَّ لَمْ يَنقُصُوكُمْ شَيْـًٔا
وَلَمْ يُظَٰهِرُوا۟ عَلَيْكُمْ أَحَدًا فَأَتِمُّوٓا۟
إِلَيْهِمْ عَهْدَهُمْ إِلَىٰ مُدَّتِهِمْ ۚ إِنَّ ٱللَّهَ
يُحِبُّ ٱلْمُتَّقِينَ ٤

4. The 10th of Dhu al-Ḥijjah is known as *Yawm al-Naḥr* (the Day of Sacrifice). According to authentic traditions, the Prophet (peace be on him) asked the audience on the occasion of *Ḥajjat al-Wādā'* (The Farewell Pilgrimage): 'Which day is it?' They replied: 'It is *Yawm al-Naḥr* (the Day of Sacrifice).' The Prophet (peace be on him) said: 'This is *Yawm al-Ḥajj al-Akbar* (the day of Greater Pilgrimage).' It is in contrast to *al-Ḥajj al-Aṣghar,* (that is, *'Umrah* or Minor Pilgrimage) that the Pilgrimage performed on the appointed dates in the month of Dhu al-Ḥijjah is called 'the Greater Pilgrimage'.

5. The Muslims were directed to maintain agreements with those who had not been guilty of violating agreements with them. Any act which contravened this idea would not be God-fearing and Muslims should abstain from it since God loves those who fear Him.

(5) But when the sacred months expire,[6] slay those who associate others with Allah in His divinity wherever you find them; seize them, and besiege them, and lie in wait for them. But if they repent and establish the Prayer and pay *Zakāh*, leave them alone.[7] Surely Allah is All-Forgiving, Ever-Merciful. (6) And if any of those who associate others with Allah in His divinity seeks asylum, grant him asylum that he may hear the Word of Allah, and then escort him to safety for they are a people bereft of all understanding.[8]

فَإِذَا ٱنسَلَخَ ٱلْأَشْهُرُ ٱلْحُرُمُ فَٱقْتُلُوا۟
ٱلْمُشْرِكِينَ حَيْثُ وَجَدتُّمُوهُمْ
وَخُذُوهُمْ وَٱحْصُرُوهُمْ وَٱقْعُدُوا۟ لَهُمْ
كُلَّ مَرْصَدٍ فَإِن تَابُوا۟ وَأَقَامُوا۟
ٱلصَّلَوٰةَ وَءَاتَوُا۟ ٱلزَّكَوٰةَ فَخَلُّوا۟
سَبِيلَهُمْ إِنَّ ٱللَّهَ غَفُورٌ رَّحِيمٌ ﴿٥﴾
وَإِنْ أَحَدٌ مِّنَ ٱلْمُشْرِكِينَ
ٱسْتَجَارَكَ فَأَجِرْهُ حَتَّىٰ يَسْمَعَ
كَلَٰمَ ٱللَّهِ ثُمَّ أَبْلِغْهُ مَأْمَنَهُۥ ذَٰلِكَ
بِأَنَّهُمْ قَوْمٌ لَّا يَعْلَمُونَ ﴿٦﴾

6. The expression 'sacred months' in the above verse means something rather different from its usual understanding, whereby fighting during those four months was prohibited. Here the expression refers merely to the four months of respite granted to the polytheists. Since it was not lawful for Muslims to attack the polytheists during those months, they were characterized as '*ḥurum*' (sacred, prohibited).

7. Apart from a disavowal of unbelief and polytheism, the Muslims are required to establish Prayers and pay *Zakāh*. Without these, their claim that they had abandoned unbelief and embraced Islam would have no credence. Abū Bakr referred to this verse as the basis of his action in response to the movement of apostasy during his reign. A group of those who had launched a rebellious movement against Islam after the death of the Prophet (peace be on him) contended that they had not renounced Islam and were even prepared to observe the Prayers. They were not prepared, however, to pay *Zakāh*. Many of the Companions were puzzled as to how the sword could be unleashed against a people who claimed to profess Islam and observed Prayers. Abū Bakr referred to the above verse which enjoins Muslims to allow such polytheists to have their way provided

(7) How can there be a covenant with those who associate others with Allah in His divinity on the part of Allah and His Messenger except those with whom you made a covenant near the Sacred Mosque?[9] Behave in a straight way with them so long as they behave straight with you for Allah loves the God-fearing. (8) How can there be any covenant with the rest who associate others with Allah in His divinity for were they to prevail against you, they will respect neither kinship nor agreement. They seek to please you with their tongues while their hearts are averse to you,[10] and most of them are wicked.[11] ▶

كَيْفَ يَكُونُ لِلْمُشْرِكِينَ
عَهْدٌ عِندَ اللَّهِ وَعِندَ رَسُولِهِۦٓ
إِلَّا الَّذِينَ عَٰهَدتُّمْ عِندَ
الْمَسْجِدِ الْحَرَامِ ۖ فَمَا اسْتَقَٰمُوا۟
لَكُمْ فَاسْتَقِيمُوا۟ لَهُمْ ۚ إِنَّ اللَّهَ يُحِبُّ
الْمُتَّقِينَ ﴿٧﴾ كَيْفَ وَإِن
يَظْهَرُوا۟ عَلَيْكُمْ لَا يَرْقُبُوا۟ فِيكُمْ
إِلًّا وَلَا ذِمَّةً ۚ يُرْضُونَكُم بِأَفْوَٰهِهِمْ
وَتَأْبَىٰ قُلُوبُهُمْ وَأَكْثَرُهُمْ
فَٰسِقُونَ ﴿٨﴾

---

they give up polytheism, establish Prayers and pay *Zakāh*. However, the injunction would not apply if they failed to fulfil any one of these three conditions.

8. If during the war any enemy expresses the desire to learn about Islam, the Muslims should provide him asylum, allow him to come to their land, and help him understand their religion. Thereafter if he decides not to accept Islam, they should escort him to wherever he wishes to go. In Islamic legal terminology, the person who enters *Dār al-Islām* under its protection is called *musta'min*.

9. This alludes to the Kinānah, Khuzā'ah and Ḍamrah tribes.

10. Although the unbelievers negotiated a peace treaty with the Muslims, their hearts were nevertheless full of treachery. Their intentions were borne out by their deeds for whenever they concluded a treaty it was apparent that they had done so only with the intention of breaking it.

(9) They have sold the revelations of Allah for a paltry price[12] and have firmly hindered people from His path.[13] Evil indeed is what they have done. (10) They neither have any respect for kinship nor for agreement in respect of the believers. Such are indeed transgressors. (11) But if they repent and establish Prayer and give *Zakāh* they are your brothers in faith. Thus do We expound Our revelations to those who know.[14] ▶

اشْتَرَوْا بِآيَاتِ اللَّهِ ثَمَنًا قَلِيلًا
فَصَدُّوا عَن سَبِيلِهِ ۚ إِنَّهُمْ سَاءَ
مَا كَانُوا يَعْمَلُونَ ﴿٩﴾ لَا يَرْقُبُونَ
فِي مُؤْمِنٍ إِلًّا وَلَا ذِمَّةً ۚ وَأُولَٰئِكَ
هُمُ الْمُعْتَدُونَ ﴿١٠﴾ فَإِن تَابُوا
وَأَقَامُوا الصَّلَاةَ وَآتَوُا الزَّكَاةَ
فَإِخْوَانُكُمْ فِي الدِّينِ ۗ وَنُفَصِّلُ الْآيَاتِ
لِقَوْمٍ يَعْلَمُونَ ﴿١١﴾

11. The unbelievers had neither consideration either for their moral obligations nor had any compunction in their transgressions.

12. On the one hand, the Book of God invited the unbelievers to virtuous conduct, to righteousness, and to the observance of Divine Law. On the other hand, the worldly life offered them ephemeral benefits which they expected to gain by giving a free, unbridled rein to their lusts. On comparing the two, they preferred the latter to the former.

13. Not only did those wicked people choose error in preference to true guidance, they even had the brazenness to try to obstruct the spread of the truth, to prevent people from responding to righteousness. They tried to gag the mouths of those who invited people to the truth. In short, they spared nothing in their efforts to prevent the establishment of a righteous way of life. They sought to make life extremely difficult for those who, convinced of the truth of their way of life, tried to sincerely follow it.

14. This reiterates the statement that if the repentance of the unbelievers is not accompanied by the establishment of Prayers and the payment of *Zakāh*, then they would not be considered as part of the Islamic fraternity on the grounds of their mere repentance. As to the Qur'ānic statement that they would become brethren in faith, it means that if they fulfil the requisite conditions, it would no longer be permissible for Muslims to fight

(12) But if they break their pledges after making them and attack your faith, make war on the leaders of unbelief that they may desist, for they have no regard for their pledged words.[15]

(13) Will you not fight[16] against those who broke their pledges and did all they could to drive the Messenger away and initiated hostilities against you? Do you fear them? Surely Allah has greater right that you should fear Him, if you are true believers. ▶

وَإِن نَّكَثُوٓا۟ أَيْمَـٰنَهُم مِّنۢ بَعْدِ
عَهْدِهِمْ وَطَعَنُوا۟ فِى دِينِكُمْ
فَقَـٰتِلُوٓا۟ أَئِمَّةَ ٱلْكُفْرِ ۙ إِنَّهُمْ
لَآ أَيْمَـٰنَ لَهُمْ لَعَلَّهُمْ يَنتَهُونَ
﴿١٢﴾ أَلَا تُقَـٰتِلُونَ قَوْمًا نَّكَثُوٓا۟
أَيْمَـٰنَهُمْ وَهَمُّوا۟ بِإِخْرَاجِ
ٱلرَّسُولِ وَهُم بَدَءُوكُمْ
أَوَّلَ مَرَّةٍ ۚ أَتَخْشَوْنَهُمْ ۚ فَٱللَّهُ
أَحَقُّ أَن تَخْشَوْهُ إِن كُنتُم
مُّؤْمِنِينَ ﴿١٣﴾

against them, and also that their lives and property would become sacred. Moreover, they would be entitled to enjoy equal rights in the Islamic society. They would be treated like other Muslims in all social and legal matters. Nor would they be discriminated against in any way, nor any obstacles placed in front of them which might impede their progress in achieving what they might be capable of achieving.

15. It appears from the context that the expression 'their oaths' stands here for their repudiation of unbelief and so their acceptance of Islam. For, in view of their previous record of treaty violation, it was simply out of the question for any new treaty to be concluded with them. In fact, their persistent violation of such treaties had brought about the proclamation from God and His Messenger that all treaties with them be annulled (see verse 1 above). The Qur'ān unequivocally declares that no treaty may be concluded with such people. The only way for such persons to be let alone was if they renounce unbelief and polytheism and perform the duties of Prayer and *Zakāh*.

This verse also contains a clear injunction with regard to apostasy. The verse does in fact hint at the apostasy movement that was to break out after a year and a half of Abū Bakr's Caliphate. In dealing with apostates Abū Bakr acted on the directive set forth in the present verse. (For a detailed discussion of apostasy see Sayyid Abū al-A'lá Mawdūdī, *Murtadd kī Sazā Islāmī Qānūn Mén* (Lahore, 1953).

(14) Make war on them. Allah will chastise them through you and will humiliate them. He will grant you victory over them, and will soothe the bosoms of those who believe; (15) and will remove rage from their hearts, and will enable whomsoever He wills to repent.[17] Allah is All-Knowing, All-Wise. ▶

قَٰتِلُوهُمْ يُعَذِّبْهُمُ ٱللَّهُ بِأَيْدِيكُمْ وَيُخْزِهِمْ وَيَنصُرْكُمْ عَلَيْهِمْ وَيَشْفِ صُدُورَ قَوْمٍ مُّؤْمِنِينَ ﴿١٤﴾ وَيُذْهِبْ غَيْظَ قُلُوبِهِمْ ۗ وَيَتُوبُ ٱللَّهُ عَلَىٰ مَن يَشَآءُ ۗ وَٱللَّهُ عَلِيمٌ حَكِيمٌ ﴿١٥﴾

16. From here on the discourse is directed to the Muslims who are exhorted to wage war and to disregard worldly interests, blood ties, and everything else, in matters relating to faith.

For a fuller appreciation of the true spirit of this part of the discourse, one should take into account the circumstances which then confronted the Muslims. At that time, Islam had no doubt gained such an ascendancy that no power in Arabia could challenge its supremacy. To the superficial eye t might well have seemed highly dangerous to nullify all agreements with the unbelievers for the following reasons:

(1) It was feared that doing many things at once – the annulment of treaties with polytheistic tribes, the ban on polytheists from performing Pilgrimage, the transference of custody of the Ka'bah to the Muslims, and the total abolition of the evil practices of the time of Ignorance – would be dangerous. It was feared that these steps might inflame even the polytheists and hypocrites into a decisive encounter against the Muslims in their attempts to defend their interests and their inherited way of life.

(2) The decision to institute *Ḥajj* as an exclusively Muslim religious rite and to ban the polytheists from entering the Ka'bah was, for the polytheists, highly controversial. This step not only offended the religious feelings of a vast section of the Arabian population, but was also detrimental to their economic interests for Makka was the centre of the Arabs' economic life.

(3) It was also feared that the declaration would put the faith of those who had embraced Islam after the Treaty of Ḥudaybīyah and the conquest of Makka to a severe test as many of their kith and kin still professed polytheism. In addition, the interests of some of them were closely linked with the *Jāhilīyah* system. A deadly blow aimed at the polytheists of Arabia

(16) Do you imagine that you will be spared without being subjected to any test? Know well that Allah has not yet determined who strove hard (in His cause), and has not taken any others beside His Messenger and the believers as his trusted allies?[18] Allah is well aware of all that you do.

أَمْ حَسِبْتُمْ أَن تُتْرَكُوا وَلَمَّا يَعْلَمِ
اللَّهُ الَّذِينَ جَٰهَدُوا مِنكُمْ وَلَمْ
يَتَّخِذُوا مِن دُونِ اللَّهِ وَلَا رَسُولِهِۦ
وَلَا الْمُؤْمِنِينَ وَلِيجَةً وَاللَّهُ خَبِيرٌ
بِمَا تَعْمَلُونَ ﴿١٦﴾

implied that recent converts to Islam would not only be required to shed the blood of those who were near and dear to them, but also to destroy the positions and privileges which they had enjoyed for centuries.

All of these apprehensions proved groundless. For, far from causing turmoil, the public disavowal of all affinities with the polytheists prompted those tribes which had still clung to polytheism to make their way to the Prophet (peace be on him). They steadily came to him, embraced Islam and pledged themselves to obey him. The delegations, comprised of ordinary tribesmen as well as chiefs and princes, came from all parts of Arabia. Once they had declared their conversion to Islam, the Prophet (peace be on him) allowed them to retain their former positions. But at the time when the new policy was being launched it was impossible for people to foresee the advantages that would follow. It should also be remembered that if the Muslims were not prepared to expend their energies for ensuring the enforcement of that decision, such advantages might not have accrued at all.

It was necessary, therefore, at this stage to urge the Muslims to fight in the cause of God, to remove the misgivings which they entertained about the new policy, and to impress upon them that they should allow no consideration to prevent them from carrying out the directives of God. This constitutes the theme of the present discourse.

17. Here the misunderstandings of those Muslims who considered that the Prophet's annulment of all agreements with the polytheists would plunge the land into a blood-bath is dispelled. It is pointed out that whilst a storm of bloody strife might well ensue, it is equally possible that the event might prompt some people to repent. This possibility was not,

(17) It does not become those who associate others with Allah in His divinity to visit and tend Allah's mosques while they bear witness of unbelief against themselves.[19] All their works have gone to waste.[20] They shall abide in the Fire. (18) It only becomes those who believe in Allah and the Last Day and establish Prayer and pay *Zakāh* and fear none but Allah to visit and tend the mosques of Allah. These are likely to be guided aright.

مَا كَانَ لِلْمُشْرِكِينَ أَن يَعْمُرُوا مَسَٰجِدَ
ٱللَّهِ شَٰهِدِينَ عَلَىٰٓ أَنفُسِهِم بِٱلْكُفْرِ
أُو۟لَٰٓئِكَ حَبِطَتْ أَعْمَٰلُهُمْ وَفِى ٱلنَّارِ
هُمْ خَٰلِدُونَ ﴿١٧﴾ إِنَّمَا يَعْمُرُ مَسَٰجِدَ
ٱللَّهِ مَنْ ءَامَنَ بِٱللَّهِ وَٱلْيَوْمِ ٱلْءَاخِرِ
وَأَقَامَ ٱلصَّلَوٰةَ وَءَاتَى ٱلزَّكَوٰةَ وَلَمْ
يَخْشَ إِلَّا ٱللَّهَ فَعَسَىٰٓ أُو۟لَٰٓئِكَ أَن
يَكُونُوا مِنَ ٱلْمُهْتَدِينَ ﴿١٨﴾

---

however, clearly spelled out. An explicit statement would, on the one hand, have made the Muslims complacent about their war preparations. On the other hand, such a statement might have negated the grim and threatening tone of the verse. Its present form alerts them to the precariousness of their situation, and sets in motion a process that might lead them to assimilate into the Islamic body-politic.

18. This is addressed to the recent converts to Islam. The verse makes it plain to them that unless they prove that they hold their faith to be dearer than their lives, properties and blood ties, then they cannot be declared true believers. On the basis of what had happened it might have been claimed that they had embraced Islam merely because it was now established as the supreme force in the land. This was the result of the true believers' valiant struggle.

19. Those who associate others in the divinity of the One True God cannot be considered legitimate custodians, servants and caretakers of those places consecrated exclusively for the worship of God. The polytheists of Arabia, by explicitly rejecting the call to monotheism and by refusing to consecrate their worship and servitude to the One True God, had forfeited their right to the custodianship of the Ka'bah which had after all been erected for the worship of God alone.

(19) Do you consider providing water to the Pilgrims and tending the Sacred Mosque equal in worth to believing in Allah and the Last Day and striving in the cause of Allah?[21] The two are not equal with Allah. Allah does not guide the wrong-doing folk. (20) The higher rank with Allah is for those who believed and migrated and strove in His cause with their belongings and their persons. It is they who are triumphant. (21) Their Lord gives them glad tidings of mercy from Him and of His good pleasure. For them await Gardens of eternal bliss. (22) Therein they shall abide for ever. Surely with Allah there is a mighty reward.

۞ أَجَعَلْتُمْ سِقَايَةَ الْحَاجِّ وَعِمَارَةَ
الْمَسْجِدِ الْحَرَامِ كَمَنْ ءَامَنَ بِاللَّهِ وَالْيَوْمِ
الْآخِرِ وَجَٰهَدَ فِي سَبِيلِ اللَّهِ لَا يَسْتَوُۥنَ
عِندَ اللَّهِ وَاللَّهُ لَا يَهْدِي الْقَوْمَ الظَّٰلِمِينَ
١٩ الَّذِينَ ءَامَنُوا وَهَاجَرُوا وَجَٰهَدُوا فِي
سَبِيلِ اللَّهِ بِأَمْوَٰلِهِمْ وَأَنفُسِهِمْ أَعْظَمُ
دَرَجَةً عِندَ اللَّهِ وَأُولَٰٓئِكَ هُمُ الْفَآئِزُونَ ٢٠
يُبَشِّرُهُمْ رَبُّهُم بِرَحْمَةٍ مِّنْهُ
وَرِضْوَٰنٍ وَجَنَّٰتٍ لَّهُمْ فِيهَا نَعِيمٌ
مُّقِيمٌ ٢١ خَٰلِدِينَ فِيهَآ أَبَدًا
إِنَّ اللَّهَ عِندَهُۥٓ أَجْرٌ عَظِيمٌ ٢٢

The Qur'ān thus lays down a principle which is of general application. The specific command itself, however, was prompted by the decision to put an end to the polytheists' custodianship of the Ka'bah and the Holy Mosque around it, and to confer it instead upon the believers.

20. No matter what service the polytheists had proffered as custodians of the House of God had gone to waste for they had tainted it with polytheism together with other practices of *Jāhilīyah*. The little good they did was outweighed by the sins they committed.

21. To act merely as the custodians and caretakers of a religious shrine and to ostentatiously perform a few religious rites with the intent of creating the impression of piety for the sake of superficial observers, was of no value in the eyes of God. A man's worth in the sight of God depends on

(23) Believers! Do not take your fathers and your brothers for your allies if they choose unbelief in preference to belief. Whosoever of you takes them as allies those are wrong-doers. (24) Tell them (O Prophet!): 'If your fathers and your sons and your brothers and your wives and your tribe and the riches you have acquired and the commerce of which you fear a slackening, and the dwellings that you love, are dearer to you than Allah and His Messenger and striving in His cause, then wait until Allah brings about His decree.[22] Allah does not guide the evil-doing folk.'

يَـٰٓأَيُّهَا ٱلَّذِينَ ءَامَنُوا۟ لَا تَتَّخِذُوٓا۟
ءَابَآءَكُمْ وَإِخْوَٰنَكُمْ أَوْلِيَآءَ إِنِ
ٱسْتَحَبُّوا۟ ٱلْكُفْرَ عَلَى ٱلْإِيمَـٰنِ ۚ
وَمَن يَتَوَلَّهُم مِّنكُمْ فَأُو۟لَـٰٓئِكَ هُمُ
ٱلظَّـٰلِمُونَ ﴿٢٣﴾ قُلْ إِن كَانَ
ءَابَآؤُكُمْ وَأَبْنَآؤُكُمْ وَإِخْوَٰنُكُمْ
وَأَزْوَٰجُكُمْ وَعَشِيرَتُكُمْ وَأَمْوَٰلٌ
ٱقْتَرَفْتُمُوهَا وَتِجَـٰرَةٌ تَخْشَوْنَ
كَسَادَهَا وَمَسَـٰكِنُ تَرْضَوْنَهَآ
أَحَبَّ إِلَيْكُم مِّنَ ٱللَّهِ وَرَسُولِهِۦ
وَجِهَادٍ فِى سَبِيلِهِۦ فَتَرَبَّصُوا۟ حَتَّىٰ
يَأْتِىَ ٱللَّهُ بِأَمْرِهِۦ ۗ وَٱللَّهُ لَا يَهْدِى
ٱلْقَوْمَ ٱلْفَـٰسِقِينَ ﴿٢٤﴾

---

his faith and the sacrifices he makes in this cause. Whoever is in possession of such qualities, regardless of his lineage, is of value to God. Conversely, those who enjoy an illustrious lineage and ceremoniously perform religious rites on appointed occasions but who are devoid of the qualities outlined above, deserve no respect whatsoever. Nor is it proper to allow the custodianship of holy places and religious institutions to remain in the hands of such worthless people merely on the basis of their hereditary claims to them.

22. It is possible that God might deprive them of the blessing of true faith and of their present pre-eminence and confer the same on some other group, making this latter group the standard-bearers of Islam and guides to righteousness in place of the former.

(25) Surely Allah has succoured you before on many a battlefield and (you have yourselves witnessed His succour to you)[23] on the day of Ḥunayn when your numbers made you proud, but they did you no good, and the earth, for all its vastness, constrained you, and you turned your backs in retreat. (26) Then Allah caused His tranquillity to descend upon His Messenger and upon the believers, and He sent down hosts whom you did not see, and chastised those who disbelieved. Such is the recompense of those who deny the truth.

لَقَدْ نَصَرَكُمُ ٱللَّهُ فِى مَوَاطِنَ
كَثِيرَةٍ وَيَوْمَ حُنَيْنٍ إِذْ
أَعْجَبَتْكُمْ كَثْرَتُكُمْ فَلَمْ
تُغْنِ عَنكُمْ شَيْـًٔا وَضَاقَتْ
عَلَيْكُمُ ٱلْأَرْضُ بِمَا
رَحُبَتْ ثُمَّ وَلَّيْتُم مُّدْبِرِينَ ﴿٢٥﴾
ثُمَّ أَنزَلَ ٱللَّهُ سَكِينَتَهُۥ عَلَىٰ رَسُولِهِۦ
وَعَلَى ٱلْمُؤْمِنِينَ وَأَنزَلَ جُنُودًا
لَّمْ تَرَوْهَا وَعَذَّبَ ٱلَّذِينَ
كَفَرُوا۟ وَذَٰلِكَ جَزَآءُ ٱلْكَٰفِرِينَ
﴿٢٦﴾

23. Those who anticipated a blood-bath throughout Arabia as a result of the annulment of agreements with the polytheists are being asked to shed their fears. They are also told that God helped the believers on earlier occasions when they were confronted with grave danger, and He was still there to help them. Had the success of the mission of Islam been dependent merely on the resources of the believers, Islam would not have spread beyond Makka and it would have certainly been wiped out in the Battle of Badr. Islam survived, however, for God was there to help it. Incidents in the past confirmed that if Islam had flourished it was due to the power of God. The believers should, therefore, feel assured that He will enable Islam to flourish as He had done before.

Allusion is made here to the Battle of Ḥunayn which took place in Shawwāl 8 A.H./630 C.E. in the Ḥunayn valley, about one year before the revelation of this verse. In this battle the Muslim army consisted of twelve thousand people – so far the strongest Muslim army. The army of the unbelievers was much smaller. Yet the archers of the Hawāzin tribe put up a very tough fight and routed the Muslim army. Only the Prophet (peace be on him) and a handful of intrepid Companions stood their ground. This enabled the Muslim army to reconsolidate its position and

(27) Then (after so chastising the unbelievers), Allah enables, whomsoever He wills, to repent.[24] Allah is All-Forgiving, All-Merciful.

(28) Believers! Those who associate others with Allah in His divinity are unclean. So, after the expiry of this year, let them not even go near the Sacred Mosque.[25] And should you fear poverty, Allah will enrich you out of His bounty, if He wills. Surely Allah is All-Knowing, All-Wise.

ثُمَّ يَتُوبُ ٱللَّهُ مِنۢ بَعۡدِ ذَٰلِكَ عَلَىٰ مَن
يَشَآءُۗ وَٱللَّهُ غَفُورٌ رَّحِيمٌ ﴿٢٧﴾
يَٰٓأَيُّهَا ٱلَّذِينَ ءَامَنُوٓاْ إِنَّمَا
ٱلۡمُشۡرِكُونَ نَجَسٌ فَلَا يَقۡرَبُواْ
ٱلۡمَسۡجِدَ ٱلۡحَرَامَ بَعۡدَ عَامِهِمۡ
هَٰذَاۚ وَإِنۡ خِفۡتُمۡ عَيۡلَةً فَسَوۡفَ
يُغۡنِيكُمُ ٱللَّهُ مِن فَضۡلِهِۦٓ إِن شَآءَۚ
إِنَّ ٱللَّهَ عَلِيمٌ حَكِيمٌ ﴿٢٨﴾

eventually win the battle. Had the outcome of the battle been different, the Muslims would have lost much more by this defeat than what they had gained by the conquest of Makka.

24. The grace and magnanimity with which the Prophet (peace be on him) treated his defeated enemies won most of them over to Islam. By references to such instances the Muslims are being told that they should have no reason to believe that circumstances would necessarily lead to the total obliteration of all the polytheists of Arabia. In view of past experiences they should rather believe that once people are deprived of the false props which enabled them to cling to *Jāhilīyah*, they will automatically move towards Islam.

25. The polytheists were not only forbidden to perform *Ḥajj*, but also to enter the precincts of the Holy Mosque. This was done so as to ensure there would be no revival of polytheism or *Jāhilīyah* in the future. That 'the polytheists are unclean' does not imply bodily impurity; rather it is their beliefs, morals, deeds, practices and customs which are unclean. Hence a ban was placed on their entry into the precincts of the Holy Mosque.

According to Abū Ḥanīfah, the importance of this verse lays with the fact that the unbelievers are no longer allowed to enter the precincts of

(29) Those who do not believe in Allah and the Last Day[26] – even though they were given the scriptures, and who do not hold as unlawful that which Allah and His Messenger have declared to be unlawful,[27] and who do not follow the true religion – fight against them until they pay tribute out of their hand and are utterly subdued.[28]

قَٰتِلُواْ ٱلَّذِينَ لَا يُؤْمِنُونَ بِٱللَّهِ وَلَا بِٱلْيَوْمِ ٱلْءَاخِرِ وَلَا يُحَرِّمُونَ مَا حَرَّمَ ٱللَّهُ وَرَسُولُهُۥ وَلَا يَدِينُونَ دِينَ ٱلْحَقِّ مِنَ ٱلَّذِينَ أُوتُواْ ٱلْكِتَٰبَ حَتَّىٰ يُعْطُواْ ٱلْجِزْيَةَ عَن يَدٍ وَهُمْ صَٰغِرُونَ ٢٩

the Holy Mosque to perform *Ḥajj* and *'Umrah*, or the religious rites of *Jāhilīyah*. However, Shāfi'ī interprets the verse in an absolute sense and rules out totally their entry into the Holy precincts. Likewise, Mālik holds that the ban was not confined to the Holy Mosque; the unbelievers may not enter any mosque. The last opinion, however, is not sound since the Prophet (peace be on him) had allowed unbelievers to enter his own mosque in Madina. (See Qurṭubī's comments on verse 28 – Ed.)

26. Although the People of the Book pretend to believe in God and the Hereafter, in fact they do not. Belief in God does not simply mean verbal affirmation of God's existence. It rather means that man should acce' God as the One and Only Lord, and should neither associate himself ı anyone else with God's being, His attributes, His claims against man, or with His authority. Nevertheless, both the Christians and Jews are guilty of doing this, their actions identified at length in the following verse. Their profession of faith is, therefore, of no use and cannot be taken as evidence of true belief in God.

Likewise, belief in the Hereafter does not just mean affirmation of man's resurrection after death. True belief in the Hereafter necessitates a firm conviction that no intercession, ransom, association with saints, or spiritual leaders will be of any use in the Next Life, nor will anyone be able to expiate for others. One should hold firm in the belief that full justice will be done in God's court where nothing else matters but one's faith and deeds. A mere verbal affirmation of belief in the Hereafter is, therefore, meaningless. The Christians and the Jews have corrupted their faith since they have distorted certain basic components of that belief. Their belief in the Hereafter is also inauthentic.

27. The People of the Book do not follow the Law revealed by God through His Messenger (peace be on him).

28. The purpose for which the Muslims are required to fight is not as one might think to compel the unbelievers into embracing Islam. Rather, their purpose is to put an end to the sovereignty and supremacy of the unbelievers so that the latter are unable to rule over men, The authority to rule should only be vested in those who follow the true faith; unbelievers who do not follow this true faith should live in a state of subordination. Unbelievers are required to pay *jizyah* (poll tax) in lieu of the security provided to them as the *Dhimmīs* ('Protected People') of an Islamic state. *Jizyah* symbolizes the submission of the unbelievers to the suzerainty of Islam. 'To pay *jizyah* of their own hands humbled' refers to payment in a state of submission. 'Humbled' also reinforces the idea that the believers, rather than the unbelievers, should be the rulers in performance of their duty as God's vicegerents.

Initially the rule that *jizyah* should be realized from all non-Muslims meant its application to Christians and Jews living in the Islamic state. Later on, the Prophet (peaçe be on him) extended it to Zoroastrians as well, granting them the status of *Dhimmīs.* Guided by the Prophet's practice the Companions applied this rule to all non-Muslim religious communities living outside Arabia.

Some nineteenth-century Muslim writers and their followers in our own times never seem to tire of their apologies for *jizyah.* But God's religion does not require that apologetic explanations be made on its behalf. The simple fact is that according to Islam, non-Muslims have been granted the freedom to stay outside the Islamic fold and to cling to their false, man-made, ways if they so wish. They have, however, absolutely no right to seize the reins of power in any part of God's earth nor to direct the collective affairs of human beings according to their own misconceived doctrines. For if they are given such an opportunity, corruption and mischief will ensue. In such a situation the believers would be under an obligation to do their utmost to dislodge them from political power and to make them live in subservience to the Islamic way of life.

It is sometimes asked: 'What do non-Muslims get in return for *jizyah*?' In our view, *jizyah* is the compensation which non-Muslims pay for the freedom they are provided to adhere to their erroneous ways while living under an Islamic state. The amount so received should be spent on the administration of that righteous state which grants them freedom and protects their rights. One of the advantages of *jizyah* is that it reminds the *Dhimmīs* every year that because they do not embrace Islam, they are not only deprived of the honour of paying *Zakāh,* but also have to pay a price – *jizyah* – for clinging to their errors.

(30) The Jews say: 'Ezra ('Uzayr) is Allah's son,'[29] and the Christians say: 'The Messiah is the son of Allah.' These are merely verbal assertions in imitation of the sayings of those unbelievers who preceded them.[30] May Allah ruin them. How do they turn away from the truth? (31) They take their rabbis and their monks for their Lords beside Allah,[31] and also the Messiah, son of Mary, whereas they were commanded to worship none but the One God. There is no god but He. Exalted be He above those whom they associate with Him in His divinity. ▶

وَقَالَتِ ٱلْيَهُودُ عُزَيْرٌ ٱبْنُ ٱللَّهِ
وَقَالَتِ ٱلنَّصَٰرَى ٱلْمَسِيحُ
ٱبْنُ ٱللَّهِ ذَٰلِكَ قَوْلُهُم
بِأَفْوَٰهِهِمْ يُضَٰهِـُٔونَ قَوْلَ
ٱلَّذِينَ كَفَرُوا۟ مِن قَبْلُ قَٰتَلَهُمُ
ٱللَّهُ أَنَّىٰ يُؤْفَكُونَ ﴿٣٠﴾
ٱتَّخَذُوٓا۟ أَحْبَارَهُمْ وَرُهْبَٰنَهُمْ
أَرْبَابًا مِّن دُونِ ٱللَّهِ وَٱلْمَسِيحَ
ٱبْنَ مَرْيَمَ وَمَآ أُمِرُوٓا۟ إِلَّا
لِيَعْبُدُوٓا۟ إِلَٰهًا وَٰحِدًا لَّآ
إِلَٰهَ إِلَّا هُوَ سُبْحَٰنَهُۥ عَمَّا
يُشْرِكُونَ ﴿٣١﴾

---

29. The Jews consider Ezra (*c.* 450 B.C.) to be the reviver of their faith. According to their tradition, it was Ezra who compiled the Torah and revived the Law which had been lost in the dark period following the death of the Prophet Soloman (peace be on him). As a result of their captivity in Babylon the Jews had become oblivious to their Scripture, Law, traditions, and national language – Hebrew. The Jews hold Ezra in great esteem for his revival of their faith. Some Jewish sects, however, revered Ezra to the point of deifying him, some even considering him the son of God. The above verse does not suggest that all Jews were guilty of this deification. It only points to the erroneous Jewish concept of God which resulted in the appearance of certain groups within the Jewish community itself who held Ezra to be the son of God.

30. 'The unbelievers of old' refers to the Egyptians, Greeks, Romans, Persians and others who had gone astray. Influenced by their thoughts, superstitions, and myths, both the Jews and Christians invented false doctrines. (For further elaboration of this point see *Towards Understanding the Qur'ān*, vol. II, *al-Mā'idah* 5, n. 101, pp. 181–5 – Ed.)

(32) They seek to extinguish the light of Allah by blowing through their mouths; but Allah refuses everything except that He will perfect His light even though the unbelievers might abhor it. (33) He it is Who has sent His Messenger with the guidance and the true religion that He may make it prevail over all religions,[32] howsoever those who associate others with Allah in His divinity might detest it. ▶

يُرِيدُونَ أَن يُطْفِـُٔوا نُورَ ٱللَّهِ
بِأَفْوَٰهِهِمْ وَيَأْبَى ٱللَّهُ إِلَّآ
أَن يُتِمَّ نُورَهُۥ وَلَوْ كَرِهَ
ٱلْكَـٰفِرُونَ ﴿٣٢﴾ هُوَ ٱلَّذِىٓ
أَرْسَلَ رَسُولَهُۥ بِٱلْهُدَىٰ وَدِينِ
ٱلْحَقِّ لِيُظْهِرَهُۥ عَلَى ٱلدِّينِ كُلِّهِۦ
وَلَوْ كَرِهَ ٱلْمُشْرِكُونَ ﴿٣٣﴾

31. As reported in a tradition, 'Adī b. Ḥātim, a Christian convert to Islam, once requested the Prophet (peace be on him) to explain the import of the following Qur'ānic statement: 'They (the Jews and Christians) take their priests and monks as lords apart from Allah.' In reply the Prophet (peace be on him) asked him: 'Is it not so that you consider unlawful whatever your priests declare to be unlawful, and consider lawful whatever your priests declare to be lawful?' 'Adī confirmed that such was the practice of the Jews and Christians. Thereupon the Prophet (peace be on him) told him that doing so amounted to 'taking them as lords apart from Allah'.

This means, according to the Qur'ān, that those who declare things to be lawful or unlawful without sanction from the Book of God, in fact place themselves in the position of God. Similarly, those who accept the right of such persons to make laws according to their will take them as their lords.

Both these charges against the Jews and the Christians – that they declared one person or another to be the son of God, and that they invested human beings with the authority to make laws independent of Revelation – have been mentioned in order to emphasize that their profession to believe in God was false. They might well be believers in the existence of God. But their concept of God is so erroneous that their belief is no better than disbelief.

32. The word used in the verse is *al-dīn* (the way). In Arabic this word signifies, as we have explained earlier (see *Towards Understanding the Qur'ān*, vol. I, *al-Baqarah* 2, n. 204), a way of life to which one subjects oneself because of one's belief that he who prescribed it enjoys supreme

(34) Believers! Many of the rabbis and monks wrongfully devour men's possessions and hinder people from the way of Allah.[33] And there are those who amass gold and silver and do not spend it in the way of Allah. Announce to them the tidings of a painful chastisement (35) on a Day when they shall be heated in the Fire of Hell, and their foreheads and their sides and their backs shall be branded with it, [and they shall be told]: 'This is the treasure which you hoarded for yourselves. Taste, then, the punishment for what you have hoarded.'

۞ يَٰٓأَيُّهَا ٱلَّذِينَ ءَامَنُوٓا۟ إِنَّ كَثِيرًا
مِّنَ ٱلْأَحْبَارِ وَٱلرُّهْبَانِ لَيَأْكُلُونَ
أَمْوَٰلَ ٱلنَّاسِ بِٱلْبَٰطِلِ وَيَصُدُّونَ
عَن سَبِيلِ ٱللَّهِ ۗ وَٱلَّذِينَ يَكْنِزُونَ
ٱلذَّهَبَ وَٱلْفِضَّةَ وَلَا يُنفِقُونَهَا
فِى سَبِيلِ ٱللَّهِ فَبَشِّرْهُم بِعَذَابٍ
أَلِيمٍ ﴿٣٤﴾ يَوْمَ يُحْمَىٰ عَلَيْهَا فِى نَارِ
جَهَنَّمَ فَتُكْوَىٰ بِهَا جِبَاهُهُمْ
وَجُنُوبُهُمْ وَظُهُورُهُمْ ۖ هَٰذَا مَا
كَنَزْتُمْ لِأَنفُسِكُمْ فَذُوقُوا۟
مَا كُنتُمْ تَكْنِزُونَ ﴿٣٥﴾

---

authority and is worthy of obedience. The verse explains that the purpose of the Prophets was to establish the supremacy of the Guidance and the Right Way revealed to them by God over and above all other systems of life. In other words, a Prophet is never sent with a sanction to let the way of life revealed to him be subjected to other ways of life. Nor is a Prophet sent to be content to exist at the sufferance of the false ways of life which hold sway over man's life. Since a Prophet is the representative of the Lord of the universe, he seeks to make the Right Way prevail. If any other way of life continues to exist, it should be satisfied with the concessions made to it by Islam. For example, the rights granted to the *Dhimmīs* to enjoy the protection offered by Islam in lieu of *jizyah*. (See *Tafhīm al-Qur'ān, al-Zumar* 39, n. 3; *al-Mu'min* 40, n. 43, and *Fuṣṣilat* 41, n. 20.)

33. The false pretenders to piety issued false religious decrees in return for pecuniary benefits, took bribes, accepted presents and offerings, and invented a variety of religious rituals that forced people to buy their salvation from them. They also extorted money from the people on every conceivable pretext, creating situations in which it would become impossible for people to escape their extortionate clutches, be the occasion one of

(36) Surely the reckoning of months, in the sight of Allah, is twelve months,[34] laid down in Allah's decree on the day when He created the heavens and the earth; and out of these months four are sacred. That is the true ordainment. Do not, therefore, wrong yourselves, with respect to these months.[35] And fight all together against those who associate others with Allah in His divinity in the manner which they fight against you all together,[36] and know well that Allah is with the God-fearing.

إِنَّ عِدَّةَ ٱلشُّهُورِ عِندَ ٱللَّهِ ٱثْنَا عَشَرَ
شَهْرًا فِي كِتَٰبِ ٱللَّهِ يَوْمَ خَلَقَ
ٱلسَّمَٰوَٰتِ وَٱلْأَرْضَ مِنْهَآ
أَرْبَعَةٌ حُرُمٌ ذَٰلِكَ ٱلدِّينُ ٱلْقَيِّمُ
فَلَا تَظْلِمُوا۟ فِيهِنَّ أَنفُسَكُمْ
وَقَٰتِلُوا۟ ٱلْمُشْرِكِينَ كَآفَّةً
كَمَا يُقَٰتِلُونَكُمْ كَآفَّةً
وَٱعْلَمُوٓا۟ أَنَّ ٱللَّهَ مَعَ ٱلْمُتَّقِينَ ٣٦

birth, marriage or death. People were made to believe that their fate was in the pretenders' hands, that they could make or ruin you. Driven by pecuniary motives alone, they led people into error and engrossed them in it. Whenever a call for reform is made, such people are the first to oppose it and use every possible device to that wicked end.

34. Ever since God created the universe, the moon has unfailingly appeared every month in the form of a crescent and then completed its full cycle ending with its disappearance from the sky. As a result of this, twelve months have always constituted a year. However, the Arabs, in accordance with their practice of *nasī'*, increased the number of months to thirteen or fourteen to enable them to interpose in the calendar a sacred month which they declared to be free of the restrictions they were required to follow during the 'sacred months'. (For further elaboration see n. 37 below.)

35. They were asked not to disregard beneficial considerations, for waging war in those months was prohibited, nor to wrong themselves by creating disorder during those days. The four months alluded to here are the months of Dhu al-Qa'dah, Dhu al-Ḥijjah and Muḥarram for *Ḥajj* (Major Pilgrimage) and Rajab for *'Umrah* (Minor Pilgrimage).

(37) The intercalation [of sacred months] is an act of gross infidelity which causes the unbelievers to be led further astray. They declare a month to be lawful in one year and forbidden in another year in order that they may conform to the number of months that Allah has declared as sacred, and at the same time make lawful what Allah has forbidden.[37] Their foul acts seem fair to them. Allah does not provide guidance to those who deny the truth.

إِنَّمَا ٱلنَّسِىٓءُ زِيَادَةٌ فِى ٱلْكُفْرِ
يُضَلُّ بِهِ ٱلَّذِينَ كَفَرُوا۟ يُحِلُّونَهُۥ عَامًا
وَيُحَرِّمُونَهُۥ عَامًا لِّيُوَاطِـُٔوا۟ عِدَّةَ مَا
حَرَّمَ ٱللَّهُ فَيُحِلُّوا۟ مَا حَرَّمَ ٱللَّهُ ۚ زُيِّنَ
لَهُمْ سُوٓءُ أَعْمَٰلِهِمْ ۗ وَٱللَّهُ
لَا يَهْدِى ٱلْقَوْمَ ٱلْكَٰفِرِينَ
٣٧

36. The Muslims are told that they are free to fight in the sacred months if the unbelievers attack them. If the unbelievers fight unitedly against the Muslims in disregard of the sacred months, the Muslims may also unitedly fight against them. (For an explanation of this verse, see *al-Baqarah* 2: 194.)

37. *Nasī'* was practised by the Arabs in two ways:

(1) In order to shed blood or to plunder, or to satisfy a blood vendetta; here they declared a sacred month to be an ordinary one, and compensated for this violation later on by declaring one of the ordinary months to be sacred.

(2) With a view to harmonizing the lunar calendar with the solar calendar the Arabs used to add a month to the lunar calendar. Their purpose in so doing was to ensure that the *Ḥajj* dates should consistently fall in the same season so that they were spared the hardship and inconvenience resulting from observation of the lunar calendar for the fixation of the *Ḥajj* dates. As a result of this practice, *Ḥajj* was performed once on its appointed date, the days on which the 9th and 10th of Dhu al-Ḥijjah truly fell, and then for the next thirty-three years it was performed on days which were fictitiously declared to be the 9th and 10th of Dhu al-Ḥijjah. Allusion to this is found in the Prophet's address during the Farewell Pilgrimage:

'The time has returned to what it was when God created the heavens and the earth.' (Bukhārī, 'Tafsīr', 'Bāb inna 'iddat al-Shuhūr 'ind Allāh ithnā 'ashar Shahran fī Kitāb Allāh' – Ed.)

By forbidding *nasī'*, a major step was taken to frustrate the principal purposes of the pre-Islamic Arabs. The first of these purposes involved, quite obviously, undisguised sin. It consisted, in practice, of legalizing what God had declared unlawful; by resorting to chicanery the Arabs attempted to give their impious act a semblance of legality. As for the second purpose (viz. to keep the *Ḥajj* permanently fixed to the solar calendar), it might seem innocuous and beneficent at first sight. In actual fact, however, even this purpose amounts to an act of rebellion against the law of God.

God chose the lunar calendar in connection with the rites of *Ḥajj* for a number of reasons, one of which seems to be that man should accustom himself to following the law of God in all possible conditions and circumstances. To take the case of Ramaḍān, because it follows the lunar calendar, it falls in different seasons. Sometimes it falls in summer, sometimes in winter, and sometimes in spring or autumn. Men of faith, however, obey God in every season, in all kinds of weather conditions, and this provides them with excellent moral training. Similarly, as the lunar calendar is followed in determining the dates of *Ḥajj*, then this also falls in different years in different seasons. People, therefore, have to undertake long journeys in varying conditions to perform Pilgrimage. This is certainly a test of their mettle and helps them acquire the capacity to remain steadfast in their obedience to God. Now, if for the sake of man's own convenience – be it in relation to tourism, business or fun – the Muslims were to decide that *Ḥajj* and Ramaḍān should always fall during the pleasant seasons of the year, this would amount to a rebellion against God; for some of God's purposes would be blatantly violated. Moreover, since Islam is a universal religion, it is inconceivable that a particular month of the solar calendar should be permanently fixed for Pilgrimage or Fasting, for some people would find it convenient whilst others, travelling from other parts of the world, would find it permanently inconvenient.

It is worth noting that the proclamation to abolish *nasī'* was made during the *Ḥajj* in 9 A.H./631 C.E. The following year, in 10 A.H./632 C.E., *Ḥajj* was performed on the appointed dates and in accordance with the lunar calendar. From that time onwards *Ḥajj* has always been performed on its due dates.

(38) Believers![38] What is amiss with you that when it is said to you: 'March forth in the cause of Allah,' you cling heavily to the earth? Do you prefer the worldly life to the Hereafter? Know well that all the enjoyment of this world, in comparison with the Hereafter, is trivial.[39] (39) If you do not march forth, Allah will chastise you grievously[40] and will replace you by another people,[41] while you will in no way be able to harm Him. Allah has power over everything. ▶

يَٰٓأَيُّهَا ٱلَّذِينَ ءَامَنُوا۟ مَا لَكُمْ
إِذَا قِيلَ لَكُمُ ٱنفِرُوا۟ فِى سَبِيلِ ٱللَّهِ
ٱثَّاقَلْتُمْ إِلَى ٱلْأَرْضِ ۚ أَرَضِيتُم
بِٱلْحَيَوٰةِ ٱلدُّنْيَا مِنَ ٱلْءَاخِرَةِ ۚ
فَمَا مَتَٰعُ ٱلْحَيَوٰةِ ٱلدُّنْيَا فِى
ٱلْءَاخِرَةِ إِلَّا قَلِيلٌ ﴿٣٨﴾ إِلَّا
تَنفِرُوا۟ يُعَذِّبْكُمْ عَذَابًا
أَلِيمًا وَيَسْتَبْدِلْ قَوْمًا غَيْرَكُمْ
وَلَا تَضُرُّوهُ شَيْـًٔا ۗ وَٱللَّهُ عَلَىٰ
كُلِّ شَىْءٍ قَدِيرٌ ﴿٣٩﴾

---

38. This verse marks the beginning of the second discourse of the *sūrah* (comprising verses 38–72). It was revealed during the preparations for the Tabūk expedition.

39. The statement that the goods of this world will count for little in the Hereafter is open to two possible interpretations. First, it may mean that on witnessing the eternal life and immeasurable bounties of the Next Life one will realize the triviality of pleasures gained in worldly life. This would make people deeply regret, despite having been duly warned and out of sheer short-sightedness, that they sacrificed the everlasting and immense bliss of the Hereafter for the ephemeral pleasures of this world.

Second, that the enjoyments of this world will be of no avail in the Next Life. For, howsoever well provided one might be with worldly goods, one has to leave them behind at the time of death. Once a man dies all his worldly possessions remain behind and no part of them can be transferred to the Next World. Whatever good will come to man's share in the Next Life will be in consideration of the sacrifices he has made in seeking God's good pleasure.

40. This verse formed the basis of a legal ruling issued by the jurists regarding *jihād*. They concluded that as long as the Muslims as a whole, or the Muslims of a particular area or a section thereof, have not been

(40) It will matter little if you do not help the Prophet, for Allah surely helped him when the unbelievers drove him out of his home and he was but one of the two when they were in the cave, and when he said to his companion: 'Do not grieve. Allah is with us.'[42] Then Allah caused His tranquillity to descend upon him, and supported him with hosts you did not see; and He humbled the word of the unbelievers. And Allah's word is inherently uppermost. Allah is All-Powerful, All-Wise. (41) March forth whether light or heavy,[43] and strive in the way of Allah with your belongings and your lives. That is best for you if you only knew it.

إِلَّا تَنصُرُوهُ فَقَدْ نَصَرَهُ ٱللَّهُ إِذْ
أَخْرَجَهُ ٱلَّذِينَ كَفَرُوا۟ ثَانِىَ
ٱثْنَيْنِ إِذْ هُمَا فِى ٱلْغَارِ إِذْ
يَقُولُ لِصَـٰحِبِهِۦ لَا تَحْزَنْ
إِنَّ ٱللَّهَ مَعَنَا ۖ فَأَنزَلَ ٱللَّهُ
سَكِينَتَهُۥ عَلَيْهِ وَأَيَّدَهُۥ
بِجُنُودٍ لَّمْ تَرَوْهَا وَجَعَلَ
كَلِمَةَ ٱلَّذِينَ كَفَرُوا۟
ٱلسُّفْلَىٰ ۗ وَكَلِمَةُ ٱللَّهِ هِىَ
ٱلْعُلْيَا ۗ وَٱللَّهُ عَزِيزٌ حَكِيمٌ ﴿٤٠﴾
ٱنفِرُوا۟ خِفَافًا وَثِقَالًا وَجَـٰهِدُوا۟
بِأَمْوَٰلِكُمْ وَأَنفُسِكُمْ فِى سَبِيلِ
ٱللَّهِ ۚ ذَٰلِكُمْ خَيْرٌ لَّكُمْ إِن كُنتُمْ
تَعْلَمُونَ ﴿٤١﴾

summoned to *jihād*, it would remain merely *farḍ bi al-kifāyah* (the collective duty of all Muslims). Thus, if some Muslims engage in *jihād*, other Muslims are absolved from that obligation. However, if the Muslims are called upon by their leader to make *jihād* – no matter whether all Muslims are so called, or the Muslims of a particular area, or a section thereof – *jihād* would become obligatory on every Muslim who has been so called upon. The matter is of such vital importance that if those who fail to perform this duty without any legitimate excuse claim to be Muslims, such a claim will not be entertained.

41. The Muslims are told to disabuse their minds of the misconception that but for them God's purposes would not be achieved. On the contrary, if they have served the cause of God they should gratefully recognize God's favour on them insofar as He has provided them with a golden opportunity to serve the cause of their faith. If they allow such an opportunity to slip,

(42) Were it a gain at hand or a short journey, they would have surely followed you, but the distance seemed too far to them.[44] Still they will swear by Allah: 'If only we could, we would surely have gone forth with you.' They merely bring ruin upon themselves. Allah knows well that they are liars.

لَوْ كَانَ عَرَضًا قَرِيبًا وَسَفَرًا قَاصِدًا لَّاتَّبَعُوكَ وَلَٰكِنۢ بَعُدَتْ عَلَيْهِمُ الشُّقَّةُ ۚ وَسَيَحْلِفُونَ بِاللَّهِ لَوِ اسْتَطَعْنَا لَخَرَجْنَا مَعَكُمْ يُهْلِكُونَ أَنفُسَهُمْ وَاللَّهُ يَعْلَمُ إِنَّهُمْ لَكَاذِبُونَ ﴿٤٢﴾

---

then God will lavish that favour on some other people. (For details of the *Hijrah* see Ibn Hishām, vol. 1, pp. 484–96. See also the comments of Qurṭubī and Ibn Kathīr on the verse – Ed.)

42. This statement occurs in connection with the migration of the Prophet (peace be on him) to Madina on the very night the Makkan unbelievers planned to kill him. A majority of Muslims had already migrated to Madina in their twos and threes. Those Muslims who remained in Makka were either helpless or were not dependable; their faith being suspect. When the Prophet (peace be on him) learned of the plot to assassinate him, he left Makka in the company of only one person, Abū Bakr. Anticipating a hot pursuit by the enemy, the Prophet (peace be on him) travelled southward instead of following the northern route which leads to Madina. He also secluded himself in a cave, Thawr, for three days.

As the Prophet (peace be on him) had anticipated, his bloodthirsty enemies began their mad pursuit. They searched every nook and cranny around Makka. Some of his pursuers even reached the mouth of the cave where the Prophet (peace be on him) was in hiding. This naturally caused Abū Bakr considerable consternation as he and the Prophet (peace be on him) were just a step away from being caught. The Prophet (peace be on him) remained unperturbed. He comforted Abū Bakr, saying: 'Grieve not, for Allah is with us.' (For relevant details of the *Hijrah* see Ibn Hishām, vol. 1, pp. 484 ff. – Ed.)

43. The directive: 'Go forth in the way of Allah, whether you are equipped lightly or heavily', is comprehensive in its meaning. In the first place, it instructs Muslims to go forth and fight in the cause of God. They should comply with this request regardless of whether they feel happy to do so or not; whether they are amply resourceful or otherwise; whether

(43) Allah forgive you! Why did you give them leave to stay behind before it became clear to you as to whom were truthful and who were liars.[45] (44) Those who believe in Allah and the Last Day will never ask your leave to be excused from striving (in the cause of Allah) with their belongings and their lives. Allah fully knows the God-fearing. (45) It is only those who do not believe in Allah and the Last Day, and whose hearts are filled with doubt that seek exemption from striving (in the cause of Allah). They keep tossing to and fro in their doubt.[46] ▶

عَفَا ٱللَّهُ عَنكَ لِمَ أَذِنتَ لَهُمْ حَتَّىٰ
يَتَبَيَّنَ لَكَ ٱلَّذِينَ صَدَقُوا۟ وَتَعْلَمَ
ٱلْكَٰذِبِينَ ﴿٤٣﴾ لَا يَسْتَـْٔذِنُكَ
ٱلَّذِينَ يُؤْمِنُونَ بِٱللَّهِ وَٱلْيَوْمِ
ٱلْءَاخِرِ أَن يُجَٰهِدُوا۟ بِأَمْوَٰلِهِمْ
وَأَنفُسِهِمْ ۗ وَٱللَّهُ عَلِيمٌۢ بِٱلْمُتَّقِينَ ﴿٤٤﴾
إِنَّمَا يَسْتَـْٔذِنُكَ ٱلَّذِينَ لَا يُؤْمِنُونَ
بِٱللَّهِ وَٱلْيَوْمِ ٱلْءَاخِرِ وَٱرْتَابَتْ قُلُوبُهُمْ
فَهُمْ فِى رَيْبِهِمْ يَتَرَدَّدُونَ ﴿٤٥﴾

---

the circumstances are favourable or adverse, and whether they are young and healthy or old and weak.

44. The idea of marching across vast stretches of desert to reach Tabūk appeared arduous for a number of reasons. Because of the prospect of an armed encounter with a power as great as that of the Romans; because the journey was to take place in the blazing heat of summer; and because the harvesting season was just at hand – this was of great importance that year when famine conditions prevailed.

45. Proffering excuses, the hypocrites asked the Prophet (peace be on him) to exempt them from *jihād*. Even though the Prophet (peace be on him) was aware of the falsity of their excuses, he granted them an exemption. This, however, did not meet with the approval of God, and the Prophet (peace be on him) was told that his leniency towards the hypocrites was not well-placed for the latter had used the exemption to disguise their hypocrisy. Had they not been exempted, their deliberate abstention from *jihād* would have revealed the hypocrites in their true colours.

(46) Had they truly intended to march forth to fight, they would have certainly made some preparation for it. But Allah was averse to their going forth,[47] so He made them lag behind, and they were told: 'Stay behind with those that are staying behind.' (47) Had they gone forth with you, they would have only added to your trouble, and would have run about in your midst seeking to stir up sedition between you, whereas there are among you some who are prone to give ears to them. Allah knows well the wrong-doers. (48) Surely they sought even earlier to stir up sedition, and turned things upside down to frustrate you until the truth came and the decree of Allah appeared, however hateful this may have been to them.

۞ وَلَوْ أَرَادُوا الْخُرُوجَ لَأَعَدُّوا لَهُ
عُدَّةً وَلَٰكِن كَرِهَ اللَّهُ انبِعَاثَهُمْ
فَثَبَّطَهُمْ وَقِيلَ اقْعُدُوا مَعَ
الْقَاعِدِينَ ﴿٤٦﴾ لَوْ خَرَجُوا فِيكُم
مَّا زَادُوكُمْ إِلَّا خَبَالًا وَلَأَوْضَعُوا
خِلَالَكُمْ يَبْغُونَكُمُ الْفِتْنَةَ
وَفِيكُمْ سَمَّاعُونَ لَهُمْ ۗ وَاللَّهُ عَلِيمٌ
بِالظَّالِمِينَ ﴿٤٧﴾ لَقَدِ ابْتَغَوُا
الْفِتْنَةَ مِن قَبْلُ وَقَلَّبُوا لَكَ
الْأُمُورَ حَتَّىٰ جَاءَ الْحَقُّ وَظَهَرَ
أَمْرُ اللَّهِ وَهُمْ كَارِهُونَ ﴿٤٨﴾

---

46. One thus learns that an encounter between the forces of Islam and unbelief serves as a touchstone for distinguishing a true believer from a hypocrite. Whenever such an encounter takes place, a sincere believer is bound to exert himself to the utmost in his support of Islam, not sparing any effort or resource in that connection. On the contrary, if a person shirks from supporting Islam and is overly concerned with saving his own skin, his conduct negates his claim to be a sincere believer.

47. God did not like that people should rise to fight in His cause unwillingly, without sincerity of purpose. The situation with the hypocrites was that they lacked the spirit of *jihād*; they had no zeal for a struggle to

(49) And among them is he who says: 'Grant me leave to stay behind, and do not expose me to temptation.'[48] Lo! They have already fallen into temptation.[49] Surely the Hell encompasses the unbelievers.[50]

وَمِنْهُم مَّن يَقُولُ ٱئْذَن لِّي
وَلَا تَفْتِنِّيٓ ۚ أَلَا فِي ٱلْفِتْنَةِ
سَقَطُوا۟ ۗ وَإِنَّ جَهَنَّمَ
لَمُحِيطَةٌۢ بِٱلْكَٰفِرِينَ
٤٩

uphold Islam. If they were to participate half-heartedly in *jihād* merely under the pressure of Muslim public opinion, or with the intent to cause mischief, this might have resulted in much greater damage as is clearly mentioned in the next verse (i.e. verse 47).

48. Some of the hypocrites even had the affrontery to seek their exemption from *jihād* by fabricating excuses weaved from religious and moral pretensions. This is well illustrated by the plea of Jadd b. Qays which has been recorded in the traditions. He told the Prophet (peace be on him) that he was infatuated with feminine beauty, a weakness which he claimed was well known to his fellow-tribesmen. He pleaded that if he were to see Roman women, he might be unable to keep himself under control. He asked, therefore, for an exemption from *jihād* in order that he remain beyond such temptations. (See Ibn Hishām, vol. 2, p. 516. See also the comments of Qurṭubī on the verse – Ed.)

49. These hypocrites made the pretence that they were afraid of evil temptations and hence should be spared being sent to the war-front. But the fact of the matter is that they were fully given over to a variety of evils – hypocrisy, lies, deceit, and pretence of piety. They sought to persuade their God of their fears from even minor temptations. But it is quite clear that withholding their support to Islam in its crucial encounter with unbelief is in itself the worst kind of evil.

50. Instead of bringing them any good, their false pretence of piety led them ultimately to Hell.

(50) If good fortune befalls you, it vexes them; and if an affliction befalls you, they turn away in jubilation and say: 'We have taken due care of our affairs in good time.' (51) Say: 'Nothing will befall us except what Allah has decreed for us; He is our Protector.' Let the believers, then, put all their trust in Allah.[51]

إِن تُصِبْكَ حَسَنَةٌ تَسُؤْهُمْ
وَإِن تُصِبْكَ مُصِيبَةٌ
يَقُولُوا قَدْ أَخَذْنَا أَمْرَنَا مِن
قَبْلُ وَيَتَوَلَّوا وَّهُمْ
فَرِحُونَ ﴿٥٠﴾ قُل لَّن
يُصِيبَنَا إِلَّا مَا كَتَبَ
اللَّهُ لَنَا هُوَ مَوْلَىٰنَا وَعَلَى اللَّهِ
فَلْيَتَوَكَّلِ الْمُؤْمِنُونَ ﴿٥١﴾

51. The above Qur'ānic passage delineates the differences in the attitude of a man of God and a man of the world. In all his actions the man of the world seeks to satisfy himself by the attainment of worldly ends. If he is able to attain those ends, his joy knows no bounds. If he fails, he feels overly dejected. Moreover, a worldly person depends on material resources alone. If material circumstances seem favourable, that boosts his spirit. In unfavourable circumstances, he feels altogether heart-broken.

A man of God, on the contrary, is prompted in all his actions by the desire to please God. Therefore, far from depending on his own strength or on material resources, he depends upon God. Regardless of whether he meets with success or suffers reverses in his struggle for the cause of the truth, he remains calm since he believes that both are essentially God given; that it is the omnipotent will of God which is at work in both cases. Adversities do not dishearten him. Success does not make him swagger. For, apart from considering both success and failure to be from God, he regards each of them as a test from God, and his attention is focused on how he might successfully pass that test.

Moreover, since his basic purposes are not of a worldly nature, he does not measure his success or failure by a worldly yardstick. The good pleasure of God being his sole end, a man of God measures his success or failure with reference to the extent to which he was able to devote his life and resources in God's cause. If a man does exert himself fully in the performance of his duty, it is immaterial whether he attains any success in this world or not. For he is convinced that even if he loses all that he has in this world – his resources, and even his life – this will not be allowed to go unrewarded by God in Whose cause he had made that sacrifice. Such a man is also not daunted by adverse circumstances, for he places his trust

(52) Tell them: 'What you await to befall upon us is nothing but one of the two good things![52] And what we await for you is that Allah visit you with chastisement from Him or chastise you at our hands. So continue waiting; we too shall wait with you.'

قُلْ هَلْ تَرَبَّصُونَ بِنَآ إِلَّآ إِحْدَى ٱلْحُسْنَيَيْنِ وَنَحْنُ نَتَرَبَّصُ بِكُمْ أَن يُصِيبَكُمُ ٱللَّهُ بِعَذَابٍ مِّنْ عِندِهِۦٓ أَوْ بِأَيْدِينَا فَتَرَبَّصُوٓا۟ إِنَّا مَعَكُم مُّتَرَبِّصُونَ ﴿٥٢﴾

in God, the Lord of all resources. Reposing his trust in God, he continues to strive with the same zeal and determination with which a worldly person strives when the circumstances seem favourable.

That is the reason why God directs the believers in the above verse to tell the hypocrites, who are enamoured of worldly life, that the basic attitude of the believers is altogether different from theirs. The two groups also entertain entirely different notions as to what causes happiness and grief. The believers derive their contentment and happiness from one source, and the hypocrites from an entirely different source.

52. The hypocrites, despite their profession of belief in Islam, refrained from openly taking sides with Islam in its encounter with unbelief. They were disposed to a 'wisdom' which ensured they remain on the fence and watch from a safe distance the outcome of the encounter between the two forces – Islam and unbelief. The result could be either the victory of the Prophet (peace be on him) and his Companions, or their total destruction by the mighty Roman army. In response to their attitude the hypocrites were told (see verse 52) that both consequences were good in the eyes of the Muslims. For if the believers emerged victorious, the good of it, for them, would be self-evident. However, even if the Muslims perished whilst sincerely striving for their cause, this is a great achievement in the eyes of a Muslim, even though the superficial judgement of the world would deride it as a disgraceful end. This is so because the criterion used by a Muslim to measure his success or failure is quite different from that used by others. A Muslim's success does not essentially consist of such worldly achievements as the conquest of a territory or the establishment of an empire. His true success depends on devoting all his physical and mental energy to upholding the Word of God. If a Muslim devotes himself to this cause, he will be reckoned successful even if the result of his efforts, from a worldly point of view, might add up to zero.

(53) Tell them: 'Whether you spend your money willingly or unwillingly,[53] it shall not find acceptance (with Allah) for you are an evil-doing folk.' (54) Nothing prevents that their expendings be accepted except that they disbelieve in Allah and His Messenger, and whenever they come to the Prayer they do so lazily, and whenever they spend they do so grudgingly. (55) Let neither their riches nor their children excite your admiration. Allah only wants to chastise them through these things in the present life,[54] and to cause them to die while they are unbelievers.[55]

قُلْ أَنفِقُوا۟ طَوْعًا أَوْ كَرْهًا لَّن
يُتَقَبَّلَ مِنكُمْ إِنَّكُمْ كُنتُمْ
قَوْمًا فَٰسِقِينَ ﴿٥٣﴾ وَمَا مَنَعَهُمْ
أَن تُقْبَلَ مِنْهُمْ نَفَقَٰتُهُمْ إِلَّآ
أَنَّهُمْ كَفَرُوا۟ بِٱللَّهِ وَبِرَسُولِهِۦ
وَلَا يَأْتُونَ ٱلصَّلَوٰةَ إِلَّا وَهُمْ
كُسَالَىٰ وَلَا يُنفِقُونَ إِلَّا وَهُمْ
كَٰرِهُونَ ﴿٥٤﴾ فَلَا تُعْجِبْكَ
أَمْوَٰلُهُمْ وَلَآ أَوْلَٰدُهُمْ إِنَّمَا
يُرِيدُ ٱللَّهُ لِيُعَذِّبَهُم بِهَا فِى
ٱلْحَيَوٰةِ ٱلدُّنْيَا وَتَزْهَقَ
أَنفُسُهُمْ وَهُمْ كَٰفِرُونَ ﴿٥٥﴾

---

53. Some of the hypocrites who were unwilling to take the risk of joining the Muslims in their *jihād,* were also keen not to lose their credibility among the Muslims by totally dissociating themselves from it since this would have amounted to a public proclamation of their 'hypocrisy'. Hence they took the position that while they would like to be exempted from actual fighting, they would be willing to make financial contributions to the cause of *jihād*.

54. Here, the real cause of hypocrisy has been pin-pointed – excessive love for their offspring and worldly possessions. Given this weakness, it was obvious that the hypocrites would ultimately be disgraced among the Muslims and lose all the prestige, influence and social status which they had hitherto enjoyed in the Arab society. For while the hereditary chiefs would lose their *locus standi,* those belonging to the lower rungs of society – the common slaves and the offspring of slaves, the ordinary cultivators and shepherds – would attain honour and status in the new social order if they remained faithful to the cause of Islam.

An illustration in point is the following incident which took place in the

(56) They swear by Allah that they belong with you whereas they are certainly not of you. They are merely a people who dread you. (57) If they could find any shelter or any cavern, or any retreat, they would turn around and rush headlong into it.[56]

وَيَحْلِفُونَ بِٱللَّهِ إِنَّهُمْ لَمِنكُمْ وَمَا هُم مِّنكُمْ وَلَٰكِنَّهُمْ قَوْمٌ يَفْرَقُونَ ﴿٥٦﴾ لَوْ يَجِدُونَ مَلْجَـًٔا أَوْ مَغَـٰرَٰتٍ أَوْ مُدَّخَلًا لَّوَلَّوْا۟ إِلَيْهِ وَهُمْ يَجْمَحُونَ ﴿٥٧﴾

time of 'Umar. Some leading members of the Quraysh, including Suhayl b. 'Amr and Ḥārith b. Hishām once called upon 'Umar. While they were seated in 'Umar's company they noticed that 'Umar received the *Anṣār* and *Muhājirūn* with great consideration and asked them to sit beside him in preference to the Quraysh notables whom he asked to move aside so that after some time they were relegated to the rear-most seats. When the Quraysh notables came out of the meeting Ḥārith addressed his colleagues thus: 'Look! How we were treated today!' To this Suhayl b. 'Amr replied: "Umar is not to be blamed for meting out this treatment to us. Rather it is our own fault. We had rejected this religion when we were invited to accept it while they [the *Anṣār* and *Muhājirūn*] readily accepted it.' They later visited 'Umar and told him: 'Today we saw how you treated us. We realize that we are to be blamed for it. Is there a way for us to make amends?' Without giving any reply 'Umar pointed to the Roman border. His message was loud and clear. If they could show the readiness to sacrifice their lives and wealth in the cause of God, this might help them regain their lost positions.

55. Apart from being subjected to worldly disgrace and ignominy, the hypocrites would undergo a greater suffering: they would not be able to enjoy the blessing of true faith till their last breath and this would be because of the hypocritical traits which they had nourished in themselves. Furthermore, after ruining their lives in this world, they would proceed from it to meet an even more calamitous end in the Next Life.

56. Almost all the hypocrites of Madina were rich and elderly people. According to the description of the hypocrites in Ibn Kathīr's *al-Bidāyah wa al-Nihāyah*, only one of them was young and absolutely none of them was poor. (See Ibn Kathīr, *al-Bidāyah wa al-Nihāyah*, vol. 3, pp. 237–41 – Ed.) They had successful businesses and sprawling estates in Madina. Their extensive experience in worldly matters had turned them into perfect time-servers. When soon after the advent of Islam in Madina a large number

(58) (O Prophet!) Some of them find fault with you in the distribution of alms. If they are given something thereof they are pleased, and if they are given nothing they are angry.[57] (59) Would that they were content with what Allah and His Messenger gave them,[58] and were to say: 'Allah suffices for us, and Allah will give us out of His bounty and so will His Messenger.[59] It is to Allah alone that we turn with hope.'[60] ▶

وَمِنْهُم مَّن يَلْمِزُكَ فِي ٱلصَّدَقَٰتِ فَإِنْ
أُعْطُوا۟ مِنْهَا رَضُوا۟ وَإِن لَّمْ يُعْطَوْا۟ مِنْهَآ
إِذَا هُمْ يَسْخَطُونَ ﴿٥٨﴾ وَلَوْ أَنَّهُمْ
رَضُوا۟ مَآ ءَاتَىٰهُمُ ٱللَّهُ وَرَسُولُهُۥ
وَقَالُوا۟ حَسْبُنَا ٱللَّهُ سَيُؤْتِينَا
ٱللَّهُ مِن فَضْلِهِۦ وَرَسُولُهُۥٓ إِنَّآ إِلَى
ٱللَّهِ رَٰغِبُونَ ﴿٥٩﴾

of its inhabitants embraced Islam with sincerity and devotion, the hypocrites found themselves in a tight corner. For, on the one hand, they found their fellow tribesmen, including some of their own sons and daughters, full of sincere devotion to Islam. In such a situation were they to reject and publicly renounce Islam, this could mean the very end of their prestige and influence. This could also invite severe opposition from members of their own household. On the other hand, if they aligned themselves with the Muslims, it was obvious that it would incur the hostility of all Arabia, and possibly of a number of neighbouring countries and empires. At the same time, they were so strongly in the grip of their own self-interest that they had lost the capacity to appreciate the truth for its own sake; they were unable to comprehend the idea of placing the truth above everything else and courting all possible risks and endangering their lives and wealth for its sake. Thus their self-interest dictated that they should profess belief in Islam in order to retain their prestige in Madina as well as to protect their estates and commercial interests. This profession of Islam was a mere sham so as to ward off the dangers inherent in sincere and unreserved identification with Islam.

The Qur'ān accurately portrays their state of mind and stresses that they had not sincerely identified themselves with the Muslims. They had willy-nilly become a part of the Muslim body-politic, merely out of the fear of economic loss. They had professed their identification with the Muslims because they were afraid of the many losses which they might incur by openly renouncing Islam while living in Madina. Such a step was not only likely to destroy their social position but might even rupture their relations with their wives and children. Also, if they decided to leave Madina, it would entail colossal material loss. So in the final analysis they did not even have any sincere devotion to unbelief which would prepare them to suffer losses for its sake.

All these factors ensured that the hypocrites stayed on in Madina, performing Prayers even though they detested it, and paying *Zakāh* even though they paid it in the spirit in which one pays a penalty. However, day in and day out their formal profession to faith in Islam made them vulnerable to the demands to engage in *jihād* against one formidable power or another, and to risk their lives and property for the sake of Islam. These demands made them so restless that they would have been happy to seek refuge in any hole and hiding place, if such were available, which promised them security for their interests.

57. For the first time in the history of Arabia all those who possessed wealth exceeding a certain minimum were asked to pay *Zakāh*. This *Zakāh* was levied on agricultural produce, cattle, merchandise, minerals, and gold and silver according to a set of varying rates of 2.5 per cent, 5 per cent, 10 per cent and 20 per cent. Since *Zakāh* was collected and spent in an organized manner, the Prophet (peace be on him) received and distributed funds on a scale previously unknown to the Arabs.

This spectacle of wealth distribution whetted the hypocrites' appetites. However, as we know, the Prophet (peace be on him), who oversaw the distribution of *Zakāh*, excluded himself and the members of his family from any share in it. How could he then tolerate that *Zakāh* should be appropriated by undeserving persons? This attitude of the Prophet (peace be on him) offended the hypocrites and evoked their spite. The hypocrites obviously could not spell out the true reason for their wrath. It was embarrassing for them to say that they were annoyed since they were not permitted to misappropriate *Zakāh* funds. They, therefore, kept their real grievance hidden and time and again found false reasons for accusing the Prophet (peace be on him) of partiality and injustice in the distribution of *Zakāh*.

58. The Qur'ān says that the hypocrites should have better felt content with the share of the spoils granted to them by the Prophet (peace be on him), with the living which they made because of the grace of God, and with the prosperity which they enjoyed.

59. The hypocrites should have felt secure economically for they were entitled, like before, to receive their due shares besides *Zakāh* out of the wealth that would come to the treasury.

60. Rather than focus one's attention on the world and its worthless riches, one should turn one's attention to God and His grace and bounty,

(60) The alms are meant only for the poor[61] and the needy[62] and those who are in charge thereof,[63] those whose hearts are to be reconciled;[64] and to free those in bondage,[65] and to help those burdened with debt,[66] and for expenditure in the way of Allah[67] and for the wayfarer.[68] This is an obligation from Allah. Allah is All-Knowing, All-Wise.

۞ إِنَّمَا ٱلصَّدَقَٰتُ لِلْفُقَرَآءِ
وَٱلْمَسَٰكِينِ وَٱلْعَٰمِلِينَ عَلَيْهَا
وَٱلْمُؤَلَّفَةِ قُلُوبُهُمْ وَفِى ٱلرِّقَابِ
وَٱلْغَٰرِمِينَ وَفِى سَبِيلِ ٱللَّهِ
وَٱبْنِ ٱلسَّبِيلِ ۖ فَرِيضَةً مِّنَ ٱللَّهِ ۗ
وَٱللَّهُ عَلِيمٌ حَكِيمٌ ٦٠

---

seeking His good pleasure. One's hopes should be centred upon Him alone; and one should be totally satisfied with whatever wealth God bestows.

61. The Qur'ānic term *faqīr* (the poor) applies to those who depend for their subsistence on others. The word includes all those who are needy regardless of whether they are so because of factors such as physical disability or old age. It also includes those who have become needy owing to accidental circumstances which have rendered them orphans, widows, unemployed, or temporarily disabled. Likewise, it also includes those who, after temporarily receiving some assistance, are likely to become self-supporting.

62. *Maskanah* from which the word *miskīn* (pl. *masākīn*) is derived, denotes helplessness, destitution. Thus *masākīn* are those who are in greater distress than the ordinary poor people. Explaining this word the Prophet (peace be on him) declared that *masākīn* are those who cannot make both ends meet, who face acute hardship and yet whose sense of self-respect prevents them from asking for aid from others and whose outward demeanour fails to create the impression that they are deserving of help. The words used in a tradition are the following: '*Miskīn* is he who lacks the resource that would suffice him, who does not look as one deserving of charity, nor does he resort to begging.' (Bukhārī, 'Zakāh', 'Bāb Qawlihī Ta'ālá lā Yas'alūn al-Nās ilḥāfa . . . ' – Ed.) In short, he is both self-respecting and poor.

63. 'Those employed to administer them' refers to those appointed by the state to collect *ṣadaqāt* (alms), to ensure the safe-keeping of the funds

collected, to maintain their accounts, and to disburse them. Even when such persons are not poor or needy, they will be compensated for their services out of the collected funds. The Qur'ānic verse (*al-Tawbah* 9: 103) which directs: 'And out of their goods take alms' indicates that the collection and disbursement of *Zakāh* constitutes one of the duties of the Islamic state.

In this connection it is noteworthy that the Prophet (peace be on him) declared it unlawful for himself and the members of his family (i.e. Banū Hāshim) to receive *Zakāh*. Hence, while the Prophet (peace be on him) worked for the collection and distribution of *Zakāh*, he did so without taking any remuneration for the work. Likewise, he laid down the rule that while it was lawful for members of his family (i.e. Banū Hāshim) to gratuitously render any service in connection with *Zakāh*, it was unlawful for them to do so in lieu of compensation. According to the rules laid down by the Prophet (peace be on him), whereas the members of his family are obligated to pay *Zakāh* like any other Muslim if they possess the prescribed minimum of wealth, it is unlawful for them to receive it even if they are poor or needy, or in debt, or wayfarers. There is some disagreement among jurists as to whether the members of the Prophet's family may receive *Zakāh* from one another. According to Abū Yūsuf, it is lawful to do so when they are poor or needy or wayfarers or in debt. But most of the jurists do not hold even this to be lawful.

64. The words وَالْمُؤَلَّفَةِ قُلُوبُهُمْ refer to those whose hearts are won over for the cause of Islam. The rule embodied in this verse is that *Zakāh* funds may be used to calm those who are actively engaged in hostile activities against Islam, or to win over the support of those who are in the unbelievers' camp. *Zakāh* may also be used for securing the loyalty of those converts to Islam about whom it might be legitimately feared that if no consideration is shown them they may revert to unbelief. It would be lawful that regular stipends or lump sum amounts be paid to such persons on a regular or temporary basis in order to secure either their support and backing for Islam, or preferably their conversion to it, or at least to neutralize such persons even if they remain in the opposite camp. Apart from *Zakāh*, money obtained from spoils and other sources of revenue may also be used for this purpose. It is not necessary that the recipients who fall into this category be paid out of *Zakāh* only if they are poor or needy. Rather, they may be paid even if they are rich.

That stipends and grants were made in the time of the Prophet (peace be on him) for reconciling the hearts of certain people to Islam is an established fact. It is, however, a controversial question whether payments for this purpose may be made after the time of the Prophet (peace be on him). Abū Ḥanīfah and his disciples are of the view that such payments are no longer permissible because this category of expenditure stands abolished since the time of the caliphate of 'Umar. Shāfi'ī holds the view that payments may be paid to sinful Muslims in order to reconcile them fully to Islam. No such payment may, however, be made to the unbelievers. Nonetheless some jurists are of the opinion that this category of expenditure is permissible whenever a genuine need for it exists. (See Qurṭubī's comments on the verse. See also Jaṣṣāṣ, vol. 3, p. 124 – Ed.)

The Ḥanafī opinion is supported by reference to an incident in the days of Abū Bakr. 'Uyaynah b. Ḥiṣn and Aqra' b. Ḥābis visited Abū Bakr and asked him to grant a piece of land. Abū Bakr complied. In order to formalize the grant they sought to have the document witnessed by some leading Companions. Some Companions obliged them. However, when they approached 'Umar for that purpose, he tore the document into pieces before their very eyes and said: 'The Prophet (peace be on him) no doubt used to pay you in order to reconcile your hearts [to Islam]. But those were the days when Islam was weak. Now Islam does not stand in need of [the support of] persons like you.' Returning to the Caliph Abū Bakr they lodged a complaint against 'Umar and even taunted him by saying: 'Who is the Caliph, you or 'Umar?' However, neither Abū Bakr nor any other Companion expressed any disapproval of 'Umar's stand. Basing their judgement on this the Ḥanafī jurists contend that since the number of Muslims has increased and Islam has become powerful enough to defend itself, this category of expenditure has lost its rationale. So, in the unanimous view of the Companions, it now stands abolished once and for all. (See Jaṣṣāṣ's comments on the verse in vol. 3, p. 124 – Ed.)

Shāfi'ī, however, makes a different plea. According to him, the Prophet (peace be on him) never paid any unbeliever out of *Zakāh* money for the purpose of reconciling his heart to Islam. Whenever he paid some unbeliever, he drew on the spoils of war. (He paid out of *Zakāh* funds only to sinful Muslims whose hearts he sought to reconcile – Ed.)

In our opinion, there seems to be no worthwhile evidence to support the view that this category of expenditure stands abolished for ever. Whatever 'Umar said in respect of the people mentioned in the above incident is perfectly justified. If at any given time the Islamic state does not consider it necessary to spend from *Zakāh* to reconcile people to Islam, it may do as it decides; expenditure on this category of people is not an obligation. On the contrary, if the need for reconciling people to Islam is seen to arise under changed circumstances, Muslims may resort to paying them from *Zakāh* funds since God has kept a provision for it. What 'Umar and the other Companions agreed, in view of the circumstances of that time, was that it was unnecessary to reconcile people to Islam by making payments from *Zakāh*. This opinion cannot, however, be made the basis for concluding that the Companions abolished for all time to come payments which had been provided for in the Qur'ān for important religious considerations.

As for Shāfi'ī's view, it seems justified to the extent that when other sources are available, the Islamic state should refrain from making use of *Zakāh* funds for this purpose. However, when it becomes necessary to draw on *Zakāh*, there seems no valid basis for making a distinction between sinful Muslims and unbelievers. For the Qur'ān has not sanctioned payments for this purpose in view of the recipient's claim to faith. Rather, payment has been allowed in consideration of certain advantages that would accrue if certain people were won over to the cause of Islam. When the circumstances are akin to those in which the Qur'ān laid down this provision, the Imām of the Muslims would be perfectly justified in making use of *Zakāh* for this purpose. If the Prophet (peace be on him) did not draw on *Zakāh* in this connection, it was because he had other funds available to him to cover the need. However, had it been unlawful to make such payments to the unbelievers the Prophet (peace be on him) would have specified this.

65. This means that *Zakāh* may be used to secure the emancipation of slaves. This may be done in two ways. First, if a slave has entered into an agreement with his master that he would be granted freedom on payment of a specified sum of money, financial assistance may be provided to him to make that payment and thus secure his freedom. Second, *Zakāh* funds may be used to buy slaves with the intention of setting them free. All jurists agree that the first of the two alternatives is lawful. As regards the second method, 'Alī, Sa'īd b. Jubayr, Layth, Thawrī, Ibrāhīm al-Nakha'ī, Sha'abī, Muḥammad b. Sīrīn, and the Ḥanafī and Shāfi'ī jurists in general hold it to be unlawful whereas Ibn 'Abbās, Ḥasan Baṣrī, Mālik, Aḥmad b. Ḥanbal and Abū Thawr consider it lawful to use *Zakāh* funds for this purpose as well.

66. Another use of *Zakāh* funds is to help those debtors – whether they are employed or unemployed, rich or poor – who would be reduced to a state of poverty if they were to pay off all their debts from the funds available to them. Several jurists are of the opinion, however, that such help should not be rendered to those who incur heavy debts either as a result of their extravagance or their spending on evil purposes. Such persons may, however, be helped from *Zakāh* funds if they repent.

67. The expression 'in the way of Allah' has a wide and general connotation and encompasses all good deeds which please God. Some authorities, therefore, believe that *Zakāh* may be spent on all good purposes. But the truth of the matter is – and this is also the view of a great majority of past scholars – that 'in the way of Allah' stands for '*jihād* in the way of Allah'. This expression signifies struggles launched with a view to overthrowing ungodly systems and replacing them by the Islamic system of life. All those who participate in this struggle may be given assistance from *Zakāh* funds, whether it be for journey expenses, for providing means of transport, for arms and equipment or for other goods relating to warfare. Such assistance may be provided even to those who are otherwise well off and need no financial assistance in connection with their own living. Likewise, help on a temporary or regular basis may be

(61) And of them there are some who distress the Prophet, saying: 'He is all ears.'[69] Tell them: 'He listens for your good.[70] He believes in Allah and trusts the believers,[71] and is a mercy for those of you who believe. A painful punishment lies in store for those who cause distress to the Messenger of Allah.'

وَمِنْهُمُ ٱلَّذِينَ يُؤْذُونَ ٱلنَّبِىَّ
وَيَقُولُونَ هُوَ أُذُنٌ ۚ قُلْ أُذُنُ
خَيْرٍ لَّكُمْ يُؤْمِنُ بِٱللَّهِ
وَيُؤْمِنُ لِلْمُؤْمِنِينَ وَرَحْمَةٌ
لِّلَّذِينَ ءَامَنُوا۟ مِنكُمْ ۚ وَٱلَّذِينَ
يُؤْذُونَ رَسُولَ ٱللَّهِ لَهُمْ عَذَابٌ
أَلِيمٌ ﴿٦١﴾

---

provided out of *Zakāh* to those who voluntarily devote themselves to this cause wholly or on a part-time basis, either for a specified period of time or permanently.

While discussing this question the jurists generally use the word *ghazw* which is equivalent to *qitāl* (fighting). This has given rise to the misconception that *Zakāh* funds may be spent exclusively on 'fighting in the cause of God'. *Jihād* is, however, an all-embracing concept which covers every kind of struggle to bring down ungodly systems of life, to uphold the Word of God, and make the Islamic system of life prevail. This struggle may be supported by *Zakāh* funds whether Islam is in its early stage of propagating its message and persuading people to embrace it or in its later stages when the struggle assumes a combative dimension.

68. A traveller, though otherwise rich, is entitled to receive help out of *Zakāh* funds if he needs such help during his journey. Some jurists, however, subject this help to the condition that the journey should not have been undertaken for an evil purpose. There is no basis, however, for such a stipulation in the Qur'ān or *Ḥadīth.* The broad principles of Islam also indicate that a person's sinfulness does not disqualify him from receiving help. Rendering assistance to sinful people in times of dire need, and a generally graceful and benevolent attitude towards them, often serves as an effective means of reforming them.

69. One of the allegations of the hypocrites against the Prophet (peace be on him) was that he allowed everybody to speak his mind and that he listened to them. Strangely enough, the hypocrites tried to give an evil interpretation to this character trait. They misconstrued it as proof of the Prophet (peace be on him) being credulous and gullible. What actually irked the hypocrites on this count was that the sincere believers informed

(62) They swear by Allah to please you, while it is Allah and His Messenger whose pleasure they should seek if they truly believe. (63) Are they not aware that Hell-fire awaits whosoever opposes Allah and His Messenger, and in it he shall abide? That surely is the great humiliation.

يَحْلِفُونَ بِاللَّهِ لَكُمْ لِيُرْضُوكُمْ
وَاللَّهُ وَرَسُولُهُۥٓ أَحَقُّ أَن يُرْضُوهُ إِن
كَانُوا مُؤْمِنِينَ ﴿٦٢﴾ أَلَمْ
يَعْلَمُوٓا أَنَّهُۥ مَن يُحَادِدِ اللَّهَ
وَرَسُولَهُۥ فَأَنَّ لَهُۥ نَارَ جَهَنَّمَ
خَٰلِدًا فِيهَا ذَٰلِكَ الْخِزْيُ
الْعَظِيمُ ﴿٦٣﴾

---

the Prophet (peace be on him) about their conspiracies, mischievous deeds and hostile talk. Incensed by this, the hypocrites protested that the Prophet (peace be on him) lent credence to the reports of down and outs.

70. The Qur'ānic response to these taunting remarks is an exhaustive one and covers two points. First, that the Prophet (peace be on him) does not pay any attention to reports that are likely to give rise to evil and mischief; he acts only on those reports which would bring good to all, the reports which are conducive to the best interests of Islam and Muslims. Second, that the Prophet's propensity to listen to everybody is in fact in the interests of the hypocrites themselves. For had the Prophet (peace be on him) not been forbearing and cool-tempered he would not have listened with patience to their false professions to faith, to their specious protestations of goodwill, to their lame excuses to justify their shying away from fighting in the way of God. Had he been otherwise, the Prophet (peace be on him) would have dealt severely with the hypocrites and would have made their life in Madina extremely difficult. In short, the hypocrites had every reason to be thankful for this trait in the Prophet's character.

71. The hypocrites are told that they are wrong in assuming that the Prophet (peace be on him) believes in all that is narrated to him. Though he listens to everybody, he trusts only the true believers. As for the reports brought to the Prophet (peace be on him) about the hypocrites, these were not carried by characterless story-tellers. Rather they were brought to the Prophet's notice by trustworthy and righteous believers.

(64) The hypocrites are afraid lest a *sūrah* should be revealed concerning them intimating to the believers what lay hidden in their hearts.[72] Tell them (O Prophet!): 'Continue your mockery if you will. Allah will surely bring to light all that the disclosure of which you dread.' (65) Should you question them what they were talking about they would certainly say: 'We were merely jesting and being playful.'[73] Tell them: 'Was it Allah and His Messenger and His revelation that you were mocking?

يَحْذَرُ الْمُنَافِقُونَ أَنْ تُنَزَّلَ
عَلَيْهِمْ سُورَةٌ تُنَبِّئُهُمْ بِمَا فِي قُلُوبِهِمْ ۚ
قُلِ اسْتَهْزِئُوا إِنَّ اللَّهَ مُخْرِجٌ
مَا تَحْذَرُونَ ﴿٦٤﴾ وَلَئِنْ
سَأَلْتَهُمْ لَيَقُولُنَّ إِنَّمَا
كُنَّا نَخُوضُ وَنَلْعَبُ ۚ قُلْ أَبِاللَّهِ
وَآيَاتِهِ وَرَسُولِهِ كُنْتُمْ
تَسْتَهْزِئُونَ ﴿٦٥﴾

---

72. Although the hypocrites did not sincerely believe in the Messengership of the Prophet (peace be on him), they were convinced, in view of their long experience, that he did have access to some supernatural source of information which apprised him of their clandestine activities. The same source, they thought, helped the Prophet (peace be on him) gain access to their closely-guarded secrets. This enabled the Prophet (peace be on him) to reveal through the Qur'ān (which, according to the hypocrites, was the Prophet's own work rather than a revelation from God) their hypocrisy as well as their nefarious designs against the Muslims.

73. When preparations for the Tabūk expedition were under way, the hypocrites used to scoff at the Prophet (peace be on him) and the Muslims. They did so with the idea of demoralizing those Muslims engaged in *jihād* preparations. Many such reports are recorded in the traditions. Of these, one goes thus: 'Some hypocrites were talking idly in their private meeting. One of them said: "Do you think that fighting against the Roman warriors is like the mutual fight among the Arabs? I am sure that no sooner than the war breaks out you will find these [Muslim] warriors tied by ropes." (See Ibn Hishām, vol. 2, p. 525 and Wāqidī, vol. 3, p. 1003; Ṭabarī, vol. 3, p. 108, and the comments of Ibn Kathīr on verses 65–6 – Ed.) To this another added: "It will be much better if, apart from that, each one of

(66) Now, make no excuses. The truth is, you have fallen into unbelief after having believed. Even if We were to forgive some of you, We will surely chastise others because they are guilty.'[74]

(67) The hypocrites, be they men or women, are all alike. They enjoin what is evil, and forbid what is good, and withhold their hands from doing good.[75] They forgot Allah, so Allah also forgot them. Surely the hypocrites are wicked. ►

لَا تَعْتَذِرُوا قَدْ كَفَرْتُم بَعْدَ إِيمَٰنِكُمْ
إِن نَّعْفُ عَن طَآئِفَةٍ مِّنكُمْ نُعَذِّبْ
طَآئِفَةً بِأَنَّهُمْ كَانُوا مُجْرِمِينَ
﴿٦٦﴾ ٱلْمُنَٰفِقُونَ وَٱلْمُنَٰفِقَٰتُ بَعْضُهُم
مِّنۢ بَعْضٍ يَأْمُرُونَ بِٱلْمُنكَرِ
وَيَنْهَوْنَ عَنِ ٱلْمَعْرُوفِ
وَيَقْبِضُونَ أَيْدِيَهُمْ نَسُوا ٱللَّهَ
فَنَسِيَهُمْ إِنَّ ٱلْمُنَٰفِقِينَ
هُمُ ٱلْفَٰسِقُونَ ﴿٦٧﴾

them is whipped a hundred times as well." (See Wāqidī, vol. 3, p. 1004 and Ibn Hishām, vol. 2, p. 525 – Ed.)* On seeing the Prophet (peace be on him) busy in *jihād* preparations, a hypocrite derisively told another: "Just look at this man! He is out to conquer the Roman and Syrian fortresses!"' (See Qurṭubī's comments on the verse – Ed.)

74. Jesters and clowns among the hypocrites could be pardoned for having indulged in such idle talk in view of their non-serious approach to life. But those hypocrites who deliberately uttered such derisive remarks with a definite view to demoralize and unnerve the Muslims undoubtedly stood guilty of committing an unpardonable crime.

75. An instinctive interest in evil, and hostility to goodness are common denominators of all hypocrites. If a person is inclined to evil, they lavish their sympathy, counsel, encouragement, and support upon him. They do

*We are not sure about the actual sources from which the author derived the statement mentioned above. The statement in the two sources that we have been able to locate seems to have a somewhat different signification. The statement in Ibn Hishām is the following:

"فقال مُخشّن بن حُمير: والله لوددتُ اني أُقاضى على ان يُضرب كُلّ [رجل](٢) منّا
مائة جلدة، وانّا ننفلتُ ان ينزل فينا قرآنٌ لمقالتكم هذه".

– Ed.

(68) Allah has promised Hell-Fire to the hypocrites, both men and women, and to the unbelievers. They shall abide in it: a sufficient recompense for them. Allah has cursed them, and theirs is a lasting torment. (69) Your ways are like the ways of those who have gone before you.[76] They were mightier than you in power, and more abundant in riches and children. They enjoyed their lot for a while as you have enjoyed your lot, and you also engaged in idle talk as they did. Their works have come to a naught in this world and in the Hereafter they are surely the losers. ►

وَعَدَ ٱللَّهُ ٱلْمُنَٰفِقِينَ وَٱلْمُنَٰفِقَٰتِ
وَٱلْكُفَّارَ نَارَ جَهَنَّمَ خَٰلِدِينَ فِيهَاۚ
هِىَ حَسْبُهُمْۚ وَلَعَنَهُمُ ٱللَّهُۖ وَلَهُمْ
عَذَابٌ مُّقِيمٌ ٦٨ كَٱلَّذِينَ مِن
قَبْلِكُمْ كَانُوٓا۟ أَشَدَّ مِنكُمْ قُوَّةً
وَأَكْثَرَ أَمْوَٰلًا وَأَوْلَٰدًا فَٱسْتَمْتَعُوا۟
بِخَلَٰقِهِمْ فَٱسْتَمْتَعْتُم بِخَلَٰقِكُمْ
كَمَا ٱسْتَمْتَعَ ٱلَّذِينَ مِن
قَبْلِكُم بِخَلَٰقِهِمْ وَخُضْتُمْ كَٱلَّذِى
خَاضُوٓا۟ۚ أُو۟لَٰٓئِكَ حَبِطَتْ
أَعْمَٰلُهُمْ فِى ٱلدُّنْيَا وَٱلْءَاخِرَةِۖ
وَأُو۟لَٰٓئِكَ هُمُ ٱلْخَٰسِرُونَ ٦٩

not fail to intercede on his behalf, and spare no eloquence in their praise of him. They join hands in his evil deeds and urge others to take part in them as well. They also encourage the evil-doer to continue in the same vein. Their attitude leaves no room for doubt that evil gratifies them to the core. For the mere sight of a good deed puts them off. The very thought of goodness distresses them. They are ill-prepared to see anybody suggest an act of goodness. When they see anyone proceed in that direction they writhe in pain. They resort to a variety of devices to obstruct people from doing good and to dissuade them from it.

Another trait common to all hypocrites is their unwillingness to spend in good causes. This characterizes not only those hypocrites who are miserly but also those who are otherwise spendthrift. The ill-gotten wealth of the hypocrites is either stored in their coffers or is squandered on unlawful pursuits. They are utterly extravagant if the purpose be evil, but are totally close-fisted if money is needed for a good cause.

76. The foregoing characterized the hypocrites in the third person. Here, suddenly, they are addressed directly in the second person.

(70) Have they not heard the accounts of those who came before them[77] – of the people of Noah and 'Ād and Thamūd, and the people of Abraham and the dwellers of Madyan (Midian), and the Ruined Cities?[78] Their Messengers came to them with clear signs. Then, it was not Allah Who caused them any wrong; they rather wronged themselves.[79]

(71) The believers, both men and women, are allies of one another. They enjoin good, forbid evil, establish Prayer, pay *Zakāh*, and obey Allah and His Messenger.[80] Surely Allah will show mercy to them. Allah is All-Mighty, All-Wise. ►

أَلَمْ يَأْتِهِمْ نَبَأُ الَّذِينَ مِن قَبْلِهِمْ
قَوْمِ نُوحٍ وَعَادٍ وَثَمُودَ وَقَوْمِ
إِبْرَاهِيمَ وَأَصْحَابِ مَدْيَنَ
وَالْمُؤْتَفِكَاتِ أَتَتْهُمْ رُسُلُهُم
بِالْبَيِّنَاتِ فَمَا كَانَ اللَّهُ لِيَظْلِمَهُمْ
وَلَٰكِن كَانُوا أَنفُسَهُمْ يَظْلِمُونَ ﴿٧٠﴾
وَالْمُؤْمِنُونَ وَالْمُؤْمِنَاتُ بَعْضُهُمْ أَوْلِيَاءُ
بَعْضٍ يَأْمُرُونَ بِالْمَعْرُوفِ وَيَنْهَوْنَ
عَنِ الْمُنكَرِ وَيُقِيمُونَ الصَّلَاةَ
وَيُؤْتُونَ الزَّكَاةَ وَيُطِيعُونَ اللَّهَ
وَرَسُولَهُ أُولَٰئِكَ سَيَرْحَمُهُمُ اللَّهُ إِنَّ اللَّهَ
عَزِيزٌ حَكِيمٌ ﴿٧١﴾

---

77. The narrative again reverts to a description of the hypocrites in the third person.

78. This refers to the areas where the people of Lot lived.

79. The Qur'ān emphasizes that earlier communities were not destroyed because God had any grudge against them which prompted Him to seek their destruction. This calamitous end was the natural result of their own actions. God gave them every opportunity to choose the right path. He gave them every opportunity to think and to understand. He sent Messengers to admonish them, and who warned them of the dire consequences of their wickedness, who explained clearly which way leads to salvation and which to destruction. But when they failed to pay any heed to these admonitions and persisted in following the wrong path, they inevitably met with disastrous consequences. This constitutes the import of the above verse: 'It is not Allah Who wrongs them; it is they who wrong themselves.'

(72) Allah has promised the believing men and believing women Gardens beneath which rivers flow. They shall abide in it. There are delightful dwelling places for them in the Gardens of Eternity. They shall, above all, enjoy the good pleasure of Allah. That is the great achievement.

(73) O Prophet![81] Strive against the unbelievers and the hypocrites, and be severe to them.[82] Hell shall be their abode – what an evil destination! ▶

وَعَدَ ٱللَّهُ ٱلْمُؤْمِنِينَ وَٱلْمُؤْمِنَٰتِ
جَنَّٰتٍ تَجْرِى مِن تَحْتِهَا ٱلْأَنْهَٰرُ
خَٰلِدِينَ فِيهَا وَمَسَٰكِنَ طَيِّبَةً فِى
جَنَّٰتِ عَدْنٍ ۚ وَرِضْوَٰنٌ مِّنَ ٱللَّهِ
أَكْبَرُ ۚ ذَٰلِكَ هُوَ ٱلْفَوْزُ ٱلْعَظِيمُ
﴿٧٢﴾ يَٰٓأَيُّهَا ٱلنَّبِىُّ جَٰهِدِ ٱلْكُفَّارَ
وَٱلْمُنَٰفِقِينَ وَٱغْلُظْ عَلَيْهِمْ ۚ
وَمَأْوَىٰهُمْ جَهَنَّمُ ۖ وَبِئْسَ
ٱلْمَصِيرُ ﴿٧٣﴾

---

80. The Muslims and hypocrites stood apart, each a separate entity. Superficially they seemed identical insofar as both groups recognized Islam as their religion and outwardly followed the same set of religious practices. Nevertheless, they differed in character, temperament, behaviour, and habits; in short, in their total orientation. In the case of the hypocrites, faith was merely a verbal claim devoid of true conviction. This claim was repudiated by their life-style. Their case is similar to that of a man who fills up a container with filth, and labels it perfume; a claim which will instantly be known to be false by the stench it gives off.

In the case of the true believers, their claim can be verified by reference to their character and conduct. The label of perfume is justified by the sweet smell! Both the hypocrites and true believers passed off as members of the same Muslim community due to the label of Islam. Nevertheless, the characteristics of the two were so radically different that they could not be considered one community. The hypocrites, by dint of their heedlessness to God, their instinctive interest in evil, their revulsion against goodness, their unwillingness to co-operate with good causes, were a community by themselves. On the other hand, the true believers – men and women – constituted a distinct community because they shared many traits. They were instinctively disposed to righteousness, they abhorred evil, and remembrance of God was the very breath of life for them. They also spent freely in the way of God, and the dominant characteristic of their life as a whole was obedience to God. These common characteristics

(74) They swear by Allah that they said nothing blasphemous whereas they indeed blasphemed,[83] and fell into unbelief after believing, and also had evil designs which they could not carry into effect.[84] They are spiteful against Muslims for no other reason than that Allah and His Messenger have enriched them through His bounty![85] So, if they repent, it will be to their own good. But if they turn away, Allah will sternly punish them in this world and in the Hereafter. None in the world will be able to protect or help them.

يَحْلِفُونَ بِٱللَّهِ مَا قَالُوا۟ وَلَقَدْ
قَالُوا۟ كَلِمَةَ ٱلْكُفْرِ وَكَفَرُوا۟
بَعْدَ إِسْلَٰمِهِمْ وَهَمُّوا۟ بِمَا لَمْ يَنَالُوا۟ۚ
وَمَا نَقَمُوٓا۟ إِلَّآ أَنْ أَغْنَىٰهُمُ ٱللَّهُ
وَرَسُولُهُۥ مِن فَضْلِهِۦۚ فَإِن يَتُوبُوا۟
يَكُ خَيْرًا لَّهُمْ ۖ وَإِن يَتَوَلَّوْا۟
يُعَذِّبْهُمُ ٱللَّهُ عَذَابًا أَلِيمًا فِى
ٱلدُّنْيَا وَٱلْءَاخِرَةِ ۚ وَمَا لَهُمْ فِى
ٱلْأَرْضِ مِن وَلِىٍّ وَلَا نَصِيرٍ
٧٤

developed a sense of common identity among them and made them quite distinct from the hypocrites.

81. This marks the beginning of the third discourse of the *sūrah* (comprising verses 73–129), which was revealed after the expedition to Tabūk.

82. So far the hypocrites had mainly been treated with tolerance and forbearance for two reasons. First, the Muslims could not afford to open a front against the enemies within while they were involved in a fight against the enemies without. Second, this policy was intended to provide an opportunity to those in the ranks of the hypocrites who were merely victims of doubt and scepticism, but were not incorrigibly corrupt. It was conceivable that some belonging to this category might attain genuine belief and conviction in Islam.

Neither of these two reasons existed any longer. The Muslims held sway over virtually the whole of Arabia and in fact a new phase of conflict with powers outside Arabia had just begun. To strike a severe blow at the enemy within had, therefore, become both possible and necessary. This step was necessary in order to prevent the internal enemies from collaborating with the external enemies and so create a difficult situation in the Muslim body-politic. The hypocrites had already been granted respite for a full nine years during which time they had had every opportunity to see, think about, make their judgements on Islam. They could have made good use of this long period of respite if they had even the slightest ability to accept the truth. The Qur'ān, therefore, declared that in addition to waging *jihād* against the unbelievers, the Muslims should also wage *'jihād'* against the hypocrites, and should henceforth treat them severely. This declaration thus marked the end of the period of leniency shown to the hypocrites.

The directive to wage *jihād* against the hypocrites and to show severity to them did not mean that Muslims should start a war against the hypocrites. Rather, the directive meant that Muslims should no longer be indulgent towards the hypocrites' nefarious activities. The previous policy of overlooking their hypocrisy had allowed the hypocrites to be considered by the generality of Muslims as part of the Muslim body-politic, which in turn had enabled them to meddle in the affairs of the Muslim society and inject their poisonous influence into it. The present directive marked the end of that policy. From now on if anyone adopted a hypocritical attitude whilst living in the midst of Muslims, their behaviour clearly showed that they owed allegiance neither to God nor to the Prophet (peace be on him), such people should be fully exposed, be subjected to public censure, be deprived of the influence and authority they had enjoyed before, be socially ostracized, and be excluded from consultation in matters relating to the affairs of the Muslim community. Nor should their witness be accepted in the courts. They should also be barred from holding public office. No deference should be shown to them on social occasions. Muslims should treat them in a way which would make them realize they had lost their prestige in the Muslim society and that no Muslim held them in esteem. If any hypocrite committed treachery, no connivance should be shown to his crime. Rather, he should be tried publicly and be awarded a befitting punishment.

This was a timely directive for its absence could well have led to the disintegration of the Islamic society. For a community that breeds hypocrites and traitors in its midst and holds them in esteem will inevitably face moral degeneration, and ultimately, total destruction. Hypocrisy is like a plague, and the hypocrite is the carrier of those germs, infecting people all around. If the rats, hypocrites, carrying the germs of plague are allowed to move about freely, this would expose the entire population to grave risk. If hypocrites hold respectable positions in society, this might motivate others to follow suit and encourage them to commit downright treachery. Such a situation is likely to make many a person entertain the idea that sincerity, honesty and true faith do not contribute to a person's success. All one has to do is make a verbal declaration of faith and then go about doing as one pleases and nothing will prevent one from flourishing. The Prophet (peace be on him) alluded to this pithily in one of his sayings: 'He

(75) Some of them made a covenant with Allah: 'If Allah gives us out of His bounty, we will give alms and act righteously.' (76) Then, when He gave them out of His bounty, they grew niggardly and turned their backs (upon their covenant).[86] (77) So He caused hypocrisy to take root in their hearts and to remain therein until the Day they meet Him because they broke their promise with Allah and because they lied. ▶

۞ وَمِنْهُم مَّنْ عَٰهَدَ ٱللَّهَ لَئِنْ
ءَاتَىٰنَا مِن فَضْلِهِۦ لَنَصَّدَّقَنَّ
وَلَنَكُونَنَّ مِنَ ٱلصَّٰلِحِينَ ﴿٧٥﴾
فَلَمَّآ ءَاتَىٰهُم مِّن فَضْلِهِۦ بَخِلُوا۟
بِهِۦ وَتَوَلَّوا۟ وَّهُم مُّعْرِضُونَ ﴿٧٦﴾
فَأَعْقَبَهُمْ نِفَاقًا فِى قُلُوبِهِمْ إِلَىٰ يَوْمِ
يَلْقَوْنَهُۥ بِمَآ أَخْلَفُوا۟ ٱللَّهَ مَا وَعَدُوهُ
وَبِمَا كَانُوا۟ يَكْذِبُونَ ﴿٧٧﴾

who shows respect to one who introduces an innovation in Islam, lends a hand to the demolition of Islam.' (For this tradition see Bayhaqī, *Shu'ab al-Īmān*, quoted in *Mishkāt al-Maṣābīḥ*, 'Bāb al-I'tiṣān, bi'l-Kitāb wa'l-Sunnah' – Ed.)

83. There is no certainty about what constitutes the 'word of unbelief' mentioned in the above verse. However, there are references in traditions to the many blasphemous utterances of the hypocrites. For example, a hypocrite is reported to have told his Muslim relatives: 'If the message delivered by him [the Prophet (peace be on him)] is really genuine, then we are worse than donkeys.' (Wāqidī, vol. 3, p. 1004 – Ed.) According to another report, during the expedition to Tabūk when a she-camel of the Prophet (peace be on him) went astray and the Muslims set about searching for it, a group of hypocrites made much fun of the incident, saying to one another: '(Just look at this man!) He brings us news about the heavens but cannot tell where his she-camel is.' (See Wāqidī, vol. 3, p. 1010; Ibn Hishām, vol. 2, p. 523 – Ed.)

84. This alludes to the conspiracies contrived by the hypocrites during the expedition to Tabūk. One of these, according to traditionists, was that the hypocrites had planned to throw the Prophet (peace be on him) into a ravine during his return from Tabūk. On learning of this evil design, the

(78) Are they not aware that Allah knows what they conceal and what they secretly discuss, and that Allah has full knowledge even of all that is beyond the reach of perception? (79) As for those who taunt the believers who voluntarily give alms and scoff at those who have nothing to give except what they earn through their hard toil,[87] Allah scoffs at them in return. A grievous chastisement awaits them. (80) (O Prophet!) It is the same whether or not you ask for their forgiveness. Even if you were to ask for forgiveness for them seventy times, Allah shall not forgive them. That is because they disbelieved in Allah and His Messenger; and Allah does not bestow His guidance on such evil-doing folk.

أَلَمْ يَعْلَمُوٓا۟ أَنَّ ٱللَّهَ يَعْلَمُ سِرَّهُمْ
وَنَجْوَىٰهُمْ وَأَنَّ ٱللَّهَ عَلَّٰمُ
ٱلْغُيُوبِ ٧٨ ٱلَّذِينَ يَلْمِزُونَ
ٱلْمُطَّوِّعِينَ مِنَ ٱلْمُؤْمِنِينَ
فِى ٱلصَّدَقَٰتِ وَٱلَّذِينَ لَا
يَجِدُونَ إِلَّا جُهْدَهُمْ فَيَسْخَرُونَ مِنْهُمْ
سَخِرَ ٱللَّهُ مِنْهُمْ وَلَهُمْ عَذَابٌ أَلِيمٌ ٧٩
ٱسْتَغْفِرْ لَهُمْ أَوْ لَا تَسْتَغْفِرْ لَهُمْ إِن
تَسْتَغْفِرْ لَهُمْ سَبْعِينَ مَرَّةً فَلَن يَغْفِرَ
ٱللَّهُ لَهُمْ ذَٰلِكَ بِأَنَّهُمْ كَفَرُوا۟
بِٱللَّهِ وَرَسُولِهِۦ وَٱللَّهُ لَا يَهْدِى
ٱلْقَوْمَ ٱلْفَٰسِقِينَ ٨٠

Prophet (peace be on him) directed his army to take a longer route through the valley while he himself followed a shorter route together with 'Ammār b. Yāsir and Ḥudhayfah b. al-Yamān. During his journey the Prophet (peace be on him) came to know that about a dozen masked hypocrites were in pursuit of him. As soon as this was known, Ḥudhayfah hastened towards them with the intention of driving them away. The hypocrites spotted this from afar and were afraid. In addition, fearing that they would be identified, they immediately took to their heels. (See Aḥmad b. Ḥanbal, vol. 5, p. 453; Wāqidī, vol. 3, pp. 1042–3 – Ed.)

Another conspiracy hatched by the hypocrites was that they secretly decided that as soon as the news would come that the Muslim army had

(81) Those who were allowed to stay behind rejoiced at remaining behind and not accompanying the Messenger of Allah. They were averse to striving in the cause of Allah with their belongings and their lives and told others: 'Do not go forth in this fierce heat.' Tell them: 'The Hell is far fiercer in heat.' Would that they understand! (82) Let them, then, laugh little, and weep much at the contemplation of the punishment for the evil they have committed!

فَرِحَ ٱلْمُخَلَّفُونَ بِمَقْعَدِهِمْ
خِلَٰفَ رَسُولِ ٱللَّهِ وَكَرِهُوٓا۟ أَن يُجَٰهِدُوا۟
بِأَمْوَٰلِهِمْ وَأَنفُسِهِمْ فِى سَبِيلِ ٱللَّهِ وَقَالُوا۟
لَا تَنفِرُوا۟ فِى ٱلْحَرِّ ۗ قُلْ نَارُ جَهَنَّمَ أَشَدُّ
حَرًّا ۚ لَّوْ كَانُوا۟ يَفْقَهُونَ ﴿٨١﴾ فَلْيَضْحَكُوا۟
قَلِيلًا وَلْيَبْكُوا۟ كَثِيرًا جَزَآءًۢ بِمَا كَانُوا۟
يَكْسِبُونَ ﴿٨٢﴾

---

been defeated by the Romans they would install 'Abd Allāh b. Ubayy as the ruler of Madina. They went about planning for this since they had not even a shred of doubt that the Muslim army was doomed. (See the comments on this verse by Qurṭubī – Ed.)

85. Prior to the migration of the Prophet (peace be on him), Madina (i.e. Yathrib) was a small Arabian town and the Aws and Khazraj, the two main clans inhabiting the town, did not enjoy any extraordinary position of authority or affluence. However, within eight or nine years of the Prophet's migration, during which the *Anṣār* exposed themselves to every kind of risk and danger and extended their full support to the Prophet (peace be on him), Madina became the capital of the whole of Arabia. The farmers belonging to the Aws and Khazraj clans became, as it were, the notables of the new society and administered the newly-founded state. Madina was flooded with affluence as a result of the conquests made by the Muslims and the attendant overflow from the spoils of war and the prosperity of trade and commerce. Alluding to this, the Qur'ān reproaches the hypocrites who, instead of being grateful to the Prophet (peace be on him) through whom they had achieved such prosperity, directed their spite and anger towards him.

86. The ingratitude of the hypocrites for which they were rebuked (see verse 74 above) is evident from their conduct. Reference has been made

(83) Then if Allah brings you face to face with a party of them, and they ask your leave to go forth (to fight in the cause of Allah), tell them: 'You shall not go forth with me, and shall never fight against any enemy along with me. You were well-pleased to remain at home the first time, so now continue to remain with those who have stayed behind.'

(84) Do not ever pray over any of them who dies, nor stand over his grave. They disbelieved in Allah and His Messenger and died in iniquity.[88] ▶

فَإِن رَّجَعَكَ ٱللَّهُ إِلَىٰ طَآئِفَةٍ مِّنْهُمْ
فَٱسْتَـْٔذَنُوكَ لِلْخُرُوجِ فَقُل لَّن
تَخْرُجُوا۟ مَعِىَ أَبَدًا وَلَن تُقَـٰتِلُوا۟ مَعِىَ
عَدُوًّا ۖ إِنَّكُمْ رَضِيتُم بِٱلْقُعُودِ أَوَّلَ
مَرَّةٍ فَٱقْعُدُوا۟ مَعَ ٱلْخَـٰلِفِينَ ﴿٨٣﴾
وَلَا تُصَلِّ عَلَىٰٓ أَحَدٍ مِّنْهُم مَّاتَ أَبَدًا
وَلَا تَقُمْ عَلَىٰ قَبْرِهِۦٓ ۖ إِنَّهُمْ كَفَرُوا۟ بِٱللَّهِ
وَرَسُولِهِۦ وَمَاتُوا۟ وَهُمْ فَـٰسِقُونَ
﴿٨٤﴾

---

to this in order to emphasize that the hypocrites were a bunch of die-hard criminals who lacked even the most rudimentary virtues such as gratefulness, acknowledgement of beneficence, and faithfulness to covenants.

87. This refers to the stinginess of the hypocrites in response to the appeal of the Prophet (peace be on him) to make contributions to the war fund on the occasion of the expedition to Tabūk. Not only that, they even made fun of the sincere believers when they gave generously. About each of them they had something to say. If wealthy Muslims donated a large amount – an amount which was in accord with or beyond their means – they accused them of insincere ostentation. And if the poor Muslims donated modest amounts out of their hard-earned income, they scoffed, saying: 'Look! Here is the farthing that will help conquer the forts of the Roman Empire!' (See the comments of Ibn Kathīr on the verse – Ed.)

88. 'Abd Allāh b. Ubayy, the ringleader of the hypocrites, died some time after the Prophet's return from Tabūk. His son, 'Abd Allāh b. 'Abd Allāh b. Ubayy, who was a sincere believer, called on the Prophet (peace be on him) and requested him to give his gown away so that it might be used as a shroud for 'Abd Allāh b. Ubayy's burial. The Prophet (peace

(85) Let not their riches or their children excite your admiration. Through these Allah seeks to chastise them in this world, and that their lives may depart them while they are unbelievers.

(86) And whenever any *sūrah* is revealed enjoining: 'Believe in Allah and strive (in His cause) along with His Messenger,' the affluent among them ask you to excuse them, saying: 'Leave us with those who will sit back at home.' (87) They were content to stay behind with the womenfolk. Their hearts were sealed, leaving them bereft of understanding.[89]

وَلَا تُعْجِبْكَ أَمْوَٰلُهُمْ وَأَوْلَٰدُهُمْ ۚ
إِنَّمَا يُرِيدُ ٱللَّهُ أَن يُعَذِّبَهُم بِهَا فِى
ٱلدُّنْيَا وَتَزْهَقَ أَنفُسُهُمْ وَهُمْ
كَٰفِرُونَ ﴿٨٥﴾ وَإِذَآ أُنزِلَتْ
سُورَةٌ أَنْ ءَامِنُوا۟ بِٱللَّهِ وَجَٰهِدُوا۟
مَعَ رَسُولِهِ ٱسْتَـْٔذَنَكَ أُو۟لُوا۟
ٱلطَّوْلِ مِنْهُمْ وَقَالُوا۟ ذَرْنَا
نَكُن مَّعَ ٱلْقَٰعِدِينَ ﴿٨٦﴾
رَضُوا۟ بِأَن يَكُونُوا۟ مَعَ
ٱلْخَوَالِفِ وَطُبِعَ عَلَىٰ قُلُوبِهِمْ
فَهُمْ لَا يَفْقَهُونَ ﴿٨٧﴾

---

be on him) generously acceded to this request. 'Abd Allāh also requested the Prophet (peace be on him) to lead the Funeral Prayer for 'Abd Allāh b. Ubayy. Acting with the same magnanimous spirit, the Prophet (peace be on him) promised to oblige. Although 'Umar tried to dissuade the Prophet (peace be on him) from doing so in view of 'Abd Allāh b. Ubayy's ignominious role in opposing Islam, the Prophet (peace be on him) ignored his protest and did not mind praying for the forgiveness of this arch-enemy of Islam. This was out of his mercy and tenderness which embraced friend and foe alike. However, as soon as the Prophet (peace be on him) rose to lead the Funeral Prayer the above verse was revealed, forbidding him to do so. (Bukhārī, 'Tafsīr', 'Bāb Qawlihī Ta'ālá istaghfir lahum aw lā tastaghfir lahum' and 'Bāb lá tuṣallī 'alá Aḥad minhum' – Ed.) For a policy had already been laid down that no further allowance should be given to the hypocrites (see verse 73). They should no longer be allowed to flourish and that there should be a total abstention from anything that might encourage them.

A rule which has been derived from this incident is that the leaders of the Muslim community should not lead or offer the Funeral Prayer of

(88) But the Messenger and those who shared his faith strove with their belongings and their lives. It is they who shall have all kinds of good. It is they who shall prosper. (89) Allah has prepared for them Gardens beneath which rivers flow. There shall they abide. That is the supreme triumph.

(90) Many of the bedouin Arabs[90] came with excuses, seeking leave to stay behind. Thus those who were false to Allah and His Messenger in their covenant remained behind. A painful chastisement shall befall those of them that disbelieved.[91]

لَٰكِنِ ٱلرَّسُولُ وَٱلَّذِينَ ءَامَنُوا۟ مَعَهُۥ
جَٰهَدُوا۟ بِأَمْوَٰلِهِمْ وَأَنفُسِهِمْ ۚ
وَأُو۟لَٰٓئِكَ لَهُمُ ٱلْخَيْرَٰتُ ۖ
وَأُو۟لَٰٓئِكَ هُمُ ٱلْمُفْلِحُونَ ﴿٨٨﴾
أَعَدَّ ٱللَّهُ لَهُمْ جَنَّٰتٍ تَجْرِى مِن
تَحْتِهَا ٱلْأَنْهَٰرُ خَٰلِدِينَ فِيهَا ۚ ذَٰلِكَ
ٱلْفَوْزُ ٱلْعَظِيمُ ﴿٨٩﴾ وَجَآءَ ٱلْمُعَذِّرُونَ
مِنَ ٱلْأَعْرَابِ لِيُؤْذَنَ لَهُمْ وَقَعَدَ
ٱلَّذِينَ كَذَبُوا۟ ٱللَّهَ وَرَسُولَهُۥ ۚ
سَيُصِيبُ ٱلَّذِينَ كَفَرُوا۟
مِنْهُمْ عَذَابٌ أَلِيمٌ ﴿٩٠﴾

notorious sinners. After the revelation of the above verse, the Prophet (peace be on him) used to inquire about the conduct of the deceased before leading any Funeral Prayer. If the deceased was a notorious sinner, he advised the relatives of the deceased to make alternative arrangements.

89. It was indeed shameful of the hypocrites that despite their physical fitness and material resourcefulness they failed to go to the battle-front to take part in the *jihād.* And this though they were behind none in claiming to be Muslims. They preferred to stay back in their homes like women when they should have been on the battlefield at that critical moment. Since they had deliberately adopted this stance, they were stripped of those noble feelings which makes a man ashamed of his unbecoming conduct.

90. The word *al-A'rāb* refers to the bedouin who either lived in the desert or in the villages around Madina.

91. If a man's profession to faith is not backed by a true affirmation of the Message of the Prophet (peace be on him), submission to God, and sincerity in devotion, it is merely an act of the tongue which does not

(91) There is no blame on the weak nor the sick nor on those who have no means for *jihād* if they stay behind provided that they are sincere to Allah and to His Messenger.[92] There is no cause for reproach against those who do good. Allah is All-Forgiving, Ever-Merciful.

لَّيْسَ عَلَى ٱلضُّعَفَآءِ وَلَا عَلَى ٱلْمَرْضَىٰ وَلَا عَلَى ٱلَّذِينَ لَا يَجِدُونَ مَا يُنفِقُونَ حَرَجٌ إِذَا نَصَحُوا۟ لِلَّهِ وَرَسُولِهِۦ ۚ مَا عَلَى ٱلْمُحْسِنِينَ مِن سَبِيلٍ ۚ وَٱللَّهُ غَفُورٌ رَّحِيمٌ ﴿٩١﴾

prevent him from according precedence to his material interests and worldly concerns over God and the religion of God. Such a profession of faith is no better than unbelief. Such people will, therefore, be treated by God in the Hereafter as unbelievers and rebels. This is notwithstanding the fact that it might not be possible in this world to declare them unbelievers since they verbally profess Islam, and hence Muslims will have no option but to treat them, on a social and legal level, as Muslims. This is because in the life of this world people can be declared unbelievers only when they are guilty of open denial, rebellion, treachery or infidelity. Hence it is difficult to judge all hypocrites, from a legal point of view, as unbelievers. But escaping the judgement of human beings in this world does not guarantee man's escape from God's judgement and punishment in the Next World.

92. This makes it clear that even those who are otherwise apparently exempt from *jihād* are in fact not automatically so on grounds of physical disability, sickness or indigence. They are exempt only when these disabilities are combined with their true loyalty to God and His Messenger. If someone lacks this loyalty, he cannot be pardoned for the simple reason that when it became obligatory for him to wage *jihād* he was sick or indigent. God does not look at such external criteria for exemption from duty. For God can examine what is at the bottom of each man's heart. He can examine both inner and outer conditions and test whether one's excuse is that of a loyal servant or of a rebel and traitor.

If several persons happen to fall sick on the eve of *jihād,* it will hardly be possible for a human being to distinguish the sickness of one from that of another. But God knows well that each case is different from the other. For instance, there will be those who, if they fall sick on the eve of *jihād,* will thank the heavens for their sickness since it has provided them with a timely excuse to stay away from the war-front. There will be others who react quite differently. They will probably lament their sickness which has

(92) Nor can there be any cause for reproach against those who, when they came to you demanding mounts to go to the battlefront, but who went back, their eyes overflowing with tears when you told them that you had no mounts for them, grieving that they had no resources to enable them to take part in fighting.[93] (93) There are grounds for reproach against those who seek leave to stay behind even though they are affluent. They are the ones who were content to be with the womenfolk who stay behind. Allah has set a seal on their hearts, leaving them bereft of understanding.

وَلَا عَلَى ٱلَّذِينَ إِذَا مَآ أَتَوْكَ
لِتَحْمِلَهُمْ قُلْتَ لَآ أَجِدُ
مَآ أَحْمِلُكُمْ عَلَيْهِ تَوَلَّوا
وَّأَعْيُنُهُمْ تَفِيضُ مِنَ ٱلدَّمْعِ
حَزَنًا أَلَّا يَجِدُوا مَا يُنفِقُونَ
﴿٩٢﴾ إِنَّمَا ٱلسَّبِيلُ عَلَى ٱلَّذِينَ
يَسْتَـْٔذِنُونَكَ وَهُمْ أَغْنِيَآءُ
رَضُوا بِأَن يَكُونُوا مَعَ ٱلْخَوَالِفِ
وَطَبَعَ ٱللَّهُ عَلَىٰ قُلُوبِهِمْ فَهُمْ لَا
يَعْلَمُونَ ﴿٩٣﴾

prevented them from doing their duty and from having the honour of taking part in *jihād*. Whereas the people of the former category will not be content with securing an exemption for themselves from fighting, but will probably also try to dissuade others from *jihād*, there will be others who, even though they themselves are unable to take part in *jihād* for reasons beyond their control, will urge others to hasten to the war-front. Likewise, while people belonging to the first category will spread all kinds of rumours in order to demoralize the believers, the people of the latter category will try to compensate for their inability by reinforcing the home front, and thus at least make some contribution to the cause of *jihād*. Though people of both categories failed to join *jihād*, God will judge them differently in view of their different attitudes. God might pardon the latter, but the former must be convicted for treachery and disloyalty even though both could present a justifiable excuse for not engaging in *jihād*.

93. Those who had a sincere desire to serve Islam but could not do so owing to some genuine reason feel as grief-stricken as a worldly person does when he has been afflicted of misfortune such as when he loses his

(94) They will put up excuses before you when you return to them. Tell them: 'Make no excuses. We will not believe you. Allah has already informed us of the truth about you. Allah will observe your conduct, and so will His Messenger; then you will be brought back to Him Who knows alike what lies beyond human perception and what lies within the reach of human perception, and He will let you know what you did. (95) When you return to them they will surely swear to you in the name of Allah that you may leave them alone. So do leave them alone;[94] they are unclean. Hell shall be their home, a recompense for what they did. ▶

يَعْتَذِرُونَ إِلَيْكُمْ إِذَا
رَجَعْتُمْ إِلَيْهِمْ قُل لَّا تَعْتَذِرُوا
لَن نُّؤْمِنَ لَكُمْ قَدْ نَبَّأَنَا ٱللَّهُ
مِنْ أَخْبَارِكُمْ وَسَيَرَى ٱللَّهُ
عَمَلَكُمْ وَرَسُولُهُۥ ثُمَّ تُرَدُّونَ
إِلَىٰ عَٰلِمِ ٱلْغَيْبِ وَٱلشَّهَٰدَةِ
فَيُنَبِّئُكُم بِمَا كُنتُمْ تَعْمَلُونَ ﴿٩٤﴾
سَيَحْلِفُونَ بِٱللَّهِ لَكُمْ إِذَا
ٱنقَلَبْتُمْ إِلَيْهِمْ لِتُعْرِضُوا عَنْهُمْ
فَأَعْرِضُوا عَنْهُمْ إِنَّهُمْ رِجْسٌ
وَمَأْوَىٰهُمْ جَهَنَّمُ جَزَآءًۢ بِمَا
كَانُوا يَكْسِبُونَ ﴿٩٥﴾

---

job or narrowly misses a treasure. Such persons would be deserving of the same reward from God as those who actually did serve the cause of Islam. For even though they might not have been able physically to contribute to the struggle in the way of God, their hearts were there. This explains why the Prophet (peace be on him), whilst returning from Tabūk, told the Companions: 'You have never undertaken a march nor crossed a valley but that some people, who are actually in Madina, were with you.' In utter surprise they asked: 'Did they do so while they were staying in Madina itself?' The Prophet (peace be on him) affirmed: 'Yes, they did so even while staying in Madina. For they had been forced by circumstances into staying back or else they would never have stayed back.' (See Bukhārī, 'Maghāzī', 'Bāb Nuzūl al-Nabī al-Ḥijr'; Muslim, 'Imārah', 'Bāb Thawāb man ḥabasahū 'an al-Ghazw Maraḍ aw 'Udhr ākhar' – Ed.)

94. Two different verbal forms of the same word *i'rāḍ* have been used in this verse. In the first instance it denotes 'to turn away' in the sense of

(96) They will swear to you in order to please you. But even if you become pleased with them, Allah will not be pleased with such an evil-doing folk.

(97) The bedouin Arabs surpass all in unbelief and hypocrisy and are most likely to be unaware of the limits prescribed by Allah in what He has revealed to His Messenger. Allah is All-Knowing, All-Wise.[95] (98) And among the bedouin Arabs there are such as regard whatever they spend (in the cause of Allah) as a fine[96] and wait for some misfortune to befall you. May ill fortune befall them! Allah is All-Hearing, All-Knowing.

يَحْلِفُونَ لَكُمْ لِتَرْضَوْا عَنْهُمْ ۖ
فَإِن تَرْضَوْا عَنْهُمْ فَإِنَّ ٱللَّهَ لَا
يَرْضَىٰ عَنِ ٱلْقَوْمِ ٱلْفَٰسِقِينَ
﴿٩٦﴾ ٱلْأَعْرَابُ أَشَدُّ كُفْرًا
وَنِفَاقًا وَأَجْدَرُ أَلَّا يَعْلَمُوا۟
حُدُودَ مَآ أَنزَلَ ٱللَّهُ عَلَىٰ رَسُولِهِۦ ۗ
وَٱللَّهُ عَلِيمٌ حَكِيمٌ ﴿٩٧﴾ وَمِنَ
ٱلْأَعْرَابِ مَن يَتَّخِذُ مَا يُنفِقُ
مَغْرَمًا وَيَتَرَبَّصُ بِكُمُ ٱلدَّوَآئِرَ ۚ
عَلَيْهِمْ دَآئِرَةُ ٱلسَّوْءِ ۗ وَٱللَّهُ
سَمِيعٌ عَلِيمٌ ﴿٩٨﴾

---

being indulgent. In the second instance it means to turn away in disgust. The word has been used in an imperative form and contains the injunction to sever all connections with those persons.

95. The word *al-A'rāb*, as we have explained earlier (see n. 90 above), signifies the bedouin – whether of the desert or the countryside – in the vicinity of Madina. For a long time they had followed a policy of opportunism with regard to the conflict between Islam and unbelief. However, as Islam established its sway over the greater part of Hijaz and Najd and the power of the tribes hostile to Islam began to weaken, they saw their interests lay in entering the fold of Islam.

Of them, only a minority embraced Islam out of true conviction and with the readiness to fulfil its demands. For a majority of these bedouin, acceptance of Islam was the outcome of sheer expediency and self-interest, sincere belief playing scarcely any part in it. They were primarily interested in the advantages that accrue to those belonging to the ruling party. But they were intensely resentful of practically everything relating to Islam.

(99) And of the bedouin Arabs are those who believe in Allah and the Last Day, and regard their spending (in the cause of Allah) as a means of drawing them near to Allah and of deserving the prayers of the Messenger. Indeed, this shall be a means of drawing near to Allah. Allah will surely admit them to His mercy. Allah is All-Forgiving, Ever-Merciful.

وَمِنَ ٱلْأَعْرَابِ مَن يُؤْمِنُ بِٱللَّهِ وَٱلْيَوْمِ ٱلْآخِرِ وَيَتَّخِذُ مَا يُنفِقُ قُرُبَٰتٍ عِندَ ٱللَّهِ وَصَلَوَٰتِ ٱلرَّسُولِ ۚ أَلَآ إِنَّهَا قُرْبَةٌ لَّهُمْ ۚ سَيُدْخِلُهُمُ ٱللَّهُ فِى رَحْمَتِهِۦٓ ۗ إِنَّ ٱللَّهَ غَفُورٌ رَّحِيمٌ ﴿٩٩﴾

They were resentful of the moral discipline which Islam imposed on them. They were unhappy with the duty placed upon them to observe Fasting. They were unhappy at the imposition of *Zakāh* on their cattle and agricultural produce. They were also disconcerted by the tight grip imposed by the many regulations which they were required to follow for the first time in their history. They also resented the idea of sacrificing their lives and property not in connection with tribal feuding or razzias, which were close to their hearts, but in the way of God.

Thus a deep sense of dissatisfaction continued to smoulder in the bedouins' hearts and a great number of them invented ever new excuses to circumvent the requirements of Islam. They were a cynical lot who cared nothing for right and wrong or for the true welfare of humanity. Theirs was a small world, confined essentially to their economic interests, their conveniences and privileges, their lands and properties, their camels and goats, and the very limited world around their tents. If they did believe in anything higher, it was a kind of superstitious reverence for saints and holy men to whom they made offerings. In return for those offerings they were supposed to guarantee them material prosperity and immunity from natural calamities. They were also expected to provide them with amulets and pray for their worldly success. Such was their outlook that they could not subscribe to a faith that would seek to subject their entire cultural, social and economic life to a rigorous moral and legal discipline, and which would also ask them to sacrifice their lives and wealth in order to promote its universal reform mission.

In the above verse the Qur'ān refers to this attitude of the bedouin who, compared with town dwellers, were relatively more prone to hypocrisy and unbelief. Town dwellers fare better since they have the opportunity to

(100) And of those who led the way – the first of the Emigrants *(Muhājirūn)* and the Helpers *(Anṣār)*, and those who followed them in the best possible manner – Allah is well-pleased with them and they are well-pleased with Allah. He has prepared for them Gardens beneath which rivers flow; therein they will abide for ever. That is the supreme triumph.

(101) As for the bedouin Arabs around you, some are hypocrites; and so are some of the people of Madina who have become inured to hypocrisy. You do not know them, but We know them.[97] We will chastise them doubly,[98] and then they shall be sent to an awesome suffering.

وَٱلسَّٰبِقُونَ ٱلْأَوَّلُونَ مِنَ
ٱلْمُهَٰجِرِينَ وَٱلْأَنصَارِ وَٱلَّذِينَ
ٱتَّبَعُوهُم بِإِحْسَٰنٍ رَّضِيَ ٱللَّهُ
عَنْهُمْ وَرَضُوا۟ عَنْهُ وَأَعَدَّ لَهُمْ
جَنَّٰتٍ تَجْرِي تَحْتَهَا ٱلْأَنْهَٰرُ
خَٰلِدِينَ فِيهَآ أَبَدًا ۚ ذَٰلِكَ ٱلْفَوْزُ
ٱلْعَظِيمُ ﴿١٠٠﴾ وَمِمَّنْ حَوْلَكُم
مِّنَ ٱلْأَعْرَابِ مُنَٰفِقُونَ ۖ
وَمِنْ أَهْلِ ٱلْمَدِينَةِ ۖ مَرَدُوا۟ عَلَى
ٱلنِّفَاقِ لَا تَعْلَمُهُمْ ۖ نَحْنُ نَعْلَمُهُمْ ۚ
سَنُعَذِّبُهُم مَّرَّتَيْنِ ثُمَّ يُرَدُّونَ
إِلَىٰ عَذَابٍ عَظِيمٍ ﴿١٠١﴾

meet learned and pious people and thus gain some knowledge of religion and its requirements. The bedouin, however, tend to engross themselves in the pursuit of their bread and butter alone, leaving them no leisure time for higher pursuits. At the end of the day they are no more than economic brutes, and as such are ignorant. In this context it may be added that movements towards apostasy and the refusal to pay *Zakāh* which broke out only a couple of years after the revelation of these verses (i.e. verses 97–9) during Abū Bakr's Caliphate, were mainly the result of the bedouins' attitude.

96. Essentially, the bedouin looked upon *Zakāh* as a kind of fine or penalty imposed upon them. Likewise, they also resented the Islamic duty of showing hospitality to strangers. The same was true of the financial contributions they were required to make in connection with *jihād*. They

(102) There are others who have confessed their faults. They intermixed their good deeds with evil. It is likely that Allah will turn to them in mercy, for Allah is All-Forgiving, Ever-Merciful. (103) (O Prophet!) Take alms out of their riches and thereby cleanse them and bring about their growth (in righteousness), and pray for them. Indeed your prayer is a source of tranquillity for them. Allah is All-Hearing, All-Knowing. (104) Are they not aware that it is Allah who accepts the repentance of His servants and takes alms, and that it is Allah Who is Oft-Relenting, Ever-Merciful? ►

وَءَاخَرُونَ ٱعْتَرَفُوا۟ بِذُنُوبِهِمْ خَلَطُوا۟
عَمَلًا صَٰلِحًا وَءَاخَرَ سَيِّئًا عَسَى ٱللَّهُ
أَن يَتُوبَ عَلَيْهِمْ إِنَّ ٱللَّهَ غَفُورٌ رَّحِيمٌ ﴿١٠٢﴾
خُذْ مِنْ أَمْوَٰلِهِمْ صَدَقَةً تُطَهِّرُهُمْ
وَتُزَكِّيهِم بِهَا وَصَلِّ عَلَيْهِمْ إِنَّ صَلَوٰتَكَ
سَكَنٌ لَّهُمْ وَٱللَّهُ سَمِيعٌ عَلِيمٌ ﴿١٠٣﴾
أَلَمْ يَعْلَمُوٓا۟ أَنَّ ٱللَّهَ هُوَ يَقْبَلُ ٱلتَّوْبَةَ
عَنْ عِبَادِهِۦ وَيَأْخُذُ ٱلصَّدَقَٰتِ وَأَنَّ
ٱللَّهَ هُوَ ٱلتَّوَّابُ ٱلرَّحِيمُ ﴿١٠٤﴾

---

made those contributions reluctantly and only with the idea of assuring the Muslims of their faithfulness rather than to please God.

97. The hypocrites had become so adept at keeping their hypocrisy hidden that despite his unusual insight even the Prophet (peace be on him) could not quite see through them.

98. The 'double punishment' mentioned in this verse will consist of the following. First, instead of gaining wealth, prestige, and honour the hypocrites will suffer worldly losses and be subjected to humiliation even though it is their excessive love of the world which led them to hypocrisy and rebellion against God. Second, the cause of Islam, which they seek to frustrate by their evil machinations, will flourish before their very eyes and despite their vicious efforts to the contrary.

(105) And tell them (O Prophet!): 'Keep working: Allah will behold your works and so will His Messenger and the believers;[99] and you shall be brought back to Him Who knows that which is beyond the reach of human perception and that which is within the reach of human perception. He will then declare to you all what you have been doing.'[100]

وَقُلِ ٱعْمَلُوا۟ فَسَيَرَى ٱللَّهُ عَمَلَكُمْ وَرَسُولُهُۥ
وَٱلْمُؤْمِنُونَ ۖ وَسَتُرَدُّونَ إِلَىٰ عَٰلِمِ
ٱلْغَيْبِ وَٱلشَّهَٰدَةِ فَيُنَبِّئُكُم بِمَا كُنتُمْ
تَعْمَلُونَ ﴿١٠٥﴾

---

99. The above Qur'ānic verse brings into sharp relief the difference between the attitudes of a hypocrite and a sinful believer. In light of this, it has to be determined how Muslims should treat people whose claim to be Muslim is false.

The verse lays down that those who profess to be Muslims, but who in fact have no sincere allegiance to God, to the religion propounded by Him, and to the Muslim community, should be treated firmly and severely if their behaviour provides incontrovertible evidence of this. If such people make contributions in the cause of God, they must not be accepted. Nor may the believers, however closely related they be, perform the Funeral Prayers of such persons and pray for their forgiveness. But, if an otherwise sincere believer commits an act inconsistent with the requirements of sincerity and confesses to it, he should be forgiven. The charity offered to him should be accepted and Prayers should be made to God for his forgiveness.

The question arises: How can a sinful believer be determined from a hypocrite, when the act which has been committed is contrary to Islam and Muslims? In our view, the following criteria, hinted at in these verses (101 ff.) could be of help in making a distinction between a sinful believer and a hypocrite:

(1) A sinful believer would be inclined to confess his faults clearly rather than try to explain them away by presenting lame excuses and far-fetched explanations.

(2) The past record of the person concerned should be looked into to see whether or not insincerity towards Islam is a regular trait of

character. If that record shows that he has on the whole been a righteous person, that his life is marked by sincere service to, and sacrifice for the cause of Islam and Muslims, and by an eagerness to excel others in good deeds, it can be safely concluded that if he committed any offence, it was not because of lack of faith and sincerity. It was merely a lapse on his part and was presumably a temporary occurrence.

(3) However, a serious lapse on the part of a person necessitates that a keen eye should be kept on his post-repentant behaviour. This is necessary to decide whether his confession of having committed a lapse and his repentance over it were merely an act of the tongue, or whether there was indeed a deep feeling of regret indicative of a change of heart. If there is convincing evidence of sincere regret and an earnest effort to make amends, and his overall conduct shows that he wants sincerely to wipe out all traces of weakness in his faith, it will be concluded that his repentance is genuine. Such repentance can be considered evidence of his true faith and sincerity.

Traditionists have mentioned the incident in which the Qur'ānic passage in question was revealed. This is reproduced here *in extenso* since it helps to better understand the verses. According to the traditionists, the verses were revealed in connection with Abū Lubābah b. 'Abd al-Mundhir and his six companions' conduct. Abū Lubābah had embraced Islam as early as the occasion of the *Bay'ah* of 'Aqabah before the Prophet's migration to Madina, and thereafter took part in the battles of Badr, Uḥud, and other military campaigns. At the time of the Tabūk expedition, however, he succumbed to the evil propensities of self and stayed back from *jihād* without any real justification. The same was true of some of his companions who were otherwise quite sincere believers. After the Prophet's return from Tabūk and on coming to learn about God's proclamation regarding those who had failed to join *jihād,* Abū Lubābah and his companions were seized by an overwhelming feeling of remorse and shame. Even before they were asked to explain their conduct, they tied themselves to a pillar and vowed to abstain from food and sleep until they were either forgiven or met with death. They underwent this self-inflicted chastisement for several days with the result that they eventually fell down unconscious. Finally, on being told that God and His Messenger had relented towards them, they went to the Prophet (peace be on him) and told him that their repentance included giving away their house – the comfort of which had rendered them heedless to the duty of *jihād* – in the way of God. The Prophet (peace be on him), however, directed them not to give away their whole property; giving away one third of it was sufficient. They instantly gave away one third, making it a *waqf* (endowment). (See the comments of Qurṭubī on verse 102 – Ed.)

If one reflects on this incident one will realize the kinds of weaknesses which are pardoned by God. Abū Lubābah and his companions were not

(106) There are others in whose regard Allah's decree is awaited: whether He will chastise or relent towards them. Allah is All-Knowing, All-Wise.[101]

(107) Then there are others who have set up a mosque to hurt the true faith, to promote unbelief, and cause division among believers, and as an ambush for one who had earlier made war on Allah and His Messenger. They will surely swear: 'We intended nothing but good', whereas Allah bears witness that they are liars. ▶

وَءَاخَرُونَ مُرْجَوْنَ لِأَمْرِ ٱللَّهِ إِمَّا
يُعَذِّبُهُمْ وَإِمَّا يَتُوبُ عَلَيْهِمْ وَٱللَّهُ
عَلِيمٌ حَكِيمٌ ﴿١٠٦﴾ وَٱلَّذِينَ
ٱتَّخَذُوا۟ مَسْجِدًا ضِرَارًا وَكُفْرًا
وَتَفْرِيقًۢا بَيْنَ ٱلْمُؤْمِنِينَ
وَإِرْصَادًا لِّمَنْ حَارَبَ ٱللَّهَ
وَرَسُولَهُۥ مِن قَبْلُ وَلَيَحْلِفُنَّ إِنْ
أَرَدْنَآ إِلَّا ٱلْحُسْنَىٰ وَٱللَّهُ يَشْهَدُ
إِنَّهُمْ لَكَٰذِبُونَ ﴿١٠٧﴾

---

chronic victims of insincerity. On the contrary, their past record showed that they were men of sincere faith. Moreover, they did not invent excuses to cover up their faults, rather they readily confessed it. Not only that, their subsequent actions made it abundantly clear that they were genuinely repentant and were eager for the atonement of their sins.

These verses (see 102 ff. – Ed.) also embody an important point. In order to atone for one's sin, it is not enough to repent merely with one's heart and tongue, important though that is. True repentance should also be evident from one's action. One way to do this is to give away a part of one's wealth to charity. This would help get rid of the evil embedded in one's self which had prompted the sin in the first place, and would increase the potential to return to the right way. For confessing to one's sin is not unlike the feeling of someone who falls into a pit. The shame and remorse felt indicate that one realizes the wretchedness of one's state of being at the bottom of the pit. The subsequent efforts to atone for one's sins by giving to charity and doing other good works amounts to an attempt to get out of the pit.

100. Man will ultimately be judged by God and no act of his will remain hidden from Him. Even if a man succeeds in keeping his hypocrisy

(108) Never stand therein. Surely a mosque founded from the first day on piety is more worthy that you should stand in it for Prayer. In it are men who love to purify themselves, and Allah loves those that purify themselves.[102] ▶

لَا تَقُمْ فِيهِ أَبَدًا ۚ لَّمَسْجِدٌ أُسِّسَ
عَلَى التَّقْوَىٰ مِنْ أَوَّلِ يَوْمٍ أَحَقُّ أَن
تَقُومَ فِيهِ ۚ فِيهِ رِجَالٌ يُحِبُّونَ
أَن يَتَطَهَّرُوا ۚ وَاللَّهُ يُحِبُّ
الْمُطَّهِّرِينَ ﴿١٠٨﴾

concealed and makes people believe that he is a sincere believer, this will not protect him from punishment for his hypocrisy.

101. The circumstances surrounding the cases of the persons referred to in the above verse were unclear: that is, it was not easy for people to determine whether they belonged to the category of sinful believers or to that of hypocrites. Judgement on these cases was, therefore, deferred. This does not mean that God was in a state of doubt and indecision about them. What this statement means is that the Muslims could take a definite position about them only on the basis of sufficient and tangible evidence. For judgements based on esoteric grounds have no validity. Only those judgements which are supported by tangible evidence and reasoning carry any weight.

102. Before the arrival of the Prophet (peace be on him) in Madina there lived a man called Abū 'Āmir. He belonged to the Khazraj clan and had converted to Christianity. Being an ascetic and a scholar of the Scriptures, Abū 'Āmir was held in great esteem by the bedouin of both Madina and the adjoining areas. His popularity among the masses was at its zenith when the Prophet (peace be on him) arrived in Madina. But his religious scholarship and ascetic way of life, rather than assisting him to recognize the truth, in fact became a hindrance. The result was that Abū 'Āmir not only failed to embrace Islam, but looked upon the Prophet (peace be on him) as his rival in the field of religious leadership.

In the beginning Abū 'Āmir cherished the hope that the hostile force of the Quraysh would be enough to nip Islam in the bud. But contrary to what he had expected, the Quraysh were badly routed in the battle of Badr. After that event, he was unable to restrain himself. He moved out of Madina the same year and began to visit different tribes and incite them against Islam. In fact he was one of the people whose vicious efforts instigated the Battle of Uḥud. It is also said that he arranged for several pits to be dug in Uḥud, and as we know, the Prophet (peace be on him) fell into one of them during the course of the battle and was badly injured. Later, when the Battle of the Ditch *(Ghazwat al-Khandaq)* took place, he took a major role in provoking many of the tribes to join the forces that invaded Madina. In all the battles that took place thereafter right up to the Battle of Ḥunayn, this Christian monk consistently allied himself with the forces of polytheism against Islam.

In the end, he utterly despaired that any power in Arabia would be able to resist the stormy onslaught of Islam. He therefore turned to Rome and warned Caesar of the impending Islamic menace. It was because of his initial efforts that Caesar commenced his preparations to invade Arabia, and on knowing of such activity the Prophet (peace be on him) decided to pre-empt it by dispatching a military expedition to Tabūk. (For further information about Abū ʻĀmir see the comments of Qurṭubī on *al-Aʻrāf* 7: 175 and *al-Tawbah* 9: 107 – Ed.) A group of hypocrites in Madina actively collaborated with Abū ʻĀmir in his efforts. They also supported Abū ʻĀmir's plan that, by taking advantage of his position as a clergyman, he should persuade Caesar as well as the Christian chiefs of northern Arabia to strike a deadly blow against Islam. On the eve of Abū ʻĀmir's departure to Rome, he was party to a decision made by a group of hypocrites in Madina to erect a mosque of their own so that they could carry on their insidious activities under the garb of religion. They thought that this religious act – building a mosque – would provide the 'Muslim' hypocrites – as distinct from the generality of Muslims – a safe meeting place for organizing themselves into a force that would carry on its activities without inviting any suspicion. The mosque was to serve as the centre for hatching conspiracies against Islam, a centre to which the agents of Abū ʻĀmir, carrying the latter's instructions, could come safely and stay in as travellers and holy men. The above verse (i.e. 107) alludes to this vile conspiracy which lay behind the building of the mosque. (See the comments of Qurṭubī on verse 107 – Ed.)

At that time there were two mosques in Madina: the mosque of Qubā which was situated on the outskirts of the town, and the Prophet's mosque which was in the heart of Madina. There was, therefore, hardly any need for another mosque. Nor were the Muslims of the day possessed of that naive religious zeal which prompts people to construct mosques as an act to ensure their heavenly rewards even if there is no need or justification for it. Not only that, there seemed no reason to expect that the construction of a new mosque would yield any positive benefit; there were, in fact, reasons to believe that it would indeed be harmful. For a new mosque was likely to create dissensions in the ranks of the Muslims and this is unacceptable under a sound Islamic dispensation. The hypocrites, knowing there was no convincing justification for a new mosque, began to put forward flimsy grounds to justify their intent. They pleaded to the Prophet (peace be on him) that such a mosque was necessary because of the difficulties of praying, congregationally, five times a day, and particularly at night in cold and rainy weather; this was especially difficult for the old

(109) Is he, then, who has
erected his structure on fear
of Allah and His good pleasure better, or he who erects
his string on the brink of a
crumbling bank,[103] so that it
crumbles down with him into
the Hell-fire? Allah does not
bestow His guidance on the
wrong-doing folk.[104] (110)
And the structure which they
have erected will ever inspire
their hearts with doubts unless it be that their very
hearts are cut into pieces.[105]
Allah is All-Knowing, All-
Wise.

أَفَمَنْ أَسَّسَ بُنْيَـٰنَهُۥ عَلَىٰ تَقْوَىٰ
مِنَ ٱللَّهِ وَرِضْوَٰنٍ خَيْرٌ أَم مَّنْ
أَسَّسَ بُنْيَـٰنَهُۥ عَلَىٰ شَفَا جُرُفٍ
هَارٍ فَٱنْهَارَ بِهِۦ فِى نَارِ جَهَنَّمَ وَٱللَّهُ
لَا يَهْدِى ٱلْقَوْمَ ٱلظَّـٰلِمِينَ ﴿١٠٩﴾
لَا يَزَالُ بُنْيَـٰنُهُمُ ٱلَّذِى بَنَوْا۟ رِيبَةً
فِى قُلُوبِهِمْ إِلَّآ أَن تَقَطَّعَ قُلُوبُهُمْ
وَٱللَّهُ عَلِيمٌ حَكِيمٌ ﴿١١٠﴾

and the disabled who lived at some distance from the Mosque of the Prophet (peace be on him).

When the mosque (called Masjid Ḍirār) – constructed on such pietistic pretexts – was ready, the hypocrites approached the Prophet (peace be on him) asking him to inaugurate the mosque by leading the Prayer there. The Prophet (peace be on him) declined, saying that he was preoccupied with the Tabūk expedition, and asked them to bide their time. (See Ṭabarī, *Ta'rīkh*, vol. 3, p. 110; Ibn Hishām, vol. 2, p. 529 – Ed.) As the Prophet (peace be on him) left for Tabūk, the hypocrites began hatching their conspiracies against Islam in the new mosque. They even decided that as soon as the Muslims were crushed by the Romans – and they were absolutely sure this was imminent – they would install 'Abd Allāh ibn Ubayy as the ruler of Madina. But the outcome of the expedition was quite different from that which the hypocrites had expected and it threw cold water on all their hopes. During his return when the Prophet (peace be on him) reached a place called Dhū Adān in the vicinity of Madina, the above verses were revealed. The Prophet (peace be on him) immediately sent a few people to Madina with the directive to raze Masjid Ḍirār to the ground before he even entered Madina.

103. The word *juruf* used in the above verse applies in Arabic usage to the bank of a river or stream, the supporting ground of which has been washed out, rendering it hollow and leaving the surface standing without

any support. This simile describes adequately the situation of ungodly people.

The structure of such peoples' lives is comparable to a building which is constructed on the river bank which has been rendered hollow by water and hence lacks foundations and strength. The simile is both apt and picturesque insofar as it brings sharply to mind a graphic enactment of the whole situation. Extending the above simile it may be said that the outward facet of worldly life in which men of all sorts – the believers and the unbelievers, the sincere and the insincere, the pious and the sinners are found at work – resembles the upper surface of the land on which all buildings are erected. The upper surface is not stable in itself since its stability depends on the support of compact soil beneath. If an ignorant, short-sighted person constructs his house on a piece of land of which the lower level has been rendered hollow by water, that construction will be fatal not only for that person, but will also make the capital invested by him in the construction of that house useless.

In exactly the same way, a person's actions are as such insignificant. Actions are only meaningful and significant if their foundation is God-fearing, if they are based upon belief in ultimate answerability to God, and upon a commitment to follow the requirements of His good pleasure. Those simpletons who are satisfied with the external glitter of worldly life and whose actions are not prompted by God-fearing, nor involve concern for God's good pleasure, themselves cause the erosion of the lower layer of soil under the building which they erect. The ultimate outcome of such an act is that the foundations are destroyed and the building collapses, bringing about the total undoing of the person concerned.

104. The 'straight way' is the one that leads to the true success and felicity of man.

105. They have committed hideous sins such as erecting 'Masjid Ḍirār' and as a result their hearts have become saturated with unbelief, and incapable of belief. The case of these people is more hopeless than of those who publicly erect temples for worship or who declare war against Islam and take part in military action aimed at the extirpation of Islam. However iniquitous these declared unbelievers might be, there remains the hope that at some stage they may be guided to the Right Way. For even though they are misguided, their behaviour shows that they are honest, sincere and courageous in their convictions. All those who possess such valuable qualities can become great assets for the cause of true faith once they are able to re-orient themselves. But there is no hope for those cowardly and crafty people who go so far as to build a 'mosque' in order to undermine the cause of Islam, and who do so with the pretension of serving the cause of Islam. They will never be guided to the Right Way. Their cynical and utterly depraved behaviour has undermined their capacity to appreciate the truth for its own sake.

(111) Surely Allah has purchased of the believers their lives and their belongings and in return has promised that they shall have Paradise.[106] They fight in the cause of Allah, and slay and are slain. Such is the promise He has made incumbent upon Himself in the Torah, and the Gospel, and the Qur'ān.[107] Who is more faithful to his promise than Allah? Rejoice then, in the bargain you have made with Him. That indeed is the mighty triumph. ▶

إِنَّ ٱللَّهَ ٱشْتَرَىٰ مِنَ ٱلْمُؤْمِنِينَ
أَنفُسَهُمْ وَأَمْوَٰلَهُم بِأَنَّ لَهُمُ
ٱلْجَنَّةَ ۚ يُقَٰتِلُونَ فِى سَبِيلِ ٱللَّهِ
فَيَقْتُلُونَ وَيُقْتَلُونَ ۖ وَعْدًا عَلَيْهِ
حَقًّا فِى ٱلتَّوْرَىٰةِ وَٱلْإِنجِيلِ
وَٱلْقُرْءَانِ ۚ وَمَنْ أَوْفَىٰ بِعَهْدِهِۦ
مِنَ ٱللَّهِ ۚ فَٱسْتَبْشِرُوا۟ بِبَيْعِكُمُ
ٱلَّذِى بَايَعْتُم بِهِۦ ۚ وَذَٰلِكَ هُوَ ٱلْفَوْزُ
ٱلْعَظِيمُ ﴿١١١﴾

---

106. When a man has true faith it involves a commitment to devote himself sincerely to God and God's promise of reward in return for that commitment. This two-way commitment has been described as a 'transaction'. What this means is that faith is not just the affirmation of a set of metaphysical propositions. It is in fact a contract according to which man places all that he has – his life, his wealth – at the disposal of God; he 'sells' them to God. In return, he accepts God's promise of Paradise in the Next Life.

In order to fully understand this point and its implications, it is necessary to explain the nature of the 'transaction' mentioned in the verse.

To start with, it is evident that God is the Owner of all that man has – his life, his wealth, his everything – for He is the Creator of man as well as of all his possessions. Viewed from this angle, any transaction of sale and purchase between man and God is, strictly speaking, out of the question. For man does not possess anything of his own which he might sell. Nor is there anything which God does not own and which would necessitate purchase on His part. Nonetheless, God has bestowed upon man free-will and freedom of choice and this is the basis of the transaction mentioned above, as we shall see.

The conferment of free-will does not alter the basic reality of God's godhead. However, it enables man to freely accept or reject the basic reality. Investing man with free-will does not mean that man has thereby been made the absolute owner of himself, of his mental and physical abilities, and of the worldly possessions that he has come to acquire. Nor does it mean that God has conferred upon man the right to utilize his native abilities and material possessions as he pleases. The conferment of free-will simply means that God does not compel man to behave in the manner prescribed by Him. Hence man can follow one of two courses: he can, if he so decides, recognize God as his true Master and in consideration of that fact use his native abilities and material possessions in the manner prescribed by God. On the other hand, he can if he so decides, disregard God as his master, arrogate to himself mastery over himself, his abilities and material possessions, and hence consider himself entitled to use his abilities and possessions in the manner he pleases.

It is here that the concept of 'transaction' becomes relevant. The 'transaction' referred to in the above verse should not convey the impression that God intends to purchase what man owns. For, God is the true owner of all that man has. Hence the 'transaction' concerns what God Himself has granted man by way of trust, and with regard to which God has given man the freedom to act either in good faith or contrary to it. It is this freedom which man holds in trust from God which He asks man to recognize – and to do so purely of his own volition rather than compulsorily. Man is the trustee and not the absolute owner, and he is asked to avoid committing any breach of this trust which, by the nature of things, man is in a position to do. When someone voluntarily makes a bargain with God, committing his life in this manner, surrendering to God the freedom which God Himself has conferred upon him, then God recompenses him for his voluntary relinquishment of freedom by granting him Paradise in the never-ending life of the Hereafter. It is the believer who, by making such a commitment with God in expectation of reward, enters into a transaction with God. Such is the substance of the transaction that it is equivalent with faith itself. Conversely, when someone refuses to make this transaction, and behaves in a manner which is inconceivable with such a transaction – then this person is an unbeliever. The technical term applied to this refusal to make the transaction is unbelief *(kufr)*.

Having considered the nature of the transaction, let us now consider its implications:

(1) God has presented man with two severe tests. First, the conferment of freedom tests man's mettle: will he acknowledge the lordship of his Creator and act gratefully towards Him or will he prove to be ungrateful and rebellious. The second, relates to whether or not man will put his trust in God, whether or not he will surrender his freedom and sacrifice his worldly advantages and pleasures in return for God's promise of Paradise and eternal felicity in the Next Life.

(2) At this stage a clear distinction ought to be made between two kinds of faith. Faith in one sense is required in order that a person be considered a member of the Muslim community. In its second sense, faith has a certain spiritual content because of which a person is

considered to be a believer in the reckoning of God. Requirements of faith in the second sense are higher than of faith in the first sense.

Faith in the first sense has, of necessity, a legal meaning. Hence verbal profession of articles of faith suffice to make a man be considered a Muslim in the legal sense. A Muslim may be declared to have gone out of the fold of Islam only if he does something which is flagrantly opposed to his profession of faith.

As for the faith which is of value in the sight of God, its requirements are quite different. Even if a person observes Prayer and Fasting, that might not be deemed enough. For if a man considers himself the absolute master of his body and soul, of his heart and mind, of his wealth and resources, and of the different things which are under his control, deeming that he has the right to use them as he pleases, then such a person is not a believer in the sight of God regardless of what others think of him. For such a person does not commit himself to the transaction mentioned in the present verse and which the Qur'ān considers to be at the very core of faith. To exert oneself and one's abilities and possessions in a way disapproved of by God and not to exert them in the manner prescribed by Him, betray a false claim to faith. For such an attitude clearly shows that either the person concerned does not consciously 'sell' his life and wealth to God, or that he still considers himself – despite the transaction he has made with God – the true owner of his possessions.

(3) This concept of faith enables us to make a clear distinction between Islamic and the un-Islamic ways of life. A Muslim who truly believes in God follows the Will of God in all walks of life. At no time does his attitude betray any claim on his part to be independent of God. True, occasionally he will commit sins, but this is only a momentary lapse where he has overlooked the implications of his transaction with God.

This transaction is not just meant for the personal lives of the believers. The collective lives of the believers should also reflect the implications and requirements of the transaction. The Muslim body-politic must not pursue a course of action, whether it be political, economic or social, in disregard of the Islamic Law. And if they ever lapse into the same kind of mistake as human beings are prone to do in their personal lives, they should again submit to God's Will and abandon any claim of the right to act independently of God. For the very notion that man has the right to work in disregard of God, that he has the right to determine what he should do and what he should not, is essentially an un-Islamic attitude even if that attitude might be adopted by those called 'Muslims'.

(4) The 'transaction' in question binds man to adhere to the Will of God alone so that it leaves no room for man to follow his own desires. To arbitrarily declare something to be the Will of God and to follow

it amounts to following one's own will rather than God's, and this militates against the basic terms of the 'transaction' between man and God. Only those individuals and groups who derive guidance for their life as a whole from the Book of God and the directives of His Messenger can be truly considered faithful to the transaction made with God.

These being the implications of the transaction with God, it is clear why the grant of reward by God to those men who live up to their commitment to Him has been deferred to the Next Life. For Paradise is not given for merely professing that one has sold one's life and possessions to God. Rather it is a reward for man's action in accordance with that profession. That is, Paradise is a reward granted to him who abstains from using his life and wealth as though he has the right to use them as he pleases. Thus, the transaction will mature only when the life of man – the seller – will come to an end and it is proved that he did truly abide by the terms of the transaction he had made with God. Then, but not before, can it be decided how he should be recompensed.

It will be illuminating to look at this matter by reference to its circumstantial context in the Qur'ān. It occurs in connection with those who claimed to be believers and yet had not lived up to that claim. When put to the test, they preferred not to sacrifice their time, wealth, material interests and lives for the sake of God and His religion. They were either lazy, insincere or downright hypocritical. The attitude demonstrated by these groups of people was subjected to a severe reproach in the Qur'ān, and the people themselves were told unequivocally that faith does not consist of a mere verbal affirmation of God's existence and unity. True profession of faith rather amounts to affirming that one's life and wealth all belong to God alone. If some people do not sacrifice their lives and wealth in compliance with God's command and use those possessions in opposition to the Will of God, their profession of faith is blatantly false. True believers are those who have sold their lives and wealth to God and regard Him as the sole Master of all their possessions. Accordingly, they are willing to sacrifice their lives and wealth unquestioningly at His behest, and refrain from expending their abilities or financial resources in disregard of His command.

107. The statement that the Torah, the Gospels and the Qur'ān assure Paradise to the believers if they sell their lives and wealth to God has been called into question on the grounds that there is no trace of such a promise in the Torah and the Gospels. Insofar as the Gospels are concerned this objection does not hold water. For Jesus makes numerous statements in the Gospels which substantively amount to what the Qur'ān says here. Consider, for instance, the following:

> Blessed are those who are persecuted for righteousness' sake, for theirs is the Kingdom of heaven (*Matthew* 5: 10).

> He who finds his life will lose it: and he who loses his life for my sake will find it (*Matthew* 10: 39).
>
> And everyone who has left houses or brothers or sisters or father or mother or children or lands for my name's sake, will receive hundred fold, and inherit eternal life (*Matthew* 19: 29).

True, the Torah in its present form does not contain any explicit promise of Paradise to those who sell their lives and wealth to God. The existing Torah is altogether shorn of the notion of Life after Death, of the Day of Judgement, and of Divine Reward and Punishment even though these doctrines have always formed an inextricable part of true faith. Absence of any reference to this promise in the Torah should not leave the impression that the original Torah did not contain such a promise. What really accounts for its omission in the extant Torah is that in the days of their all-round degeneracy the Jews became too worldly and materialistic to conceive of any reward other than a worldly one. They, therefore, debased all reference in the Scriptures to promises of reward for obedience by forcing upon these a worldly interpretation. As for the descriptions of Paradise, they construed them to be descriptions of Palestine, the land of their dreams. Nevertheless we find in the Torah such statements as the following:

> Hear, O Israel: The Lord our god is one Lord; and you shall love the Lord your God with all your heart, and with all your soul, and with all your might (*Deuteronomy* 6: 4–5).
>
> Is not he your father, who created you, who made you and established you? (*Deuteronomy* 32: 6).

When it comes to God's reward for being faithful to the covenant with Him, it is interpreted by the Jews to mean Palestine. When a land flowing with milk and honey is mentioned (see *Deuteronomy* 6: 3), it is given a purely earthly interpretation. This anomaly can be explained by reference to the fact that the extant Torah is neither complete nor free from distortions since it embodies man's additions such as the exegetical notes of theologians side by side with the Word of God. In the Torah extraneous elements have become so mixed up with the original divine revelation that it is simply impossible to distinguish the original divine elements from national traditions, racial prejudices and superstitions, dreams and aspirations, and legal deductions. (See *Towards Understanding the Qur'ān*, vol. I, *Āl 'Imrān* 3, n. 2, pp. 233–5 – Ed.)

(112) Those who constantly turn to Allah in repentance,[108] who ever worship Him, who praise Him, who go about the world to serve His cause,[109] who bow down to Him, who prostrate themselves before Him, who enjoin what is good and forbid what is evil, and who keep the limits set by Allah.[110] To such believers announce glad tidings.

ٱلتَّٰٓئِبُونَ ٱلْعَٰبِدُونَ
ٱلْحَٰمِدُونَ ٱلسَّٰٓئِحُونَ
ٱلرَّٰكِعُونَ ٱلسَّٰجِدُونَ
ٱلْءَامِرُونَ بِٱلْمَعْرُوفِ
وَٱلنَّاهُونَ عَنِ ٱلْمُنكَرِ
وَٱلْحَٰفِظُونَ لِحُدُودِ ٱللَّهِ ۗ وَبَشِّرِ
ٱلْمُؤْمِنِينَ ١١٢

108. The word *tā'ibūn* used in the above verse may be translated literally as 'those who turn to God in repentance'. However, the context in which this word occurs indicates that repentance is a recurring characteristic of believers, implying that far from repenting once, they constantly turn to God in repentance. We have tried to convey this nuance in the translation of the verse.

The need to repent time and time again stems from the fact that man is prone to become oblivious to the transaction which he has made with God. For by all appearances it looks as though man himself is the master of his life and wealth. As compared with this, the notion that God is the true master of man's life and wealth seems abstract. A believer may, therefore, often lapse into momentary forgetfulness of his transaction with God and behave in a manner counter to its spirit. What marks out a true believer, however, is that at the very moment he becomes aware of his lapse, he repents over his obliviousness, his unconscious defiance of the requirements of the transaction he has made with God. (For an understanding of 'transaction' see n. 106 above – Ed.) Full of regret he turns to his Lord asking for pardon, and renews the commitment he has made to Him.

This recurrent turning to God in repentance, this constant striving to return to the course of obedience and submission ensures the permanence and vitality of a person's faith. Given man's inherent frailties it seems that had there been no repentance, it would have been virtually impossible for man to remain continually faithful to the terms of the transaction he has made with God. Hence the believer has not been portrayed in the Qur'ān as one who, once he adopts the course of obedience to God, never suffers a lapse. What is praiseworthy about the believer is that after every lapse he returns to the same course – obedience to God.

Mentioning 'repentance' as a characteristic of a believer is also quite significant in the present context. For in the preceding verses the address was directed to those who had acted in a manner inconsistent with the requirements of their faith. Hence, after explaining the true nature and requisites of faith, they are told that turning to God in repentance is an unmistakable characteristic of the believer. Far from persisting in his deviation, no sooner does a believer become conscious of his lapse, than he turns to God in repentance.

109. The word *al-sā'iḥūn* used in the text has been interpreted by some commentators of the Qur'ān as *al-ṣā'imūn,* i.e. those who fast. (Both Ibn Kathīr and Qurṭubī mention this as one of the meanings of the word *al-sā'iḥūn* – Ed.) But that is an extended rather than a literal meaning of the word. The tradition in which the Prophet (peace be on him) is reported to have explained it to mean 'those who fast', lacks authenticity. What, therefore, seems appropriate is to interpret the word *al-sā'iḥūn* in its literal sense: 'those who move about the earth (in the cause of Allah)'.

The addition of the words 'in the cause of Allah' to qualify the words 'those who move about' is quite justified. There are several instances in the Qur'ān when a word has been used in its literal sense but which has also been qualified by its purpose – its being for the sake of God. One notable example is the use of the word *infāq,* which literally means 'to spend', and is not restricted in Arabic usage to spending 'in the way of God'. But that is the sense in which it has been used in the Qur'ān even when there is no specific reference to that effect. Hence, the word *al-sā'iḥūn* signifies all those who move about the earth for higher purposes rather than in mere pursuit of pleasure and enjoyment: who engage in journeys to seek the good pleasure of God, in journeys which are for the sake of *jihād,* in journeys for establishing and upholding God's religion, in journeys involving migration from a region under the dominance of unbelief, in journeys to spread the true faith, to reform men, to acquire useful knowledge, to observe the signs of God, or to seek a lawful livelihood.

This characteristic of a believer – that he moves about in the cause of God – has been especially mentioned so as to emphasize to those who failed to join *jihād* despite their claim to be believers, that when a true believer is summoned to *jihād* he simply cannot enjoy the cosy comfort of his home. On the contrary, a true believer moves about the earth and exerts himself so as to make the true religion prevail.

110. It is a characteristic of the believers that they faithfully observe the limits prescribed by God in all matters, whether these relate to doctrine or modes of worship, to ethics and morality or to social, cultural, economic or political life, or to the laws of war and peace. They act both individually and collectively in strict conformity with the limits set by God. They neither transgress these limits by giving free rein to their desires, nor replace Divine Law by something man-made.

(113) After it has become clear that they are condemned to the Flaming Fire,[111] it is not for the Prophet and those who believe to ask for the forgiveness of those who associate others with Allah in His divinity even if they be near of kin. (114) And Abraham's prayer for the forgiveness of his father was only because of a promise which he had made to him.[112] Then, when it became clear to him that he was an enemy of Allah he dissociated himself from him. Surely Abraham was most tender-hearted, much-forbearing.[113]

مَا كَانَ لِلنَّبِيِّ وَالَّذِينَ آمَنُوٓا أَن
يَسْتَغْفِرُوا لِلْمُشْرِكِينَ وَلَوْ كَانُوٓا
أُولِي قُرْبَىٰ مِن بَعْدِ مَا تَبَيَّنَ لَهُمْ
أَنَّهُمْ أَصْحَٰبُ الْجَحِيمِ ﴿١١٣﴾ وَمَا
كَانَ اسْتِغْفَارُ إِبْرَٰهِيمَ لِأَبِيهِ
إِلَّا عَن مَّوْعِدَةٍ وَعَدَهَآ إِيَّاهُ فَلَمَّا
تَبَيَّنَ لَهُۥٓ أَنَّهُۥ عَدُوٌّ لِّلَّهِ تَبَرَّأَ مِنْهُ إِنَّ
إِبْرَٰهِيمَ لَأَوَّٰهٌ حَلِيمٌ ﴿١١٤﴾

'To strictly guard the limits prescribed by Allah' also means that those limits are enforced and none may be allowed to transgress. Hence, the true believers are those who not only themselves observe the limits prescribed by God, but also exert themselves so as to establish and safeguard those limits in the world and try to ensure that they are not violated.

111. If a person prays to God for someone's pardon it implies, first of all, sympathy and concern for the offender, and a belief that the offence is pardonable. Such an attitude towards an offender who is otherwise faithful is quite all right. But to sympathize with, and love those who have indulged in open rebellion and to consider that rebellion pardonable is quite a different matter. Such an attitude is not only wrong in principle but leaves one's loyalty open to doubt. Were we to pray for someone's pardon merely on grounds of kinship, it would mean that we hold our tie of kinship to be more important than our loyalty to God. It also shows that our loyalty to God is not unallied for we desire that God should be influenced by the love we have for His rebels, that He should at least pardon our relatives even if He hurls all other criminals into Hell.

All such things are wrong, are inconsistent with the dictates of sincere devotion and loyalty to God, and are discordant with the spirit of true faith which requires absolute love and devotion to God. True faith requires that we should consider God's friends as our friends and God's enemies as our own enemies. It is significant that the verse in question does not say that Muslims should not seek pardon for those who ascribe divinity to others than God. The verse rather characterizes it as something unbecoming of the Prophet (peace be on him) and the believers (*al-Tawbah* 9: 113).

What is thus suggested is that the believers themselves should have such loyalty and sincerity for God that it prevents them from entertaining any sympathy for those who have rebelled against Him. It is noteworthy that the words of the verse are: 'It is not fitting for the Prophet and those who believe that they should pray for forgiveness for those who ascribe divinity to others than Allah.' The expression seems to say to people: 'What good is there if you refrain from praying for forgiveness for such people because We asked you not to? Nay, your religious commitment and your conscience should be so sensitive about such matters as to make you instinctively feel that it is not befitting for you at all to sympathize with the rebels of God or to consider their crime pardonable.'

It may, however, be clarified that the kind of sympathy which is forbidden those who have rebelled against God is sympathy which interferes with, and prevents one from fulfilling one's religious obligations. So far as human sympathy is concerned – consideration, compassion and affection – far from it being forbidden, it is praiseworthy for a believer to possess such attributes. The worldly obligations that one owes to one's kinsmen – whether they are believers or unbelievers – must be fulfilled. Likewise, those in distress – the needy, the sick, the injured, the orphans – must be helped irrespective of their religious faith. In such matters any discrimination between a believer and an unbeliever is out of the question.

112. Here allusion is made to the Prophet Abraham (peace be on him) who said to his unbelieving father as he severed his ties with him:

> Abraham said: 'Peace be to you. I will pray to my Lord for your forgiveness. For He is to me Most Gracious' (*Maryam* 19: 47).
>
> Except the saying of Abraham to his father: 'I shall certainly pray for your forgiveness though I have no power to get anything for you from Allah' (*al-Mumtaḥanah* 60: 4).

It was in view of the above promise that Abraham prayed for his father's forgiveness:

> And forgive my father, for indeed he is among those gone astray, and do not disgrace me on the Day when (all men) will be raised, the Day when neither wealth nor children will avail, but only he (will prosper) who brings to Allah a sound heart (*al-Shu'arā'* 26: 86–9).

(115) It is not Allah's way to cause people to stray in error after He has guided them and until He has made clear to them what they should guard against.[114] Surely Allah knows everything. (116) Allah's deed is the Kingdom of the heavens and the earth. He it is who confers life and causes death. You have no protector or helper besides Allah.

وَمَا كَانَ ٱللَّهُ لِيُضِلَّ قَوْمًۢا
بَعْدَ إِذْ هَدَىٰهُمْ حَتَّىٰ يُبَيِّنَ لَهُم
مَّا يَتَّقُونَ ۚ إِنَّ ٱللَّهَ بِكُلِّ شَىْءٍ عَلِيمٌ
﴿١١٥﴾ إِنَّ ٱللَّهَ لَهُۥ مُلْكُ ٱلسَّمَٰوَٰتِ
وَٱلْأَرْضِ ۖ يُحْىِۦ وَيُمِيتُ ۚ وَمَا
لَكُم مِّن دُونِ ٱللَّهِ مِن
وَلِىٍّ وَلَا نَصِيرٍ ﴿١١٦﴾

As for the prayer of Abraham for his father's forgiveness its guarded terms should be noted. Moreover, no sooner had Abraham realized that he was praying for the forgiveness of one who had publicly rebelled against God and who was hostile to the religion of God, than he gave up praying for his forgiveness. Also, as a true believer should do in such a situation, he dissociated himself from the person who had rebelled against God, even though that person was none other than his own father who had brought him up with much compassion and tenderness.

113. The word *awwāh* used in respect of Abraham in the above verse denotes a tender-hearted, lamenting, tearful and wistful person. The other word which has been used here – *ḥalīm* – denotes someone who can keep control over himself, who does not lose control of himself in anger, hostility and opposition, and who does not transgress the limits of moderation in love and friendship.

Both words have been very appropriately employed here for Abraham and convey a set of meanings. Abraham was very tender-hearted *(awwāh)*, so he shuddered at the very thought of his father ending up as fodder for Hell, and hence he prayed for his forgiveness. At the same time, the fact that Abraham was a person who kept control over himself *(ḥalīm)*, is borne out by the fact that he prayed for his father even though the latter had perpetrated cruelties on him while trying to dissuade him from the way of Islam. Also, being God-fearing and of temperate disposition, Abraham was not carried away by feelings of love for his father to the extent of exceeding the appropriate limits. Realizing that his father had rebelled against God, Abraham dissociated himself from him.

114. In dealing with men, God first explains to them the doctrines and practices which they should shun. However, if they persist in their wrong

(117) Surely Allah has relented towards the Prophet, and towards the *Muhājirūn* (Emigrants) and the *Anṣār* (Helpers) who stood by him in the hour of distress[115] when the hearts of a party of them had well-nigh swerved.[116] (But when they gave up swerving from the right course and followed the Prophet) Allah relented towards them.[117] Surely to them He is Most Tender, Most Merciful. ►

لَقَد تَّابَ ٱللَّهُ عَلَى ٱلنَّبِيِّ
وَٱلْمُهَـٰجِرِينَ وَٱلْأَنصَارِ
ٱلَّذِينَ ٱتَّبَعُوهُ فِى سَاعَةِ
ٱلْعُسْرَةِ مِنۢ بَعْدِ مَا كَادَ
يَزِيغُ قُلُوبُ فَرِيقٍ مِّنْهُمْ ثُمَّ
تَابَ عَلَيْهِمْ ۚ إِنَّهُۥ بِهِمْ رَءُوفٌ
رَّحِيمٌ ﴿١١٧﴾

ways, God withholds Himself from guiding them and lets them follow the wrong ways they choose to follow.

This verse embodies a basic principle which can help one understand all those Qur'ānic verses in which both guiding people to the right way and causing people to go astray are mentioned as God's own acts. To provide guidance on God's part consists of enunciating the Right Way through His Prophets and Scriptures, and then enabling those who are willing to follow that way to do so. Likewise, God's act of causing people to go astray means that God does not compel those who insist on not following the Right Way after it has been made plain to them, and enables them to proceed in the direction they have decided to proceed in.

115. God pardoned minor omissions on the part of the Prophet (peace be on him) and his Companions. The Prophet's lapse (see n. 45 above), consisted of granting exemption to those who had sought his permission although they were fully able to make *jihād*.

116. This refers to some sincere and devoted Companions who initially shrank from *jihād*. However, being genuine believers and true lovers of Islam, they were able to overcome their initial reluctance and fear.

117. This is an assurance that God will not take them to task for their momentary dereliction of duty. For God does not punish man for a weakness which does not manifest itself in action and which he himself is later able to overcome and correct.

(118) And He also relented towards the three whose cases had been deferred.[118] When the earth, for all its spaciousness, became constrained to them, and their lives became a burden to them, and they realized that there was no refuge from Allah except in Him, He relented towards them that they may turn back to Him. Surely, it is Allah Who is Much-Forgiving, Ever-Merciful.[119]

وَعَلَى ٱلثَّلَٰثَةِ ٱلَّذِينَ خُلِّفُوا۟ حَتَّىٰٓ إِذَا
ضَاقَتْ عَلَيْهِمُ ٱلْأَرْضُ بِمَا رَحُبَتْ
وَضَاقَتْ عَلَيْهِمْ أَنفُسُهُمْ وَظَنُّوٓا۟
أَن لَّا مَلْجَأَ مِنَ ٱللَّهِ إِلَّآ إِلَيْهِ ثُمَّ
تَابَ عَلَيْهِمْ لِيَتُوبُوٓا۟ ۚ إِنَّ ٱللَّهَ هُوَ
ٱلتَّوَّابُ ٱلرَّحِيمُ ١١٨

118. When the Prophet (peace be on him) returned to Madina after the expedition to Tabūk, those who had stayed behind came to him offering all sorts of excuses for not having joined the expedition. Eighty of them were hypocrites and only three were sincere Muslims. The hypocrites made lame excuses which the Prophet (peace be on him) accepted at their face value and excused them. Then came the turn of the three sincere Muslims who confessed their fault explicitly without reference to extenuating circumstances. The Prophet (peace be on him) deferred his decision on their cases and directed the Muslims not to have any association with them till God settled the matter. The present verse embodies the decision that God made in their case. (It may be noted that this incident is different from the one mentioned earlier whereby seven Companions subjected themselves to punishment before their indictment, see n. 99 above.)

119. The three Companions referred to in this verse are those who stayed behind – Ka'b b. Mālik, Hilāl b. Umayyah and Murārah b. Rabī'. Apart from their firm belief in Islam and the many sacrifices they had earlier made in its cause, Hilāl and Murārah had also taken part in the Battle of Badr – an indubitable testimony of their unflinching faith in Islam. As for Ka'b b. Mālik, though he did not have the privilege of participating in the Battle of Badr, he had accompanied the Prophet (peace be on him) on all other military campaigns. Notwithstanding their illustrious services to the cause of Islam in the past, they were reproached severely for having slacked off in their duty to join the *jihād* to which all the able-bodied Muslims had been summoned. After his return from Tabūk, the Prophet (peace be on him) asked all Muslims to sever their ties with these three.

Forty days later even their wives were asked to part company with them. The anguish they then suffered in Madina – their home town – has been graphically set forth in the above verse. After having undergone the tormenting social boycott for a full fifty days, they were eventually pardoned by God.

The following is the incident as it was related by Ka'b to his son, 'Abd Allāh many years later when Ka'b was old and blind, and 'Abd Allāh used to hold his hand to walk him around:

> Preparations for the expedition to Tabūk were afoot, and whenever the Prophet (peace be on him) appealed to the Muslims to take part in *jihād,* I prepared myself to go forth. But on returning home I would always say to myself that it was a bit early; when the time to depart would come, it would take me no time to get ready. Time passed by and the hour for the army to proceed arrived, but I had not made my preparations. I said to myself: 'Let the army move out, and I will catch up with it in a day or two.' But the same slackness prevented me from proceeding till the time for accompanying the others was past.
>
> What tormented me most was that the only persons with whom I had remained behind in Madina were either the hypocrites or the disabled whom God had excused from *jihād.*
>
> When the Prophet (peace be on him) returned, he always used to go to the mosque first and pray two *rak'ahs* and then sit down to receive people. When the Prophet (peace be on him) did so, those who had stayed behind came to him, making excuses and taking oaths (to support their statements). In all there were more than eighty people. The Prophet (peace be on him) accepted their apparent claims and let them take a pledge of fealty (*bay'ah*). He also prayed to God for their forgiveness. As to whether those statements were true or not, he left that to God's judgement.
>
> When my turn came, I went forth to the Prophet (peace be on him) and greeted him. The Prophet smiled and said:
>
> 'What prevented you from going to *jihād*?' I said: 'O Messenger of Allah! Had I been sitting with any other person than you, I would have resorted to specious explanations to calm his anger and so that my excuses would have been accepted before my leaving. For I have the gift of eloquence. But, by God, I am sure that if I lie to gratify you this would certainly bring God's wrath upon me. And if I tell you the truth, and this truth angers you, I seek only a felicitous end with God. For, by God, I have no valid excuse. By God, never was I stronger and more resourceful than at the moment when I stayed back.'
>
> The Prophet (peace be on him) said: 'As for this one, he has indeed spoken the truth. So wait until God decides in your case.' Some persons of the Salimah tribe walked, following me, and said: 'By God, we did not know that you had sinned ever before. If you were incapable of making excuses to the Messenger of God (peace be on him) as the

others who had stayed behind did, then the Prophet's prayer for your forgiveness would have been enough to efface your sins.'

They continually approached me until I thought of going back to the Messenger of God (peace be on him) and contradicting my own statement. Then I said to them: 'Did he [i.e. the Prophet (peace be on him)] receive the same kind of answer from any other person as he received from me?' They said: 'Two other persons met the Prophet (peace be on him) and both said like you said, and they were told the same as you were told.' I asked: 'Who are those two?' They said: 'Murārah ibn Rabī' al-'Amrī and Hilāl ibn [Umayyah] al-Wāqifī.' They thus spoke of two Muslims who took part in the battle of Badr and were exemplary men. When they mentioned to me the actions of these two, I firmed up in my determination to maintain my truthful statement.

Then the Prophet (peace be on him) prohibited people to talk to the three of us from among those who had remained behind from *jihād.* So people avoided us, people changed towards us so much so that the whole world seemed to have changed. It was no longer the same earth that I had known. We remained in this state for fifty nights. As for the two of my companions, they surrendered to the changed state of affairs, confined themselves to their houses, and wept continuously. But I was the youngest and the most persevering of them all. I used to go out, pray with the Muslims, go about the market place, and none would speak to me. I would visit the Prophet (peace be on him) and greet him while he would be in his assembly after prayer and I would ask myself: 'Did he move his lips to answer the greeting or not?' Then I would pray close to him and stealthily glance at him. When I began praying, he would look at me, but when I glanced at him, he turned his face away. When this harsh punishment from the Muslims continued for some time I once climbed the wall of Abū Qatādah – he was the son of my uncle and the dearest person to me – and greeted him. By God, even he did not answer the greeting. I said to him: 'Abū Qatādah, I ask you in the name of God: Do I love God and His Messenger (peace be on him)?' He remained silent. I repeated the question, imploring him to answer. He again kept silent. Once again I repeated the question, imploring him to answer. He only said: 'God and His Messenger (peace be on him) know better.' On hearing this, tears flowed from my eyes, and I climbed down the wall. While I was walking through the market-place a Nabataean of Syria, who had come to Madina to sell foodstuff, said: 'Who will lead me to Ka'b ibn Mālik?' People began to gesture, pointing in my direction until he came to me and gave me the letter of the Ghassanid prince. Since I was a scribe I read the letter and to my surprise I found in it [the following message]: 'I have come to learn that your companion [i.e. the Prophet (peace be on him)] has been harsh to you. God has not placed you in an abode of humiliation, or in a position where your rights and dignity might be violated. Join us, and we shall sympathize with you.' When I read this I said: 'This is also a test!' So I headed to the baking oven and heated it up [and threw the letter in it].

And when forty of the fifty days passed and no revelation came, suddenly an envoy of the Prophet (peace be on him) advanced towards me and said: 'The Messenger of God orders you to stay away from your wife.' I said: 'Should I divorce her or what should I do?' He said: 'Just stay away from her; do not be close to her.' He also sent envoys to the other two companions even as he had sent them to me. So I said to my wife: 'Go and stay with your family and remain with them until God decides this matter . . . '

Then on the morning after fifty nights had passed and when I had performed Morning Prayer on the roof of one of our houses and was sitting in the state described by God [in His Book] – the state in which my soul had become a burden and the earth despite its vastness had become constricted for me – [see verse 118] – I heard suddenly the cry of a crier [Abū Bakr, according to reports], who had climbed Sal [a mountain in Madina] saying at the top of his voice: 'Ka'b ibn Mālik, rejoice at the good news.' I fell prostrate and knew that the moment of deliverance had come. The Prophet (peace be on him) announced to people at the time of the Morning Prayer that God had accepted our repentance, and people went forth announcing the good news. I headed towards the Messenger of God (peace be on him) and crowds of people met us on the way, congratulating us on the acceptance of our repentance. When I entered the mosque and greeted the Messenger of God (peace be on him) he said – his face beaming with joy – 'Rejoice at the best day of your life since your mother gave birth to you.' I asked the Prophet (peace be on him): 'Is this pardon from you or from God?' The Prophet (peace be on him) said: 'No; it is from God, the Mighty, the Exalted.' Then as I sat before him I said: 'O Messenger of God! As a part of my repentance I should give charity out of my wealth for the sake of God and His Messenger.' The Prophet said: 'Retain a part of your property; that is better for you.' I said: 'I will hold my share in Khaybar.' I continued: 'O Messenger of God! God delivered me out of this trial because of my truthfulness. Now an aspect of my repentance is that I shall speak nothing but the truth as long as I live.' (*Riyāḍ al-Ṣāliḥīn,* ed. Subḥī al-Ṣāliḥ, 3rd edition, 1976, Beirut, pp. 57 ff. The story has been summarily mentioned in Bukhārī, 'Tafsīr', 'Bāb Sūrat al-Barā'ah'. For a detailed description see Ibn Hishām, vol. 2, pp. 531–7; Wāqidī, vol. 3, pp. 1049–55; and Qurṭubī's comments on verse 118 – Ed.)

Full as this incident is of lessons, it especially brings home the following points to every Muslim.

First, that whenever there is a conflict between Islam and unbelief, it is imperative that a Muslim identify with Islam and actively participate in the struggle on its behalf. This is of such crucial importance that even if a Muslim fails to actively support Islam in such a struggle, let alone if he supports the forces of unbelief, that even if this happens just once in a life-time and without any *male fides,* his life-long record of righteous behaviour and religious devotion are liable to go to waste. The matter is so grave that even lapses of persons of proven integrity and faith – men who had actively participated in the battles of Badr, Uḥud, Khandaq (Ditch) and Ḥunayn – were not condoned.

Second, that any slackness in performing one's duty should not be taken lightly. For trivial slackness can lead to sins of a grave nature, and a Muslim cannot claim acquittal on the grounds that what lay at the core of the matter was slackness rather than any act with evil intent.

The episode narrated above also provides us with a valuable insight into the spirit of the society which had developed under the able leadership of the Prophet (peace be on him). The episode shows that on the one hand there were the hypocrites, who were known for their treachery, and yet their lame excuses were entertained and their failings overlooked. The reason for this had to do with the fact that no good was ever expected of them; their treachery was too well-known to elicit complaint.

On the other hand, there was a limited number of trustworthy Muslims, persons of proven integrity who were guilty of not participating in *jihād*. They confessed their fault and were subjected to a severe reproach. The reason for the treatment meted out to them was not that there was any doubt about the sincerity of their faith. The point of reproach was precisely that even though they were sincere, they had behaved in a manner becoming only of a hypocrite. These sincere Muslims, to use the famous expression employed by Jesus, were the salt of the earth. And if they themselves came bereft of salt, from where would one obtain it?

What is particularly noteworthy about the incident is the behaviour of both the leader and the followers, including the defaulters. The way in which the leader awarded the punishment, and the remarkable manner in which it was received by the defaulters, and again the manner in which the whole community enforced it. The role of each is so superb that one is hard put to decide who occupies pride of place in the incident.

The leader, no doubt, decided to pronounce a harsh punishment. But the spirit actuating his decision was that of love and compassion rather than of anger and hatred. His eyes seemed fiery like those of a raging father, yet the corner of his eyes revealed that any hostility towards the defaulter was simply out of the question. It was his misbehaviour that had wounded the heart. Were he to make amends, he would become as dear as he always was. The conduct of the defaulter was exemplary in its own way. He writhes in pain at the harsh punishment awarded him, but that does not prompt him to swerve from the path of obedience. Nor is he seized by a fit of arrogance and haughtiness. Not only does his attitude remain free from open affrontery to his leader; he does not even nurse a grievance against him in his heart. As a result of the incident, his love for, and devotion to the leader is in fact increased. All through those fifty agonizing days if there was one thing that he restlessly thirsted for it was the glow of affection in the eyes of the Prophet (peace be on him), which he cherished as his last source of hope. That look of affection in the Prophet's eyes was his last hope in life and was no less dear to him than a patch of cloud in the sky to a drought-stricken farmer.

The exemplary discipline and the high moral spirit displayed by the whole Muslim community also calls for admiration. No sooner had the Prophet (peace be on him) put the defaulter under reproach than all Muslims severed their ties with him. No one, not even his kith and kin and close friends, talked to him in private, let alone in public. Even his wife parted company with him. He implored them in the name of God to tell him if his integrity was suspect. But even his life-long friends curtly told him to turn to God and to His Messenger (peace be on him) for the answer. The members of the Islamic community not only displayed a high level of discipline but their moral standards were also so high that even during this crisis not a single person slandered the defaulter who had fallen from grace. On the contrary, each member of the community felt a deep concern for his brother in disgrace and looked forward to his early redemption. And as soon as he was pardoned, each of them flocked to his house to heartily felicitate him. This constitutes the model of a righteous community, the community that the Qur'ān seeks to establish in this world.

Viewed from this background, the verse in question highlights the point that the pardoning of the three Companions and the spirit of compassion and love shown them, was the result of the high degree of sincerity displayed by them during their fifty-day ordeal. Had their offence been followed by a show of arrogance and haughtiness, and had they greeted the Prophet's award of punishment with anger and hostility as does an egotist whose pride is wounded, the attitude of the community towards them would certainly have been different. Likewise, had the defaulters behaved during their period of punishment as though they would have preferred to leave the community rather than endure an action that hurt their pride, or if they had kept themselves busy during those fifty days trying to spread disaffection among the community and seeking to wean away the disgruntled elements from the Muslim body-politic, then they would surely have been expelled once and for all from the fold of Islam. They would have been left to wander in the wilderness of their egotism, to engage in self-worship as they pleased, and be deprived for ever of the honour to take part in the struggle to uphold the Word of God.

The three Companions of the Prophet (peace be on him) however, behaved differently. Even though the options of rebellion and disobedience were obviously open to them, they proved by their action that their devotion to God was total, and that such devotion left no room for them to worship any other god, not even their own ego. Their conduct also made it plain that they were fully committed to the Muslim body-politic; that regardless of what happened to them there was no question of any backsliding. No

(119) Believers! Have fear of Allah and stand with those that are truthful. (120) It did not behove the people of Madina and the bedouin Arabs around them that they should refrain from accompanying the Messenger of Allah and stay behind and prefer their own security to his. For whenever they suffer from thirst or weariness or hunger in the cause of Allah, and whenever they tread a place which enrages the unbelievers; (whenever anything of this comes to pass) a good deed is recorded in their favour. Allah does not cause the work of the doers of good to go to waste. (121) Likewise, each amount they spend, be it small or large, and each journey they undertake, shall be recorded in their favour so that Allah may bestow upon them reward for their good deeds.

يَٰٓأَيُّهَا ٱلَّذِينَ ءَامَنُوا۟ ٱتَّقُوا۟ ٱللَّهَ
وَكُونُوا۟ مَعَ ٱلصَّٰدِقِينَ ﴿١١٩﴾
مَا كَانَ لِأَهْلِ ٱلْمَدِينَةِ وَمَنْ
حَوْلَهُم مِّنَ ٱلْأَعْرَابِ أَن يَتَخَلَّفُوا۟
عَن رَّسُولِ ٱللَّهِ وَلَا يَرْغَبُوا۟ بِأَنفُسِهِمْ
عَن نَّفْسِهِۦ ذَٰلِكَ بِأَنَّهُمْ لَا
يُصِيبُهُمْ ظَمَأٌ وَلَا نَصَبٌ
وَلَا مَخْمَصَةٌ فِى سَبِيلِ ٱللَّهِ وَلَا
يَطَـُٔونَ مَوْطِئًا يَغِيظُ
ٱلْكُفَّارَ وَلَا يَنَالُونَ مِنْ
عَدُوٍّ نَّيْلًا إِلَّا كُتِبَ لَهُم بِهِۦ
عَمَلٌ صَٰلِحٌ إِنَّ ٱللَّهَ لَا يُضِيعُ
أَجْرَ ٱلْمُحْسِنِينَ ﴿١٢٠﴾ وَلَا يُنفِقُونَ
نَفَقَةً صَغِيرَةً وَلَا كَبِيرَةً وَلَا
يَقْطَعُونَ وَادِيًا إِلَّا كُتِبَ
لَهُمْ لِيَجْزِيَهُمُ ٱللَّهُ أَحْسَنَ مَا
كَانُوا۟ يَعْمَلُونَ ﴿١٢١﴾

matter how they were treated in the Muslim community, it was in that community that they would live and in it that they would die. They were willing to bear disgrace in their own community rather than consider the highest positions of honour and prestige outside of it.

Given this excellent conduct, was there any other course left for the community but to warmly embrace such men? This explains the compassion and kindness which characterizes verse 118 of the Qur'ān which mentions the pardoning of these Companions: '. . . Allah turned to them (in mercy) that they might turn to Him (in repentance).' The verse in question portrays

(122) It was not necessary for the believers to go forth all together (to receive religious instructions), but why did not a party of them go forth that they may grow in religious understanding, and that they may warn their people when they return to them, so that they may avoid (wrongful attitudes)?[120]

۞ وَمَا كَانَ ٱلْمُؤْمِنُونَ لِيَنفِرُوا۟
كَآفَّةً ۚ فَلَوْلَا نَفَرَ مِن كُلِّ فِرْقَةٍ
مِّنْهُمْ طَآئِفَةٌ لِّيَتَفَقَّهُوا۟ فِى ٱلدِّينِ
وَلِيُنذِرُوا۟ قَوْمَهُمْ إِذَا رَجَعُوٓا۟ إِلَيْهِمْ
لَعَلَّهُمْ يَحْذَرُونَ ١٢٢

graphically that their Lord had first turned His attention away from the three fallen servants. But He saw that instead of running away, they remained at His portal with broken hearts. Moved by this show of loyalty, God's love and kindness was aroused to a state of rapturous passion and the Lord came out to bring back the delinquent servants to His mansion.

120. For a better appreciation of the above verse, it should be read in conjunction with verse 97 above:

> The bedouin Arabs surpass in unbelief and hypocrisy, and are most likely to be unaware of the limits prescribed by Allah in what He has revealed to His Messenger.

This verse states that the desert Arabs were generally victims of hypocrisy because of their ignorance, that being cut off from centres of knowledge and unable to enjoy the company of scholars, they were ignorant of the limits laid down by Islam. In the present verse the Muslims are told what steps they should take so as to remedy the situation. The directive that is given here is not to allow the bedouin to remain steeped in their age-old ignorance. Systematic efforts should be made to remove their ignorance and to develop an Islamic consciousness among them. This did not necessitate the migration *en masse* of the bedouin to Madina in quest of knowledge. Rather, a few drawn from each desert village and tribe were required to visit such seats of learning as Makka and Madina, to study Islam, and to try to create an awakening and consciousness among their people upon their return.

It was an important and timely directive aimed at strengthening the Islamic movement. For in its earlier phase when Islam was a new phenomenon and was pressing its way gradually through a hostile environment, there was no need for such a directive. In the early phase anyone who embraced Islam did so after thoroughly understanding it and becoming fully convinced of its truth. However, when the Islamic movement gained momentum and established its hegemony on a piece of land, whole armies of people began entering its fold. Of these, only a few fully understood the implications and requirements of the Islamic faith. Many of them were prompted by the herd instinct, driven by the prevalent popular current towards Islam.

This rapid spread of Islam was apparently a source of strength for Islam since the number of its adherents swelled day by day. However, a great many of those converts to Islam, devoid as they were of true Islamic consciousness and understanding and of the sincere spirit to follow its moral standards, were not very helpful for the Islamic order. On the contrary, such a development was harmful as became evident during the preparations for the expedition to Tabūk. The moment when the Islamic movement spread at such a pace was chosen by God to issue directives that would assist its consolidation as well. The way forward lay in educating and training people drawn from every section of the population so that on their return they may, in turn, educate and train their own people. If this could be done it would ensure that Islamic consciousness and knowledge of Islamic injunctions would spread on a wide scale among the Muslims.

A clarification in this connection seems necessary. The directive laid down in the verse does not simply aim at spreading literacy, at developing the capacity to read books. The verse rather enunciates the purpose to be promoting an understanding of Islam to the extent whereby people eschew un-Islamic attitudes of life. This is the aim of education which God has laid down for Muslims for all times to come. This aim should serve as the criterion of success or failure of every educational effort that the Muslims may ever make. This does not mean that Islam is not concerned with spreading literacy or developing basic educational skills, or imparting worldly knowledge. What we wish to emphasize is that the distinctive educational objective of Islam is to impart an education that develops among Muslims a profound understanding of Islam. Even if all Muslims become highly educated and each of them attains the heights of scientific achievement as those of Einstein and Freud, such an education would be a curse according to Islam if it neither promotes among the Muslims a good understanding of Islam nor helps them refrain from un-Islamic attitudes.

The actual words used in the verse are also quite significant: *li yatafaqqahū fī al-dīn*. Unfortunately in the later period of Muslim history the purpose of the verse was misconceived and the effects of this misconception continue to vitiate the system of religious education, nay the very religious life of the Muslims. To reiterate and clarify, the purpose of education as laid down in the verse is to develop an understanding of Islam, to gain insight into its system, its nature and spirit, to develop mental attitudes and practical conducts which are in consonance with the spirit of Islam.

(123) Believers! Fight against the unbelievers who live around you;[121] and let them find in you sternness.[122] Know that Allah is with the God-fearing.[123] (124) And whenever a new *sūrah* is revealed some of the hypocrites ask the believers (in jest): 'Whose faith has increased because of this?' As for those who believe, it will certainly increase their faith, and they are joyful over that. ▶

يَا أَيُّهَا الَّذِينَ آمَنُوا قَاتِلُوا الَّذِينَ
يَلُونَكُم مِّنَ الْكُفَّارِ وَلْيَجِدُوا
فِيكُمْ غِلْظَةً وَاعْلَمُوا أَنَّ اللَّهَ مَعَ
الْمُتَّقِينَ ﴿١٢٣﴾ وَإِذَا مَا أُنزِلَتْ
سُورَةٌ فَمِنْهُم مَّن يَقُولُ أَيُّكُمْ
زَادَتْهُ هَٰذِهِ إِيمَانًا فَأَمَّا الَّذِينَ
آمَنُوا فَزَادَتْهُمْ إِيمَانًا وَهُمْ
يَسْتَبْشِرُونَ ﴿١٢٤﴾

Unfortunately a serious misconception has found its way into the Muslim society. The Muslims at some stage in their history became convinced that the purpose of the verse was to encourage them to learn *fiqh* (Jurisprudence), which is the root word used in the present verse and signifies 'understanding'. Now, jurisprudence gradually developed into a branch of knowledge and was called *Fiqh*. It concerned itself with the external and formal rules of human conduct, without necessarily being concerned with their spirit and purpose. This concern with the formal rules of external behaviour should have formed only a part of the Muslims' intellectual activity, but instead it became an all-absorbing pre-occupation. It would need volumes to speak of the harm done to Islam and Muslims by this intellectual deviation. Suffice it to say here that this misconception made the Muslims focus all their attention on the skeleton of Islam as distinct from its spirit. This also bred a soulless religious formalism which was regarded as the zenith of Muslim religious life.

121. The above verse, taken at face value, might be interpreted to mean that the responsibility for fighting against the enemy falls, in the first instance, on Muslims whc live nearest the enemy territory. However, on reading the verse in conjunction with the succeeding passage it appears that the reference is to fighting against the hypocrites, the enemy within the Islamic society. The hypocrites were clearly established and their interaction with different sections of the Islamic population had caused much damage. It had already been urged in the opening part of the discourse (see verse 73 ff. above) that *jihād* should be waged in order to

(125) As for those whose hearts are affected with the disease (of hypocrisy), every new *sūrah* added a fresh abomination to their abomination.[124] They remained unbelievers till their death. (126) Do they not see that they are tried every year once or twice?[125] Yet they neither repent nor take heed. ▶

وَأَمَّا ٱلَّذِينَ فِي قُلُوبِهِم مَّرَضٌ
فَزَادَتْهُمْ رِجْسًا إِلَىٰ رِجْسِهِمْ
وَمَاتُواْ وَهُمْ كَٰفِرُونَ ﴿١٢٥﴾
أَوَلَا يَرَوْنَ أَنَّهُمْ يُفْتَنُونَ فِي
كُلِّ عَامٍ مَّرَّةً أَوْ مَرَّتَيْنِ
ثُمَّ لَا يَتُوبُونَ وَلَا هُمْ
يَذَّكَّرُونَ ﴿١٢٦﴾

rid Islam of the internal enemy. The same directive is now being reiterated at the end of the discourse in order to shake Muslims into realizing the importance of the matter and to urge them to wage *jihād* to crush these enemies and to disregard all ethnic, family and social ties which they have shared with them.

It is worth noting that in the previous injunction on the subject (see verse 73 above), the Muslims had been commanded to launch *jihād* against the hypocrites and unbelievers whereas in the present verse the word *qitāl* is used. This latter usage suggests that the Muslims should spare no effort in their drive to crush the hypocrites. Likewise, it should also be noted that whereas in the earlier verse (i.e. 73), both hypocrites and unbelievers are mentioned, the present verse mentions only the unbelievers. This is so because the hypocrites, whose unbelief had become crystal clear, had no right to claim any relief on grounds of their formal profession to faith.

122. The lenient policy shown the hypocrites so far should now be given up. (See also verse 73 above where substantively the same directive was given.)

123. The note of warning to the Muslims contained in the above verse has two different meanings, and perhaps both are intended. First, the Muslims are warned that making any allowance to the hypocrites in view of their personal, social and business ties with them, is inconsistent with God-fearing behaviour. It is not possible to fear God and at the same time have relationships of deep friendship and love with His enemies. If Muslims care for God's support and favour they should give up those relationships. Second, the Muslims are warned that God's command to be stern towards and fight against the hypocrites should not mean disregard of moral and humanitarian considerations. For, regardless of what they do, Muslims are

(127) And whenever a *sūrah* is revealed, they glance at each other as though saying: 'Is anyone watching?' Then they slip away.[126] Allah has turned away their hearts for they are a people who are bereft of understanding.[127]

وَإِذَا مَآ أُنزِلَتْ سُورَةٌ نَّظَرَ بَعْضُهُمْ
إِلَىٰ بَعْضٍ هَلْ يَرَىٰكُم مِّنْ أَحَدٍ
ثُمَّ ٱنصَرَفُوا۟ صَرَفَ ٱللَّهُ قُلُوبَهُم
بِأَنَّهُمْ قَوْمٌ لَّا يَفْقَهُونَ ﴿١٢٧﴾

always required to act within the limits prescribed by God. Transgression of these limits will render them undeserving of God's support.

124. For a detailed discussion of the increase and decrease in faith, hypocrisy and unbelief, see *al-Anfāl* 8, n. 2 above.

125. Circumstances often arose which made it possible to test the claim of the hypocrites to be believers, and invariably their claim was proved hollow. From time to time, for instance, a Qur'ānic injunction would be revealed in opposition to their instinctive desires. Occasionally, they would be faced with a demand of faith which was prejudicial to their worldly interests. Sometimes circumstances would place them in a situation of conflicting loyalties and they were forced to make a clear choice: did they hold God, God's Messenger and God's religion dearer than their personal, family and tribal interests? At times war would break out and one's loyalty was put to the test: to what extent was one prepared to sacrifice life, property, time and energy for the sake of the religion which one claimed to believe in? On all such occasions the filth of hypocrisy that lay hidden behind a cloak of false profession to faith came to the surface. In fact on such occasions when the hypocrites cast aside the obligations of faith, they became more hardened in their hypocrisy.

126. Whenever a *sūrah* was revealed to the Prophet (peace be on him), he recited it at a public gathering of Muslims. While the Prophet (peace be on him) recited it, the true believers listened to it in rapturous attention. The hypocrites, however, behaved at such gatherings in an altogether different way. They attended these meetings as it was obligatory for every believer to do so and their absence would have exposed their hypocrisy. Nonetheless, they evinced no interest in the Prophet's recitation, and their presence was only ever half-hearted. Their only concern was to register their physical presence at the gathering, and they would depart at the first

(128) There has come to you a Messenger of Allah from amongst yourselves; one who grieves at your suffering losses, who is ardently desirous of your welfare, and who is tender and merciful to those that believe.

(129) Yet, if they should turn away, then tell them: 'Allah is sufficient for me; there is no God but Him. In Him I have put my trust. He is the Lord of the Mighty Throne.'

لَقَدْ جَآءَكُمْ رَسُولٌ
مِّنْ أَنفُسِكُمْ عَزِيزٌ عَلَيْهِ
مَا عَنِتُّمْ حَرِيصٌ عَلَيْكُم
بِالْمُؤْمِنِينَ رَءُوفٌ
رَّحِيمٌ ﴿١٢٨﴾ فَإِن تَوَلَّوْا فَقُلْ
حَسْبِيَ اللَّهُ لَآ إِلَٰهَ إِلَّا هُوَ
عَلَيْهِ تَوَكَّلْتُ وَهُوَ رَبُّ
الْعَرْشِ الْعَظِيمِ ﴿١٢٩﴾

---

opportunity. The above Qur'ānic verse presents a graphic account of their conduct.

127. The Qur'ān demonstrates the utter foolishness of the hypocrites insofar as they were ignorant of their true interests and welfare, oblivious to their salvation, and absolutely ignorant of the great favour God had shown them by revealing the Qur'ān and sending His Prophet (peace be on him). Engaged in their trivial pursuits and narrow interests, they could not see that by embracing the true faith they could assume not only the leadership of all mankind in this life, but also attain eternal felicity in the Next. Their behaviour deprived them of the opportunity to benefit from the vast, unlimited treasures of faith which could have led them to eternal happiness, success, power and greatness. The hypocrites were indeed altogether unfortunate to miss this golden opportunity while the true believers availed themselves fully of it.

Glossary of Terms

Ahl al-Dhimmah (or *Dhimmīs*) are the non-Muslim subjects of an Islamic state who have been guaranteed protection of their rights – life, property and practise of their religion, etc. – by the Muslims.

Ahl al-Ḥadīth refers to the group of scholars in Islam who pay relatively greater importance to 'traditions' than to other sources of Islamic doctrine such as *qiyās,* and tend to interpret the traditions more literally and rigorously. The term has also come to be used lately for a group of Muslims in the Indo-Pakistan subcontinent who are close to the Hanbalī school in theology, and claim to follow no single school on legal matters.

Ahl al-Kitāb, literally 'People of the Book', refers to the followers of Divine Revelation before the advent of the Prophet Muḥammad (peace be on him).

Anṣār means 'the Helpers'. In Islamic parlance the word refers to the Muslims of Madina who helped the *Muhājirūn* of Makka in the process of the latter's settling down in the new environment.

Al-A'rāb signifies the bedouin – whether of the desert or the countryside – in the vicinity of Madina. For a long time they had followed a policy of opportunism with regard to the conflict between Islam and unbelief. However, as Islam established its sway over the greater part of Ḥijāz and Najd and the power of the tribes hostile to Islam began to weaken, they saw their interests lay in entering the fold of Islam. For details see *Sūrah* 9, nn. 90 and 95.

'Arsh: literally throne. It is quite difficult to appreciate fully its exact nature. It may stand for dominion and authority and that God's ascending the Throne signifies His actual taking over the reins of the universe after having created it. Whatever the exact meaning of the expression '(Allah) ascended the Throne', the main thrust of the verse is that God is not just the creator of the universe, but is also its sovereign and ruler; that after creating the universe He did not detach Himself from, nor become indifferent to, His creation.

On the contrary, He effectively rules over the universe as a whole as well as every part of it. All power and sovereignty rest with Him. Everything in the universe is fully in His grip and is subservient to His will. For a detailed discussion see *Sūrah* 7, n. 41.

Aṣḥāb al-A'rāf (Heights) will be the people who are neither righteous enough to enter Paradise nor wicked enough to be cast into Hell. They will, therefore, dwell at a place situated between the two.

Al-Asmā' al-Ḥusnā, literally meaning the 'most excellent names' used of God, express His greatness and paramountcy, holiness, purity, and the perfection and absoluteness of all His attributes.

Barakah signifies growth and increase. The notions of elevation and greatness as well as of permanence and stability are also an essential part of the word's meaning.

Dār al-Ḥarb (Domain of War) refers to the territory under the hegemony of unbelievers, which is on terms of active or potential belligerency with the Domain of Islam, and presumably hostile to the Muslims living in its domain.

Dār al-Kufr (Domain of Unbelief) refers to the territory under the hegemony of the unbelievers.

Dhimmī (see *Ahl al-Dhimmah*).

Dīn: the core meaning of *dīn* is obedience. As a Qur'ānic technical term, *dīn* refers to the way of life and the system of conduct based on recognizing God as one's sovereign and committing oneself to obey Him. According to Islam true *dīn* consists of living in total submission to God, and the way to do so is to accept as binding the guidance communicated through the Prophets.

Farḍ bi al-Kifāyah signifies a collective duty of the Muslim community so that if some people carry it out no Muslim is considered blameworthy; but if no one carries it out all incur a collective guilt.

Fawāḥish applies to all those acts whose abominable character is self-evident. In the Qur'ān all extra-marital sexual relationships, sodomy, nudity, false accusation of unchastity, and taking as one's wife a woman who had been married to one's father, are specifically reckoned as shameful deeds. In *Ḥadīth,* theft, taking intoxicating drinks and begging have been characterized as *fawāḥish* as have many other brazenly evil and indecent acts.

Fī sabīl Allāh (in the way of Allah) is a frequently used expression in the Qur'ān which emphasizes that good acts should be done exclusively to please God. Generally the expression has been used in the Qur'ān in connection with striving or spending for charitable purposes.

Fisq: transgression; consists of disobedience to the command of God.

Furqān signifies that which enables one to distinguish between true and false; between real and fake.

Ḥadīth: the word *ḥadīth* literally means communication or narration. In the Islamic context it has come to denote the record of what the Prophet (peace be on him) said, did, or tacitly approved. According to some scholars, the word *ḥadīth* also covers reports about the sayings and deeds, etc. of the Companions of the Prophet in addition to the Prophet himself. The whole body of traditions is termed *Ḥadīth* and its science *'Ilm al-Ḥadīth.*

Ḥajj (Major Pilgrimage) is one of the five pillars of Islam, a duty one must perform during one's life-time if one has the financial resources for it. It resembles *'Umrah* (q.v.) in some respects, but differs from it insofar as it can be performed during certain specified dates of Dhu al-Ḥijjah alone. In addition to *ṭawāf* and *sa'y* (which are also required for *'Umrah*), there are a few other requirements but especially one's 'standing' *(wuqūf)* in 'Arafāt during the day-time on 9th of Dhu al-Ḥijjah. For details of the rules of *Ḥajj,* see the books of *Fiqh.*

Ḥijābah refers to the function of keeping the key of the Ka'bah, which has traditionally been considered a matter of great honour in Arabia.

Hijrah signifies migration from a land where a Muslim is unable to live according to the precepts of his faith to a land where it is possible to do so. The *hijrah par excellence* for Muslims is the *hijrah* of the Prophet (peace be on him) which not only provided him and his followers refuge from persecution, but also an opportunity to build a society and state according to the ideals of Islam.

Iḥrām refers to the state in which the Pilgrim is held to be from the time he performs certain prescribed rituals making his entry into the state of *Iḥrām* (literally 'prohibiting'). *Iḥrām* is so called in view of the numerous prohibitions that ought to be observed (e.g. abstention from all sex acts, from the use of perfume, from hunting or killing animals, cutting the beard or shaving the head, cutting the nails, plucking blades of grass or cutting green trees.)

Ijmā' refers to the consensus of eminent scholars *(mujtahidūn)* of Islam in a given age. *Ijmā'* comes next to the Qur'ān and the *Sunnah* as a source of Islamic doctrines.

Imām signifies the leader, and in its highest form, refers to the head of the Islamic state. It is also used with reference to the founders of the different systems of theology and law in Islam.

'Ishā' (Night) Prayer signifies the prescribed Prayer which is performed after the night has well set in.

Ithm denotes negligence, dereliction of duty and sin. For details see *Sūrah* 7, n. 25.

Jāhilīyah denotes all those world-views and ways of life which are based on rejection or disregard of heavenly guidance communicated to mankind through the Prophets and Messengers of God; the attitude of treating human life – either wholly or partly – as independent of the directives of God.

Jihād literally means 'to strive' or 'to exert to the utmost'. In Islamic parlance it signifies all forms of striving, including armed struggle, aimed at making the Word of God prevail.

Jinn are an independent species of creation about which little is known except that unlike man, who was created out of earth, the *jinn* were created out of fire. But like man, a Divine Message has also been addressed to them and they too have been endowed with the capacity, again like man, to choose between good and evil, between obedience or disobedience to God.

Jizyah: Unbelievers are required to pay *jizyah* (poll tax) in lieu of security provided to them as the *Dhimmīs* (Protected People) of an Islamic state, and their exemption from military service and payment of *Zakāh*. *Jizyah* symbolizes the submission of the unbelievers to the suzerainty of Islam.

Kaffārah means atonement, expiation.

Kāfir signifies one who denies or rejects the truth, i.e. who disbelieves in the message of the Prophets. Since the advent of Muḥammad (peace be on him), anyone who rejects his Message is a *kāfir*.

Khums: literally one-fifth. One-fifth of the spoils of war is earmarked for the struggle to exalt the Word of God and to help the orphans, the needy, the wayfarer and the Prophet's kinsmen. Since the Prophet (peace be on him) devoted all his time to the cause of Islam, he was not in a position to earn his own living. Hence a part of *khums* was allocated for the maintenance of the Prophet (peace be on him) as well as for his family and the relatives dependent upon him for financial support.

Makr signifies a secret strategy of which the victim has no inkling until the decisive blow is struck. Until then, the victim is under the illusion that everything is in good order.

Ma'rūf refers to the conduct which is accepted as good and fair by human beings in general.

Miskīn (pl. *masākīn*) denotes helplessness, destitution. Thus *masākīn* are those who are in greater distress than the ordinary poor people. Explaining this word the Prophet (peace be on him) declared that *masākīn* are those who cannot make both ends meet, who face acute hardship and yet whose sense of self-respect prevents them from asking for aid from others and whose outward demeanour fails to create the impression that they are deserving of help.

Nasab means family, lineage, descent.

Naṣārá is the name given to the followers of the Christian faith both in the Qur'ān and *Ḥadīth*.

Nasī': it was practised by the Arabs in two ways: (1) In order to shed blood or to plunder, or to satisfy a blood vendetta; here they declared a sacred month to be an ordinary one, and compensated for this violation later on by declaring one of the ordinary months to be sacred. (2) With a view to harmonizing the lunar calendar with the solar calendar the Arabs used to add a month to the lunar calendar. Their purpose in so doing was to ensure that the *Ḥajj* dates should consistently fall in the same season so that they were spared the hardship and inconvenience resulting from observation of the lunar calendar for the fixation of the *Ḥajj* dates.

Nubūwah means prophethood.

Nusuk signify ritual sacrifice as well as other forms of devotion and worship.

Qiblah signifies the direction to which all Muslims are required to turn when offering their prescribed Prayers, namely towards the Ka'bah.

Sabbath, which means Saturday, was declared for the Israelites as the holy day of the week. God declared the Sabbath as a sign of the perpetual covenant between God and Israel. (*Exodus* 31: 12–16.) The Israelites were required to strictly keep the Sabbath which meant that they may not engage in any worldly activity; they may not cook, nor make their slaves or cattle serve them. Those who violated these rules were to be put to death. The Israelites, however, publicly violated these rules. For further details see *Sūrah* 7, n. 123.

Shahīd in Islamic parlance means martyr.

Sharī'ah signifies the entire Islamic way of life, especially the Law of Islam.

Shirk consists of associating anyone or anything with the Creator either in His being, or attributes, or in the exclusive rights (such as worship) that He has against His creatures.

Shukr means thankfulness. In Islam, it is a basic religious value. Man owes thanks to God for almost an infinite number of things. He owes thanks to God for all that he possesses – his life as well as all that makes his life pleasant, enjoyable and wholesome. And above all, man owes thanks to God for making available the guidance which can enable him to find his way to his salvation and felicity.

Siqāyah signifies the function of providing water to the Pilgrims in the Pilgrimage season. *Siqāyah,* like *ḥijābah* (q.v.), was an office of great honour.

Sunnah Prayers are prayers which are considered recommended in view of the fact that the Prophet (peace be on him) either performed them often and/or made statements about their meritorious character.

Ṭāghūt literally denotes the one who exceeds his legitimate limits. In Qur'ānic terminology it refers to the creature who exceeds the limits of his creatureliness and arrogates to himself godhead and lordship. In the negative scale of values, the first stage of man's error is *fisq* (i.e. disobeying God without necessarily denying that one should obey Him). The second stage is that of *kufr* (i.e. rejection of the very idea that one ought to obey God). The last stage is that man not only rebels against God but also imposes his rebellious will on others. All those who reach this stage are *ṭāghūt*.

Tawbah basically denotes 'to come back; to turn towards someone'. *Tawbah* on the part of man signifies that he has given up his disobedience and has returned to submission and obedience to God. The same word used in respect of God means that He has mercifully turned to His repentant servant so that the latter has once more become an object of His compassionate attention.

Ulū al-amr include all those entrusted with directing Muslims in matters of common concern.

Ummī signifies the 'unlettered'. It is also used to refer to those who do not possess Divine revelation.

'Umrah (Minor Pilgrimage) is an Islamic rite and consists of Pilgrimage to the Ka'bah. It consists essentially of *Ihrām* (q.v.), *ṭawāf* (i.e. circumambulation) around the Ka'bah (seven times), and *sa'y* (i.e. running) between Ṣafā and Marwah (seven times). It is called minor *ḥajj* since it need not be performed at a particular time of the year and its performance requires fewer rituals than the *Ḥajj* proper.

Waḥy refers to Revelation which consists of communicating God's Messages to a Prophet or Messenger of God. The highest form of revelation is the Qur'ān of which even the words are from God.

Walāyah denotes the relationship of kinship, support, succour, protection, friendship, and guardianship. It signifies also the relationship of mutual support between the Islamic state and its citizens, and between the citizens themselves. For details see *Sūrah* 8, n. 50.

Wuḍū' refers to the ablution made before performing the prescribed Prayers. It requires washing (1) the face from the top of the forehead to the chin and as far as each ear; (2) the hands and arms up to the elbow; (3) wiping with wet hands a part of the head; and (4) washing the feet to the ankle.

Zakāh (Purifying Alms) literally means purification, whence it is used to express a portion of property bestowed in alms, as a means of purifying the person concerned and the remainder of his property. It is among the five pillars of Islam and refers to the mandatory amount that a Muslim must pay out of his property. The detailed rules of *zakāh* have been laid down in books of *Fiqh*.

Ẓālim is the wrong-doer, he who exceeds the limits of right, the unjust.

Zinā means illegal sexual intercourse and embraces both fornication and adultery.

Ẓulm literally means placing a thing where it does not belong. Technically, it refers to exceeding the right and hence committing wrong or injustice.

Biographical Notes

Al-'Abbās ibn Mirdās al-Sulamī, d. *circa* 18 A.H./*circa* 639 C.E., was the son of the famous poetess al-Khansā'. He embraced Islam before the conquest of Makka.

'Abbās ibh 'Ubādah ibn Naḍlah, d. 3 A.H./624 C.E., was a Companion of the Khazraj tribe who was martyred in the Battle of Uḥud.

'Abd Allāh ibn 'Abbās see Biographical Notes vols. I and II.

'Abd Allāh ibn 'Abd Allāh ibn Ubayy ibn Salūl, was a Companion of the Prophet (peace be on him). He was the son of 'Abd Allāh ibn Ubayy, who was the ring-leader of the Hypocrites of Madina. Unlike the father, however, the son was intensely sincere in his profession of faith.

'Abd Allāh ibn Mas'ūd see Biographical Notes vols. I and II.

'Abd Allāh ibn Ubayy see Biographical Notes vols. I and II.

'Abd Allāh ibn 'Umar see Biographical Notes vols. I and II.

'Abd al-Raḥmān ibn 'Awf, d. 32 A.H./652 C.E., one of the earliest converts to Islam, was one of the most highly regarded Companions of the Prophet (peace be on him), one of the ten Companions who, according to the Prophet, would be admitted to Paradise. 'Abd al-Raḥmān was a prosperous merchant who acquired great wealth of which he spent generously in the cause of God.

Abū Bakr, 'Abd Allāh ibn 'Uthmān abī Quḥāfah see Biographical Notes vols. I and II.

Abū Ḥanīfah, al-Nu'mān ibn Thābit see Biographical Notes vol. I.

Abū Sufyān, Ṣakhr ibn Ḥarb ibn Umayyah see Biographical Notes vol. I.

Abū Thawr, Ibrāhīm ibn Khālid al-Kalbī, d. 240 A.H./854 C.E., one of the companions of Shāfi'ī, was a well-known jurist who wrote several works of note.

Abū Yūsuf, Ya'qūb ibn Ibrāhīm see Biographical Notes vol. II.

'Adī ibn Ḥātim see Biographical Notes vol. II.

Aḥmad ibn Ḥanbal see Biographical Notes vols. I and II.

Akīdir ibn 'Abd al-Malik al-Kindī, d. 12 A.H./633 C.E., was the ruler of Dawmat al-Jandal (al-Jawf). After the death of the Prophet (peace be on him), Akīdir went back on the agreement between him and the Prophet whereupon the Caliph Abū Bakr despatched Khālid ibn al-Walīd who attacked and conquered Dawmat al-Jandal.

'Alī ibn abī Ṭālib see Biographical Notes vols. I and II.

'Ammār ibn Yāsir see Biographical Notes vol. II.

'Amr ibn 'Anbasah ibn Khālid, a Companion who embraced Islam in Makka and then returned to his own tribe, Sulaym. He joined the Prophet (peace be on him) in Madina after the Battle of Ḥunayn. After the death of the Prophet (peace be on him) 'Amr settled down in Syria and remained there till his death.

Al-Anṣārī, Abū Qatādah al-Ḥārith ibn Ruba'ī, was a Companion of the Prophet (peace be on him) who valiantly took part in the Battle of Uḥud and the subsequent military encounters. During the Caliphate of 'Alī he was appointed governor of Makka.

Al-Aqra' ibn al-Ḥābis, d. 31 A.H./651 C.E., a Companion of the Tamīm tribe, who was among the noted leaders of the Arabs before the advent of Islam. He took part in the battles of Ḥunayn and Ṭā'if and in the conquest of Makka. He also took part in most of the battles along with Khālid ibn al-Walīd.

As'ad ibn Zurārah ibn 'Adas, d. 1 A.H./622 C.E., a Madīnan of the Najjār tribe, who embraced Islam before *Hijrah*.

'Aṭā' ibn abī Rabāḥ see Biographical Notes vols. I and II.

Awzā'ī, 'Abd al-Raḥmān ibn 'Amr see Biographical Notes vol. II.

Al-Bukhārī, Muḥammad ibn Ismā'īl see Biographical Notes vols. I and II.

Farwah ibn 'Amr al-Judhamī, d. 10 A.H./655 C.E., the governor of the Byzantines over the territory lying between the Gulf of 'Aqabah and Yanbu', who embraced Islam after the expedition of Tabūk.

Ḥamzah ibn 'Abd al-Muṭṭalib, d. 3 A.H./625 C.E., an uncle of the Prophet (peace be on him) and one of the leaders of the Quraysh, who embraced Islam before *Hijrah,* and became a major source of strength for it. He fought valiantly in the Battle of Badr and was martyred in the Battle of Uḥud and is regarded as one of the great heroes of Islam.

Al-Ḥārith ibn Hishām al-Mughīrah al-Makhzūmī, d. 18 A.H./639 C.E., was a Companion of the Prophet (peace be on him) who embraced Islam on the day Makka was conquered. During the Caliphate of 'Umar, al-Ḥārith migrated to Syria where he continually took part in *jihād* until his death in the famous Plague of 'Amwās.

Al-Ḥārith al-Lihbī, d. 8 A.H./629 C.E., a Companion of the Prophet (peace be on him) whom he sent to Buṣrá with his letter. When al-Ḥārith reached Mu'tah (near al-Kark in present day Jordan) he was killed by the local ruler with cruelty. The expedition of Mu'tah took place as a result of this incident.

Al-Ḥasan al-Baṣrī see Biographical Notes vols. I and II.

Hilāl ibn Umayyah ibn 'Āmir was one of the three Companions who stayed behind in Madina instead of joining the expedition to Tabūk. Like the other two Companions, Hilāl also repented and his repentance was accepted by God. (See the Qur'ān, *Tawbah* 9: 118 and *Towards Understanding the Qur'ān*, n. 119 of the same *sūrah*.)

Hūd was an Arabian Prophet of the 'Ād, a people who lived in al-Aḥqāf in northern Ḥadramawt. Hūd has been mentioned in the Qur'ān several times. For the Qur'ānic references to Hūd see the Qur'ān 7: 65-72.

Hudhayfah ibn al-Yamān see Biographical Notes vol. II.

Ibn Hishām, 'Abd al-Malik see Biographical Notes vol. I.

Ibn Kathīr, Ismā'īl ibn 'Umar see Biographical Notes vols. I and II.

Ibn Sīrīn, Muḥammad see Biographical Notes vols. I and II.

Ibrāhīm al-Nakha'ī see Biographical Notes vols. I and II.

Al-Jaṣṣāṣ, Aḥmad ibn 'Alī see Biographical Notes vol. I.

Ka'b ibn al-Ashraf see Biographical Notes vol. I.

Ka'b ibn Mālik al-Anṣārī, d. 50 A.H./670 C.E., was a Companion of the Prophet (peace be on him) and a noted poet. He took part in many battles and was one of the strongest supporters of 'Uthmān when the latter faced opposition.

Ka'b ibn 'Umayr al-Ghifārī, d. 8 A.H./629 C.E., one of the prominent Companions of the Prophet (peace be on him) who was sent by him on a military expedition on which he was martyred.

Kurz ibn Jābir al-Fihrī (d. 8 A.H./629 C.E.), before embracing Islam was one of the Makkan chiefs who carried out a raid on the outskirts of Makka. He later embraced Islam and was martyred on the day of the conquest of Makka.

Al-Layth ibn Sa'd see Biographical Notes vol. II.

Madyan was the ancestor of an Arabian tribe of that name who lived before the time of Moses. The town of Madyan on the Red Sea acquired that name from him and his offspring. Madyan was also the habitat of the people called 'Ād mentioned in the Qur'ān.

Mālik ibn Anas see Biographical Notes vols. I and II.

Al-Miqdād ibn 'Amr alias ibn al-Aswad, d. 33 A.H./653 C.E., was one of the seven earliest converts to Islam. Al-Miqdād earned great fame for his bravery.

Mu'āwiyah ibn abī Sufyān see Biographical Notes vol. II.

Murārah ibn Rabī' al-Anṣarī, a Companion of the Aws tribe, was one of the three Companions who stayed behind in Madina instead of joining the expedition to Tabūk. He, like the other Companions, repented and his repentance was accepted by God. (See the Qur'ān, *Tawbah* 9: 118 and *Towards Understanding the Qur'ān*, n. 119 of the same *sūrah*.)

Al-Rāzī, Muḥammad ibn 'Umar Fakhr al-Dīn, d. 606 A.H./1210 C.E., was one of the most famous exegetes of the Qur'ān and the most outstanding scholar of his time who was well-versed in both religious and rational sciences.

Sa'd ibn Mu'ādh, d. 5 A.H./626 C.E., was a Madīnan Companion and one of the leaders of the Aws tribe. He fought valiantly in many battles and was martyred in the Battle of Khandaq (or Trench).

S'ad ibn abī Waqqāṣ, 50 A.H./670 C.E., was one of the heroes of early Islam who took part in many battles during the life of the Prophet (peace be on him). His fame, however, rests on leading the Muslim army to the conquest of Iraq during the Caliphate of 'Umar.

Sa'īd ibn Jubayr see Biographical Notes vol. II.

Sa'īd ibn al-Musayyib see Biographical Notes vols. I and II.

Ṣāliḥ was an Arabian Prophet of the Thamūd, a people who have been mentioned many a time in the Qur'ān. Ṣāliḥ lived before the Prophets Moses and Shu'ayb. His mission was to direct his people to righteousness. But they refused to respond to the call of Shu'ayb whereupon they were destroyed.

Ṣayfī ibn 'Āmir ibn al-Aslat, d. 1 A.H./622 C.E., was a pro-Islamic poet, orator and warrior. He was opposed to idol-worship and was considering embracing Islam but died apparently before he could make up his mind.

Al-Sha'bī, 'Āmir ibn Shuraḥbīl see Biographical Notes vol. II.

Al-Shāfi'ī, Muḥammad ibn Idrīs see Biographical Notes vols. I and II.

Shu'ayb, an Arabian Prophet of Madyan (q.v.), was from the progeny of the Prophet Abraham. He lived in the period before Moses and after the Prophets Hūd and Ṣāliḥ. His tomb is said to be in Ḥittīn in Palestine.

Shuraḥbīl ibn 'Amr was a Christian tribal chief who was a satrap of the Caesar over Buṣrá. He was responsible for putting the Prophet's envoy, Hārith ibn 'Umayr, to the sword – an incident which led to the Battle of Mu'tah.

Suhayl ibn 'Amr, d. 18 A.H./639 C.E., embraced Islam on the day Makka was conquered. Earlier he was the representative of the Quraysh when they negotiated a peace agreement with the Prophet (peace be on him) in Ḥudaybiyah.

Ṭalhah ibn 'Ubayd Allāh ibn 'Uthmān, d. 36 A.H./656 C.E., was one of the ten Companions whom the Prophet (peace be on him) declared to be among the People of Paradise. He was among the earliest converts to Islam, and was noted for his bravery and generosity. He was killed in the civil war during the Caliphate of 'Alī.

Al-Thawrī, Sufyān ibn Sa'īd see Biographical Notes vol. II.

'Ubaydah ibn al-Ḥārith, d. 2 A.H./624 C.E., was one of the heroes of the Quraysh who embraced Islam quite early. He took part in the Battle of Badr and was martyred.

'Umar ibn al-Khaṭṭāb see Biographical Notes vols. I and II.

Umayyah ibn Khalaf ibn Wahb, d. 2 A.H./624 C.E., of the Lu'ayy tribe, one of the most influential leaders of the Quraysh and an inveterate enemy of Islam, was put to the sword in the Battle of Badr.

Umayyah ibn abī al-Ṣalt, d. 5 A.H/626 C.E., was a poet and savant of Ṭā'if. He went to Damascus before the advent of Islam and was well-versed in the ancient lore. He always abstained from intoxicating drinks and idol worship. After the Battle of Badr, Umayyah returned to Ṭā'if from Damascus and lived there till his death.

'Uthmān ibn 'Affān see Biographical Notes vols. I and II.

'Uyaynah ibn Ḥiṣn, a Companion who soon after the death of the Prophet (peace be on him) renounced Islam and joined the ranks of Ṭulayḥah al-Asadī, a false claimant to prophethood. 'Uyaynah fought the Muslim army and was taken captive.

Al-Zubayr ibn al-'Awwām ibn Khuwaylid, d. 36 A.H./656 C.E., was one of the most prominent Companions, and one of those ten about whom the Prophet (peace be on him) had given the good news of Paradise. He took part in the civil war in the Caliphate of 'Alī and was killed.

Al-Zuhrī, Muhammad ibn Shihāb see Biographical Notes vols. I and II.

Bibliography

Abū Dā'ūd, Sulaymān ibn al-Ash'ath al-Sijistānī, *al-Sunan.*

Al-Bukhārī, Abū 'Abd Allāh Muḥammad ibn Ismā'īl, *al-Jāmi' al-Ṣaḥīḥ.*

Al-Dāraquṭnī, 'Alī ibn 'Umar, *al-Sunan,* 4 vols., Beirut, 'Ālam al-Kutub, n.d.

Al-Dārimī, Abū Muḥammad 'Abd Allāh ibn 'Abd al-Raḥmān, *al-Sunan,* 2 vols., Cairo, Dār al-Fikr, 1978.

Al-Fīrūzābādī, *al-Qāmūs al-Muḥīṭ*, Cairo, al-Ḥalabī, 1952. Second Edition.

The Holy Bible, Revised Standard Edition, New York, 1952.

Ibn al-'Arabī, Abū Bakr, *Aḥkām al-Qur'ān.*

Ibn Hishām, Abū Muḥammad 'Abd al-Malik, *Sīrah,* eds. Muṣṭafá al-Saqqā et al., II edition, Cairo, 1955.

Ibn Isḥāq, *The Life of Muḥammad,* tr. and notes by A. Guillaume, Oxford University Press, 1955.

Ibn Kathīr, *Mukhtaṣar Tafsīr Ibn Kathīr,* ed. Muḥammad 'Alī al-Ṣābūnī, 7th edition, 3 vols., Beirut, 1402/1981.

Ibn Mājah, Abū 'Abd Allāh Muḥammad ibn Yazīd al-Qazwīnī, *al-Sunan.*

Ibn Manẓūr, *Lisān al 'Arab*, Beirut, Dar Ṣader, n.d.

Ibn Rushd, *Bidāyat al-Mujtahid,* 2 vols., Cairo, n.d.

Ibn Sa'd, Abū 'Abd Allāh Muḥammad, *Al-Ṭabaqāt al-Kubrá,* 8 vols., Beirut, 1957–60.

Ibn Taymīyah, Taqī al-Dīn, *Majmū' al-Fatāwá Ibn Tymīyah,* ed. Muḥammad ibn 'Abd al-Raḥmān ibn Qāsim, 37 vols., Riyadh, 1398.

Al-Jaṣṣāṣ, Abū Bakr, *Aḥkām al-Qur'ān*, 3 vols., Cairo, 1347 A.H.

Al-Jazīrī, 'Abd al-Raḥmān, *al-Fiqh 'alá al-Madhāhib al-Arba'ah*, 5 vols., Beirut, Dār Iḥyā' al-Turāth, 1980.

Mālik ibn Anas, *al-Muwaṭṭa'*, ed. Muḥammad Fu'ād 'Abd al-Bāqī, 2 vols., Cairo, 1951.

Muslim, ibn al-Ḥajjāj, *al-Ṣaḥīḥ*.

Al-Nasā'ī, Abū 'Abd al-Raḥmān Aḥmad ibn Shu'ayb, *al-Sunan*.

Al-Nawawī, Yaḥyá ibn Sharaf, *Al-Arba'īn*.

Al-Qurṭubī, *al-Jāmi' li Aḥkām al-Qur'ān*, 8 vols., Cairo, Dār al-Sha'b, n.d.

Al-Ṣābūnī, Muḥammad 'Alī, *Ṣafwat al-Tafāsīr*, 3 vols., 4th edition, Beirut, 1402/1981.

Al-Ṣāliḥ, Ṣubḥī, *Mabāḥith fī 'Ulūm al-Qur'ān*, Beirut, 1977.

Al-Ṭabarī, Muḥammad b. Jarīr, *Tafsīr*.

Al-Tirmidhī, Abū 'Īsá Muḥammad ibn 'Īsá, *al-Jāmi' al-Ṣaḥīḥ*.

Al-Wāqidī, Muḥammad ibn 'Umar, *al-Maghāzī*, ed. M. Jones, 3 vols., Cairo, 1966.

Wensinck, A.J., *Concordance et indices de la tradition musulmane*, 7 vols., Leiden, 1939–1969.

Subject Index

Aaron (Hārūn):
- His mention in the Qur'ān, 69.
- Acting for Moses during his absence, 78.
- Israelites take to idol-worship, 83.
- Jews' allegation against him, 82.

Abraham (Ibrāhīm):
- His people, 230.
- His qualities, 263.
- Why he prayed for his father's forgiveness, 262–3.

'Ād:
- Their land and history, 42–3.
- Made successors after the people of Noah, 42.
- Their main error, 43.
- Their attitude towards the Prophet Hūd and its consequences, 40, 44–5.

Adam (Ādam):
- Story of Adam and Eve, 7–15.
- The prostration before Adam was in his capacity as the representative of all mankind, 7.
- Refutation of the charge of polytheism against them, 108–10.

Admonition (*Dhikr*):
- Used for the Qur'ān, 38, 42.
- Used in the sense of remembering God, 116–17.
- How to remember God, 115–16.
- Command to remember Him much, 156.
- Used in the sense of reminder, 3, 101.

Advent of the Last Day, 106, 107.

Ahl al-Kitāb (see People of the Book).

Al-Ākhirah (see Hereafter).

– It is not allowed to pray for their forgiveness, 261–2.
– Their entry into mosques, 200–1.

Āyah, pl. *Āyāt* (Sign, signs):
– Evil consequences of their rejection, 22, 26, 30, 40–2, 44, 73, 80, 102, 104, 160.
– Signs of God's power, 15, 36, 69, 72, 79, 101.
– Purpose of expounding them, 101.
– As miracles, 46–7, 63, 65–6, 69, 72, 115.
– What happens to those who reject them, 6, 102.
– Those who reject it are wrong-doers, 227.
– God expounds them for those who have knowledge, 20.
– Meaning of 'selling these for a paltry price', 192.
– God's mercy is deserved by those who have faith in them, 84.
– They are for exalting man, 102.
– Their impact on the believers, 137–8.

Balance:
– Weighing of one's deeds on the Day of Judgement, 6–7.

Banū Isrā'īl (see Israel, the Children of).

Barakah (Growth, Increase):
– Its meaning and explanation, 34–5.
– Meaning of the statement that God is full of *barakah*, 34.

Battle of Badr:
– Its causes, 119–27.
– Its significance, 125, 140–1, 144.
– What was the aim of the unbelievers?, 126, 144, 157–9.
– Unbelievers' army, 157.
– Strength of the unbelievers' army, 127.
– In what circumstance the Prophet (peace be on him) decided to go to war, 126–8.
– The Prophet's aim, 128.
– What was God's purpose?, 139, 155.
– Muslims' condition at the time, 138, 155.
– The Muslim army's strength, 131.
– Muslims' preparations for war, 129–30.
– How did it start?, 139–40.
– The Prophet's (peace be on him) prayer, 132.
– Satan was with the unbelievers but he deserted them on seeing the divine scourge, 158.
– How did God help the Muslims?, 141, 156.
– How were the Muslims tested?, 143.
– Sacrifices made by both the *Muhājirūn* and *Anṣār*, 128–32.
– Hypocrites' attitude, 128, 159.
– Attitude of the Madinan Jews, 160–1.

Causes of Going Astray:
- Blind following, 16, 43, 98.
- Forgetting God, 116–17.
- Taking satans rather than God as guardian, 19.
- Forgetting the Hereafter, 30.
- Misconception that some intercession will help one escape God's punishment, 95.
- Not using properly the faculty of reasoning, 80, 104, 144.
- Indifference to God's signs, 73, 79.
- Fallacious view of history and failure to draw lessons from it, 59–60, 61–2.
- Persistent rejection of the truth, 61–2, 63, 66–7, 72, 73, 109–10.
- Arrogance, 9, 22, 26, 73, 109–10.
- To hold God responsible for one's misdeeds, 11.
- Non-serious attitude towards religion, 30.
- To hold others responsible for one's misdeeds, 71.
- To be engrossed in this worldly life, 31.
- To believe that the pursuit of truth spells material doom, 57.
- Influence of the misguided nations, 74–5.
- Misconception that a man cannot be God's Messenger, 38, 42.
- Forgetting the Prophets' teachings, 92.
- Following one's desires rather than the divine knowledge, 102–3.
- Tampering with God's Law, 207–8.

Christians:
- Their main error, 201, 203–4.

Companions of the Prophet (peace be on him):
- The Qur'ān's unequivocal testimony to their excellence in faith, 173.
- Their sacrifices in the Battle of Tabūk, 177–83.
- They realized the implications of their association with the Prophet (peace be on him), 120–1.
- Their sacrifices in the Battle of Badr, 120–32.
- The Qur'ānic promise that they will enter Paradise, 245.
- Their efforts for preserving the Qur'ān, 175.
- Their discipline and exemplary conduct, 265–72.

Corruption (*Fasād*):
- What is corruption in the land?, 35–6.
- It is forbidden, 35–6, 47, 54.
- Who are the corrupters?, 63, 77.
- They should not be followed, 77.

Covenant:
- Its broad meaning in the Qur'ān, 62.
- The primordial covenant, 98–101.
- The covenant between man and God at the time one embraces faith, 254–7.
- Breaking it is a major sin, 160.

- The believer should set his eyes on the good of the Hereafter alone, not the worldly gains, 168.
- Loyalty to God and His Messenger being a necessary condition, 240.
- The believers should hold the Prophet dearer than their own life, 271.
- They should not lag behind in the conflict against disbelief, 211–12, 271.
- They should not take unbelievers as friends, 198.
- The believers should help one another, 173.
- They should not pray for the forgiveness of a disbelieving relative, 261–2.
- The believers should have trust in God alone, 16.
- Criterion of a believer's success and failure, 216.
- For them God is sufficient, 165.
- Difference between the believer and the unbeliever, 165, 215–16.
- Difference between the believer and the hypocrite, 231–2.
- Difference between a sinful believer and a hypocrite, 247.
- How to distinguish between a sinful believer and a hypocrite, 247–8.
- Difference between a true believer and the one who verbally professes Islam, 239–40, 254–5.
- Its impact on one's conduct, 70–1.
- It is good for both the worlds, 56–7, 59.
- All the bounties of both the worlds are exclusively for the believers, 20.
- The believers to overawe the enemies of Allah, 164.
- God accepts the repentance of believers, 83.
- God's mercy is attained by those who believe in His signs, 85–6.
- Good recompense for faith and righteous deeds, 27, 138, 231, 239, 254.
- God's favours on believers, 143, 144, 271.
- Glad tidings for believers, 259.

Striving in the Cause of God (*Jihād*):
- Its meaning, 232–4.
- What is it?, 224–5.
- Difference between *Jihād* and *Qitāl,* 225.
- Its importance in Islam, 180, 193, 198, 271.
- Criterion for one's faith, 212, 217–18, 239, 247–9, 269–72.
- Its exalted place, 197–8, 271.
- Its reward, 271.
- Those who avoid it are hypocrites, 212.
- It is best for believers, 210.
- Use of *Zakāh* for it, 224–5.
- Against hypocrites and unbelievers, 232–4.

Fighting in the Way of God (*Qitāl fī Sabīl Allāh*):
- The purpose and rationale of war in Islam, 135–7, 146–7, 153, 177, 202.
- Its significance, 254, 271.
- A requirement of the covenant between a believer and God, 254–7.
- To avoid it betrays a disbelieving and hypocritical attitude, 235–8.
- Believers should not lag behind in this, 213, 265–72.
- A compulsory duty for those summoned by the Islamic state, 209–10.

– In participating in it one should not give any consideration to inconvenience or hardship, 211–12.

Fir'awn (see Pharaoh).

Forgiveness:
– Who will get it?, 138, 169, 173.
– Who will not get it?, 235.
– Its conditions, 147, 152.
– Not to pray for the forgiveness of polytheists, 261–2.

God:
– Most Merciful of the merciful, 82.
– All-Seeing, 153.
– Oft-Relenting, 246, 265.
– All-Wise, 140, 158, 165, 168, 169, 194, 200, 210, 221, 230, 243, 249, 252.
– Best of those who judge, 54, 55.
– Best of those who forgive, 84.
– Best of those who scheme, 149.
– Lord of the Universe, 32, 37, 42, 63, 109.
– All-Compassionate, 83, 93, 168, 169, 190, 200, 240, 244, 246, 264, 265.
– All-Hearing, 112, 143, 155, 159, 165, 243, 246.
– Severe in punishment, 141, 146, 158, 159.
– Most tender, 264.
– All-Mighty, 158, 165, 168, 210, 230.
– He knows alike what lies beyond human perception and what lies within the reach of human perception, 242, 297.
– All-Knowing, 112, 143, 155, 159, 165, 169, 194, 200, 221, 243, 246, 249, 252.
– All-Forgiving, 83, 168, 169, 190, 200, 240, 244, 246.
– Lord of abounding bounty, 147.
– Blessed, 32.
– All-Powerful, 159.
– Has full knowledge even of all that is beyond the reach of perception, 235.
– Has the most excellent names, 104.
– The human eye can never see Him, 77.
– Swift in chastisement, 93.
– His word is inherently uppermost, 210.
– No one is more faithful to his promise than Him, 254.
– An excellent Protector and an excellent Helper, 153.
– Protector of believers, 215.
– No other god than Him, 37, 40, 45, 52, 75, 87, 203, 277.
– Only He deserves all worship, 37, 40, 45, 52, 75, 87, 203
– Help should be sought only from Him, 70.
– Refuge should be sought only from Him, 112.
– To call upon Him with fear and longing, 35.

– Everyone should fear Him, 193.
– To trust in Him, 165, 215, 277.
– One should strive his utmost to please Him, 243.
– Sufficient, 165, 277.
– Earning His good pleasure is a great achievement, 231.
– Those taking others than Him as their guardians have gone astray, 19.
– No master other than Him, 4.
– His mercy encompasses everything, 84.
– The general rule underlying His governance is mercy, not wrath, 85.
– Accepts the repentance of His servants, 246.
– No protector or helper besides Him, 263.
– Man is accountable to Him, 5.
– He is not unjust in the least to His creatures, 158, 230.
– He does not allow the reward of the righteous men to go to waste, 96, 271.
– His reward is more than one's good deeds, 271.
– He never enjoins any indecency, 16.
– He does not like those who go to excesses, 19, 35.
– He is not pleased with an evil-doing folk, 243.
– He does not love the treacherous, 161.
– Who incurs His wrath?, 44, 82, 142.
– No one can harm Him, 209.
– He loves those who purify themselves, 250.
– He loves the pious, 189.
– He created everything, 32, 108, 206.
– His is the command, 32.
– His is the creation, 32, 70, 87, 263, 277.
– To Him are all matters referred for decision, 156.
– He has power over all things, 153, 209.
– His design is incontrovertible, 104.
– No one can overcome Him, 161, 187, 189.
– No one can challenge Him, 144.
– Help comes from Him alone, 140, 167.
– He enforces His designs, 61, 104.
– He grants life and deals death, 87, 263.
– He bestows the earth on whom He chooses, 70.
– He rewards and afflicts whomsoever He wishes, 84, 194, 200, 249.
– Signs of His power and wisdom, 32, 36.
– He has knowledge of all things, 55, 173, 235, 263.
– He is cognizant of all one does, 6, 171, 195.
– He knows what is hidden in the breasts, 145, 155.

God's Decree (*Taqdīr*):
– God decrees one's prosperity and misfortune, 71.
– God enriches whom He wills, 200.
– God grants victory, 167.
– God bestows cordiality and unity, 166.

Islamic Law:
- No one other than God can declare things lawful or unlawful, 204.
- Tampering with God's Law is an act of disbelief, 207.
- On the basis of mere doubt no action should be taken against anyone, 250.

Islamic Laws of War:
- Its development, 135–7.
- Reform in the laws of war, 136–7.
- War to be stopped if the enemy embraces Islam, 190.
- Minimum conditions for one's acceptance of Islam, 190–1, 192–3.
- Spoils of war and its distribution, 135–7, 154.
- Share of God, His Messenger and his kinsmen, 154.
- *Jizyah*, 202.

Islamic Society:
- Its constituents, 174.
- Essential conditions for its membership, 192–3.
- How should the believers behave?, 265–72.
- Muslims should help one another, 173.
- To set things right between themselves, 135.
- Not to quarrel with one another, 156.
- To obey the command, 135, 144, 145, 156.
- Not to be knowingly unfaithful to trusts, 148
- Attitude towards the wicked and transgressors, 237–9.
- Men of doubtful integrity should be watched, 247–9.
- Harmful effects of the inclusion of hypocrites in society, 213–14, 232–4.
- Attitude towards hypocrites, 232–4, 237–40, 247–9, 275.

Islamic State:
- Its educational policy, 272–4.
- Its policy about hypocrites, 232–4, 275.
- All Muslims of the Islamic state are bound by the agreement signed by the Islamic state, 173.
- How can the Muslims living in a non-Islamic state be helped?, 172.
- An important provision in Islamic constitutional law, 171.
- It should act with courage and bravery, 165.

Israel, The Children of, Israelites (Banū Isrā'īl):
- Their history is full of lessons, 64.
- Their Egyptianized outlook, 74–5, 81–2.
- Moses asks Pharaoh to release them, 64–5, 72.
- Pharaoh's persecution of them, 71, 75.
- The two periods of persecution, 71.
- God's promise to make them rulers, 70.
- God exalted them above all, 75.
- Their exodus from Egypt, 74–5.
- The point at which they crossed the Red Sea, 74.
- Their demand for a false god soon after the exodus, 74.

Preaching:
- How to disseminate the message, 2, 101–2, 112–14.

Prophethood:
- Why man needs it, 15–18.
- All Messengers were human beings, 38, 42.
- Ignorant people have always refused to believe that Messengers can be human beings, 38, 42.
- One laying a false claim to it is the worst wrong-doer, 22.
- How Messengers are prepared to receive the revelation, 75.
- Messengers are granted the knowledge which others do not possess, 38.
- Purpose of their advent, 35–6, 100–1.
- Allegory of rain used for them, 36–7.
- Success is contingent on obeying them, 22.
- Messengers are reliable, 42.
- They are sincere to their people, 38, 42, 49, 56.
- They say nothing except the truth, 63.
- Same mission and message of all Messengers, 37, 40, 42, 45, 52, 75.
- They are not to obey other human beings, 67.
- They reform not only religion but transform the whole of life, 67.
- To obey God and His Messenger, 135, 144, 145, 156, 230.
- Why they are granted miracles, 65–6.
- They present their message fearlessly, 137–8.
- Distinction between the people addressed by the Prophet directly and indirectly, 40–2.
- Opposing them amounts to opposing God which incurs severe punishment, 141.
- When are the rejectors of Messengers punished?, 147.
- Punishment for distressing the Messenger, 225.
- Punishment for hypocrisy towards the Messenger, 2.
- End of those who challenge God and His Messenger, 225.
- Evil recompense for rejecting the Messengers, 22, 39, 44, 48, 51, 56, 59, 61, 230.
- Disbelievers in Messengers will be full of remorse in the Hereafter, 31.
- That the Messengers were truthful will be manifest in the Hereafter, 27, 31.

Prosperity (*Falāḥ*):
- How to attain it, 42, 156.
- Who attains it?, 6, 85, 239.
- How is it the great achievement?, 231, 239, 245, 254.

Prostration (*Sajdah*):
- How many *Sajdah* are in the Qur'ān?, 117.
- Its rationale and rules, 117–18.

Punishment:
- Punishment in this world, 5.
- Its law, 5, 37–8, 41–2, 47, 57, 59–60, 71, 72–3, 90–6, 104, 146, 150, 160, 209.

Subject Index

Talmud, 49.

Taqwá (Piety; Fear of God):
– Its meaning, 38, 40, 96.
– Without faith it cannot be achieved, 84.
– Its requirements, 135, 160, 189, 206, 271, 274.
– Characteristics of the pious and their attitude, 11, 112–14, 168, 212.
– God loves the pious, 189.
– God is with the pious, 206, 274.
– God's mercy for them, 84.
– Meaning of the garment of piety, 16–17.
– Its good recompense, 22, 38, 59, 70, 94, 147.

Tasbīḥ:
– Its meaning and explanation, 117.

Test:
– Its purpose, 94.
– It is of crucial importance for people, 84–5.
– How God tests man, 71, 84, 91, 148.
– How are the believers tested?, 75, 143.
– It distinguishes between a believer and a hypocrite, 275.

Thamūd:
– God made them successors after 'Ād, 47.
– Their history and land, 45–7.
– Their attitude towards the Prophet Ṣalīḥ and their end, 45–9.

Throne (*'Arsh*):
– Meaning of the statement that 'God ascended the Throne', 33.
– The Mighty Throne, 277.

Torah (Tawrāh):
– Its commands in the Tablets, 78.
– Its contents, 83.
– Its reference to the Prophet Muḥammad (peace be on him), 86.

Transgression (*Fisq*):
– Who are the transgressors?, 62, 78, 91, 192, 198, 217, 235, 243.
– Their punishment in this world, 62, 78, 91.
– They are denied guidance, 198, 235.
– God will not be pleased with them, 243.

Transmigration of souls: 25–6.

Trust in God:
– A requirement of faith, 137.
– Trust in the All-Mighty, 158.
- A source of strength, 55.

Utter Loss:
- Who will end in utter loss?, 6–7, 31, 56, 61, 81, 102, 152, 229.

Vain Deeds:
- Its meaning, 80.
- Whose deeds are vain?, 79, 196, 229.

Vicegerency (*Khilāfah*):
- Man testified before God's vicegerency was bestowed on him, 97.
- 'Ād made successors after the people of Noah, 42
  Thamūd made successors after 'Ād, 47
- Promise to the Israelites, 70.

Worship of God, Service to God (*'Ibādah*):
- Its exposition, 204–5.
- To follow someone unquestioningly amounts to worshipping him, 203, 204.
- To worship One God alone, 204.
- God alone is to be worshipped, 37, 40, 45, 52, 204.
- Its proper mode, 18–19.
- Main difference between the worship of polytheists and Muslims, 18–19.

Wrong-doing:
- Sin and disobedience, 10, 12, 89, 92, 146.
- Amounts to wronging one's self, 206.
- Rejecting God's signs, 26, 64, 102, 160.
- Making a false claim to prophethood, 22.
- Associating others with God in His divinity, 80, 81.
- Disbelieving in the Hereafter, 28.
- Hindering men from the path of God, 28.
- Hypocrites commit it, 213, 252.
- Those who love unbelievers are wrong-doers, 198.
- They are not granted guidance, 197, 252.
- God's curse upon the wrong-doers, 28.
- End of the wrong-doers, 27, 89, 160.

Zakāh:
- Its mention in the Qur'ān, 196, 230.
- God shows mercy to those who pay it, 84.
- It has been part of the divine religion, 84.
- It reaches God, 246.
- As a means of purification, 246.
- Its importance in Islam, 190–1, 192–3.
- Abū Bakr's waging war against those who refused to pay it, 190–1.
- The transformation it brought about in the life of the Arabs, 220.
- Its collection is a duty of the Islamic state, 246.
- Who can get it?, 221–5.
- Forbidden for Banū Hāshim, 225.
- Can Banū Hāshim give it to one another?, 222.

General Index